ALCONBURY
INDEX TO STREETS

Alconbury House C.2
ALCONBURY WESTON B.1
Ash End C.2

Beech End B.2
Bell Lane B.2
Blackbird Way B.2
Bramble End B.2
Brook close B.2
Brookside B.2
Buckworth Road A.1

Chapel Lane B.2
Chequers Close A.1
Church Way, Alconbury .B.2
Church Way,
    Alconbury Weston A.1
Coulson Way B.2
Crown Gardens B.2

Elm End B.2

Field Close B.1
Ford End B.2
Frumetty Lane B.2

Globe Lane A.3

Hamerton Road A.1
Hawthorn End B.2
Highfield Avenue A.1
High Street Alconbury .B.2
High Street,
    Alconbury Weston A.1
Hillfield B.1

Lark Way B.2

Manor Lane B.1
Maple End B.2
Mill Lane B.2

North Road A.1

Oak End C.2
Old Glebe B.1

Palmer Lane B.2
Polecat Lane B.1

Red Lion Close B.2
Robin Terrace B.2
Rusts Lane B.2

School Lane B.2
Sharps Lane B.2
Sparrow Drive B.2
Spinney Lane B.2
Spires End A.1
Spring Field Road A.1
Starling Close B.2

Tanglewood A.1
The Acre B.2
The Leys B.2
The Maltings B.1
The Paddocks B.1

Vinegar Hill A.1

West Close A.1
Wheatsheaf Road A.1
Willow End B.2
Willow Farm Close A.1

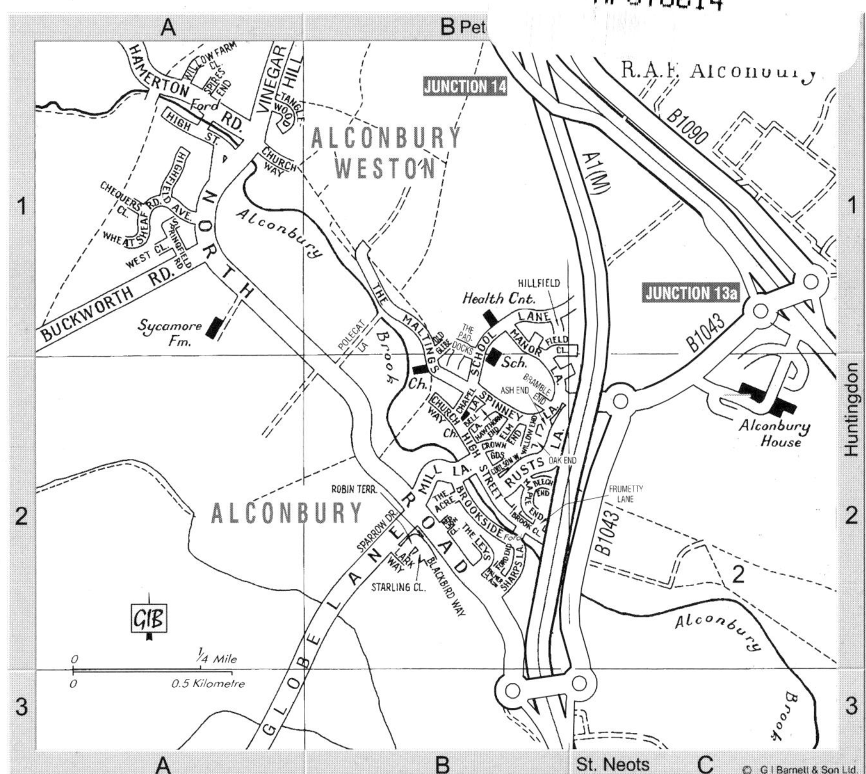

GREAT AND LITTLE STUKELEY

GREAT AND LITTLE STUKELEY
INDEX TO STREETS

Beech Avenue B.2

Camoys Close B.2
Chestnut Green B.2
Church Close B.2
Church Road B.2
Church Way A.1

Elm Road B.2
Ermine Street A.1

Green End B.2
Hill Close B.2

Low Road A.1

Mill Close A.1
Mill Road A.1
Montagu Road B.2
Moorfield Way B.2

Owl End B.2

Park View B.2
Pringle Court A.1
Pringle Way A.1

R.A.F. Alconbury B.1

Sanders Close A.1

West View B.2

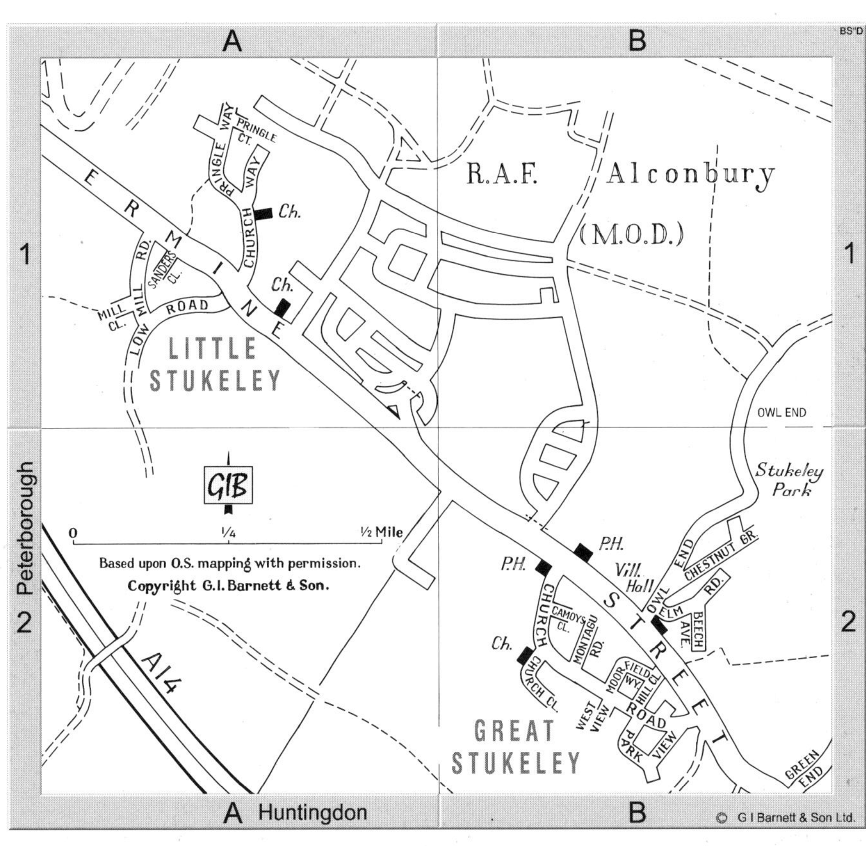

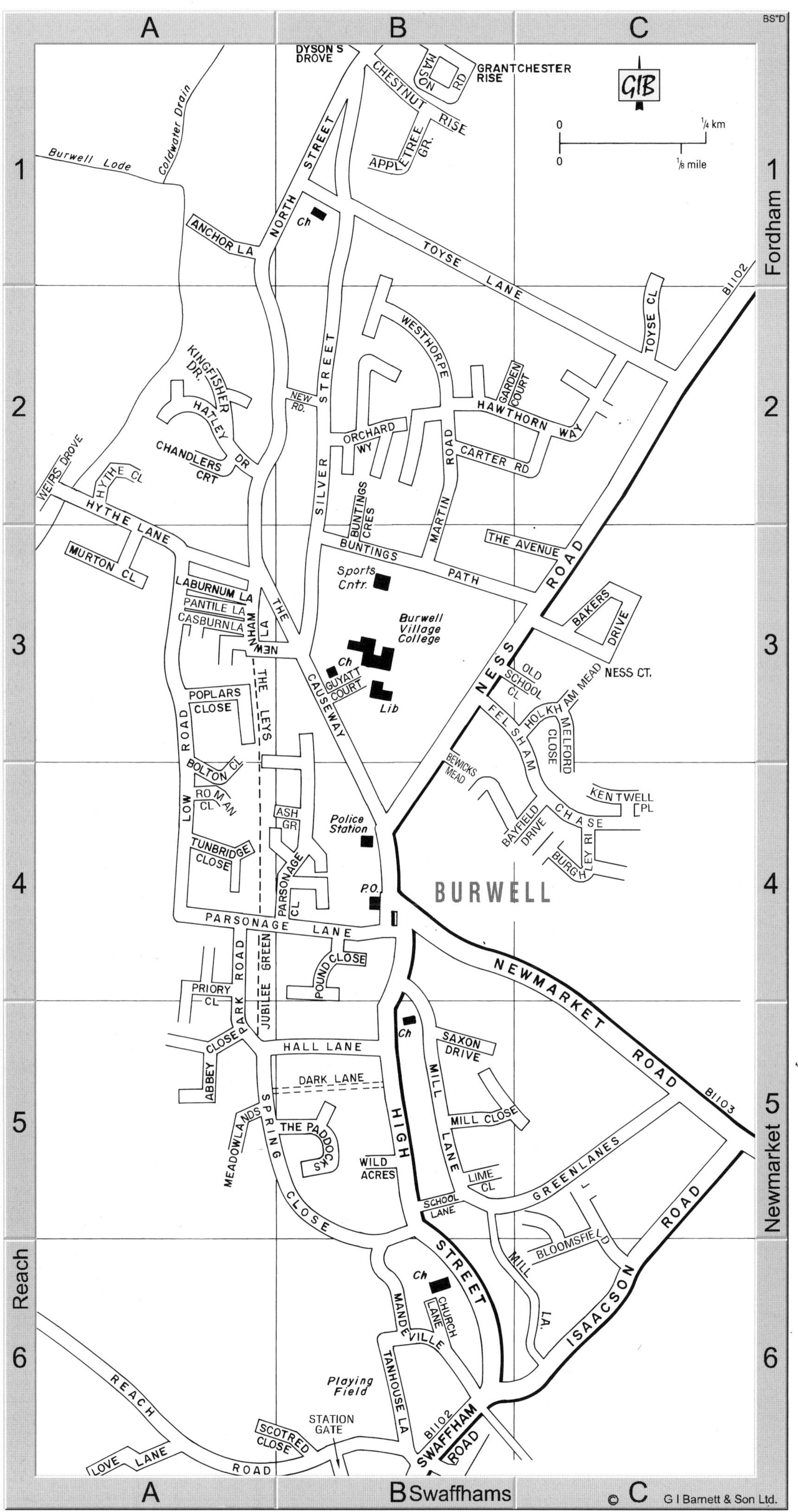

BURWELL INDEX

Abbey Close ....,A.5
Anchor Lane A.1
Appletree Grove B.1
Ash Grove B.4

Bakers Drive C.3
Bayfield Drive B.4
Bewicks Mead B.3
Bloomsfield C.6
Blton Close A.4
Buntings Crescent B.2
Buntings Path B.3
Burghley Rise C.4

Carter Road.....................B.2
Casburn Lane A.3
Chandlers Court A.2
Chestnut Rise B.1
Church Lane B.6

Dark Lane B.5
Dyson's Drove B.1

Felsham Chase B.3

Garen Court.....................B.2
Grantchester Rise B.1
Greenlanes C.5
Guyatt Court B.3

Hall Lane B.5
Hatley Drive A.2
Hawthorn Way B.2
High Street......................B.5
Hockham Mead C.3
Hythe Close A.2
Hythe Lane A.2

Isaacson Road C.6

Jubilee Green A.5

Kentwell Place.................C.4
Kingfisher Drive A.2

Laburnum Lane A.3
Lime Close......................B.5
Love Lane A.6
Low Road A.4

Mandeville B.6
Martni Road.....................B.2
Mason Road B.1
Meadowlands A.5
Melford Close C.3
Mill Close B.5
Mill Lane B.5
Murton Close A.3

Ness Court C.3
News Road B.3
New Road B.2
Newmarket Road..............B.4
Newham Lane A.3
North Street B.1

Old School Close C.3
Orchard Way B.2

Pantile Lane....................A.3
Park Road A.5
Parsonage Close.............B.4
Parsonage Lane A.4
Poplars Close A.3
Pound Close A.4
Priory Close A.4

Reach Road.....................A.6
Roman Close...................A.4

Saxon Drive.....................B.5
School Lane.....................B.5
Scotred Close A.6
Silver Street....................B.2
Spring Close A.5
Station Gate....................B.6
Swaffham Road................B.6

Tanhouse Lane B.6
The Avenue C.3
The Causeway B.3
The Leys A.3
The Paddocks B.5
Toyse Lane B.1
Tunbridge Close A.4

Weirs Drove....................A.2
Westhorpe B.2
Wild Acres B.5

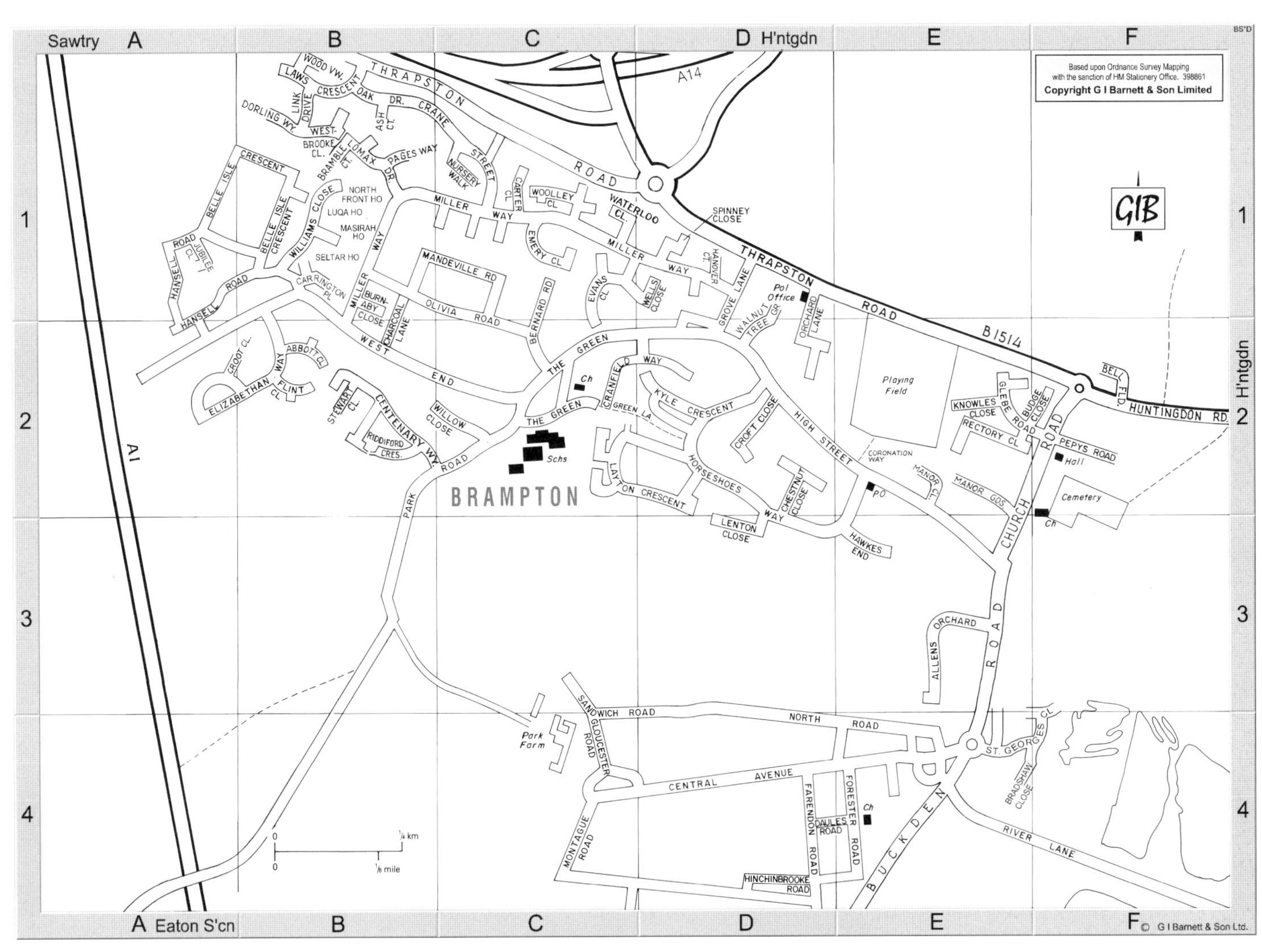

BRAMPTON INDEX TO STREETS

Abbot Close B.2
Allens Orchard E.3
Ash Court B.1

Bell field F.2
Belle Isle Crescent A.1
Bernard Road C.2
Bradshaw Close E.4
Bramble Court B.1
Buckden Road E.4
Budge Close E.2
Burnaby Close E.1

Carrington Place B.1
Carter Close C.1
Central Avenue D.4
Charcoal Lane B.2
Chestnut Close D.2
Church Road E.3
Coronation Way E.2

Crane Street C.1
Cranfield Way C.2
Croft Close D.2
Croot Close A.2

Daules Road D.4
Dorling Way B.1

Elizabeth Way A.2
Emery Close C.1
Evans Close C.1

Farendon Road D.4
Flint Close B.2
Forester Road E.4

Glebe Road E.2
Gloucester Road C.4
Green Lane C.2
Grove Lane D.1

Hanover Court D.1
Hansell Road A.1
Hawkes End E.3
High Street D.2
Hinchinbrooke Road ... D.4
Horseshoes Way D.2
Huntingdon Road F.2

Jubilee Close A.1

Knowles Close E.2
Kyle Crescent D.2

Laws Crescent B.1
Layton Crescent C.2
Lenton Close D.3
Link Drive B.1
Lomax Drive B.1
Luqa House B.1

Manderville Road C.1
Manor Close E.2
Manor Gardens E.2
Masirah House B.1
Miller Way B.1
Montague Road C.4

North Front House B.1
North Road D.4
Nursey Walk C.1

Oak Drive B.1
Olivia Road C.1
Orchard Lane D.2

Pages Way B.1
Park Road B.2
Pepys Road F.2
Rectory Road E.2
River Lane E.4

St. Georges Close E.4
Sandwich Road C.3
Seltar House B.1
Spinney Close D.1
Stewart Close B.2

The Green C.2
Thrapston Road D.1

Walnut Tree Grove D.2
Waterloo Close C.1
Wells Close D.1
West End B.2
Westbrooke Close B.1
Williams Close B.1
Willow Close C.2
Wood View B.1
Woolley Close C.1

CHATTERIS INDEX TO STREETS

Alma Terrace A.3
Angood's Lane B.2
Ash Grove B.2
Augustus Way C.2

Beaufort Drive B.1
Beckett Way B.2
Birch Avenue C.3
Birch Close C.3
Birch Fen Drove D.4
Black Horse Lane B.2
Blackmill Road B.5
Blackthorn Close B.5
Bridge Street B.1
Burnsfield Street A.3
By-Pass C.1

Campole Drove D.4
Chantry Close C.2
Chapel Lane A.2
Church Lane B.3

Church Walk C.3
Clare Street A.3
Coach House Court ... B.3
Cox's Lane B.2
Cricketers Way C.4
Curlew Avenue C.2
Cygnet Drive B.2

Dean Drove D.5
Delve Terrace D.2
Dock Road B.1
Doddington Road ... A.1
Drake Avenue B.2

East Park Street B.3
East Wood Estate .. B.5
Eastbourne Close .. B.5
Eastbourne Road .. B.5
Eastern By-Pass ... C.1
Eden Crescent B.4

Fairview Avenue A.5
Fairview Crescent A.5
Fairview Drive A.5
Fairview Gardens A.5
Fairway A.5
Fen View A.4
Fenland Way A.3
Fenton Way B.1
Furrowfield Road B.2

Gibside Avenue A.5
Gipson Close A.2
Glebe Close C.3
Green Park D.3
Grenadiers Drvie ... B.1
Gull Way B.2

Haighs Close A.3
Harold Heading Close .. B.4
Heronshaw B.2
High Street B.2

Hilda Clark Close B.5
Hinchingbrooke Drive .. A.4
Honeysome Road A.3
Horsegate Gardens ... B.3
Huntingdon Road A.3
Huntingdon Road A.4

Ireton's Way D.4

James Gage Close A.4
Johnson Way B.2

King Edward Road B.3
Kingfisher Close B.1

Larham Way A.2
Linden Drive B.4
Lindsells Walk B.2
Little Acre Fen Drove .. A.5
Lode Way B.1
Lyons Court B.3

Mallard Close B.2
Manor Gardens C.4
Marion Way B.5
Market Hill B.3
Marritt Close A.2
Mayfly Close A.5
Meadow Close B.5
Millfield Close B.5

New Road C.2
Newlands Road D.2

Old Auction Yard B.3
Oldforge Gardens ... B.3

Park Street B.3
Parkers Close B.2
Parkside C.4
Pecks Yard B.2
Plover Close B.2
Pound Road A.1

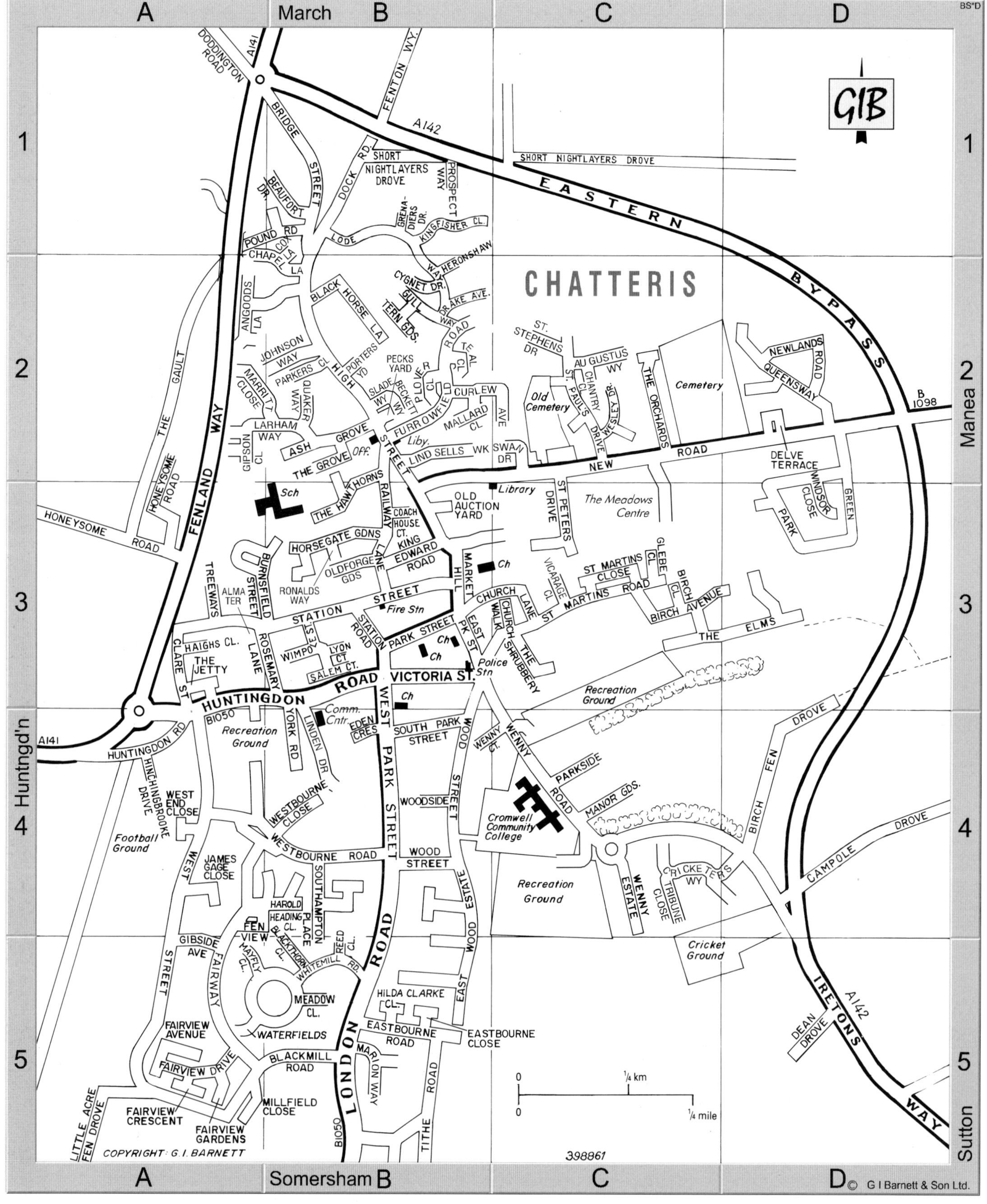

CHATTERIS INDEX TO STREETS (Continued)

Porters Yard B.2
Prospect Way B.1

Quaker Way B.2
Queensway D.2

Railway Lane B.3
Reed Close B.5
Ronalds Way B.3
Rosemary Lane A.3

Salem Court B.3

Shortnightlayers Drove . .B.1
Slade Way B.2
South Park Street B.4
Southampton Place B.4
St. Martins Close C.3
St. Martins Road C.3
St. Pauls Drive C.2
St. Peters Drive C.3
St. Stephen's Close C.2
Station Road B.3
Station Street B.3
Swan Drive C.2

Teal Close B.2
Tern Gardens B.2
The Elms C.3
The Gault A.2
The Grove B.2
The Hawthorns B.3
The Jetty A.3
The Orchards C.2
The Shrubbery C.3
Tithe Road B.5
Treeways A.3
Tribune Close C.4

Vicarage Close C.3
Victoria Street B.3

Waterfields A.5
Wenny Court B.4
Wenny Estate C.4
Wenny Road C.4
Wesley Drive C.2
West End Close A.4
West Park Street B.4
West Street A.4
Westbourne Close B.4

Westbourne Road B.4
Whitemill Road B.5
Wimpole Street B.3
Windsor Close D.3
Wood Street B.4
Woodside B.4

York Road B.4

FULBOURN
INDEX TO STREETS

All Saints Road C.2
Alec Rolph Close B.1
Apthorpe Street D.1

Babraham Road C.3
Balsham Road D.3
Barnsfield D.3
Barrett's Yard D.2
Bird Farm Road C.2
Breckenwood Road B.1
Brunswick Court B.2

Cambridge Road A.2
Caraway Road B.2
Chaplin's Close C.2
Cherry Orchard B.2
Church Lane D.2
Cow Lane C.1
Cox's Drove C.1

Dogget's Lane D.3
Dunmowe Way C.2
Farmers Row C.2

Fromont Close C.3
Fulbourn Old Drift A.2
Fulbourn Road B.1

Geoffrey Bishop
 Avenue D.3
Grandridge Close C.2
Greater Foxes C.2

Haggis Gap C.2
High Street D.2
Highfield Gate C.1
Hinton Road B.2
Hollmans Road C.2
Home Close C.2
Home End D.3
Impett's Lane D.3

Jeeves Acre D.3

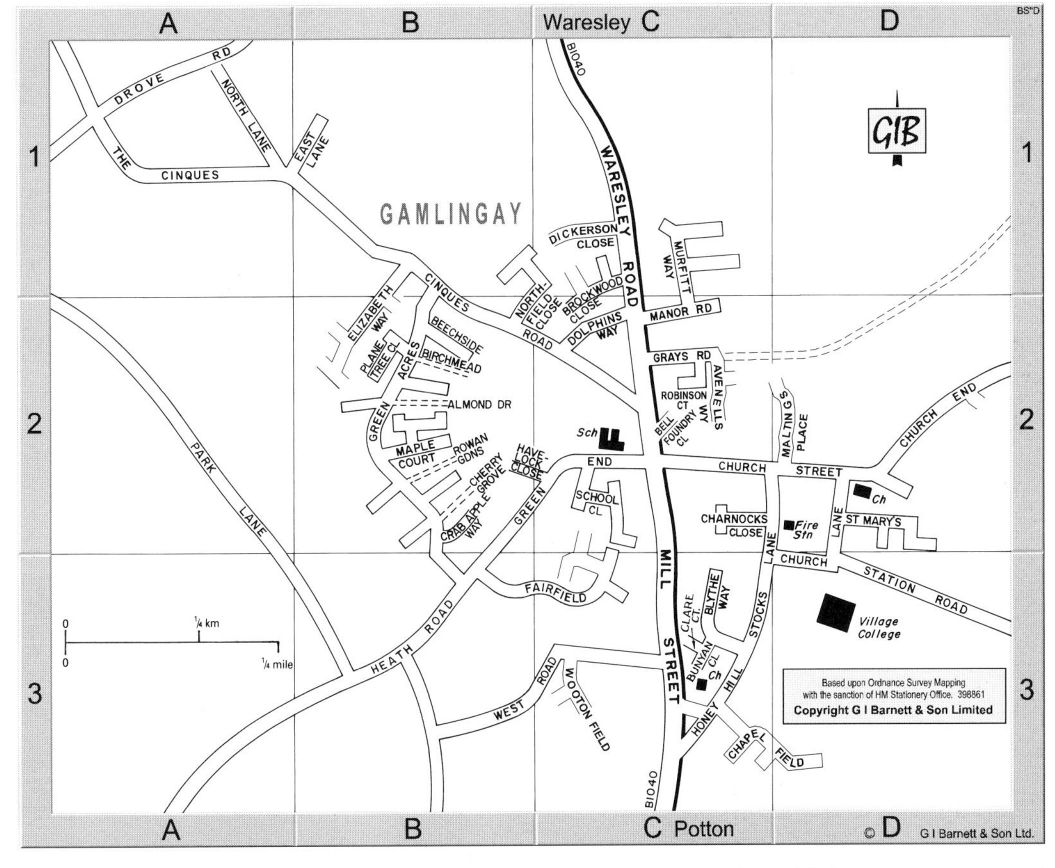

Ludlow Lane D.2

Manor Walk D.2
March's Close C.2
Northfield D.2

Oslar's Way C.2

Pettits Close D.2
Pierce Lane C.2

St. Vigors Road C.2
Sanders Lane D.3
School Lane D.2
Shelford Road B.3
Stansfield Gardens C.2

Station Road D.2
Stonebridge Lane D.2
Swifts Corner C.2

Teversham Road B.1
The Chantry D.2
The Cornway C.2
The Croft C.2

The Haven C.2
The Maples B.2
Thomas Road B.2
Town Close C.2

Weston Grove B.2
Wilbraham Road D.1
Windmill Lane C.2

GAMLINGAY

GAMLINGAY
INDEX TO STREETS

Almond Drive B.2
Avenells Way C.2

Beechside B.2
Bell Foundry Close C.2
Birchmead B.2
Blythe Way C.3
Brockwood Close C.2
Bunyan Close C.3

Chapel Field C.3
Charnocks Close C.2
Cherry Grove B.2
Church End D.2
Church Lane D.3
Church Street C.2
Cinques Road B.1
Clare Court C.3
Crab Apple Way B.2

Dolphins Way C.2
Drove Road A.1

East Lane B.1
Elizabeth Way B.2

Fairfield C.3

Grays Road C.2
Green Acres B.2
Green End B.2

Havelock Close B.2
Heath Road B.3
Honey Hill C.3

Maltings Place D.2
Manor Road C.2
Maple Court B.2
Mill Street C.3
Murfitt Way C.1

North Field Close B.2

North Lane A.1

Park Lane A.2
Plane Tree Close B.2

Robinson Court C.2
Rowan Gardens B.2

St. Mary's D.2

School Close C.2
Station Road D.3
Stock Lane C.3

The Cinques A.1

Waresley Road C.1
West Road B.3

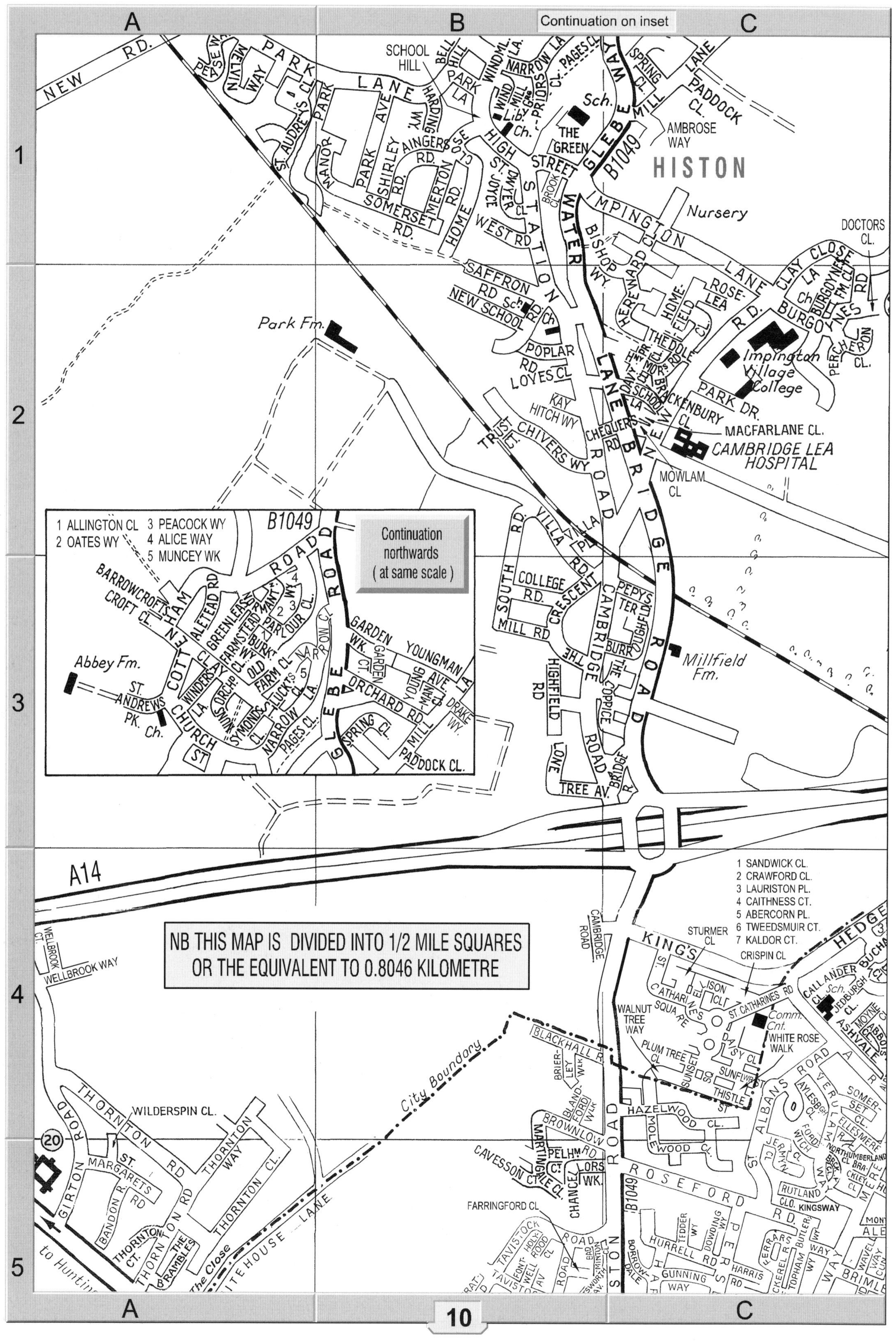
Continuation on inset
A
B
C
HISTON
NEW RD.
PEASE WAY
MELVIN WAY
PARK
ST. AUDREY'S CL.
MANOR
PARK AVE.
SHIRLEY RD.
AINGERS RD.
MERTON RD.
HOME CLOSE
PARK LANE
HARDING WY.
SCHOOL HILL
BELL HILL
PARK LA.
WINDML. LA.
NARROW LA.
WIND MILL LA.
PRIORS CL.
PAGES CL.
SPRING CL.
LANE
PADDOCK CL.
Lib.
Ch.
Sch.
THE GREEN
GLEBE WAY
B1049
MILL
AMBROSE WAY
DOCTORS CL.
SOMERSET RD.
JOYCE CL.
DWYER CL.
HIGH STREET
WEST RD.
STATION RD.
WATER LANE
BISHOP WY.
IMPINGTON LANE
Nursery
CLAY CLOSE
LA.
BURGOYNE FM. CL.
PERCHERON CL.
SAFFRON RD.
NEW SCHOOL
Sch.
Ch.
HEREWARD
HOME-FIELD
ROSE-LEA
R D.
BURGOYNES RD.
Park Fm.
POPLAR RD.
LOVES CL.
KAY HITCH WY.
CHEQUERS
DAVY RD.
THE DOLE
MORS RD.
SCHOOL LA.
BRACKENBURY CL.
PARK DR.
Impington Village College
MACFARLANE CL.
CAMBRIDGE LEA HOSPITAL
B1049
Continuation northwards
(at same scale)
BARROWCROFT
CROFT CL.
COTTENHAM RD.
ALETEAD RD.
GREENLEAS
FARMSTEAD CL.
PARLOUR WAY
BURK
OLD FARM CL.
Abbey Fm.
ST. ANDREWS PK.
Ch.
WINDERS LA.
SYMONDS CL.
LUCK'S CL.
NARROW LA.
PAGES CL.
CHURCH ST.
ORCH.
GARDEN WK.
GARDEN CT.
YOUNGMAN AVE.
YOUNG CL.
DRAKE WY.
ORCHARD RD.
GLEBE ROAD
SPRING CL.
MILL
PADDOCK CL.
TRUE ST.
CHIVERS WY.
VILLA PL.
SOUTH RD.
MILL RD.
COLLEGE RD.
CRESCENT
HIGHFIELD RD.
THE COPPICE
CAMBRIDGE ROAD
PEPYS TER.
BURK
HIGH CL.
THE
MOWLAM CL.
Millfield Fm.
LONE TREE AV.
BRIDGE
A14
1 SANDWICK CL.
2 CRAWFORD CL.
3 LAURISTON PL.
4 CAITHNESS CT.
5 ABERCORN PL.
6 TWEEDSMUIR CT.
7 KALDOR CT.
NB THIS MAP IS DIVIDED INTO 1/2 MILE SQUARES
OR THE EQUIVALENT TO 0.8046 KILOMETRE
1 ALLINGTON CL
2 OATES WY
3 PEACOCK WY
4 ALICE WAY
5 MUNCEY WK
Wellbrook CT.
WELLBROOK WAY
City Boundary
CAMBRIDGE ROAD
HEDGE
KING'S
STURMER CL.
CRISPIN CL.
ST. CATHARINES
ELY CL.
ISON CL.
SQUARE
ST. CATHARINES RD.
Comm. Cnt.
WHITE ROSE WALK
CALLANDER
Sch.
JEDBURGH RD.
MOYNE CL.
ASHVALE
BUCHAN
WALNUT TREE WAY
PLUM TREE CL.
SUNSET CL.
SUNFLOWER
THISTLE ST.
DAISY CL.
BLACKHALL RD.
BRIER-LEY
BLAND-FORD WK.
HAZELWOOD CL.
MOLE WOOD CL.
ALBANS ROAD
VERULAM
SOMERSET RD.
ELLESMERE CL.
NORTHUMBERLAND
THORNTON RD.
WILDERSPIN CL.
GIRTON ROAD
ST. MARGARETS RD.
BRANDON RD.
THORNTON CT.
THE BRAMBLES
THORNTON WAY
THORNTON CL.
The Close
WHITEHOUSE LANE
to Huntingdon
20
BROWNLOW
PELHAM RD.
MARTINGALE
CAVESSON
CHANCELLORS WK.
FARRINGFORD CL.
TAVISTOCK
WELL HOUSE
WELL HOOD CL.
ROSEFORD ROAD
BORROWDALE
PERS
B1049
HURRELL RD.
TEDDER WY.
DOWDING WY.
GUNNING WAY
HARRIS RD.
KINGSWAY
RUTLAND RD.
TOPHAM
BUTLER WAY
WAVELL
BRIMLEY
10

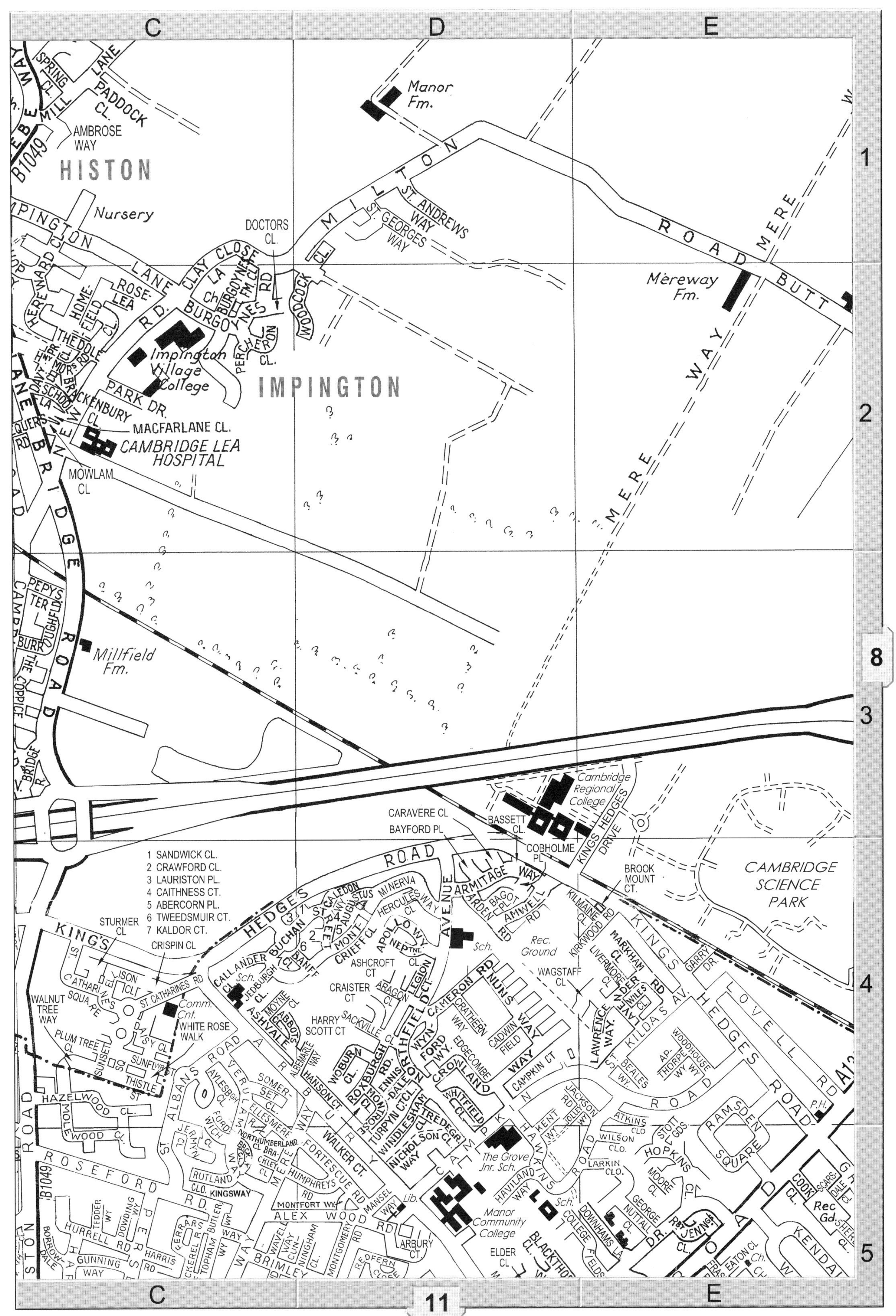
C
D
E
1
2
8
3
4
5
Manor Fm.
MILTON
ROAD
MERE WAY
MERE BUTT WY.
Mereway Fm.
HISTON
Nursery
SPRING CL.
MILL
LANE
PADDOCK CL.
AMBROSE WAY
B1049
GLEBE WAY
IMPINGTON LANE
HEREWARD
HOME FIELD
ROSE LEA
THE DOLE
MORS
SCHOOL LA.
DAVY RD.
BRACKENBURY CL.
LANE
QUERS RD.
CAMBRIDGE ROAD
BRIDGE RD.
PARK DR.
CLAY CLOSE
BURGOYNES
LA. FM. CL.
BURGOYNE RD.
Ch.
DOCTORS CL.
PERCHERON CL.
HERON CL.
WOODCOCK CL.
ST. GEORGES WAY
ST. ANDREWS WAY
Impington Village College
IMPINGTON
MACFARLANE CL.
CAMBRIDGE LEA HOSPITAL
MOWLAM CL.
PEPYS TER
LITCHFIELD RD.
BURR
THE COPPICE
Millfield Fm.
BRIDGE RD.
CAMBRIDGE REGIONAL COLLEGE
CARAVERE CL
BAYFORD PL
BASSETT CL.
COBHOLME PL.
KINGS HEDGES DRIVE
BROOK MOUNT CT.
CAMBRIDGE SCIENCE PARK
1 SANDWICK CL.
2 CRAWFORD CL.
3 LAURISTON PL.
4 CAITHNESS CT.
5 ABERCORN PL.
6 TWEEDSMUIR CT.
7 KALDOR CT.
STURMER CL.
CRISPIN CL.
KING'S
ST. CATHARINES
ISON CL.
ST. CATHARINES RD.
SQUARE
WALNUT TREE WAY
DAISY CL.
Comm. Cnt.
WHITE ROSE WALK
PLUM TREE CL.
SUNFLWR.
SUNSET
THISTLE ST.
HAZELWOOD CL.
MOLE WOOD CL.
ROSEFORD RD.
HISTON ROAD
B1049
TEDDER WY.
DOVIDING
HURRELL RD.
HARRIS RD.
GUNNING WAY
DALE
BORROW
HEDGES ROAD
CALEDON ST.
AUGUSTUS CL.
BUCHAN ST.
BANFF
MONT CL.
CRIEFF CL.
ASHCROFT CT.
CRAISTER CT.
MINERVA CL.
HERCULES WY.
APOLLO WY.
NEPTNE.
LEGION CT.
ARAGON CL.
ARMITAGE WAY
LILY WAY
AVENUE
GARDEN RD.
BAGOT PL.
AMWELL RD.
KILMAINE CL.
KIRKWOOD RD.
LIVERMORE RD.
MARKHAM CL.
ALEXANDER AV.
NILES
LAWRENCE WAY
ST. BEALES WY.
KILDAS AV.
KINGS HEDGES ROAD
LOVELL RD.
GARRY DR.
WOODHOUSE WY.
THORPE PL.
AP.
Rec. Ground
WAGSTAFF CL.
CAMPKIN CT.
NUNS WAY
CAMERON RD.
CROMWELL RD.
NORTHFIELD
FORD WY.
EDGECOMBE RD.
CRATHERN WAY
CADWIN FIELD
WHITFIELD
TREDEGAR RD.
NICHOLSON WAY
WINDLESHAM
CALLANDER CL.
JEDBURGH CL.
MOYNE CL.
ABBOTS
ASHVALE
ALBEMARLE RD.
WOBURN
ROXBURGH RD.
ENNIS RD.
DALTON
TURPYN CT.
HANSON CT.
HARRY SACKVILLE
SCOTT CT.
ALBANS ROAD
VERULAM WAY
AYLESBURY
FORD
NORTHUMBERLAND
BRICKLEY
SOMER SET
ELLESMERE
HUMPHREYS RD.
FORTESCUE RD.
WALKER CT.
MANSEL WAY
Lib.
HAVILAND WAY
HAWKINS ROAD
KENT RD.
JACKSON RD.
ATKINS CLO.
WILSON CLO.
STOTT GDS.
HOPKINS CL.
MOORE
LARKIN CLO.
RAMSDEN SQUARE
GEORGE NUTTALL CL.
JENNET
DOWNHAMS LA.
COLLEGE FIELDS
Manor Community College
ELDER CL.
BLACKTHORN
The Grove Jnr. Sch.
ARBURY CT.
ALEX WOOD RD.
BRIMLEY
MONTFORT WY.
KINGSWAY
RUTLAND CLO.
JERMY
TOPHAM BUTLER WY.
WAVELL WAY
NINGHAM CL.
MONTGOMERY RD.
REDFERN CL.
WAVENEY
EATON CL.
COOKE CL.
Rec. Gd.
KENDAL WAY
A1
11

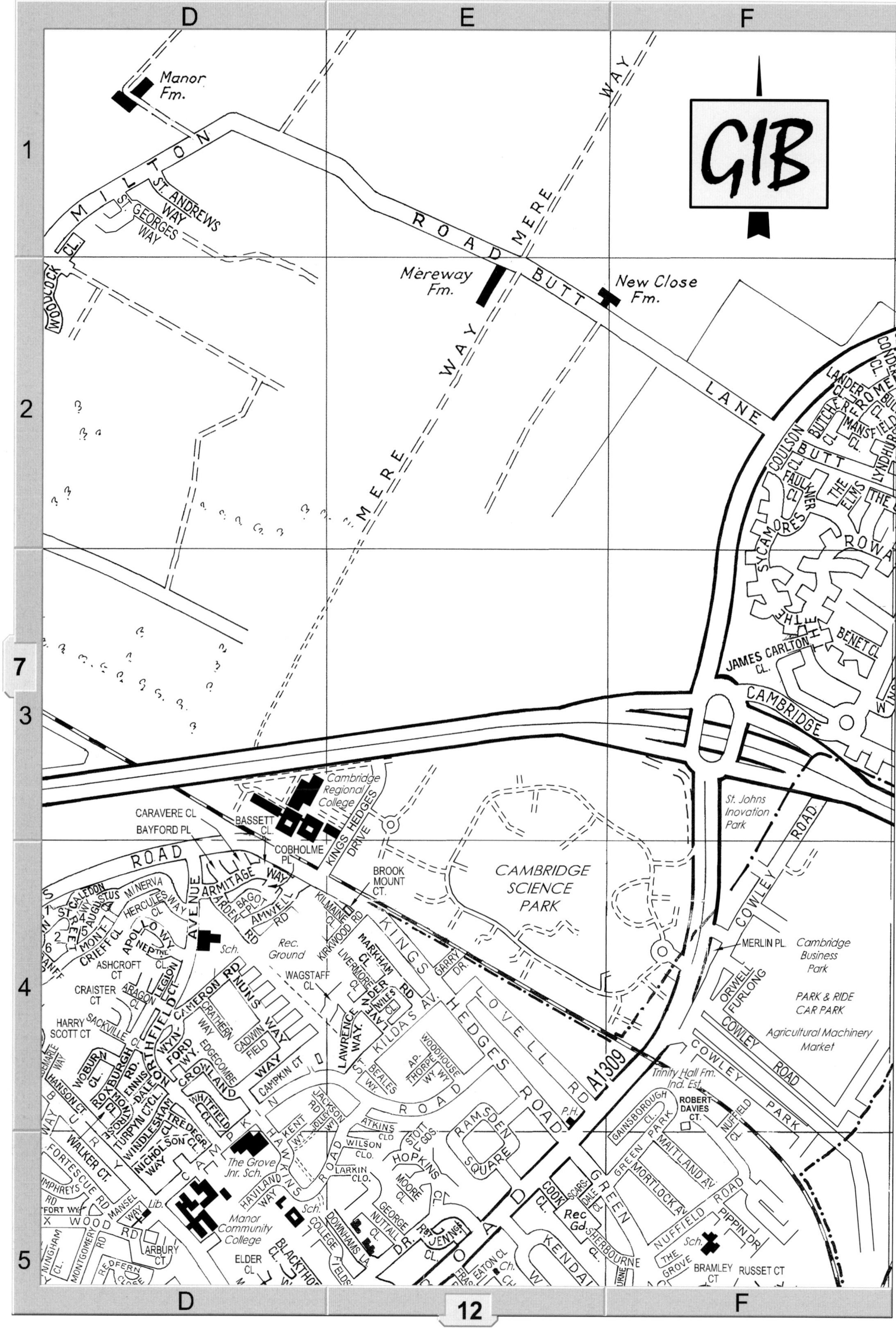

D
E
F
1
Manor Fm.
MILTON
ST. ANDREWS WAY
ST. GEORGES WAY
WOODLOCK CL.
ROAD
MERE BUTT
MERE WAY
Mereway Fm.
New Close Fm.
LANE
GIB
CONDER CL.
LANDER MEWS
CROFT CL.
BUTCHER CL.
MANSFIELD CL.
COULSON CL.
FAULKNER CL.
LYNDHURST
SYCAMORES
THE ELMS
THE
ROWA
BENET CL.
HL
JAMES CARLTON CL.
CAMBRIDGE
2
7
3
Cambridge Regional College
CARAVERE CL.
BAYFORD PL
BASSETT CL.
COBHOLME PL.
KINGS HEDGES DRIVE
BROOK MOUNT CT.
St. Johns Inovation Park
COWLEY ROAD
CAMBRIDGE SCIENCE PARK
ROAD
ST. CALEDON
AUGUSTUS WAY
MINERVA CL.
HERCULES WAY
ARMITAGE WAY
ARDEN CL.
BAGOT CL.
AMWELL RD.
KILMAINE CL.
KIRKWOOD RD.
AVENUE
APOLLO WY.
NEPTNE.
MONT
CRIEFF CL.
ASHCROFT CT.
ARAGON CL.
LEGION CL.
CRAISTER CT.
SACKVILLE CL.
HARRY SCOTT CT.
WYNFORD
ROXBURGH RD.
DALE
CAMERON WAY.
EDGECOMBE CL.
CROWLAND
CRATHERN WAY
NUNS WAY
CADWIN FIELD
Sch.
Rec. Ground
WAGSTAFF CL.
LIVERMORE CL.
MARKHAM RD.
DER
ILES
LAWRENCE WAY.
CAMPKIN CT.
KILDAS AV.
BEALES WY.
AP. THORPE WY.
WOODHOUSE WY.
GARRY DR.
KINGS HEDGES ROAD
LOVELL ROAD
A1309
MERLIN PL.
Cambridge Business Park
ORWELL FURLONG
PARK & RIDE CAR PARK
Agricultural Machinery Market
COWLEY ROAD
COWLEY PARK
4
WOBURN CL.
ENNIS CL.
EASORN.
TURPYN CT.
WINDLESHAM CL.
WHITFIELD CL.
NICHOLSON WAY
HAWKINS WAY
JACKSON CL.
KENT CL.
ATKINS CLO.
WILSON CLO.
LARKIN CLO.
STOTT GDS.
HOPKINS
MOORE CL.
RAMSDEN SQUARE
Trinity Hall Fm. Ind. Est.
P.H.
GAINSBOROUGH CL.
GREEN
MAITLAND AV.
MORTLOCK AV.
ROBERT DAVIES CT.
NUFFIELD DR.
PIPPIN DR.
5
WALKER CT.
FORTESCUE RD.
HUMPHREYS RD.
MANSEL WAY
Lib.
WOOD RD.
ARBURY CT.
MONTGOMERY RD.
REDFERN CLOSE
The Grove Jnr. Sch.
HAVILAND WAY
Manor Community College
ELDER CL.
BLACKTHORN
DOWNHAMS LA.
COLLEGE FIELDS
GEORGE NUTTALL CL.
JENNS
DALE
R. JENNS DR.
COOK CL.
Rec Gd.
SHERBOURNE
KENDA
SCARS CL.
THE GROVE
BRAMLEY CT.
RUSSET CT.
Sch.
NUFFIELD ROAD
D
F

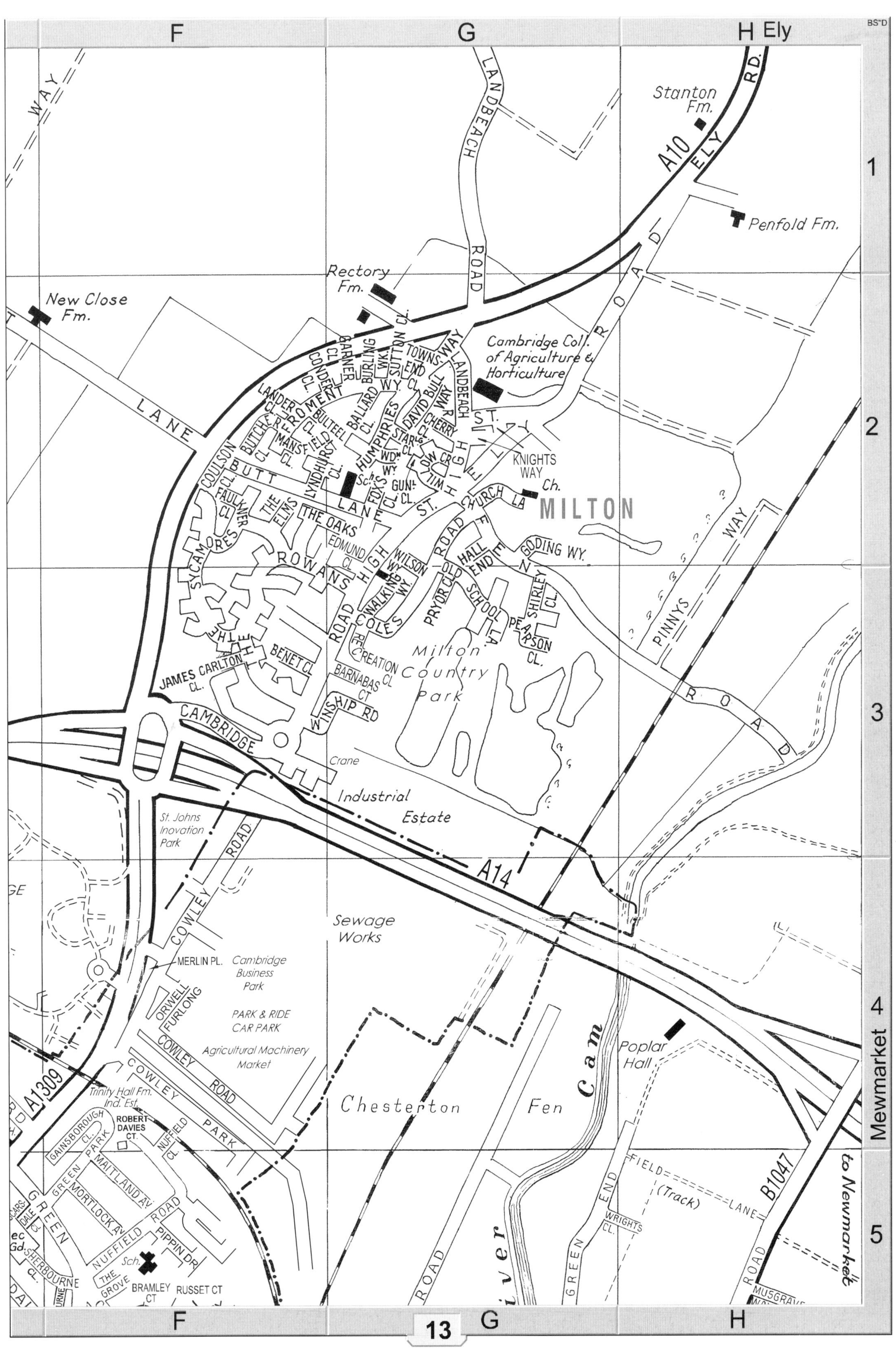
F
G
H Ely
BS"D
WAY
New Close Fm.
LANE
Stanton Fm.
A10
ELY RD.
Penfold Fm.
LANDBEACH ROAD
Rectory Fm.
Cambridge Coll. of Agriculture & Horticulture
GARNER CL.
CONDER CL.
LANDER MENT
BUTCHER CL.
CHERRY CL.
MANSFIELD CL.
BUTT
BULTEEL CL.
BALLARD CL.
HUMPHRIES
LYNDHURST CL.
FROST CL.
COULSON
BURLINGTON WK.
SUTTON CL.
TOWNS END
LANDBEACH WY.
DAVID BULL CL.
CHERRY CL.
STARS
TIM
LOW CR.
WD"N CL.
GUN" CL.
FOX'S CL.
Sch.
STAR CL.
CHURCH LA.
KNIGHTS WAY
MILTON
Ch.
PINNYS WAY
FAULKNER CL.
SYCAMORES
THE ELMS
THE OAKS
EDMUND CL.
ROWANS
HIGH
LANE
ST.
WILSON WY.
WALKING WY.
COLES
PRYOR OLD
OLD SCHOOL LA.
HALL END
GODING WY.
SHIRLEY CL.
PEARSON CL.
THE
ROAD
JAMES CARLTON CL.
BENET CL.
BARNABAS CT.
CREATION CL.
WINSHIP RD
Milton Country Park
Crane
CAMBRIDGE
ROAD
Industrial Estate
St. Johns Inovation Park
A14
COWLEY ROAD
Sewage Works
MERLIN PL.
Cambridge Business Park
ORWELL FURLONG
PARK & RIDE CAR PARK
Agricultural Machinery Market
A1309
Cam
Poplar Hall
Mewmarket
Trinity Hall Fm. Ind. Est.
GAINSBOROUGH CL.
ROBERT DAVIES CT.
NUFFIELD CL.
COWLEY ROAD
COWLEY PARK
GREEN PARK
MAITLAND AV.
MORTLOCK AV.
NUFFIELD ROAD
PIPPIN DR.
Sch.
THE GROVE
BRAMLEY CT.
RUSSET CT.
SHERBOURNE CL.
Chesterton Fen
GREEN END
WRIGHTS CL.
FIELD LANE
(Track)
B1047
ROAD
MUSGRAVE
to Newmarket
1
2
3
4
5
F
G
H

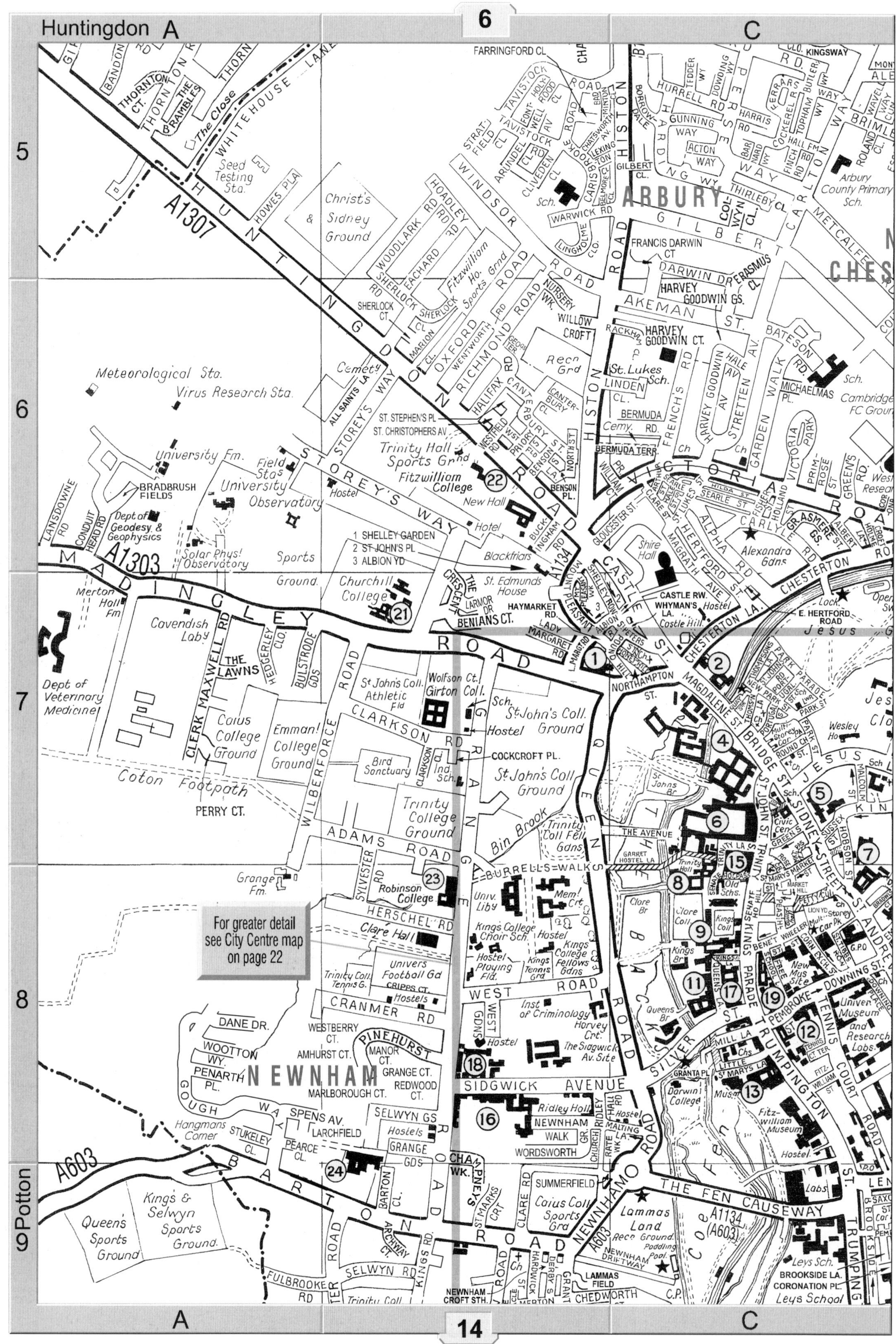

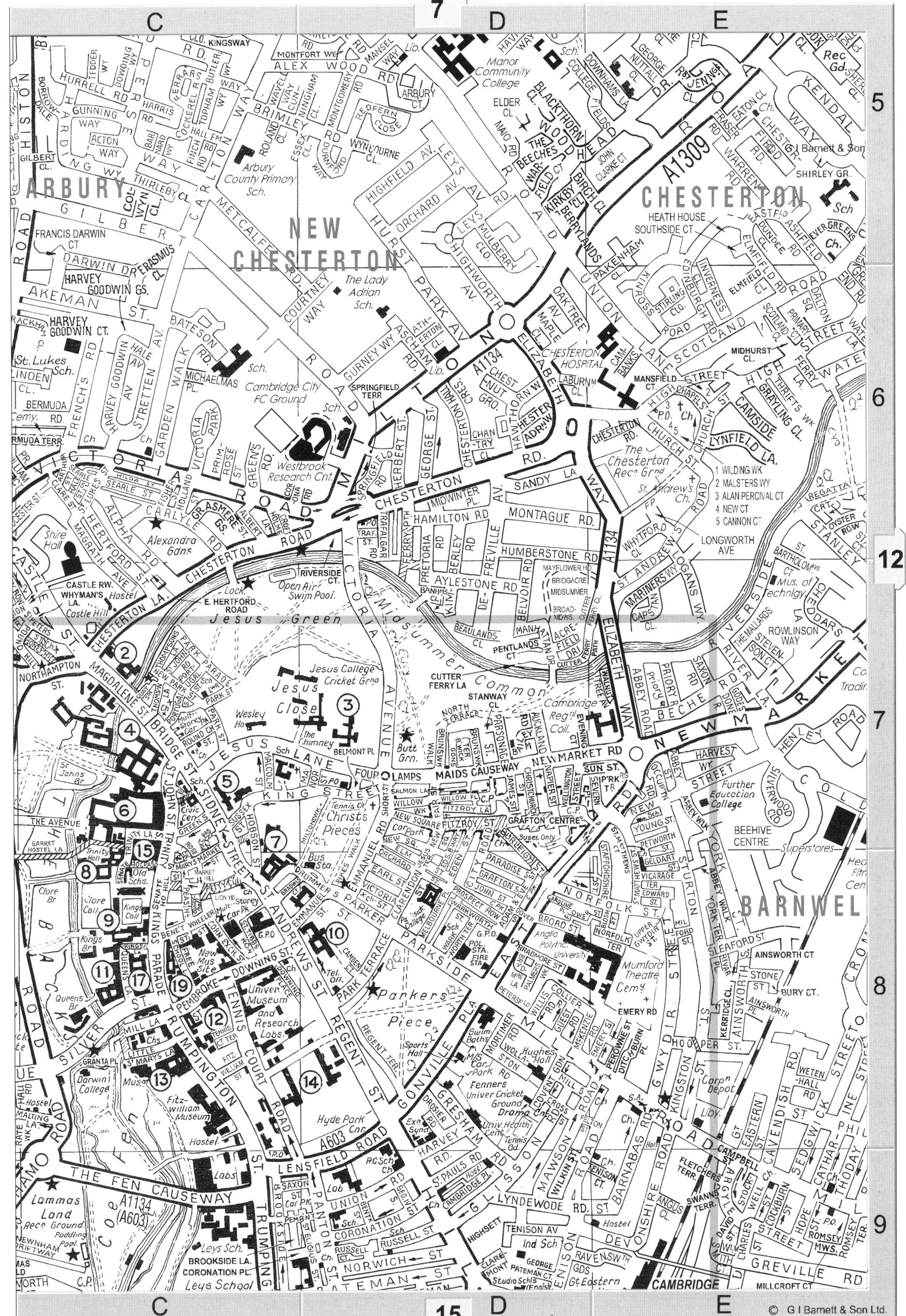

ARBURY
NEW CHESTERTON
CHESTERTON
BARNWELL
CAMBRIDGE
Manor Community College
Arbury County Primary Sch.
The Lady Adrian Sch.
Chesterton Hospital
Cambridge City FC Ground
Westbrook Research Cnt.
The Chesterton Recn Grnd
St Andrew's Ch.
1 Wilding Wk
2 Malsters Wy
3 Alan Percival Ct
4 New Ct
5 Cannon Ct
Longworth Ave
Heath House
Southside Ct
Midsummer Common
Jesus Green
Jesus College Cricket Grnd
Jesus Close
Cambridge Regl Coll.
St Johns Br
The Avenue
Christ's Pieces
Grafton Centre
Further Education College
Beehive Centre
Superstores
Parkers Piece
Mumford Theatre
Univer Museum and Research Labs
Fitzwilliam Museum
Darwin College
Hyde Park Cnr
Anglia Polytec Universh
Lammas Land Recn Ground
THE FEN CAUSEWAY
Leys School
Coronation Pl.
Brookside La.
A603
A1134
A1309
A1134
NEWMARKET RD
CHESTERTON ROAD
VICTORIA ROAD
HILLS ROAD
GONVILLE PLACE
REGENT STREET
TRUMPINGTON
HUNTINGDON ROAD
MILTON ROAD
HISTON ROAD
© G I Barnett & Son Ltd.

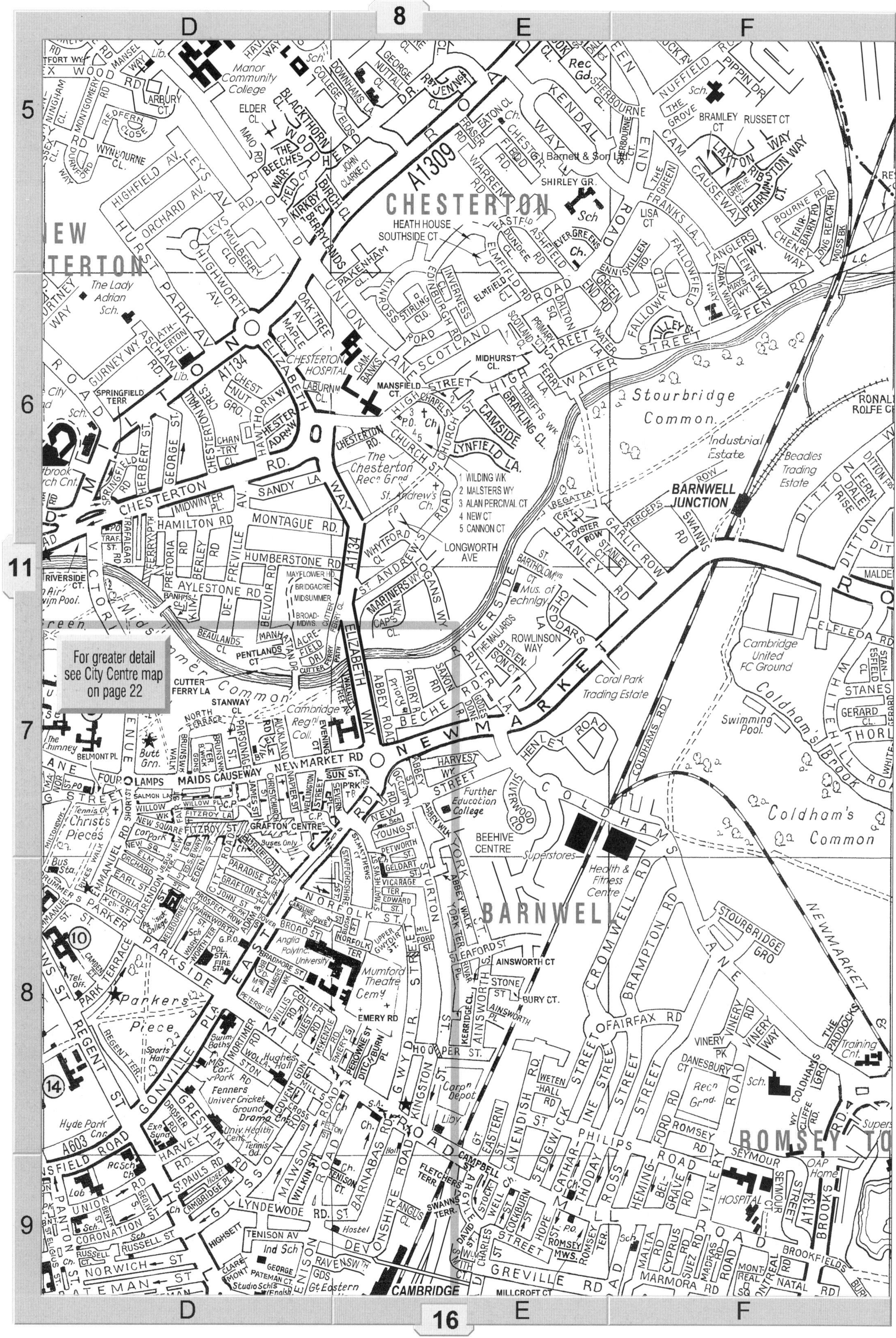
8
D
E
F
5
Manor Community College
WOOD
RD
ARBURY
CT.
ELDER
CL.
BLACKTHORN WOOD HEAD
COLLEGE FIELDS
DOWNHAMS LA.
GEORGE NUTTALL
DR.
JENNY'S
A1309
CHESTERTON
HEATH HOUSE
SOUTHSIDE CT
Rec Gd.
SHERBOURNE
NUFFIELD
PIPPIN DR
The GROVE
BRAMLEY CT
RUSSET CT
LAXTON WAY
RIBSTON WAY
PEARMOTON CT.
J Barnett & Son Ltd
SHIRLEY GR.
CHESTER FIELD RD.
WARREN RD
FRASER RD
FRANKS LA.
LISA CT
EVERGREENS
BOURNE RD
FAIR RD
CHENEY WY.
LONG REACH RD
ANGLERS WY.
HIGHFIELD AV.
LEYS AV.
HIGHWORTH AV.
LEYS AV.
MULBERRY CLO.
BIRCH CL.
BERRYLANDS
KIRKBY CT.
UNION
PAKENHAM
KINROSS CLO.
EDINBURGH ROAD
STIRLING CLO.
INVERNESS
ELMFIELD CL.
ELMFIELD RD
DALTON SQ.
EASTFIELD
DUNDEE CL.
SCOTLAND RD
PRIMARY
Ch.
EVER GREEN END RD
ENNISKILLEN
FALLOWFIELD
WATER LA.
FALLOWFIELD
FEN RD
NEW CHESTERTON
ORCHARD AV.
HURST PARK AV
The Lady Adrian Sch.
GURNEY WY.
ASCHAM RD.
ELIZABETH WAY
OAK TREE AV.
MAPLE AV.
CHESTERTON HOSPITAL
CAM BANKS
LABURNM CL.
MANSFIELD CT.
HIGH STREET
SCOTLAND ROAD
MIDHURST CL.
GRAYLING CL.
CAMSIDE
WATER STREET
Stourbridge Common
Industrial Estate
Beadles Trading Estate
DITTON
FERN DALE RISE
RONALD ROLFE CR
6
City Sch.
SPRINGFIELD TERR
CHESTERTON
SPRINGFIELD RD
HERBERT ST.
GEORGE ST.
CHESTERNHALL
CRES.
HAWTHORN WY
CHESTNUT GRO.
CHEST NUT
ELIZABETH
CHANTRY CL.
CHESTERTON RD.
The Chesterton Rec. Grnd
St. Andrew's Ch. FP
CHURCH ST.
P.O.
Ch.
LYNFIELD LA.
1 WILDING WK
2 MALSTERS WY
3 ALAN PERCIVAL CT
4 NEW CT
5 CANNON CT
REGATTA CT.
St. BARTHOLOM'WS
Mus. of technlgy
STANLEY RD
GARLIC ROW
SWANNS RD
ROW
BARNWELL JUNCTION
DITTON
MALDE
Midbrook Church Cnt.
TRAFALGAR ST.
FERRY PTH
HAMILTON RD.
MIDWINTER PL.
SANDY LA.
MONTAGUE RD.
WHYTFORD CL.
ST. ANDREWS RD
LOGANS WY
LONGWORTH AVE
MARINERS WY
CAPSTAN CL.
STANWAY RD
CHEDDARS
STANLEY RD
OYSTER ROW
11
RIVERSIDE
Open Air Swim Pool.
PRETORIA RD
BERLEY RD
FREVILLE RD
HUMBERSTONE RD.
MAYFLOWER RD
BRIDGACRE
MIDSUMMER
BROAD MDWS.
NEW CT
ACRE FIELD
RIVERSIDE
The MALLARDS
ROWLINSON WAY
STEVEN SON CT
Cambridge United FC Ground
ELFLEDA RD
STANES FIELD
Midsummer Common
AYLESTONE RD.
DE FREVILLE
BELVOIR RD
BANHAMS
KIM
BEAULANDS CL.
PENTLANDS CT.
MANHATTAN DRI
CUTTER FERRY
ELIZABETH WAY
WALNUT TREE
ABBEY ROAD
BECHE
SAXON RD
PRIORY RD
DOWE
GONES
NEWMARKET
Coral Park Trading Estate
Cambridge United FC Ground
Swimming Pool.
GERARD CL.
THORL
WHITEHILL BROOK
For greater detail see City Centre map on page 22
CUTTER FERRY LA
STANWAY CL.
NORTH TERRACE
AUCKLAND RD
PARSONAGE ST.
Cambridge Regl Coll.
EVENING
PRIORY RD
BECHE ROAD
SAXON RD
HENLEY ROAD
COLDHAMS RD
Coldham's Common
7
The Chimney
BELMONT PL.
Butt Grn.
BRUNSWK TER.
BRUNSWK ST.
NEWMARKET RD
SUN ST.
P'RK
NEW
HARVEST WY
STREET
Further Education College
SILVERWOOD CO.
COLDHAMS
FOUR LAMPS
MAIDS CAUSEWAY
SALMON LA.
WILLOW
NEW SQUARE
FITZROY ST.
WILLOW PL.
FITZROY LA.
GRAFTON CENTRE
C.P.
Buses Only
SEVERN
NAPIER ST.
ST. MATTHEWS
YOUNG ST.
PETWORTH ST.
GELDART ST.
VICARAGE TER
STURTON ST.
BEEHIVE CENTRE
Superstores
LANE
Christs Piece's
Tennis Ct.
NEW SQUARE
NEW ST.
EMMANUEL RD
SHORT ST.
CHRISTCHURCH ST.
JAMES ST.
CORN EXCH
PARADISE ST.
BURLEIGH ST.
STAFFORDSHIRE ST.
NORFOLK ST.
NEW ST.
EDWARD ST.
EDWARD ST.
MILFORD ST.
ABBEY WK
YORK ST.
ABBEY WALK
Health & Fitness Centre
BARNWELL
STOURBRIDGE GRO
8
Bus Sta.
ORCHARD ST.
EARL ST.
VICTORIA ST.
CLARENDON ST.
PROSPECT ROW
JOHN ST.
PARADISE ST.
GRAFTON ST.
DOVER ST.
CAROLINE
NORFOLK TER
NORFOLK ST.
BROAD ST.
UPPER GWYDIR ST.
SLEAFORD ST.
STONE ST.
AINSWORTH CT
BURY CT.
AINSWORTH ST.
KERRIDGE CL.
CROMWELL RD
BRAMPTON RD
STOURBRIDGE GRO
VINERY WAY
THE PADDOCKS
Training Cnf.
PARKER ST.
EMMANUEL RD
Tel. Off.
P.O.
CAMDEN
PARKER TERRACE
PARKSIDE
MELBOURNE PL.
WARKWORTH TER
Sch
POL. STA.
FIRE STA.
G.P.O.
Anglia Polytechnic University
BRADMORE ST.
PALMERS
STAFFORDSHIRE
GWYDIR STREET
MILL FORD ST.
HOOPER ST.
STONE ST.
AINSWORTH ST.
WETEN HALL RD
STREET OF FAIRFAX RD
VINERY PK
VINERY
DANESBURY CT
Sch.
10
Parkers Piece
REGENT TERRACE
REGENT ST.
Sports Hall
Swim Baths
MORTIMER RD
WOLLA STON RD
Car Park
Hughes Hall
MACKENZIE RD
MILL RD
GUEST RD
PEROWNE ST.
DITCHBURN PL.
Carpn Depot
STREET
STREET
STREET
STREET
COLDHAMS LGRO
VINERY RD
Recn Grnd.
DOWNING
14
GONVILLE PL.
GRESHAM RD
PARKSIDE
Fenners Univer Cricket Ground
Drama Cnc.
COVENT GARDEN
Univ. Health Cent.
Tennis Gd.
MILL RD
FELTON ST.
S.A.
CROSS ST.
Ch.
Liby.
SEDGWICK STREET
CATHAR INE STREET
THODAY STREET
PHILIPS ROAD
HEMINGFORD ROAD
ROSS STREET
ROMSEY RD
FORD RD
BEL GRAVE RD
CYPRUS RD
VINERY ROAD
A1134
SEYMOUR STREET
OAP Home
9
Hyde Park Cnr.
A603
MANSFIELD RD
UNION RD
CORONATION ST.
GRESHAM ROAD
HARVEY RD.
S. PAULS RD
CAMBRIDGE PL.
LYNDEWODE RD.
TENISON AV.
TENISON RD
DEVONSHIRE RD
RAVENSW'TH GDNS
WILKIN ST.
MAWSON RD
DONISTHORPE
BARNBAS RD
DEVONSHIRE ROAD
ST.
ANGUS ST.
SWANNS TER.
FLETCHERS TERR.
CAMPBELL RD
ARGYLE STREET
STOCKWELL ST.
HOPE ST.
ROMSEY TER.
ROMSEY MWS.
MALTA RD
SUEZ RD
MADRAS RD
MONT REAL RD
NATAL RD
BROOKFIELDS
ROMSEY TOWN
NORWICH ST.
RUSSELL ST.
HIGHSETT
Ind Sch
CLAREMONT
PATEMAN CT
Studio Schle (English)
George Gt Eastern
GREVILLE RD
MILLCROFT CT
MARMORA RD
CAMBRIDGE
16

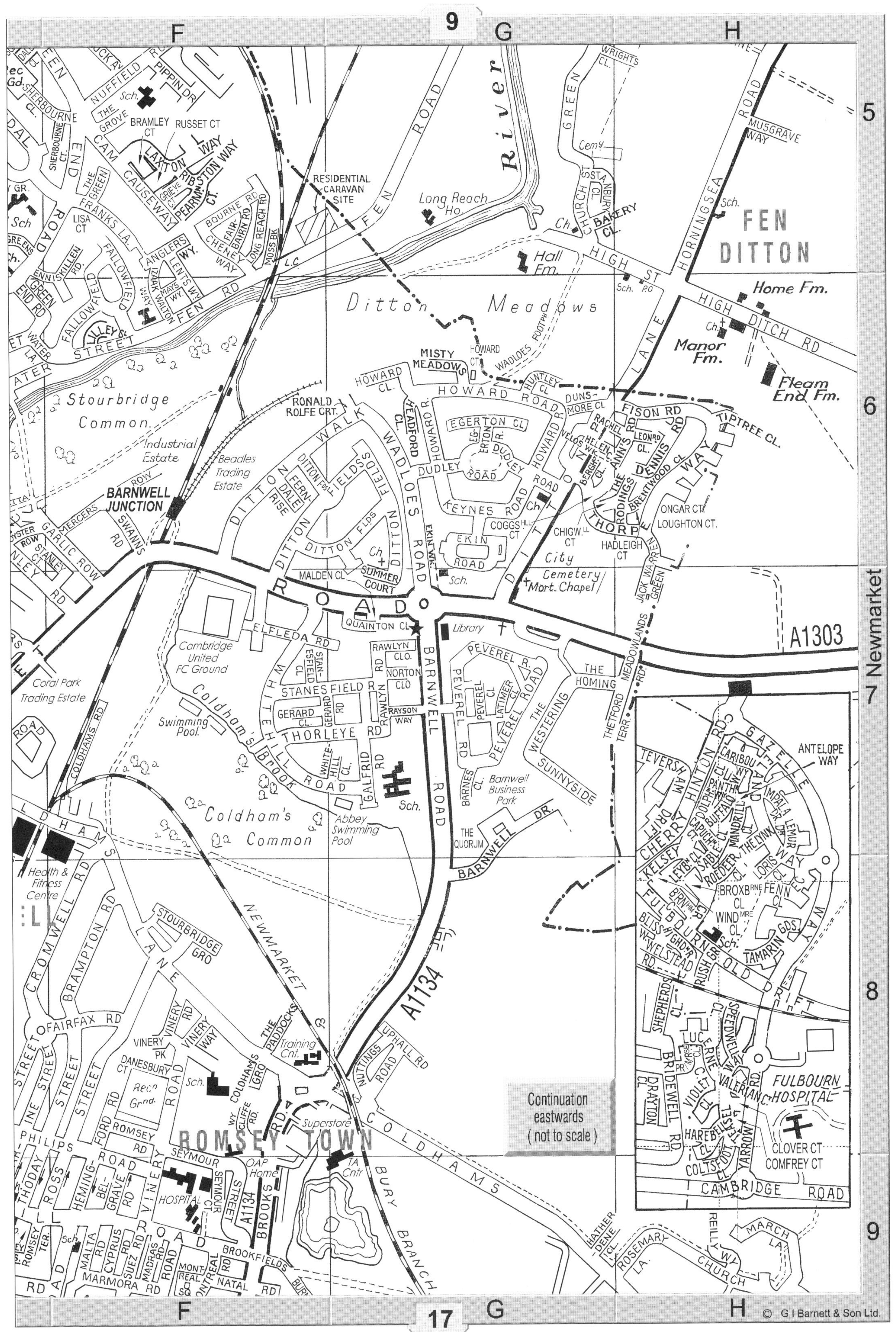
FEN DITTON
ROMSEY TOWN
BARNWELL JUNCTION
Stourbridge Common
Ditton Meadows
Coldham's Common
River
FEN ROAD
HIGH ST
HIGH DITCH RD
HORNINGSEA ROAD
MUSGRAVE WAY
Home Fm.
Manor Fm.
Fleam End Fm.
Hall Fm.
Long Reach Ho.
MISTY MEADOWS
HOWARD ROAD
HOWARD CL.
EGERTON CL.
DUDLEY ROAD
KEYNES ROAD
EKIN ROAD
HEADFORD CL.
WADLOES ROAD
DITTON FIELDS
DITTON WALK
FERNDALE RISE
RONALD ROLFE CRT.
BEADLES TRADING ESTATE
Industrial Estate
FISON RD
TIPTREE CL.
DENNIS RD
LEONARD RD
RACHEL CL
ANN'S CL
THORPE WAY
THE RODINGS
BRENTWOOD CL.
ONGAR CT
LOUGHTON CT.
HADLEIGH CT
CHIGWELL CT
COGGSHILL CT
City Cemetery
Mort. Chapel
MALDEN CL
SUMMER COURT
QUAINTON CL
Library
RAWLYN CLO.
NORTON CLO
RAWLYN RD
RAYSON WAY
STANESFIELD RD
GERARD CL.
GERARD RD
THORLEYE RD
GALFRID RD
WHITEHILL CL.
WHITEHILL ROAD
ELFLEDA RD
Cambridge United FC Ground
Coral Park Trading Estate
Swimming Pool
Abbey Swimming Pool
PEVEREL RD
PEVEREL CL.
LATIMER CL.
WESTERING ROAD
THE WESTERING
SUNNYSIDE
THE HOMING
THETFORD TERR.
MEADOWLANDS RD.
BARNES CL.
Barnwell Business Park
THE QUORUM
BARNWELL DR.
BARNWELL ROAD
A1303
A1134 Newmarket
NEWMARKET ROAD
COLDHAMS ROAD
COLDHAMS LANE
CROMWELL RD
BRAMPTON RD
STOURBRIDGE GRO
VINERY RD
VINERY WAY
VINERY PK
DANESBURY CT
Recn Grnd.
THE PADDOCKS
Training Cnt.
UPHALL RD
NUTTINGS ROAD
Superstore
SEYMOUR STREET
CLIFFE RD
ROMSEY RD
BELGRAVE RD
CYPRUS RD
SUEZ RD
MADRAS RD
MONTREAL RD
NATAL RD
MARMORA RD
BROOKFIELDS
PHILIPS ROAD
THODAY STREET
ROSSOM TER.
HEMINGFORD RD
OAP Home
Hospital
TA Cntr
BURY BRANCH
TEVERSHAM DRIFT
HINTON RD
GAZELLE WY
ANTELOPE WAY
CHERRY KELSEY
CARIBOU CL
BUFFALO CL
MANDRILL
BROXBOURNE CL
FENN WIND CL.
TAMARIN GDNS.
LORIS WAY
THE LYNX
FULBOURN OLD DRIFT
BLISS WAY
WELSTEAD RD
SHEPHERDS CL
LUCERNE CL
SPEEDWELL CL
BRIDEWELL RD
DRAYTON CL
VIOLET CL
HAREBELL CL
COLTSFOOT CL
VALERIAN CL
YARROW
FULBOURN HOSPITAL
CLOVER CT
COMFREY CT
CAMBRIDGE ROAD
HATHER DENE
ROSEMARY LA.
REILLY WY
CHURCH
MARCH LA.
RESIDENTIAL CARAVAN SITE
FRANKS LA.
FALLOWFIELD
NUFFIELD RD
THE GROVE
BRAMLEY CT
RUSSET CT
LAXTON WAY
RIBSTON WAY
PEARMAIN CT.
CHENEY WAY
ANGLERS WY.
IZAAK WALTON WAY
GREEN END RD
SHERBOURNE CL.
LISA CT
Continuation eastwards (not to scale)

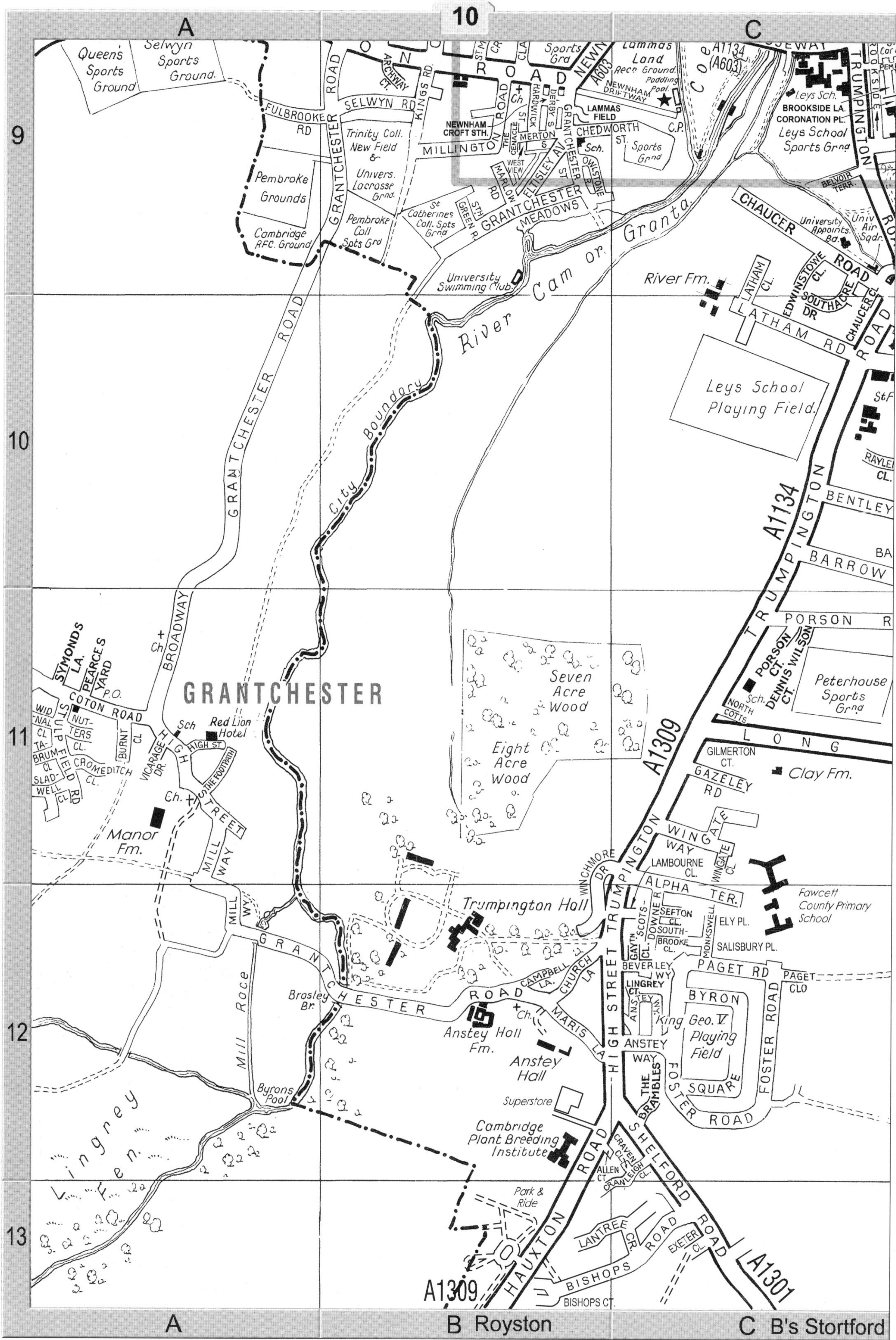
10
A
B Royston
C B's Stortford
Queen's Sports Ground
Selwyn Sports Ground
Pembroke Grounds
Cambridge R.F.C. Ground
Pembroke Coll Spts Grd
FULBROOKE RD
SELWYN RD
GRANTCHESTER ROAD
KINGS RD.
Trinity Coll. New Field &
Univers. Lacrosse Grnd.
St. Catherines Coll. Spts Grnd
MILLINGTON
NEWNHAM CROFT STH.
ARCHWAY
THE CENACLE
MARLOW RD.
WEST VIEW
5TH GREEN R.
GRANTCHESTER MEADOWS
GRANTCHESTER
ELTISLEY AV.
ST.
MERTON
HARDWICK
DERBY S.
CLA
Sports Grd
NEWN
A603
A603
LAMMAS FIELD
CHEDWORTH ST.
Sports Grnd
Sch.
OWLSTONE
Lammas Land
Newnham Driftway
Recn Ground Paddling Pool
C.P.
CAUSEWAY
A1134 (A603)
Coe Fen
Leys Sch.
BROOKSIDE LA. CORONATION PL.
Leys School Sports Grnd
TRUMPINGTON RD
BELVOIR TERR.
University Swimming Club.
River Cam or Granta
City Boundary
River Fm.
CHAUCER ROAD
University Appoints. Bd.
Univ Air Sqdr.
EDWINSTOWE CL.
SOUTHACRE DR.
LATHAM CL.
LATHAM RD.
CHAUCER CL.
ROAD
Leys School Playing Field.
St F
RAYLE CL.
A1134
TRUMPINGTON
BENTLEY
BARROW
BA
PORSON R
PORSON CT.
DENNIS WILSON CT.
NORTH COTTS
Sch.
Peterhouse Sports Grnd
A1309
LONG
GILMERTON CT.
GAZELEY RD
Clay Fm.
SYMONDS LA.
PEARCES YARD
P.O.
COTON ROAD
BROADWAY
Ch.
WIDNAL CL
STUPFIELD
BRUM CL
SLADWELL CL
TA-
NUTTERS CL.
BURNT CL
CROMEDITCH CL.
RD.
GRANTCHESTER
Sch.
Red Lion Hotel
HIGH ST.
HIGH STREET
VICARAGE DR.
THE FOOTPATH
Ch.
Manor Fm.
MILL WAY
MILL WY.
Brosley Br.
Mill Race
GRANTCHESTER ROAD
Byrons Pool
Lingrey Fen
Seven Acre Wood
Eight Acre Wood
Trumpington Hall
WINCHMORE DR.
ALPHA TER.
GAYTN CL.
SCOTS CL.
DOWNER
SEFTON CL.
SOUTHBROOKE CL.
MONKSWELL
ELY PL.
SALISBURY PL.
WINGATE WAY
LAMBOURNE CL.
WINGATE CL.
Fawcett County Primary School
TRUMPINGTON
CAMPBELL LA.
CHURCH LA.
MARIS LA.
Ch.
Anstey Hall Fm.
Anstey Hall
Superstore
Cambridge Plant Breeding Institute
HIGH STREET TRUMPINGTON
BEVERLEY WY.
ANSTEY CT.
LINGREY CT.
King
Anstey Way
THE BRAMBLES
PAGET RD.
PAGET CLO
BYRON SQUARE
Geo. V Playing Field
FOSTER ROAD
FOSTER ROAD
SHELFORD ROAD
HAUXTON ROAD
GRAVEL CT.
ALLEN CT.
CRANLEIGH
LANTREE CR.
BISHOPS RD
BISHOPS CT.
EXETER CL.
A1301
A1309
Park & Ride
A
B
C

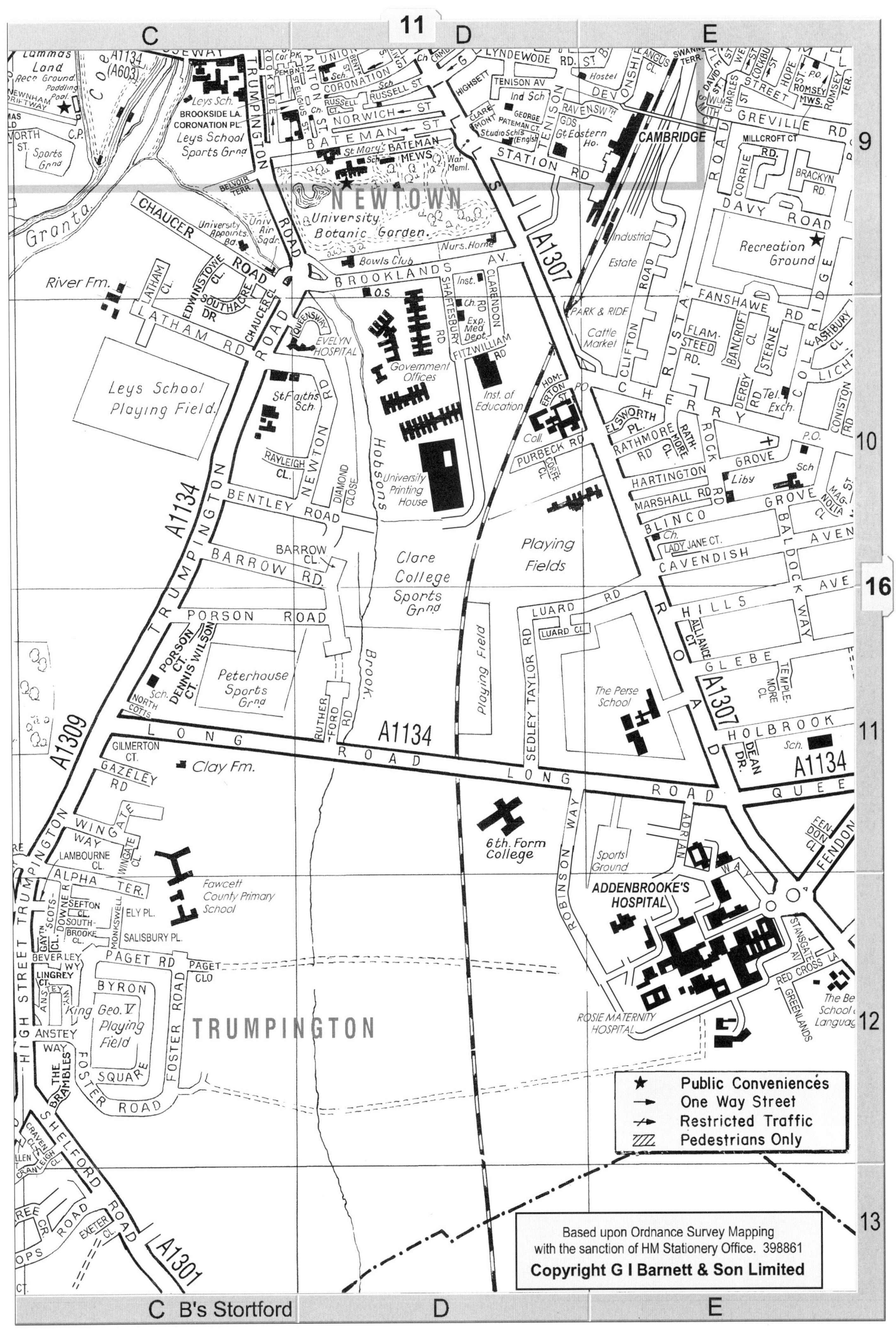
CAMBRIDGE
NEWTOWN
TRUMPINGTON
University Botanic Garden.
Leys School Sports Grnd
Leys School Playing Field.
Clare College Sports Grnd.
Peterhouse Sports Grnd.
University Printing House
Government Offices
Inst. of Education
Playing Fields
Playing Field
Addenbrooke's Hospital
Rosie Maternity Hospital
Sports Ground
6th. Form College
The Perse School
Fawcett County Primary School
King Geo. V Playing Field
Byron Square
The Brambles
Recreation Ground
River Fm.
Clay Fm.
Evelyn Hospital
St Faiths Sch.
St Mary's Sch.
Leys Sch.
Coronation Pl.
Bowls Club
Park & Ride
Cattle Market
Industrial Estate
Lammas Land
Rec. Ground
Paddling Pool.
Newnham Driftway
Sports Grnd
C.P.
War Meml.
Nurs. Home
Ind Sch
Tenison Av
Hostel
Gt. Eastern Ho.
Station Rd
Coll.
Liby
Sch
P.O.
Tel. Exch.
O.S.
Exp. Med. Dept.

A1134 (A603)
Granta
Coe
CHAUCER ROAD
LATHAM RD
LATHAM CL.
EDWINSTOWE CL.
SOUTHACRE DR
CHAUCER CL.
QUEENSWAY
NEWTON RD
RAYLEIGH CL.
BENTLEY ROAD
DIAMOND CLOSE
BARROW CL.
BARROW RD.
PORSON ROAD
PORSON CT.
DENNIS WILSON CT.
NORTH COTTS
TRUMPINGTON ROAD
A1134
A1309
GILMERTON CT.
GAZELEY RD
WINGATE WAY
WINGATE CL.
LAMBOURNE CL.
ALPHA TER.
SEFTON CL.
DOWNER CL.
SOUTHBROOKE CL.
MONKSWELL
ELY PL.
SALISBURY PL.
GWYN CL.
SCOTS CL.
BEVERLEY WY
LINGREY CT.
ANSTEY WAY
HIGH STREET TRUMPINGTON
PAGET RD
PAGET CLO
FOSTER ROAD
ANSTEY WAY
FOSTER ROAD
SHELFORD ROAD
GRAVEL
CRANLEIGH
EXETER CL.
A1301
LONG ROAD
A1134
RUTHERFORD RD
Brook.
Hobsons Brook
UNION RD
CORONATION ST
NORWICH ST
BATEMAN ST
RUSSELL ST
BATEMAN MEWS
PANTON ST
PEMBROKE ST
ST ELIGIUS ST
SELWYN
BROOKLANDS AV.
SHAFTESBURY RD
CLARENDON RD
Ch. RD
FITZWILLIAM RD
HIGHSETT
LYNDEWODE RD.
TENISON AV
TENISON RD
STATION RD
CLAREMONT
PATEMAN CT.
STUDIO Schls (Englsh)
RUSSELL ST
HOMERTON
PURBECK RD
CORFE
A1307
DEVONSHIRE RD
ANGUS ST
SWANN TERR.
CAMBRIDGE
GREVILLE RD
DAVY ROAD
CORRIE RD
MILLCROFT CT
BRACKYN RD.
CHARLES ST
HOPE ST
ROMSEY TER.
ROMSEY MWS.
COCKBURN ST
DAVY ST
WM.
WILM.
CLIFTON RD
RUSTAT RD
CHERRY ROAD
FANSHAWE RD
FLAMSTEED RD.
BANCROFT CL
STERNE CL
ELSWORTH PL.
RATHMORE RD
RATHMORE CL.
DERBY RD
HARTINGTON GROVE
MARSHALL RD
BLINCO GROVE
LADY JANE CT.
CAVENDISH RD
LUARD RD
LUARD CL
SEDLEY TAYLOR RD
HILLS ROAD
ALLIANCE CT
GLEBE RD
TEMPLE MORE CL.
HOLBROOK RD
DEAN DR.
A1307
A1134
QUEEN
ROBINSON WAY
ADRIAN WAY
STANSGATE AV
RED CROSS LA
GREENLANDS
FENDON RD
FENDON CL
BALDOCK WAY
GROVE
CONISTON CL
MAGNOLIA CL
COLERIDGE RD
LICHFIELD RD
ASHBURY CL
QUEEN EDITH'S
The Bell School of Languages
Evelyn Hospital
Coldhams

★ Public Conveniences
→ One Way Street
⇥ Restricted Traffic
▨ Pedestrians Only

Based upon Ordnance Survey Mapping
with the sanction of HM Stationery Office. 398861
Copyright G I Barnett & Son Limited

B's Stortford

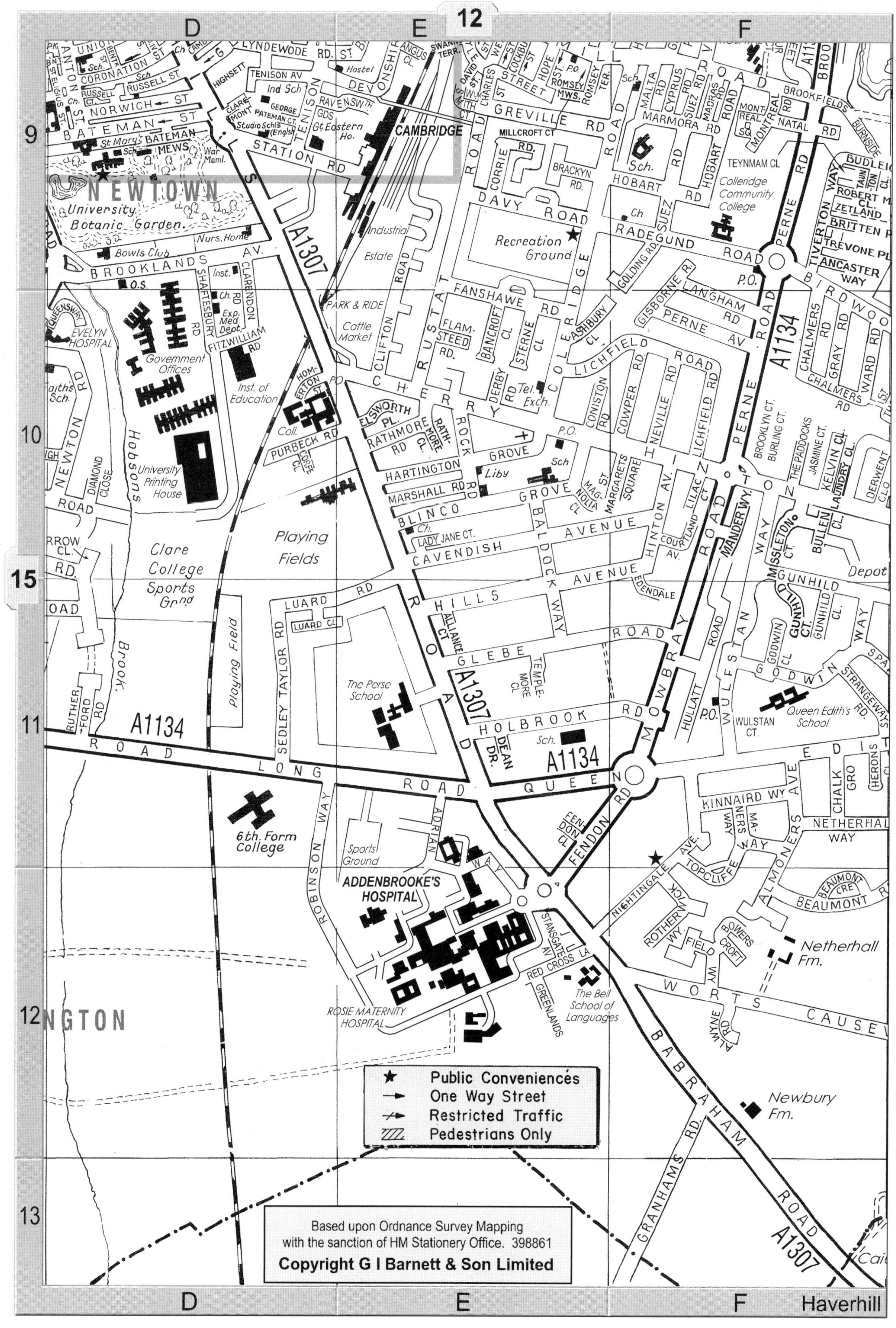
12
D
E
F
UNION
CORONATION ST
RUSSELL ST
NORWICH ST
BATEMAN
St Mary's BATEMAN
MEWS
NEWTOWN
University
Botanic Garden.
Bowls Club
O.S.
BROOKLANDS AV.
SHAFTESBURY RD
CLARENDON RD
FITZWILLIAM RD
Inst.
QUEENSWAY
EVELYN Hospital
NEWTON ROAD
DIAMOND CLOSE
Government Offices
Inst. of Education
HOBSONS
University Printing House
Clare College Sports Grnd
Brook
RUTHERFORD
A1134 ROAD
SEDLEY TAYLOR RD
LUARD RD
LUARD CL.
Playing Field
Playing Fields
The Perse School
6th. Form College
ROBINSON WAY
Sports Ground
ADDENBROOKE'S HOSPITAL
ADRIAN WAY
ROSIE MATERNITY HOSPITAL
NGTON
LYNDEWODE RD. ST.
TENISON AV
Ind Sch
Claremont
PATEMAN CT
Studio Schls (Engl)
STATION ROAD
DEVONSHIRE
RAVENSWTH
GDS
Gt Eastern Ho.
Hostel
ANGUS CL
SWANN TERR.
CAMBRIDGE
Industrial Estate
Park & Ride
Cattle Market
CLIFTON ROAD
CHERRY
RUSTAT
FANSHAWE RD
FLAM-STEED RD.
BANCROFT CL
STERNE CL
DERBY RD
RATH-MORE RD.
Tel. Exch.
ELSWORTH PL.
RATHMORE RD
HARTINGTON
MARSHALL RD
BLINCO
LADY JANE CT.
HILLS ROAD
ALLIANCE CT.
GLEBE
TEMPLE-MORE CL
HOLBROOK RD
DEAN DR.
A1307
A1134
ROCK ROAD
GROVE
Liby
GROVE
BALDOCK WAY
AVENUE
CAVENDISH AVENUE
COLERIDGE
ST. MAG. NOLIA CL
ST MARGARETS SQUARE
CONISTON RD
COWPER RD
NEVILLE RD
HINTON AV.
COURTLAND AV.
EDENDALE
MOWBRAY ROAD
QUEEN
FENDON CL
FENDON ROAD
STANSGATE AV.
RED CROSS LA
GREENLANDS
The Bell School of Languages
GREVILLE RD
MILLCROFT CT
CORRIE RD.
BRACKYN RD.
DAVY ROAD
Recreation Ground
RADEGUND ROAD
HOBART RD
SUEZ RD
GOLDING RD
GISBORNE R.
LANGHAM RD
PERNE AV
ASHBURY CL
LICHFIELD
COMPER RD
NEVILLE RD
LICHFIELD RD
LILAC CT
PERNE ROAD
MANDER WY.
WULFSTAN WAY
HULLATT
P.O.
WULSTAN CT.
GODWIN CL
GODWIN WAY
Queen Edith's School
HOPE STREET
ROMSEY MWS
ROMSEY TER.
MALTA RD
CYPRUS RD
SUEZ RD
MADRAS RD
Sch.
Colleridge Community College
MARMORA RD
TEYNMAM CL
PERNE ROAD
A1134
CHALMERS RD
GRAY RD
WARD RD
CHALMERS RD
BROOKLYN CT.
BURLING CT.
THE PADDOCKS
JASMINE CT.
KELVIN CL.
LAUNDRY CL.
BULLEN CL.
DERWENT CLO
MISSLETON CT.
GUNHILD CT.
GUNHILD WAY
GUNHILD CL.
Depot
STRANGEWAYS RD.
BIRDWOOD
ANCASTER WAY
BUDLEIG
IVERTON
ZETLAND
BRITTEN PL
TREVONE PL
ROBERT M
TAUN TON
MONTREAL RD
NATAL RD
BURNSIDE
BROOKFIELDS
KINNAIRD WY
MA-NERS WAY
ALMONERS AVE
CHALK GRO
HERONS
NETHERHALL WAY
TOPCLIFFE WAY
NIGHTINGALE AVE
BEAUMONT CRE
BEAUMONT
ROTHER WYCK
BOWERS FIELD
BOWERS CROFT
Netherhall Fm.
WORTS CAUSE
AYLWYNE RD
BABRAHAM ROAD
GRANHAMS RD
Newbury Fm.
A1307
Cai
Public Conveniences
One Way Street
Restricted Traffic
Pedestrians Only
Based upon Ordnance Survey Mapping
with the sanction of HM Stationery Office. 398861
Copyright G I Barnett & Son Limited
D
E
F
Haverhill

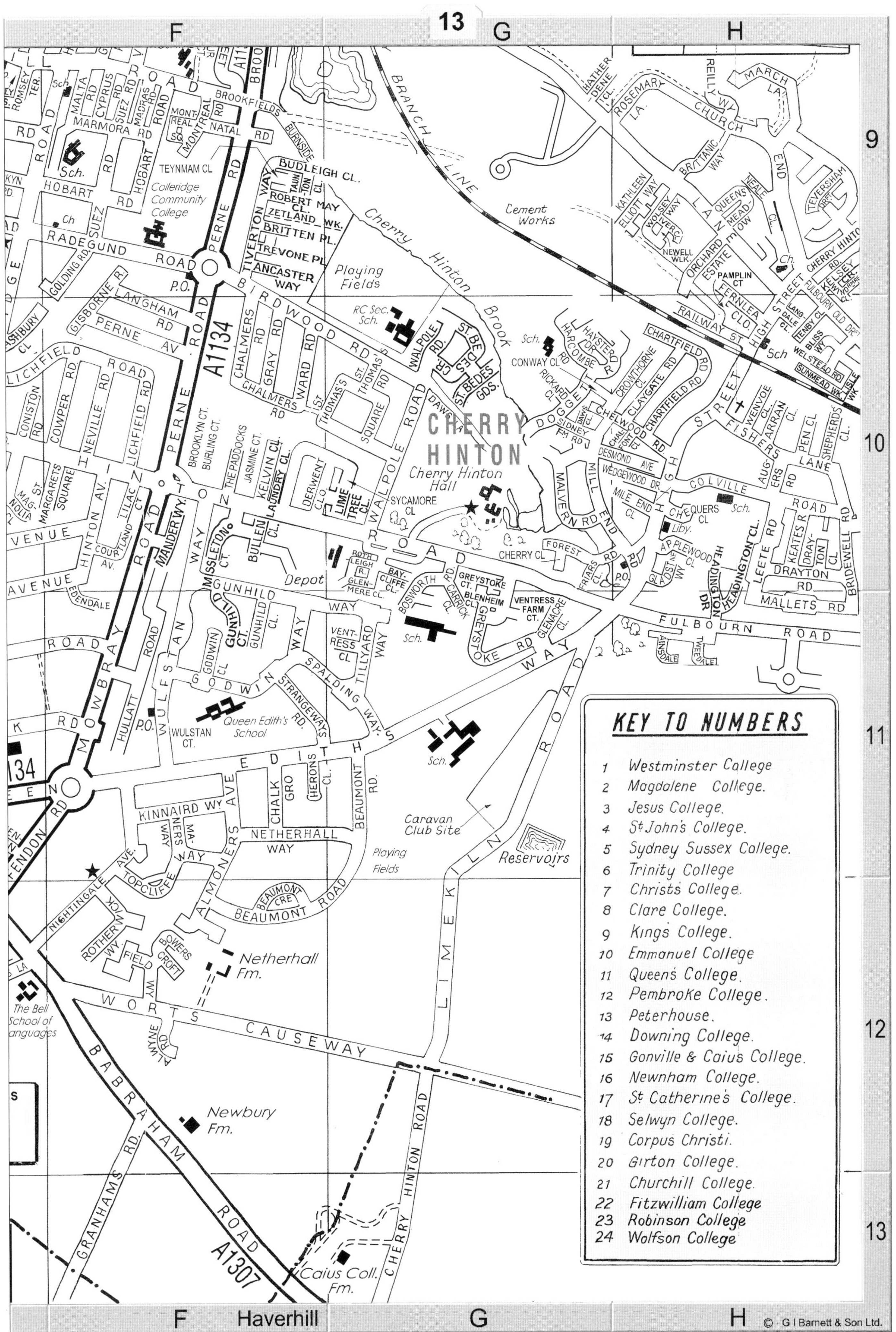
13
F
G
H
9
10
11
12
13
CHERRY HINTON
KEY TO NUMBERS
1   Westminster College
2   Magdalene College.
3   Jesus College.
4   St John's College.
5   Sydney Sussex College.
6   Trinity College
7   Christ's College.
8   Clare College.
9   Kings College.
10 Emmanuel College
11 Queen's College.
12 Pembroke College.
13 Peterhouse.
14 Downing College.
15 Gonville & Caius College.
16 Newnham College.
17 St Catherine's College.
18 Selwyn College.
19 Corpus Christi.
20 Girton College.
21 Churchill College.
22 Fitzwilliam College
23 Robinson College
24 Wolfson College
Haverhill
© G I Barnett & Son Ltd.

CAMBRIDGE INDEX TO STREETS

ABBEY RD. E7
ABBEY ST. E7
ABBEY WK. E7
ABBOTS CL. C4
ABERCORN PL. D4
ACREFIELD DR. D7
ACTON WY. C5
ADAM & EVE ST. D8
ADAMS RD. B7
ADDENBROOKE'S HOSPITAL ......
....E12
ADRIAN WY. E11
AINGERS RD. B1
AINSDALE H11
AINSWORTH CT. E8
AINSWORTH PL. E8
AINSWORTH ST. E8
AKEMAN ST. C6
ALAN PERCIVAL CT. E6
ALBEMARLE WY. D4
ALBERT ST. C6
ALBION RD. B7
ALBION YARD B7
ALETEAD RD. ....HISTON INSET
ALEX WOOD RD. C5
ALICE WY. ....HISTON INSET
ALL SAINTS LA. B6
ALLEN CT. B12
ALLIANCE CT. E11
ALLINGTON CL. ....HISTON INSET
ALMONERS AVE. F12
ALPHA RD. C6
ALPHA TER. C11
ALWYNE RD. F12
AMBROSE WAY C1
AMHURST CT. B8
AMWELL RD. D4
ANCASTER WY. F9
ANGLERS WY. F5
ANGUS CL. E9
ANN'S RD. H6
ANSTEY WY. C12
ANTELOPE WY. ....CHERRY
....................................HINTON INSET
APOLLO WY. D4
APPLEWOOD CL. H10
APTHORPE WY. E4
ARAGON CL. D4
ARBURY C5
ARBURY CT. D5
ARBURY RD. C4-D5
ARCHWAY CT. B9
ARDEN RD. D4
ARGYLE ST. E9
ARMITAGE WY. D4
ARRAN CL. H10
ARTHUR ST. C6
ARUNDEL CL. B5
ASCHAM RD. D6
ASHBURY CL. E10
ASHCROFT CT. D4
ASHFIELD RD. E5
ASHVALE C4
ATHERTON CL. D6
ATKINS CL. E4
AUCKLAND RD. D7
AUGERS RD. H10
AUGUSTUS CL. D4
AYLESBOROUGH CL. C4
AYLESTONE RD. D7

BABRAHAM RD. F12
BADMINTON CL. B5
BAGOT PL. D4
BAILEY MS. D7
BAKERY CL. G5
BALDOCK WY. E10
BALLARD CL. G2
BANCROFT CL. E10
BANDON RD. A5
BANHAMS CL. D7
BARNABAS CT. G3
BARNARD WY. C5
BARNES CL. G7
BARNWELL E8
BARNWELL DR. G8
BARNWELL RD. G7
BARROW CL. D10
BARROW RD. C10
BARROWCROFTS HISTON INSET
BARTON CL. B9
BARTON RD A9
BASSETT CL. D4
BATEMAN MEWS D9
BATEMAN ST. D9
BATESON RD. C6
BAYCLIFFE CL. G10
BAYFORD PL. D4

BEALES WY. E4
BEAULANDS CL. D7
BEAUMONT CR. F12
BEAUMONT RD. F12
BECHE RD. E7
BEEHIVE CENTRE E7
BELGRAVE RD. F9
BELL HILL B1
BELMONT PL. D7
BELMORE CL. B5
BELVOIR RD. D7
BELVOIR TER. C9
BENET CL. F3
BENE'T ST. C8
BENIANS CT. B7
BENSON PL. B6
BENSON ST. B6
BENTINCK ST. D9
BENTLEY RD. C10
BERGHOLT CL. G6
BERMUDA RD. C6
BERMUDA TER. B6
BERRYLANDS D5
BEVERLEY WY. C12
BIRCH CL. D5
BIRDWOOD RD. F9
BISHOP WY. C2
BISHOPS CT. B13
BISHOPS RD. B13
BLACKHALL RD. B4
BLACKTHORN CL. D5
BLANDFORD WK. B4
BLENHEIM CL. G11
BLINCO GR. E10
BLISS WY ....CHERRY
....................................HINTON INSET
BLISS WY. H10
BLOSSOM ST. E8
BORROWDALE C5
BOSWORTH RD. G11
BOURNE RD. F5
BOWERS CROFT F12
BRACKENBURY CL. C2
BRACKLEY CL. C5
BRACKYN RD. E9
BRADBUSH FIELDS A6
BRADMORE ST. D8
BRADWELLS CT. C8
BRAMLEY CT. F5
BRAMPTON RD. F8
BRENTWOOD CL. H6
BRIDEWELL RD. ....CHERRY
....................................HINTON INSET
BRIDEWELL RD. H10
BRIDGACRE D7
BRIDGE RD. C2
BRIDGE RD. C3
BRIDGE ST. C8
BRIERLEY WK. B4
BRIMLEY WY. C5
BRITTANIC WY. H9
BRITTEN PL. F9
BROAD ST. D8
BROADMEADOWS D7
BROADWAY A11
BROOK CL. B1
BROOK MOUNT CT. E4
BROOKFIELDS F9
BROOKLANDS AVE. D9
BROOKLYN CT. F10
BROOKS RD. F9
BROOKSIDE C9
BROOKSIDE LA. C9
BROWNLOW RD. B4
BROXBOURNE CL. ....CHERRY
....................................HINTON INSET
BRUNSWICK GDS. D7
BRUNSWICK TER. D7
BRUNSWICK WK. D7
BUCHAN ST. C4
BUCKINGHAM RD. B6
BUDLEIGH CL. F9
BUFFALO WY. ....CHERRY
....................................HINTON INSET
BULLEN CL. F10
BULSTRODE GDS. A7
BULTEEL CL. F2
BURGOYNES FARM CL. C2
BURGOYNES RD. C2
BURKETT WY. ......HISTON INSET
BURLEIGH ST. D7
BURLING CT. F10
BURLING WK. G2
BURNHAM CL. ....CHERRY
....................................HINTON INSET
BURNSIDE F9
BURNT CL. A11
BURRELLS WK. B8

BURROWFIELD C3
BURY CT. E8
BUTCHER CL. F2
BUTLER WY. C5
BUTT LA. E2-F2
BYRON SQ. C12

CADWIN FIELD D4
CAITHNESS CT. D4
CALEDON WY. D4
CALLANDER CL. C4
CAM CAUSEWAY F5
CAMBANKS E6
CAMBRIDGE BUSINESS PARK F4
CAMBRIDGE PL. D9
CAMBRIDGE RD. ......CHERRY
....................................HINTON INSET
CAMBRIDGE RD. (HISTON) B3
CAMBRIDGE RD.(MILTON) F3
CAMBRIDGE SCIENCE PARK ..E4
CAMDEN CT. D8
CAMERON RD. D4
CAMPBELL LA. B12
CAMPBELL ST. E9
CAMPKIN CT. D4
CAMPKIN RD. D5
CAMSIDE E6
CANNON CT. E6
CANTERBURY CL. B6
CANTERBURY ST. B6
CAPSTAN CL. E7
CAPUCHIN CT. ....CHERRY
....................................HINTON INSET
CARAVERE CL. D4
CARIBOU WY. ....CHERRY
....................................HINTON INSET
CARISBROOK RD. B5
CARLTON WY. C5
CARLYLE RD. C6
CAROLINE PL. D8
CARRICK CL. G11
CASTLE ROW C7
CASTLE ST. C6
CATHARINE ST. E9
CAVENDISH AVE. E10
CAVENDISH RD. D6
CAVESSON CT. B5
CHALFONT CL. H10
CHALK GR. F11
CHALMERS RD. F10
CHAMPNEYS WK. B8
CHANCELLORS WK. B5
CHANTRY CL. D6
CHAPEL ST. E6
CHARLES ST. E9
CHARTFIELD RD. H10
CHATSWORTH AVE. B5
CHAUCER CL. C10
CHAUCER RD. C9
CHEDDARS LA. E7
CHEDWORTH ST. B9
CHELWOOD RD. G10
CHENEY WY. F5
CHEQUERS CL. H10
CHEQUERS RD. B2
CHERRY CL. (MILTON) G2
CHERRY CL. (CHERRY HINTON)..
....G10
CHERRY HINTON G10
CHERRY HINTON RD. ......CHERRY
....................................HINTON INSET
CHERRY HINTON RD.
  (CHERRY HINTON) H9
CHERRY HINTON RD. E10
CHERRY HINTON RD.
  (BARBAHAM) G13
CHESTERFIELD RD. E5
CHESTERTON E5
CHESTERTON HALL CR. D6
CHESTERTON LA. C7
CHESTERTON RD. D6-E6
CHESTNUT GR. D6
CHIGWELL CT. G6
CHIVERS WY. B2
CHRISTCHURCH ST. D7
CHURCH END H9
CHURCH LA. (MILTON) G2
CHURCH LA.
  (TRUMPINGTON) B12
CHURCH RATE WK. B8
CHURCH ST. (CHESTERTON) ..E6
CHURCH ST. (FEN DITTON) ...G5
CHURCH ST. (HISTON) ....
....................................HISTON INSET
CITY RD. D8
CLARE RD. B9
CLARE ST. C6
CLAREMONT D9

CLARENDON RD. D9
CLARENDON ST. D8
CLARKSON CL. B7
CLARKSON RD. B7
CLAY CL. LA. C2
CLAY ST. ....HISTON INSET
CLAYGATE RD. H10
CLERK MAXWELL RD. A7
CLIFTON RD. E10
CLIVEDEN CL. B5
CLOVER CT. ....CHERRY
....................................HINTON INSET
COBHOLME PL. D4
COCKBURN ST. E9
COCKCROFT PL. B7
COCKEREL RD. C5
COGGESHALL CT. G6
COLDHAMS GR. F8
COLDHAMS LA. E7
COLDHAMS RD. F7
COLERIDGE RD. E10
COLES RD. G3
COLLEGE FIELDS D5
COLLEGE RD. B3
COLLIER RD. D8
COLTSFOOT CL. ....CHERRY
....................................HINTON INSET
COLVILLE RD. H10
COLWYN CL. C5
COMFREY CT. ....CHERRY
....................................HINTON INSET
CONDER CL. F2
CONDUIT HEAD RD. A6
CONISTON RD. E10
CONWAY CL. G10
COOK CL. E5
CORFE CL. D10
CORN EXCHANGE ST. C8
CORONA RD. C6
CORONATION PL. C9
CORONATION ST. D9
CORRIE RD. E9
COTTENHAM RD...HISTON INSET
COTTON RD. A11
COULSON CL. F2
COURTLAND AVE. F10
COVENT GARDEN D8
COWLEY PARK F4
COWLEY RD. F4
COWPER RD. F10
CRAISTER CT. D4
CRANLEIGH CL. C12
CRANMER RD. B8
CRATHERN WY. D4
CRAVEN CL. C12
CRAWFORD CL. D4
CRISPIN CL. C4
CROFT CL. ....HISTON INSET
CROFT HOLME LA. C6
CROME DITCH CL. A11
CROMWELL RD. E8
CROSS ST. D8
CROWLAND WY. D4
CROWTHORNE CL. H10
CUNNINGHAM CL. D5
CUTTER FERRY CL. D7
CUTTER FERRY LA. D7
CUTTER FERRY PATH D7
CYPRUS RD. F9

DAISY CL. C4
DALTON SQ. E6
DANE DR. A8
DANESBURY COURT F8
DARWIN DR. C5
DAVEY CL. C2
DAVID BULL WY. G2
DAVID ST. E9
DAVY RD. E9
DAWS CL. G10
DAWS LA. G10
DE FREVILLE AVE. D7
DEAN DR. E11
DENNIS RD. H6
DENNIS WILSON CT. C11
DERBY RD. E10
DERBY ST. B9
DERWENT CL. F10
DESMOND AVE. G10
DEVONSHIRE RD. E9
DIAMOND CL. D10
DITCHBURN PL. E8
DITTON FIELDS F6-G6
DITTON LA. G7
DITTON WK. F6
DOCTORS CL. C2
DOGGETT RD. G10
DOLPHIN CL. ....CHERRY

....................................HINTON INSET
DOVER ST. D8
DOWDING WY. C5
DOWNE RD. C12
DOWNHAMS LA. E5
DOWNING PL. C8
DOWNING ST. C8
DRAKE WY. ....HISTON INSET
DRAYTON CL. ....CHERRY
....................................HINTON INSET
DRAYTON CL. H10
DRAYTON RD. H10
DROSIER RD. D8
DRUMMER ST. C8
DUDLEY RD. G6
DUNDEE CL. E5
DUNSMORE CL. G6
DURNFORD WY. D5
DWYER-JOYCE CL. B1

EACHARD RD. B6
EARL ST. D8
EAST HERTFORD RD. C7
EAST RD. D8
EASTFIELD E5
EATON CL. E5
EDEN ST. D8
EDEN ST. BACKWAY D8
EDGECOMBE D4
EDINBURGH RD. E6
EDMUND CL. G2
EDWARD ST. E8
EDWINSTOWE CL. C9
EGERTON CL. G6
EGERTON RD. G6
EKIN RD. G6
EKIN WK. G6
ELAND WY. ....CHERRY
....................................HINTON INSET
ELDER CL. D5
ELFLEDA RD. F7
ELISON CL. C4
ELIZABETH WY. D6
ELLESMERE RD. C4
ELM ST. D7
ELMFIELD CL. E6
ELMFIELD RD. E5
ELSWORTH PL. E10
ELTISLEY AVE. B9
ELY PL. C12
ELY RD. (MILTON) G2-H1
EMERY RD. E8
EMERY ST. E8
EMMANUEL RD. D8
EMMANUEL ST. C8
ENNISDALE CL. D4
ENNISKILLEN RD. E5
ERASMUS CL. C5
ESSEX CL. D5
EVENING COURT D7
EVERGREENS........................E5
EXETER CL. C13

FAIR ST. D7
FAIRBAIRN RD. F5
FAIRFAX RD. F8
FALLOWFIELD F5
FANSHAWE RD. E10
FARMSTEAD CL. ..HISTON INSET
FARRINGFORD CL................B5
FAULKNER CL. F2
FELTON ST. D8
FEN DITTON H5
FEN RD. (MILTON) G2
FEN RD. F6-G5
FENDON CL. E11
FENDON RD. E11
FENNEC CL. ....CHERRY
....................................HINTON INSET
FERNDALE RISE F6
FERNLEA CL. H9
FERRARS WY. C5
FERRY LA. E6
FERRY PATH D6
FIELD LA. H5
FIELD WAY F12
FINCH RD. C5
FISHER ST. C6
FISHERS LA. H10
FISON RD. H6
FITZROY LA. D7
FITZROY ST. D7
FITZWILLIAM RD. D10
FITZWILLIAM ST. C8
FLAMSTEED RD. E10
FLETCHERS TER. E9
FLOWER ST. D8
FONTWELL AVE. B5

FORDWICH CL. ...C5
FOREST RD. ...G10
FOSTER RD. ...C12
FOUR LAMPS ...D7
FOX'S CL. ...G2
FRANCIS DARWIN CT. ...C5
FRANKS LA. ...F5
FRASER RD. ...E5
FREE SCHOOL LA. ...C8
FRENCH'S RD. ...C6
FRIARS CL. ...G10
FROMENT WY. ...F2
FULBOURN OLD DRIFT ..CHERRY HINTON INSET
FULBOURN OLD DRIFT ...H9
FULBOURN RD. ...H11
FULBROOKE RD. ...A9

GAINSBOROUGH CL. ...F5
GALFRID RD. ...G7
GARDEN CT. ...HISTON INSET
GARDEN WK. ...HISTON INSET
GARDEN WK. ...C6
GARLIC ROW ...F6
GARNER CL. ...G2
GARRET HOSTEL LA. ...C7
GARRY DR. ...E4
GAYTON CL. ...C12
GAZELEY RD. ...C11
GAZELLE WY. ...CHERRY HINTON INSET
GELDART ST. ...E8
GEORGE IV ST. ...D9
GEORGE NUTTALL CL. ...E5
GEORGE PATEMAN CT. ...D9
GEORGE ST. ...D6
GEORGES TER. ...B6
GERARD CL. ...F7
GERARD RD. ...F7
GILBERT CL. ...C5
GILBERT RD. ...C5
GILMERTON CT. ...C11
GIRTON RD. ...A5
GISBORNE RD. ...F10
GLADSTONE WY. ...H10
GLEBE RD. ...HISTON INSET
GLEBE RD. ...E11
GLEBE WY. ...B1
GLENACRE CL. ...G11
GLENMERE CL. ...G10
GLISSON RD. ...D9
GLOUCESTER ST. ...B6
GODESDONE RD. ...E7
GODING WY. ...G2
GODWIN CL. ...F11
GODWIN WY. ...F11
GOLDING RD. ...F9
GONVILLE PL. ...D8
GOUGH WY. ...A8
GRAFTON CENTRE ...D7
GRAFTON ST. ...D8
GRANTCHESTER ...A11
GRANTCHESTER RD. ...A12-B12
GRANGE CT. ...B8
GRANGE GDS. ...B8
GRANGE RD. ...B7-B8
GRANHAMS RD. ...F13
GRANTA PL. ...C8
GRANTCHESTER MEADOWS ..B9
GRANTCHESTER RD. ...A10-B9
GRANTCHESTER ST. ...B9
GRASMERE GDS. ...C6
GRAY RD. ...F10
GRAYLING CL. ...E6
GREAT EASTERN ST. ...E8
GREEN END ...G5
GREEN END RD. ...E6
GREEN PARK ...F5
GREEN ST. ...C7
GREENLANDS ...E12
GREENLEAS ...HISTON INSET
GREEN'S RD. ...C6
GRESHAM RD. ...D8
GREVILLE RD. ...E9
GREYSTOKE CT. ...G10
GREYSTOKE RD. ...G11
GRIEVE CT. ...F5
GUEST RD. ...D8
GUNHILD CL. ...F11
GUNHILD CT. ...F11
GUNHILD WY. ...F10
GUNNELL CL. ...G2
GUNNING WY. ...C5
GURNEY WY. ...D6
GWYDIR ST. ...E8

HADLEIGH CT. ...H6
HALE AVE. ...C6

HALE ST. ...C6
HALIFAX RD. ...B6
HALL END ...G2
HALL FARM RD. ...C5
HAMILTON RD. ...D6
HANSON CT. ...D4
HARCOMBE RD. ...G10
HARDING WY. ...B1
HARDWICK ST. ...B9
HAREBELL CL. ...CHERRY HINTON INSET
HARRIS RD. ...C5
HARRY SCOTT CT. ...D4
HARTINGTON GR. ...E10
HARVEST WY. ...E7
HARVEY GOODWIN AVE. ...C6
HARVEY GOODWIN CT. ...C6
HARVEY GOODWIN GDS. ...C6
HARVEY RD. ...D8
HATHERDENE CL. ...G9
HAUXTON RD. ...B13
HAVILAND WY. ...D5
HAWKINS RD. ...D5
HAWTHORN WY. ...D6
HAYMARKET RD. ...B7
HAYSTER DR. ...G10
HAZELWOOD CL. ...C4
HEADFORD CL. ...G6
HEADINGTON DR. ...H10
HEATH HOUSE ...E5
HEDGELEY CL. ...A7
HELEN CL. ...G6
HEMINGFORD RD. ...F9
HENLEY RD. ...E7
HENRY MORRIS RD. ...C2
HERBERT ST. ...D6
HERCULES CL. ...D4
HEREWARD CL. ...C2
HERONS CL. ...F11
HERSCHELL RD. ...B8
HERTFORD ST. ...C6
HESTER ADRIAN WY. ...D6
HIGH DITCH RD. ...H6
HIGH ST. (CHERRY HINTON)..H10
HIGH ST. (CHESTERTON) ...E6
HIGH ST. (FEN DITTON) ...G5
HIGH ST. (GRANCHESTER) ...A11
HIGH ST. (HISTON) ...B1
HIGH ST. (MILTON) ...G2
HIGH ST. TRUMPINGTON ...C12
HIGHDENE RD. ...CHERRY HINTON INSET
HIGHFIELD AVE. ...D5
HIGHFIELD RD. ...B3
HIGHSETT ...D9
HIGHWORTH AVE. ...D5
HILDA ST. ...C6
HILLS AVE. ...E11
HILLS RD. ...D9-E11
HINTON AVE. ...F10
HISTON ...C1
HISTON RD. ...B6
HOADLEY RD. ...B5
HOBART RD. ...F9
HOBSON ST. ...C7
HOLBROOK RD. ...E11
HOLLAND ST. ...C6
HOLYROOD CL. ...B5
HOME CL. ...B1
HOMEFIELD CL. ...C2
HOMERTON ST. ...D10
HONEY HILL ...C7
HOOPER ST. ...E8
HOPE ST. ...E9
HOPKINS CL. ...E5
HORNINGSEA RD. ...H5
HOWARD CL. ...G6
HOWARD CT. ...G6
HOWARD RD. ...G6
HOWES PL. ...A5
HULLATT RD. ...F11
HUMBERSTONE RD. ...D6
HUMPHREYS RD. ...C5
HUMPHRIES WY. ...G2
HUNTINGDON RD. ...A5
HUNTLEY CL. ...G6
HURRELL RD. ...C5
HURST PARK AVE. ...D5

IMPALA DR. ...CHERRY HINTON INSET
IMPINGTON ...C2
IMPINGTON LA. ...B1
INVERNESS CL. ...E6
IVER CL. ...H9
IZAAK WALTON WY. ...F5

JACKSON RD. ...D4

JAMES CARLTON CL. ...F3
JAMES ST. ...D7
JASMINE CT. ...F10
JEDBURGH CL. ...C4
JERMYN CL. ...C5
JESUS LA. ...C7
JESUS TER. ...D8
JOHN CLARKE CT. ...E5
JOHN ST. ...D8
JOLLEY WY. ...D4

KALDOR CT. ...C4
KATHLEEN ELLIOTT WY. ...H9
KAY HITCH WY. ...B2
KEATES RD. ...H10
KELSEY CR. ...CHERRY HINTON INSET
KELSEY CR. ...H9
KELVIN CL. ...F10
KENDAL WY. ...E5
KENT WY. ...D4
KERRIDGE CL. ...E8
KEYNES RD. ...G6
KILMAINE CL. ...E4
KIMBERLEY RD. ...D7
KING ST. ...C7
KING'S HEDGES DR. ...C4
KING'S HEDGES RD. ...C4-E4
KINGS LA. ...C8
KINGS PARADE ...C8
KINGS RD. ...B9
KINGSTON ST. ...E8
KINGSWAY ...C5
KINNAIRD WY. ...F11
KINROSS RD. ...E6
KIRKBY CL. ...D5
KIRKWOOD RD. ...E4
KNIGHTS WY. ...G2

LABURNUM CL. ...D6
LADY JANE CT. ...E10
LADY MARGARET RD. ...B7
LAMBOURNE CL. ...C12
LAMMAS FIELD ...B9
LANDBEACH RD. ...G1
LANDER CL. ...F2
LANGDALE CL. ...H10
LANGHAM RD. ...F10
LANSDOWNE RD. ...A6
LANTREE CR. ...B13
LARCHFIELD ...B8
LARKIN CL. ...E5
LARMOR DR. ...B7
LATHAM CL. ...C9
LATHAM RD. ...C10
LATIMER CL. ...G7
LAUNDRY CL. ...F10
LAURISTON PL. ...C4
LAVENDER RD. ...E4
LAWRENCE WY. ...E4
LAXTON WY. ...F5
LEETE RD. ...H10
LEGION CT. ...D4
LEMUR DR. ...CHERRY HINTON INSET
LENSFIELD RD. ...C9
LENTS WY. ...F5
LEONARD CL. ...H6
LEXINGTON CL. ...B5
LEYBURN CL. ...CHERRY HINTON INSET
LEYS AVE. ...D5
LEYS RD. ...D5
LICHFIELD RD. ...F10
LILAC CT. ...F10
LILLEY CL. ...F6
LILSE WK. ...H10
LIME TREE CL. ...G10
LIMEKILN RD. ...G12
LINDEN CL. ...C6
LINGHOLME CL. ...B5
LINGREY CT. ...C12
LION YARD ...C8
LISA CT. ...F5
LITTLE ST MARY'S LA. ...C8
LIVERMORE CL. ...E4
LOGANS WY. ...E7
LONE TREE AVE. ...B3
LONG RD. ...C11
LONG REACH RD. ...F5
LONGWORTH AVE. ...E6
LORIS CT. ...CHERRY HINTON INSET
LOUGHTON CT. ...H6
LOVELL RD. ...E4
LOVES CL. ...B2
LOWER PARK ST. ...C7
LUARD CL. ...D11

LUARD RD. ...D11
LUCERNE CL. ...CHERRY HINTON INSET
LUCKETTS CL. ...HISTON INSET
LYNDEWODE RD. ...D9
LYNDHURST CL. ...F2
LYNFIELD LA. ...E6

MACFARLANE CL. ...C2
MADINGLEY RD. ...A6-B7
MAGDALENE ST. ...C7
MAGNOLIA CL. ...E10
MAGRATH AVE. ...C6
MAIDS CAUSEWAY ...D7
MAIO RD. ...D5
MAITLAND AVE. ...F5
MALCOLM ST. ...C7
MALDEN CL. ...G7
MALSTERS WAY ...E6
MALTA RD. ...F9
MALTING LA. ...C8
MALTSTERS WY. ...E6
MALVERN RD. ...G10
MANDER WY. ...F10
MANDRILL CL. ...CHERRY HINTON INSET
MANERS WY. ...F11
MANHATTAN DR. ...D7
MANOR CT. ...B8
MANOR PARK ...B1
MANOR ST. ...D7
MANSEL WY. ...D5
MANSFIELD CL. ...F2
MANSFIELD CT. ...E6
MAPLE CL. ...D6
MARCH LA. ...H9
MARINERS WY. ...E7
MARION CL. ...B6
MARIS LA. ...B12
MARKET HILL ...C8
MARKET PASSAGE ...C7
MARKET ST. ...C8
MARKHAM CL. ...E4
MARLBOROUGH CT. ...B8
MARLOW RD. ...B9
MARMORA RD. ...F9
MARSHALL RD. ...E10
MARTINGALE CL. ...B4
MAWSON RD. ...D9
MAYFLOWER HOUSE ...D7
MAYS WY. ...F6
MCKENZIE RD. ...D8
MELBOURNE PL. ...D8
MELVIN WY. ...A1
MERCERS ROW ...F6
MERE WY. ...E2-E1
MERE WY. ...C5
MERLIN PL. ...F4
MERTON RD. ...B1
MERTON ST. ...B9
METCALFE RD. ...C5
MICHAELMAS PL. ...C6
MIDHURST CL. ...E6
MIDSUMMER ...D7
MIDWINTER PL. ...D6
MILE END CL. ...H10
MILFORD ST. ...E8
MILL END RD. ...G10
MILL LA. (HISTON) ...C1
MILL LA. ...HISTON INSET
MILL LA. (CAMBRIDGE) ...C8
MILL RD. (SOUTH HISTON) ...B3
MILL RD. ...D8
MILL ST. ...D8
MILL WY. ...A11-A12
MILLCROFT CT. ...E9
MILLINGTON RD. ...B9
MILTON ...G2
MILTON COUNTRY PARK ...G3
MILTON RD. ...D6
MILTON RD. (IMPINGTON) ...D1
MILTONS WALK ...D7
MINERVA WY. ...D4
MISSLETON CT. ...F10
MISTY MEADOWS ...G6
MOLEWOOD CL. ...C4
MONKSWELL ...C12
MONTAGUE RD. ...D6
MONTCRIEF CL. ...D4
MONTGOMERY RD. ...D5
MONTREAL RD. ...F9
MONTREAL SQ. ...F9
MONTROSE CL. ...D4
MOORE CL. ...E5
MORTIMER RD. ...D8
MORTLOCK AVE. ...F5
MOSS BANK ...F5
MOUNT PLEASANT ...B6

MOUNT PLEASANT WK. ...B7
MOWBRAY RD. ...F11
MOWLAM CL. ...C2
MOYNE CL. ...C4
MULBERRY CL. ...D5
MUMFORD THEATRE ...E8
MUNCEY WALK ...HISTON INSET
MUSGRAVE WY. ...H5

NAPIER ST. ...D7
NARROW CL. ...HISTON INSET
NARROW LA. ...B1
NARROW LA. ...HISTON INSET
NATAL RD. ...F9
NEALE CL. ...H9
NEPTUNE CL. ...D4
NETHERHALL WY. ...F11
NEVILLE RD. ...F10
NEW CT. ...E6
NEW PARK ST. ...C7
NEW RD. (HISTON) ...A1
NEW RD. (IMPINGTON) ...C2
NEW SCHOOL RD. ...B2
NEW SQ. ...D7
NEW ST. (BARNWELL) ...E7
NEWELL WK. ...H9
NEWMARKET RD. ...D7-E7
NEWNHAM ...A8
NEWNHAM CROFT SOUTH ...B9
NEWNHAM DRIFTWAY ...C9
NEWNHAM RD. ...B9
NEWNHAM WK. ...B8
NEWTON RD. ...D10
NEWTOWN ...D9
NICHOLSON WY. ...D5
NIGHTINGALE AVE. ...F12
NORFOLK ST. ...D8
NORFOLK TER. ...E8
NORMANTON WY. HISTON INSET
NORTH COTTAGES ...C11
NORTH ST. ...B6
NORTH TER. ...D7
NORTHAMPTON ST. ...C7
NORTHFIELD AVE. ...D4
NORTHUMBERLAND CL. ...C5
NORTON CL. ...G7
NORWICH ST. ...D9
NUFFIELD CL. ...F4
NUFFIELD RD. ...F5
NUN'S ORCHARD..HISTON INSET
NUNS WY. ...D4
NURSERY WK. ...B6
NUTTERS CL. ...A11
NUTTINGS RD. ...G8

OAK TREE AVE. ...D6
OATES WY. ...HISTON INSET
OCCUPATION RD. ...E7
OLD FARM CL. ...HISTON INSET
OLD SCHOOL LA. ...G3
ONGAR CT. ...H6
ORCHARD AVE. ...D5
ORCHARD ESTATE ...H9
ORCHARD RD. ...HISTON INSET
ORCHARD ST. ...D8
ORWELL FURLONG ...F4
OWLSTONE RD. ...B9
OXFORD RD. ...B6
OYSTER ROW ...E6

PADDOCK CL. ...C1
PADDOCK CL. ...HISTON INSET
PAGES CL. ...B1
PAGES CL. ...HISTON INSET
PAGET CL. ...C12
PAGET RD. ...C12
PAKENHAM CL. ...E6
PALMERS WK. ...D8
PAMPLIN CT. ...H10
PANTHER WY. ...CHERRY HINTON INSET
PANTON ST. ...D9
PARADISE ST. ...D8
PARK AVE. ...B1
PARK DR. ...C2
PARK LA. ...A1
PARK PARADE ...C7
PARK ST. ...C7
PARK TER. ...D8
PARKER ST. ...D8
PARKES TER. ...E7
PARKSIDE ...D8
PARLOUR CL. ...HISTON INSET
PARR CL. ...C2
PARSONAGE ST. ...D7
PEACOCK WY. ...HISTON INSET
PEARCE CL. ...A8
PEARCES YARD ...A11

CAMBRIDGE INDEX TO STREETS (Continued)

PEARMAIN CT. ...F5
PEARSON CL. ...G3
PEAS HILL ...C8
PEASE WY. ...A1
PELHAM CT. ...B5
PEMBERTON TER. ...C9
PEMBROKE ST. ...C8
PEN CL. ...H10
PENARTH PL. ...A8
PENTLANDS CT. ...D7
PEPYS TER. ...C3
PERCHERON CL. ...C2
PERNE AVE. ...F10
PERNE RD. ...F9-F10
PEROWNE ST. ...E8
PERRY CT. ...A7
PERSE WY. ...C5
PETERSFIELD ...D8
PETTY CURY ...C8
PETWORTH ST. ...E7
PEVEREL CL. ...G7
PEVEREL RD. ...G7
PIKES WK. ...D8
PINEHURST ...B8
PINNYS WY ...H3
PIPPIN RD. ...F5
PLUM TREE CL. ...C4
POPLAR RD. ...B2
PORSON CT. ...C11
PORSON RD. ...C11
PORTUGAL ST. ...C7
POUND HILL ...C7
PRETORIA RD. ...D7
PRIMARY CT. ...E6
PRIMROSE CL. ...CHERRY HINTON INSET
PRIMROSE ST. ...C6
PRINCE WILLIAM CT. ...C6
PRIORS CL. ...B1
PRIORY RD. ...E7
PRIORY ST. ...B6
PROSPECT ROW ...D8
PRYOR CL. ...G3
PURBECK RD. ...D10

QUAINTON CL. ...G7
QUAYSIDE ...C7
QUEEN EDITH'S WY. ...E11
QUEENS' LA. ...C8
QUEENS MEADOW ...H9
QUEENS RD. ...B7
QUEENSWAY ...D10

RACHEL CL. ...G6
RACKMAN CL. ...C6
RADEGUND RD. ...F9
RAILWAY ST. ...H10
RAMSDEN SQ. ...E4
RATHMORE CL. ...E10
RATHMORE RD. ...E10
RAVENSWORTH GDS. ...D9
RAWLYN CL. ...G7
RAWLYN RD. ...G7
RAYLEIGH CL. ...C10
RAYSON WY. ...G7
RECREATION CL. ...G3
RED CROSS LA. ...E12
REDFERN CL. ...D5
REDWOOD CT. ...B8
REGATTA CT. ...E6
REGENT ST. ...D8
REGENT TER. ...D8
REILLY WY. ...H9
RIBSTON WY. ...F5
RICHMOND RD. ...B6
RICKARD CL. ...G10
RIDLEY HALL RD. ...B8
RIVAR PL. ...E8
RIVER LA. ...E7
RIVERSIDE ...E7
RIVERSIDE CT. ...D6
ROBERT DAVIES CT. ...F4
ROBERT JENNINGS CL. ...E5
ROBERT MAY CL. ...F9
ROBINSON WY. ...D12
ROCK RD. ...E10
ROEDEER CL. ...CHERRY HINTON INSET
ROLAND CL. ...C5
ROMSEY MEWS ...E9
ROMSEY RD. ...F8
ROMSEY TER. ...E9
ROMSEY TOWN ...F8
RONALD ROLFE CT. ...G6
ROSE CR. ...C7
ROSEFORD RD. ...C5
ROSELEA ...C2
ROSEMARY LA. ...H9

ROSS ST. ...E9
ROTHERWICK WY. ...F12
ROTHLEIGH RD. ...G10
ROUND CHURCH ST. ...C7
ROWLINSON WY. ...E7
ROXBURGH RD. ...D4
RUSH GR. ...CHERRY HINTON INSET
RUSSELL CT. ...D9
RUSSELL ST. ...D9
RUSSET CT. ...F5
RUSTAT RD. ...E10
RUTHERFORD RD. ...D11
RUTLAND CL. ...C5

SABLE CL. ...CHERRY HINTON INSET
SACKVILLE CL. ...D4
SAFFRON RD. ...B2
SALISBURY PL. ...C12
SALMON LA. ...D7
SANDWICK CL. ...D4
SANDY LA. ...D6
SAXON RD. ...E7
SAXON ST. ...C9
SCARSDALE CL. ...E5
SCHOOL HILL ...B1
SCHOOL LA. ...C2
SCOTLAND CL. ...E6
SCOTLAND RD. ...E6
SEARLE CL. ...C6
SEDGWICK ST. ...E9
SEDLEY TAYLOR RD. ...D11
SEFTON CL. ...C12
SELWYN GS. ...B8
SELWYN RD. ...B9
SENATE HOUSE HILL ...C8
SENATE HOUSE PASSAGE ...C8
SEVERN PL. ...E7
SEYMOUR CT. ...F9
SEYMOUR ST. ...F8
SHAFTESBURY RD. ...D9
SHELFORD RD. ...C12
SHELLEY GARDEN ...B7
SHELLEY RD. ...B6
SHEPHERDS CL. ...CHERRY HINTON INSET
SHEPHERDS CL. ...H10
SHERBOURNE CL. ...E5
SHERBOURNE CT. ...F5
SHERLOCK CL. ...B6
SHERLOCK CT. ...B6
SHERLOCK RD. ...B6
SHIRLEY CL. ...G3
SHIRLEY GR. ...E5
SHIRLEY RD. ...B1
SHORT ST. ...D7
SIDGWICK AVE. ...B8
SIDNEY FARM RD. ...G10
SIDNEY ST. ...C7
SILVER ST. ...C8
SILVERWOOD CL. ...E7
SLADWELL CL. ...A11
SLEAFORD ST. ...E8
SOMERSET CL. ...C4
SOMERSET RD. ...B1
SOUTH GREEN RD. ...B9
SOUTH RD. ...B3
SOUTHBROOKE CL. ...C12
SOUTHSIDE CT. ...C6
SPALDING WY. ...F11
SPEEDWELL CL. ...CHERRY HINTON INSET
SPENS AVE. ...A8
SPRING CL. ...C1
SPRING CL. ...HISTON INSET
SPRINGFIELD RD. ...D6
SPRINGFIELD TER. ...D6
ST ALBANS RD. ...C5
ST ANDREWS PARK ...HISTON INSET
ST ANDREW'S RD. ...E7
ST ANDREW'S ST. ...C8
ST ANDREWS WY. ...D1
ST AUDREY'S CL. ...A1
ST BARNABAS RD. ...F5
ST BARTHOLOMEW'S CT. ...E6
ST BEDES CR. ...G10
ST BEDES GDS. ...G10
ST CATHERINES ROAD ...C4
ST CATHERINES SQ. ...C4
ST CHRISTOPHERS AVE. ...B6
ST ELGIUS ST. ...D9
ST JOHN ST. ...C7
ST JOHN'S PL. ...C7
ST KILDAS AVE. ...E4
ST LUKES ST. ...C6
ST MARGARET'S RD. ...A5

ST MARGARET'S SQ. ...F10
ST MARKS CT. ...B9
ST MARY'S ST. ...C8
ST MATTHEWS CT. ...E7
ST MATTHEWS ST. ...E8
ST PAUL'S RD. ...D9
ST PETER'S ST. ...C7
ST PHILIPS RD. ...E8
ST STEPHEN'S PL. ...B6
ST THOMAS'S RD. ...G10
ST THOMAS'S SQ. ...G10
ST TIBBS ROW ...C8
ST. GEORGES WAY ...D1
STANBURY CL. ...G5
STANESFIELD CL. ...F7
STANESFIELD RD. ...F7
STANLEY RD. ...E6
STANSGATE AVE. ...E12
STANWAY CL. ...D7
STARLING CL. ...G2
STATION RD. (CAMBRIDGE) ...D9
STATION RD. (HISTON) ...B1
STERNE CL. ...E10
STEVENSON CT. ...E7
STIRLING CL. ...E6
STOCKWELL ST. ...E9
STONE ST. ...E8
STOREY'S WY. ...B6
STOTT GDS. ...E5
STOURBRIDGE GR. ...F8
STRANGEWAYS RD. ...F11
STRATFIELD CL. ...B5
STRETTEN AVE. ...C6
STUKELEY CL. ...A8
STULP FIELD RD. ...A11
STURMER CL. ...C4
STURTON ST. ...E8
SUEZ RD. ...F9
SUMMER CT. ...G7
SUMMERFIELD ...B9
SUN ST. ...E7
SUNFLOWER ST. ...C4
SUNMEAD WK. ...H10
SUNNYSIDE ...G7
SUNSET SQ. ...C4
SUSSEX ST. ...C7
SUTTON CL. ...G2
SWANN'S RD. ...F6
SWANNS TER. ...E9
SYCAMORE CL. ...G10
SYLVESTER RD. ...B8
SYMONDS CL. ...HISTON INSET
SYMONDS LA. ...A11

TABRUM CL. ...A11
TAMARIN GDS. ...CHERRY HINTON INSET
TAUNTON CL. ...F9
TAVISTOCK RD. ...B5
TEASEL WY. ...CHERRY HINTON INSET
TEDDER WY. ...C5
TEMPLEMORE CL. ...E11
TENBY CL. ...H10
TENISON AVE. ...D9
TENISON CT. ...E9
TENISON RD. ...D9
TENNIS CT. RD. ...C8
TENNIS CT. TER. ...C8
TEVERSHAM DRIFT ...CHERRY HINTON INSET
TEVERSHAM DRIFT ...H9
TEYNHAM CL. ...F9
THE AVE. ...C7
THE BEECHES ...D5
THE BRAMBLES ...A5
THE BRAMBLES ...C12
THE CENACLE ...B9
THE COPPICE ...C3
THE CRESCENT (HISTON) ...B3
THE CRESCENT ...B7
THE DOLE ...C2
THE ELMS ...F2
THE FEN CAUSEWAY ...C9
THE FOOTPATH ...A11
THE GREEN (HISTON) ...B1
THE GROVE ...F5
THE HOMING ...G7
THE LAWNS ...A7
THE LYNX ...CHERRY HINTON INSET
THE MALLARDS ...E7
THE OAKS ...F2
THE PADDOCKS (ROMSEY TOWN) ...F8
THE PADDOCKS ...F10
THE QUORUM ...G7
THE RODINGS ...H6

THE ROWANS ...F3
THE SYCAMORES ...F3
THE WESTERING ...G7
THETFORD TER. ...G7
THIRLEBY CL. ...C5
THISTLE ST. ...C4
THODAY ST. ...E9
THOMPSONS LA. ...C7
THORLEYE RD. ...F7
THORNTON CL. ...A5
THORNTON CT. ...A5
THORNTON RD. ...A4-A5
THORNTON WY. ...A5
THORPE WY. ...G6
THRIFTS WK. ...E6
TILLYARD WY. ...G11
TIPTREE CL. ...H6
TIVERTON WY. ...F9
TOPCLIFFE WY. ...F11
TOPHAM WY. ...C5
TOWNSEND CL. ...G2
TRAFALGAR RD. ...D6
TRAFALGAR ST. ...D6
TREDEGAR CL. ...D4
TREVONE PL. ...F9
TRINITY LA. ...C7
TRINITY ST. ...C7
TRUMPINGTON ...C12
TRUMPINGTON RD. ...C9-C11
TRUMPINGTON ST. ...C8
TRUST CT. ...B2
TURPYN CT. ...D5
TWEEDALE ...H11
TWEEDSMUIR CT. ...D4

UNION LA. ...E6
UNION RD. ...D9
UPHALL RD. ...G8
UPPER GWYDIR ST. ...E8

VALERIAN CT. ...CHERRY HINTON INSET
VELOS WK. ...G6
VENTRESS CL. ...G11
VENTRESS FARM CT. ...G11
VERULAM WY. ...C4
VICARAGE DR. ...A11
VICARAGE TER. ...E8
VICTORIA AVE. ...D6
VICTORIA PARK ...C6
VICTORIA RD. ...C6
VICTORIA ST. ...D8
VILLA PL. ...B2
VILLA RD. ...B2
VINERY PARK ...F8
VINERY RD. ...F9-F8
VINERY WY. ...F8
VIOLET CL. ...CHERRY HINTON INSET

WADLOES RD. ...G6
WAGSTAFF CL. ...E4
WALKER CT. ...D4
WALPOLE RD. ...G10
WARD RD. ...F10
WARFIELD CT. ...D5
WARKWORTH ST. ...D8
WARKWORTH TER. ...D8
WARREN RD. ...E5
WARWICK RD. ...B5
WATER LA. ...B1
WATER LA. (CHESTERTON) ...E6
WATER ST. ...E6
WAVELL WY. ...C5
WEDGEWOOD DR. ...H10
WELLBROOK CT. ...A4
WELLBROOK WY. ...A4
WELLINGTON ST. ...D7
WELSTEAD RD. ...CHERRY HINTON INSET
WELSTEAD RD. ...H10
WENTWORTH RD. ...B6
WENVOE CL. ...H10
WEST GDS. ...B8
WEST RD. (HISTON) ...B1
WEST RD. ...B8
WEST VIEW ...B9
WESTBERRY CT. ...B8
WESTFIELD LA. ...B6
WESTFIELD RD. ...B6
WETENHALL RD. ...E8
WHEELER ST. ...C8
WHITE ROSE WK. ...C4
WHITEHILL CL. ...G7
WHITEHILL RD. ...F7
WHITEHOUSE LA. ...A5
WHITFIELD CL. ...D4
WHYTFORD CL. ...E6

WIDNAL CL. ...A11
WILBERFORCE RD. ...A7
WILDERSPIN CL. ...A5
WILDING WK. ...E6
WILES CL. ...E4
WILKIN ST. ...D9
WILLIAM SMITH CT. ...E9
WILLIS RD. ...D8
WILLOW CR. ...G2
WILLOW CROFT ...B6
WILLOW PL. ...D7
WILLOW WK. ...D7
WILSON CL. ...E5
WILSON WY. ...G2
WINCHMORE DR. ...B11
WINDERMERE CL. ...CHERRY HINTON INSET
WINDERMERE CL. ...H9
WINDERS LA. ...HISTON INSET
WINDLESHAM CL. ...D5
WINDMILL GRANGE ...B1
WINDMILL LA. ...B1
WINDSOR RD. ...B5
WINGATE CL. ...C11
WINGATE WY. ...C11
WINSHIP RD. ...F3
WOBURN CL. ...D4
WOLLASTON RD. ...D8
WOLSEY LA. ...H9
WOODCOCK CL. ...D2
WOODHEAD DR. ...D5
WOODHOUSE WY. ...E4
WOODLARK RD. ...B5
WOODMANS WY. ...G2
WOOTTON WY. ...A8
WORDSWORTH GR. ...B8
WORTS CAUSEWAY ...F12
WRIGHTS CL. ...G5
WULFSTAN CT. ...F11
WULFSTAN WY. ...F11
WYCLIFFE RD. ...F8
WYNBOURNE CL. ...D5
WYNFORD WY. ...D4

YARROW RD. ...CHERRY HINTON INSET
YORK ST. ...E7
YORK TER. ...E8
YOUNG ST. ...E7
YOUNGMAN AVE. ...HISTON INSET
YOUNGMAN CL. ...HISTON INSET

ZETLAND WK. ...F9

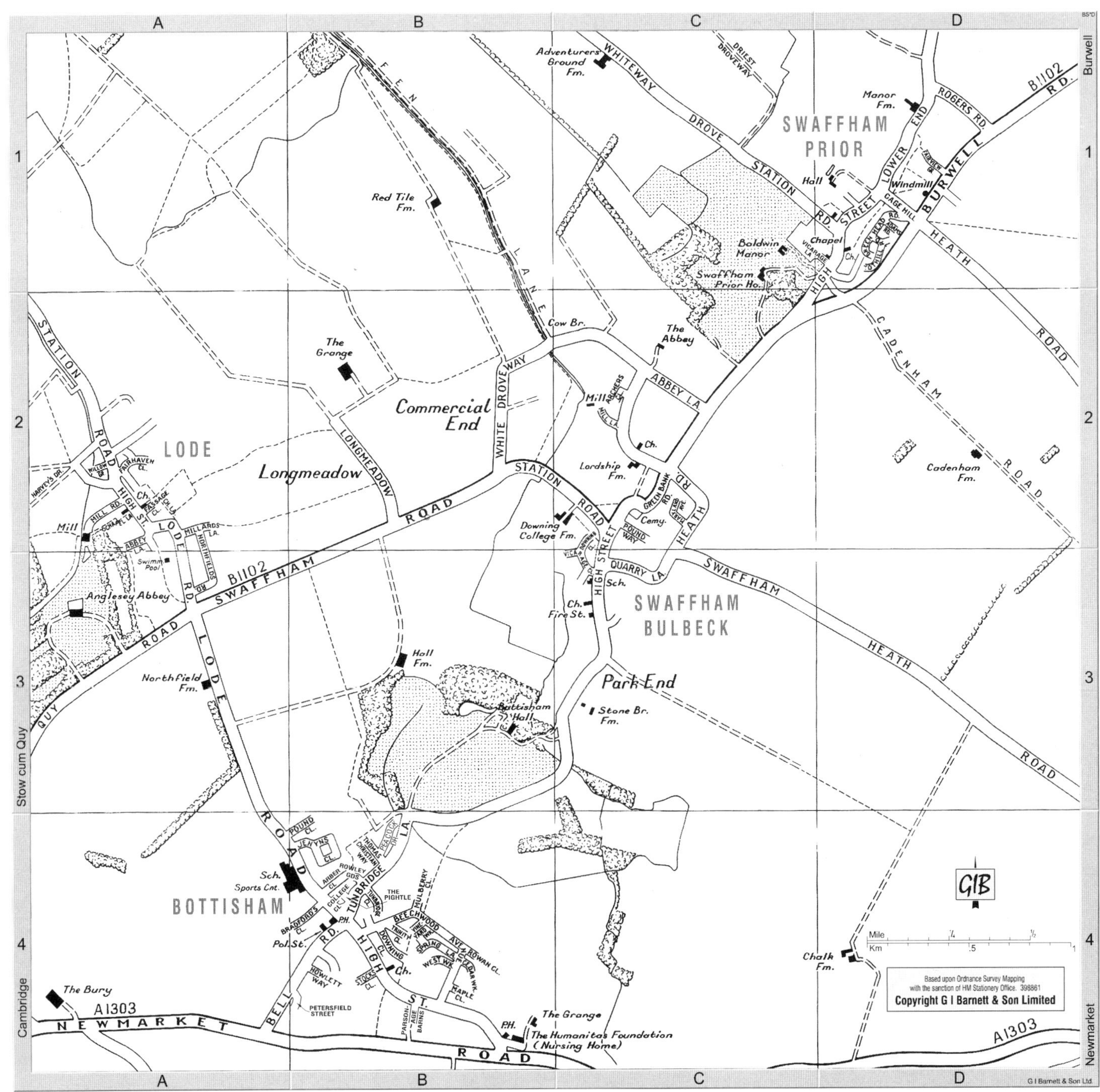

BOTTISHAM/SWAFFHAM BULBECK/SWAFFHAM PRIOR/LODE INDEX TO STREETS

Abbey Lane, Lode A.2
Abbey Lane,
   Swaffham Bulbeck C.2
Adams Road D.1
Anglesey Abbey A.3
Arber Close B.4
Archers Close C.2

Beechwood Avenue B.4
Bell Road A.4
BOTTISHAM A.4
Bottisham Hall B.3
Bradford's Close B.4
Burwell Road D.1

Cadenham Road D.2
Cage Hill D.1
Cedar Walk B.4
Chapel Lane A.2
Church Lane A.2
College Close B.4
Commercial End B.2

Downing Close,
   Bottisham B.4
Downing Close,
   Swaffham Bulbeck C.2
Driest Droveway C.1

Fairhaven Close A.2
Fairview Green D.1
Fassage Close A.2
Fen Lane B.1

Green Bank Road C.2
Green Head Road D.1

Harvey's Drive A.2
Heath Road,
   Swaffham Bulbeck C.2
Heath Road,
   Swaffham Prior D.1
High Street, Bottisham B.4
High Street, Lode A.2
High Street,
   Swaffham Bulbeck C.3
High Street,
   Swaffham Prior D.1
Howlett Way B.4

Jenyns Close B.4

LODE A.2
Lode Road A.3
Longmeadow B.2
Lower End D.1

Maple Close B.4
Maryland Avenue C.2
Mill Lane C.2
Mill Road A.2
Millards Lane A.2
Mulberry Close B.4

Newmarket Road A.4
Northfields Road A.2

Park End C.3
Parsonage Barns B.4
Peacock Drive B.4
Petersfield Street B.4
Pound Close B.4
Pound Way C.2

Quarry Lane C.3
Quy Road A.3

Rogers Road D.1
Rowan Close B.4
Rowley Gardens B.4

Spring Lane B.4
Station Road, Lode A.2
Station Road,
   Swaffham Bulbeck B.2

Station Road,
   Swaffham Prior C.1
Stocks Close B.4
SWAFFHAM BULBECK C.3
SWAFFHAM PRIOR D.1
Swaffham Heath Road C.3
Swaffham Road A.3

The Abbey C.2
The Grange, Bottisham B.4
The Grange,
   Swaffham Bulbeck B.2
The Pightle B.4
Thomas Christian Way B.4
Tothill Road D.1
Trinity Close B.4
Tunbridge Close B.4
Tunbridge Lane B.4

Vicarage Close C.3
Vicarage Lane D.1
Vineyard Walk B.4

West Walk B.4
Willow Grove A.2
White Droveway B.2
Whiteway Drive C.1

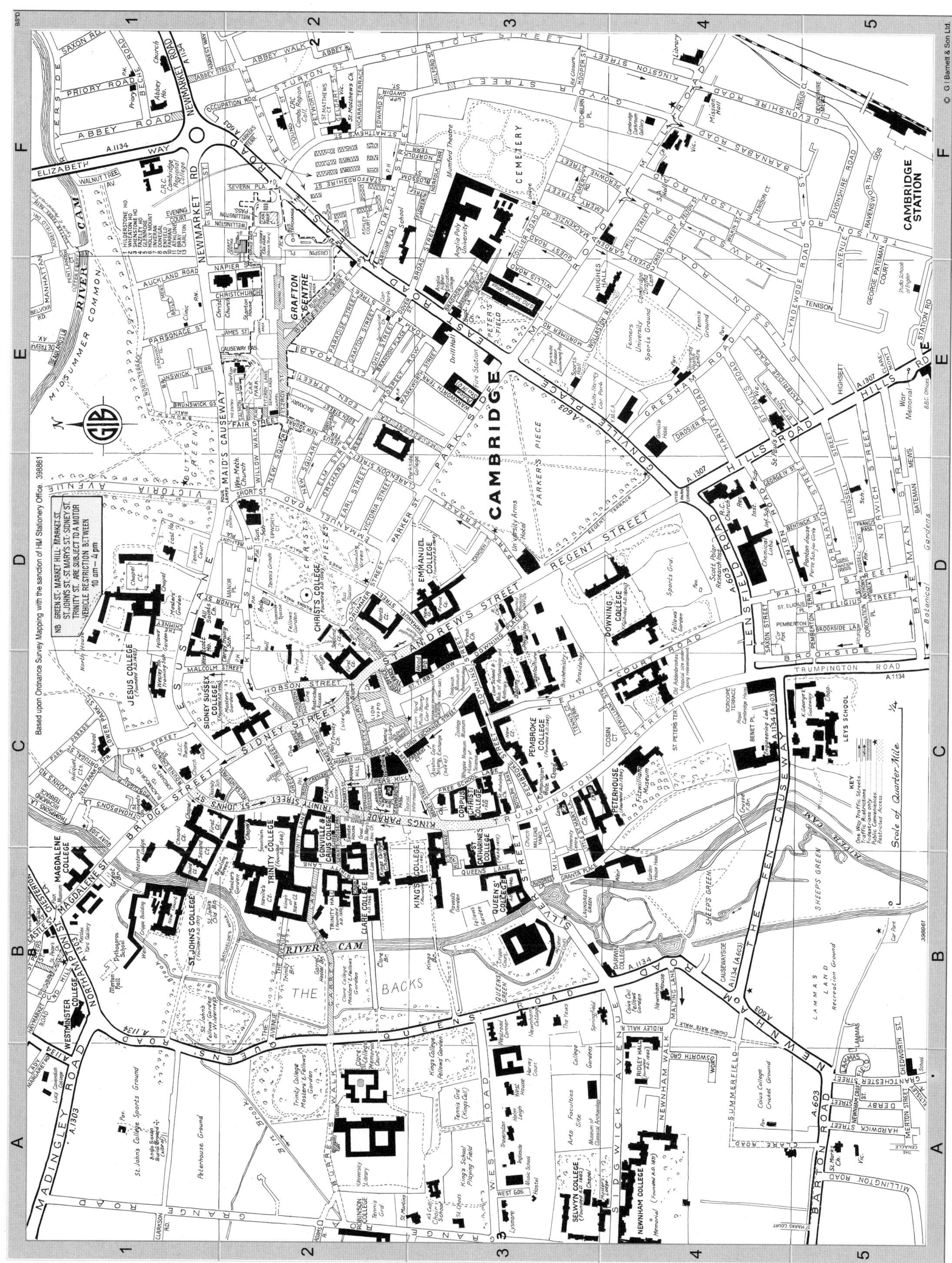

CAMBRIDGE CITY CENTRE INDEX TO STREETS

Abbey House F.1
Abbey Road F.1
Abbey Street F.1
Abbey Walk F.2
Acrefield Drive F.1
Adam and Eve Street F.3
Adams Road A.2
All Saints Church D.1
All Saints Passage C.2
Anglia Higher
    Education College E.3
Angus Close F.4
Arts Faculties Site A.3
Ashley Court F.2
Athlone F.2
Auckland Road F.1
Austin Friary C.3

B.B.C Offices E.5
Baily Mews F.1
Barnabas Road F.4
Barnwell Gate C.2
Barton Road A.5
Batchelor's Walk B.2
Bateman Mews D.5
Bateman Street D.5
Beauland's Close F.1
Beche Road E.4
Belmont Place D.2
Belvoir Road F.1
Benet Place C.4
Benet Street C.3
Bentinck Street D.4
Blackmoor Head Yard C.1
Blossom Street F.3
Botolph Lane C.3
Bradmore Lane E.3
Bradmore Street E.3
Bradwells Court C.2
Brandon Place E.2
Brass Rubbing Centre B.1
Bray F.2
Bridge Street C.1
Broad Street F.3
Brookside C.4
Brookside Lane D.5
Brunswick Gardens E.1
Brunswick Terrace E.1
Brunswick Walk E.1
Burleigh Place E.2
Burleigh Street E.2
Burrell's Walk A.2
Bus Station D.2
Butts Green D.1

Caius College,
    Cricket Ground A.4
C.C.F.E Canbridge
    College of Further
    Education F.1/F.2
Cambridge Darkroom
    Gallery F.4
Cambridge Place F.4
Cambridge Station F.5
Cambridgeshire Technical
    College F.3
Camdon Court D.3
Cariton F.2
Caroline Place F.2
Castle Street B.1
Causeway Passage B.4
Causewayside B.4
Cemetary F.3
Central Schools D.2
Chedworth Street A.5
Chemical Laboratories D.4
Chesterton Lane B.1
Chesterton Street B.1
Christ Church F.1
Christchurch Street E.1
Christ's College D.2
Christ's Lane D.2
Christ's Pieces D.2
Church Rate Walk B.4
City Road E.2
Clare Bridge B.2
Clare College B.2
Clare College Memorial
    Court A.2
Claremont E.5
Clarendon Street D.2
Clarkson Road A.1
Clergy Training School D.2
Cobble Yard F.2
Coe Fen Terrace C.4
Collier Road F.3
Corn Exchange C.3
Corn Exchange Street C.2
Coronation Mews D.5

Coronation Street D.5
Corpus Christi College C.3
Corpus Christi College
    Sports Ground A.3
Cosin Court C.4
County Hall C.2
Covent Garden E.4
Craft Centre F.2
Cripps Court B.3
Crispin Place F.2
Cross Street F.5
Crusoe Bridge C.4
Cutter Ferry Lane E.1
Cutter Ferry Path F.1

Darwin College................B.4
De Treville Avenue E.1
Derby Street A.5
Devonshire Mews F.5
Devonshire Road F.5
Ditchburn Place...............F.3
Divinity School C.1
Donegal..........................F.2
Dover Street E.2
Downing College D.4
Downing Place D.3
Downing Street................C.3
Drill Hall E.3
Drosier Road E.4
Drummer Street D.2

Earl Street D.2
East House......................D.1
East Road........................E.3
Eden Street E.2
Eden Street Backway........E.2
Edward Street F.2
Elizabeth Way F.1
Elm Street D.2
Eltisley Avenue A.5
Emery Road F.3
Emery Street F.3
Emmanuel College...........D.3
Emmanuel Road D.2
Emmanuel Street D.3
Enfield F.2
Engineering Laboratory C.4
Epworth Court D.2

Fair Street.......................E.2
Ferran F.2
Fazeley House F.2
Felton Street F.4
Fire Station E.3
Fish Ponds Close B.1
Fisher Court B.3
Fitzroy Lane E.2
Fitzroy Street E.2
Fitzwilliam Museum C.4
Fitzwilliam Street C.3
Flower Street...................F.3
Folk Museum B.1
Four Lamps D.2
Francis Passage D.5
Free School Lane.............C.3

Garnet Hostel Bridge B.2
Garret Hostel Lane...........B.2
Geldart Street F.2
George IV Street D.4
George Pateman Court......F.5
Gifford Place C.2
Glenmore F.2
Glisson Road E.4
Gonville and Caius
    College B.2
Gonville Hotel..................E.4
Gonville Place E.4
Grafton Centre E.2
Grafton House E.1
Grafton Street..................E.2
Grange Road A.3
Granta Place B.3
Grantchester Street A.5
Great Bridge....................B.1
Great Eastern House F.5
Great St. Marys
    Church C.2
Green Street....................C.2
Gresbarn Road................E.4
Guest Road......................F.3
Guildhall C.2
Guildhall Place C.2
Guildhall Street................C.2
Gwydir Street F.3

Hardwick Street A.5
Harvest Way F.1
Harvey Court A.3

Harvey Road F.4
Haymarket Road B.1
HEAD POST OFFICE C.3
Highsett D.5
Hilderstone House F.2
Hills Road........................D.4
Hobson Street C.2
Hobson Passage C.2
Holly Mount F.2
Holm Leigh A.3
Holy Trinity Church...........C.2
Honey Hill B.1
Hooper Street F.3
Hughes Hall E.3
Hyde Park Corner D.4

Ingleside A.3
Inveran F.2

James Street E.1
James Street E.2
Jesus College..................C.1
Jesus Lane C.1
Jesus Terrace E.2
John Street E.2
Jordans Yard C.1

Kettles Yard Gallery B.1
King George V
    Gateway.....................C.5
King Street C.2
King's Bridge B.3
King's College B.3
King's College
    Choir School A.3
King's Court B.2
King's Lane B.3
King's Parade C.3
Kingston Street F.4

Lady Margaret Road.........A.1
Lammas Court A.5
Lammas Field..................A.5
Lammas Lane..................B.5
Laundress Green B.3
Laundress Lane B.3
Lensfield.........................D.4
Lensfield Road D.4
Leys School C.5
Lion yard C.2
Little St. Mary Yard...........C.3
Lower Park Street C.1
Lucy Cavendish College....A.1
Lyndewood Road E.4
Lysmore A.3

Mackenzie Road F.3
Madingley Road A.1
Magdalene College B.1
Magdalene Street.............B.1
Maids Causeway D.3
Malcolm Street C.1
Malting Lane B.4
Manhatten Drive...............E.1
Manor Place D.2
Manor Street D.2
Market Hill C.2
Market Passage C.2
Market Street C.2
Mawson Road E.4
Melbourne Place E.3
Merton Hall B.1
Merton Street A.5
Milford Street...................F.3
Mill Lane B.3
Mill Road E.3
Mill Street F.4
Millers Yard.....................B.3
Millers Yard.....................C.3
Millington Road.................A.5
Milton's Walk D.2
Mortimer Road E.3
Museum of Archaeology....C.3
Museum of Classical
    Archaeology A.3

Napier Street....................F.1
Neviles Court B.2
New Park Street................C.1
New Square D.2
New Street F.2
Newmarket Road E.1
Newham College A.4
Newham Cottage B.3
Newham Croft Street A.5
Newham House B.4
Newham Road B.4
Newham Walk A.4
Norfolk Street...................F.2

Norfolk Terrace F.3
North House.....................C.1
North Terrace E.1
Northampton Street B.1
Norwich Street D.5
Occupation Road F.1
Orchard Street D.2

Palmer's Walk E.3
Panton Hosue D.5
Panton Street D.4
Paradise Street................E.2
Park Parade C.1
Park Side D.3
Park Street C.1
Park Terrace D.3
Parker Street D.2
Parkers Place D.3
Parker's Terrace F.2
Parkside College E.2
Parkside Indoor
    Swimming Pool E.3
Parsonage Street E.1
Parsons Court C.3
Peas Hill C.2
Pemberton Place D.5
Pemberton Terrace...........D.5
Pembroke Street C.3
Pentlands Court E.1
Perowne Street F.4
Peterhouse.....................C.4
Peterhouse Ground A.1
Peter's Field E.3
Petty Cury C.2
Petworth Street F.2
Pikes Walk D.2
Police Station E.3
Portland Place E.2
Portugal Place C.1
Portugal Street C.1
Post Office Terrace C.2
Pound Hill B.1
Priory Road F.1
Prospect Row E.2
Pythagoras School B.1

Quay Side C.1
Queen Ann Terrace E.4
Queen's College B.3
Queen's Green B.3
Queen's Lane B.3
Queen's Road A.2

Regent Street..................D.3
Regent Terrace................D.3
Richmond Terrace C.1
Ridley Hall A.4
Ridley Hall Road...............B.4
Riverside F.1
Robinson College A.2
Rose Crescent C.2
Round Church Street C.1
Royal Cambridge Hotel C.4
Russell Court D.5
Russell Street...................D.5

St. Andrews Street C.2
St. Anthony's Walk D.5
St. Barnabas Church.........F.4
St. Botolph's Church C.3
St. Catherines College B.3
St. Chads A.3
St. Clements Church C.1
St. Eligius Street...............D.5
St. Eligius Place D.5
St. Giles B.1
St. Johns College B.1
St. Johns College
    Sports Ground.............A.1
St. Johns Old Bridge B.1
St. Johns Road.................C.1
St. Johns Street C.2
St. Marks Church A.5
St. Marks Court A.5
St. Martins C.2
St. Marys Passage C.2
St. Marys Street C.2
St. Matthews Church.........F.2
St. Matthews Street...........F.2
St. Michaels Church..........C.2
St. Pauls Church D.4
St. Pauls Road E.4
St. Pauls Walk E.4
St. Peters Church B.1
St. Peters Street..............B.1
St. Peter's Terrace C.4
St. Tibbs Row C.3
Salmon Lane....................F.2
Saxon Road F.1

Scott Polar Research
    Institute D.4
Scroope Terrace...............C.4
Sedgewick Museum..........C.3
Selwyn College................A.3
Senate House Hill C.2
Senate House Passage ...B.2
Severn Place....................F.2
Sheeps Green B.4
Shenstone House F.2
Short Street D.2
Sidgwick Avenue A.4
Sidney Street C.2
Sidney Sussex College C.1
Silver Street B.3
Small Bridge....................B.3
Springfield.......................B.3
Staffordshire Street F.2
Stanton House E.2
Station Road....................E.5
Studio Schools
    of English E.5
Sturton Street F.2
Summerfield A.4
Sun School D.2
Sun Street F.1
Sussex Street C.2

Tenison Avenue F.5
Tenison Court F.4
Tenison Road F.5
Tennis Court Road C.3
Tennis Court Terrace C.3
The Avenue B.2
The Backs B.2
The Cenacle A.5
The Chimney D.1
The Fen Causeway B.4
The Yews B.3
Thompsons Lane C.1
Thorpe House...................A.3
Tourist Information C.2
Training College F.3
Traverston A.3
Trinity Bridge B.2
Trinity College..................B.2
Trinity Hall.......................B.2
Trinity Lane......................B.2
Trinity Street....................C.2
Trumpington Gate C.3
Trumpington Street...........C.3

Union Road D.4
Union Society's
    Rooms........................C.1
University Arms Hotel........D.3
University Centre B.3
University Health
    Centre E.4
Upper Gwydir Street F.2

Vicaarage Terrace.............F.2
Victoria Avenue D.1
Victoria Street..................D.2

Walnut Treet Avenue.........F.1
Warkworth Street E.2
Warkworth Terrace E.3
Wellington Passage F.2
Wellington Street...............F.2
Welsley House Training
    School........................C.1
West Gardens A.3
West House A.3
West Road A.3
Westcott House C.1
Westminster College B.1
Westroad Corner B.3
Wheaton House F.2
Wheeler Street C.2
Whipple Museum C.3
Wilkin Street F.4
Willis Road E.3
Willow Place E.2
Willow Walk D.2
Wollaston Road E.3
Wordsworth Grove A.4

Young Street F.2

Zoology Museum C.3

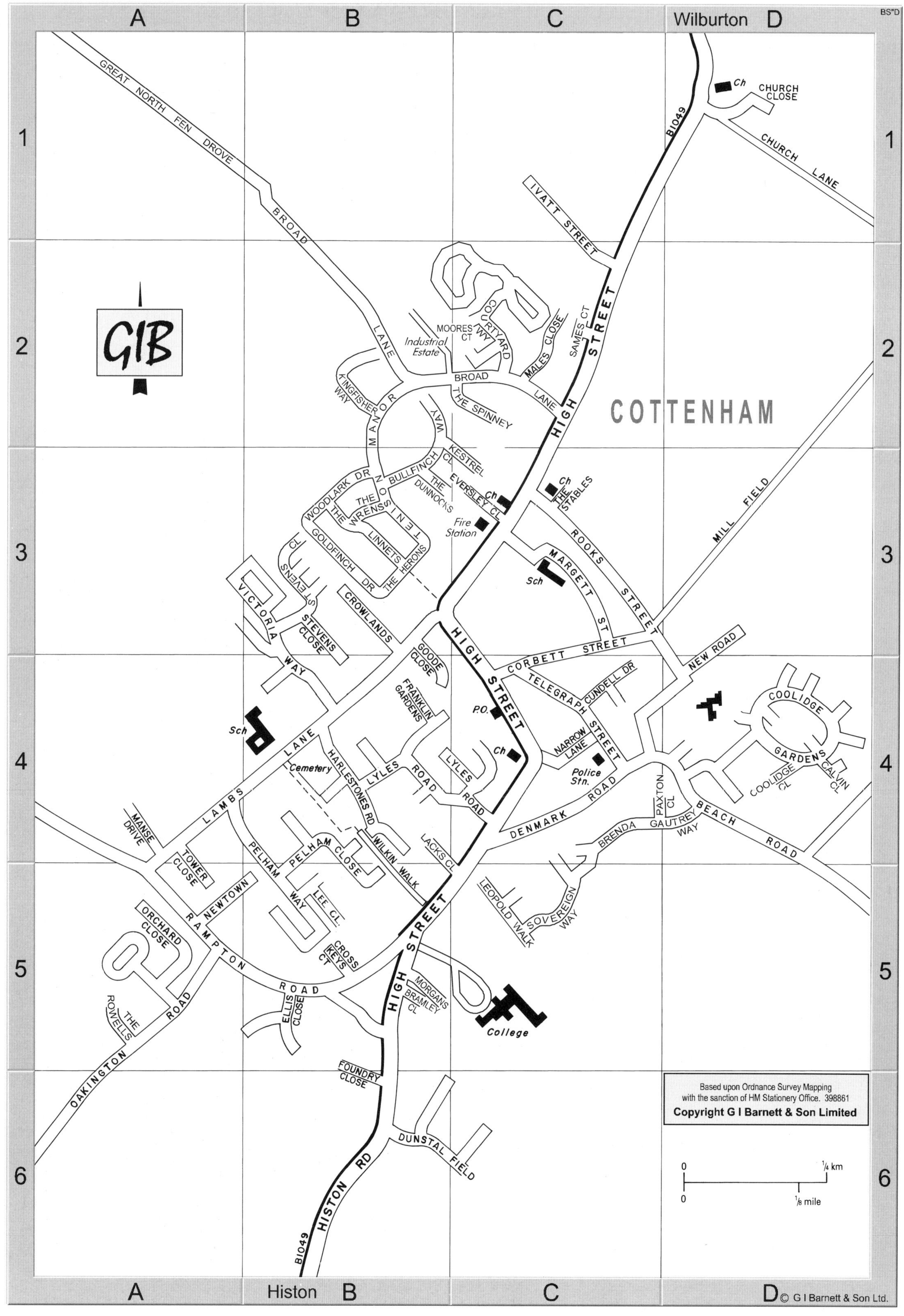
Wilburton
A B C D
BS"D
GIB
GREAT NORTH FEN DROVE
BROAD
B1049
Ch
CHURCH CLOSE
CHURCH LANE
IVATT STREET
COURTYARD WAY
MOORES CT
Industrial Estate
MALES CLOSE
SAMES CT
HIGH STREET
LANE
BROAD
THE SPINNEY
LANE
COTTENHAM
KINGFISHER WAY
MANOR
KESTREL
CL
EVERSLEY CL
Ch
MILL FIELD
WOODLARK DR
TEN SONS
BULLFINCH
THE DUNNOCKS
Ch
THE STABLES
WRENS
THE LINNETS
THE HERONS
Fire Station
ROOKS STREET
GOLDFINCH DR
CROWLANDS
Sch
MARGETT ST
NEW ROAD
VICTORIA WAY
STEVENS CL
STEVENS CLOSE
CORBETT STREET
COOLIDGE GARDENS
GOODE CLOSE
HIGH STREET
TELEGRAPH STREET
CUNDELL DR
COOLIDGE CL
CALVIN CL
Sch
FRANKLIN GARDENS
P.O.
NARROW LANE
PAXTON CL
BEACH ROAD
LAMBS LANE
Cemetery
HARLESTONES RD
LYLES ROAD
LYLES ROAD
Ch
Police Stn.
DENMARK ROAD
BRENDA
GAUTREY WAY
MANSE DRIVE
WILKIN WALK
LACKS CL
TOWER CLOSE
PELHAM WAY
PELHAM CLOSE
LEE CL.
LEOPOLD WALK
SOVEREIGN WAY
NEWTOWN
ORCHARD CLOSE
RAMPTON ROAD
CROSS KEYS CT
HIGH STREET
MORGANS
BRAMLEY CL
College
THE ROWELLS
ELLIS CLOSE
ROAD
OAKINGTON
FOUNDRY CLOSE
DUNSTAL FIELD
B1049
HISTON RD
Histon
Based upon Ordnance Survey Mapping
with the sanction of HM Stationery Office. 398861
Copyright G I Barnett & Son Limited
0 1/4 km
0 1/8 mile
© G I Barnett & Son Ltd.

COTTENHAM INDEX TO STREETS

Beach Road D.5
Bramley Close B.5
Brenda Gautrey Way C.4
Broad Lane B.1
Bullfinch Way B.3

Calvin Close D.4
Church Close D.1
Church Lane D.1
Coolidge Close D.4
Coolidge Gardens D.4
Corbett Street C.4
Courtyard Way C.2
Cross Keys Court B.5
Crowlands B.3
Cundell Drive C.4

Denmark Road C.4
Dunstal Field B.6

Ellis Close B.5

Eversley Close C.3

Foundry Close B.3
Franklin Gardens B.4

Goldfinch Drive B.3
Goode Close B.4

Harlestones Road B.4
High Street C.2
Histon Road B.6

Ivatt Street C.1

Kestrel Close C.2
Kingfisher Way B.3

Lacks Close B.4
Lambs Lane A.4
Lee Close B.5
Leopold Walk C.5

Lyles Road B.4

Males Close C.2
Manse Drive A.4
Margett Street C.3
Mill Field D.3
Moores Court C.2
Morgans B.5

Narrow Lane C.4
New Road D.4
Newtown A.5

Oakington Road A.6
Orchard Close A.5

Paxton Close C.4
Pelham Close B.4
Pelham Way B.4

Rampton Road A.5

Rooks Street C.3
Sames Court C.2
Sovereign Way C.5
Stevens Close B.3

Telegraph Street C.4
Tenison Manor B.3
The Dunnocks B.3
The Herons B.3
The Linnets B.3
The Rowells A.5
The Spinneys C.2
The Stables C.3
The Wrens B.3
Tower Close A.4

Victoria Way B.3

Wilkin Way B.4
Woodlark Drive B.3

ELY INDEX TO STREETS

Abbots Way........................B.4
Abbott Thurston Avenue E.3
Alexander Chase AA.6
Althorpe Court....................B.5
Angel Drove D.9
Angel Square D.8
Annesdale E.8
Appleby Park D.4
Archery Crescent E.6
Arundell D.4
Ash Grove G.4
Aspen Close F.4

Back Hill D.7
Back Lane E.7
Bartholomews Walk D.9
Barton Mews......................D.7
Barton Road C.7
Barton Square D.7
Beald Way..........................A.6
Beech Lane........................E.5
Bell Close D.5
Bell Holt E.6
Benedict Street B.4
Bentham Way E.3
Beresford Road...................A.6
Bernard Street B.6
Birch Close F.4
Bishop Laney Drive F.2
Bishop Wynn Close E.7
Bohemond Street E.5
Bray's Lane........................E.6
Bridge Road E.8
Broad Street E.7
Brooke Grove A.5
Buckingham Drive...............E.3
Buckthorn G.4
Butchers Row D.6
Butt Drove..........................E.2

Cam Drive..........................B.3
Cambridge Road.................B.7
Cambridgeshire Close B.6
Canterbury Way A.7
Canute Crescent.................E.2
Carey Close G.3
Castlehythe........................D.8
Chantry Lane D.6
Chapel Street C.6
Chequer Lane.....................D.6
Chief Street........................C.6
Chris. Tye Close B.5
Church Lane.......................C.6
Churchill Close A.6
Clayway F.4
Collier Close AA.6
Columbine Road.................A.4
Compton Fields F.3
Crauden Gardens................E.5
Cresswells Lane..................F.6
Cromwell Road...................C.6
Cutter Lane........................E.7

Dalton Way D.4
Darwin Close A.6
Davison Road F1
Deacon's Lane E.5
Dean Peacock Court F.3
Debden Green A.6
Dolphin Lane......................E.6
Dovehouse Close D.8
Downham Road C.4
Dunstan Street B.4

Egremont Street C.5
Elmfield.............................C.5
Engine Yard B.6
Etheldreda Street A.6

Fairfax Court.......................C.5
Falcon Mews......................B.4
Felton Way F.3
Fieldside............................B.6
Fitzgerald Close F1
Fleetwood D.4
Forehill E.6
Frankland Walk F.3

Gas Lane D.8
Gilbert Scott Drive F.2
Goodwin Grove G.2
Green Lane.........................D.6
Guelder Rose G.4
Gunning Road G.1

Hamilton Road B.7
Heaton Close G.2
Heaton Drive G.2
Henley Way G4
Hereward Street A.6
Herons Close B.4
Hertford Close AA7
Hervey Close A.7
High Barns.........................F.4
High Street D.6
Hills Lane B.6
Holly Walk..........................G.4
Houghton Gardens B.7
Hurst Lane AA.3
Hythe Lane E.7

James Essex Avenue E.2
James Essex Close E.2
John Amner Close D.4
Jubilee Terrace E.7
Juniper Drive G.4

Kent Close B.5
Kilkenny Avenue F.1
Kiln Lane G5
King Edgar Close E.2
Kings Avenue F.2

Langham Way F.2
Lansdowne Close A.7

Larkfield Road F.4
Leicester Close AA7
Lisle Close.........................F.5
Lisle Lane E.6
Little Lane B.6
Longchamp Drive G.3
Longfields A.7
Lumley Close F2
Lynn Road D.5
Lynton Close E.3
Lynton Drive E.3

Mallow Close B.3
Market Place......................E.6
Market Street D.6
Mawson Close B.7
Mayfield Close B.5
Meldon Place D.4
Merlin Drive.......................B.5
Militia Way C.7
Minster Place D.6
Morton Close F1
Mulberry Way F.4

Nene Road C.3
New Barns Avenue E.4
New Barns Road E.5
Newnham Street.................D.6
Nigel Road..........................F.1
Norfolk Road AA7
Northwold C.5
Nutholt Lane D.5

Old Brewery Close E.6
Osier Close........................E.7
Oxford Close......................C.7

Page Court E.4
Palace Green D.6
Parade Lane C.7
Philippa Close....................E.2
Pilgrims Way A.8
Potter's Lane D.8
Prickwillow Road.................E.5
Priests Meadow Court C.5
Priors Court........................B.4

Quai d'Orsay......................E.8
Quayside............................E.7
Queen Adelaide Way...........F.9
Queen Emma Walk..............E.3

Ramsey Road F.4
Ravens Court C.4
Redman Close G.2
Ribe Court C.5
Riverside Walk E.7
Robins Close B.4
Roswell View F.5

Ship Lane E.7
Silver Street C.6

Simeon Close.....................G.1
Sir James Black Road D.9
Southern Link Road C.9
Spencer Croft F.3
Springhead Lane F.5
Springhead Lane F.6
St. Andrews Way B.4
St. Audreys Way D.4
St. Catherine's C.5
St. Ethelwolds Close...........A.6
St. Johns Street A.6
St. Martins Walk E.5
St. Mary's Court C.6
St. Marys Street C.6
St. Ovins Green B.5
St. Thomas Place D.9
Station Road......................D.8
Steeple Row D.6
Stour Green D.3
Stuntney Causeway E.9
Suffolk Close AA8
Summerhayes G4
Sycamore Lane G.4

Teasel Drive A.4
Tennyson Place A.5
The Chase A.7
The Gallery D.6
The Paddock D.5
The Range C.6
The Turnpike.......................B.8
The Vineyards.....................E.6
Thirlby Gardens..................F.2
Tower Road.........................B.7
Trinity Close C.5

Upherd's Lane C.5

Victoria Street E.7
Vineyard Way E.5

Walsingham Way A.5
Warwick Drive.....................AA.8
Waterside E.7
Welland Place.....................C.3
West End B.6
West End Mews B.6
West Fen Road...................A.5
Wheatsheaf Close A.7
Wilford Drive F.3
Williams Close E2
Willow Grove F.6
Willow Walk........................E.6
Windmill Close A.7
Wissey Way C.3
Witchford Road...................A.8
Woolpack Yard D.5
Wrens Close B.5

York Way............................A.8

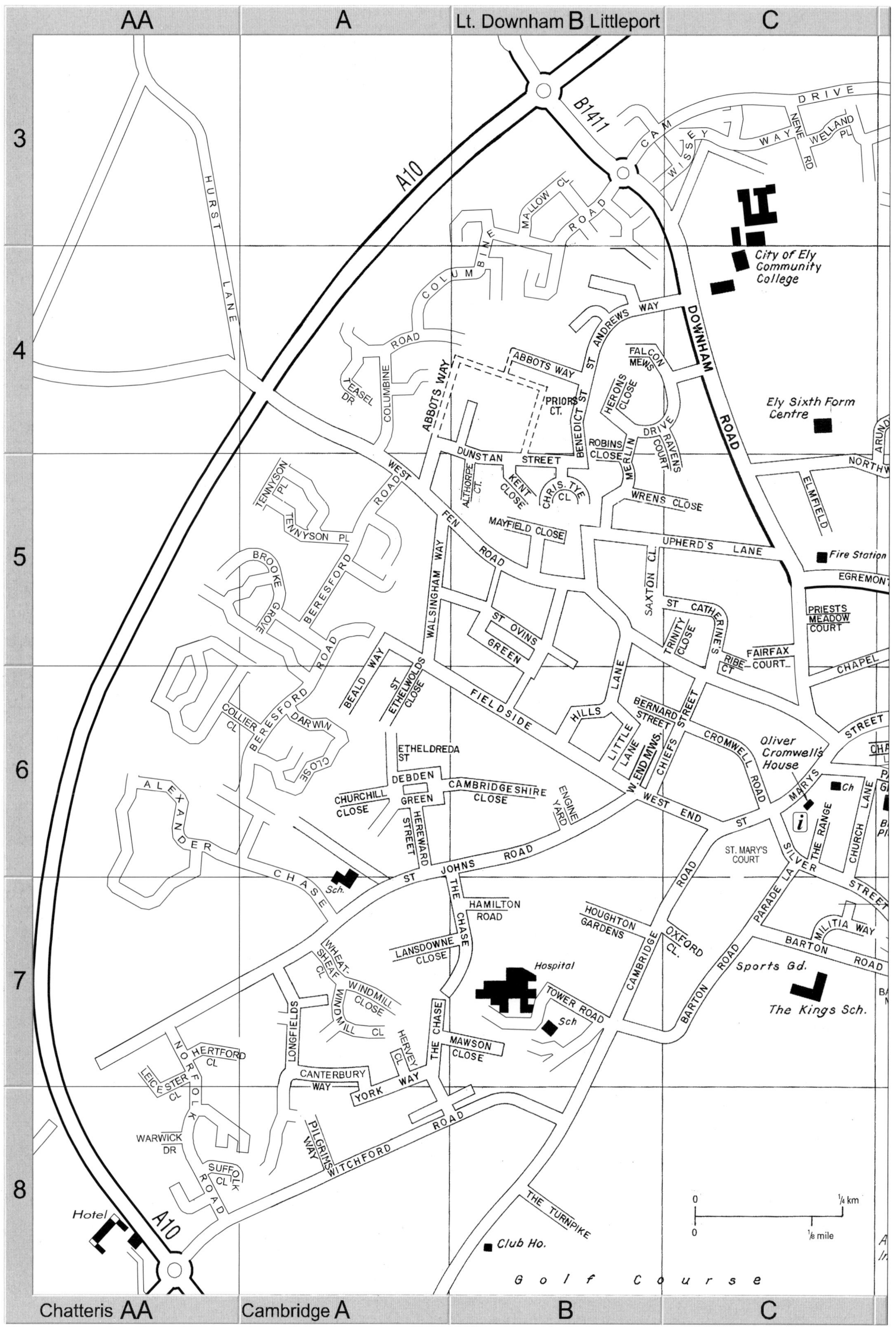

AA
A
Lt. Downham B Littleport
C
HURST LANE
A10
B1411
CAM
WISSEY WAY
NENE RD
WELLAND PL
DRIVE
City of Ely Community College
COLUMBINE ROAD
MALLOW CL
St ANDREWS WAY
FALCON MEWS
DOWNHAM ROAD
Ely Sixth Form Centre
ARUND
NORTHW
ABBOTS WAY
ABBOTS WAY
PRIORS CT.
HERONS CLOSE
MERLIN
RAVENS COURT
DRIVE
YEASEL DR
COLUMBINE ROAD
WEST ROAD
DUNSTAN STREET
BENEDICT ST
ROBINS CLOSE
WRENS CLOSE
ELMFIELD
ALTHORPE CT.
KENT CLOSE
CHRIS TYE CL
CHRIS. TYE CL
TENNYSON PL
TENNYSON PL
FEN ROAD
MAYFIELD CLOSE
UPHERD'S LANE
Fire Station
EGREMONT
BROOKE GROVE
BERESFORD ROAD
WALSINGHAM WAY
St OVINS GREEN
SAXTON CL
ST CATHERINE'S
TRINITY CLOSE
PRIESTS MEADOW COURT
COLLIER CL
BERESFORD CLOSE
DARWIN
BEALD WAY
St ETHELWOLDS CLOSE
FIELDSIDE
HILLS LANE
LITTLE
BERNARD STREET
RIBE CT
FAIRFAX COURT
CHAPEL
STREET
ETHELDREDA ST
DEBDEN GREEN
CAMBRIDGESHIRE CLOSE
ENGINE YARD
W END MWS.
CHIEFS
CROMWELL ROAD
Oliver Cromwell's House
CHA
ALEXANDER CHASE
CHURCHILL CLOSE
HEREWARD STREET
WEST END ST
MARYS
Ch
THE RANGE
CHURCH LANE
B PL
Sch.
St JOHNS ROAD
ST. MARY'S COURT
SILVER
i
STREET
HAMILTON ROAD
THE CHASE
HOUGHTON GARDENS
OXFORD CL.
ROAD
PARADE LA.
MILITIA WAY
LANSDOWNE CLOSE
Hospital
CAMBRIDGE ROAD
BARTON ROAD
BARTON ROAD
Sports Gd.
BA
WHEAT-SHEAF CL
WINDMILL CLOSE
WINDMILL CL
HERVEY CL
TOWER ROAD
Sch
The Kings Sch.
LONGFIELDS
THE CHASE
MAWSON CLOSE
NORFOLK
HERTFORD CL
CANTERBURY WAY
YORK WAY
LEICESTER CL
WARWICK DR
SUFFOLK CL
PILGRIMS WAY
WITCHFORD ROAD
A10
THE TURNPIKE
0   ¼ km
0   ⅛ mile
Hotel
Club Ho.
Golf Course
A
In
Chatteris AA
Cambridge A
B
C
3
4
5
6
7
8

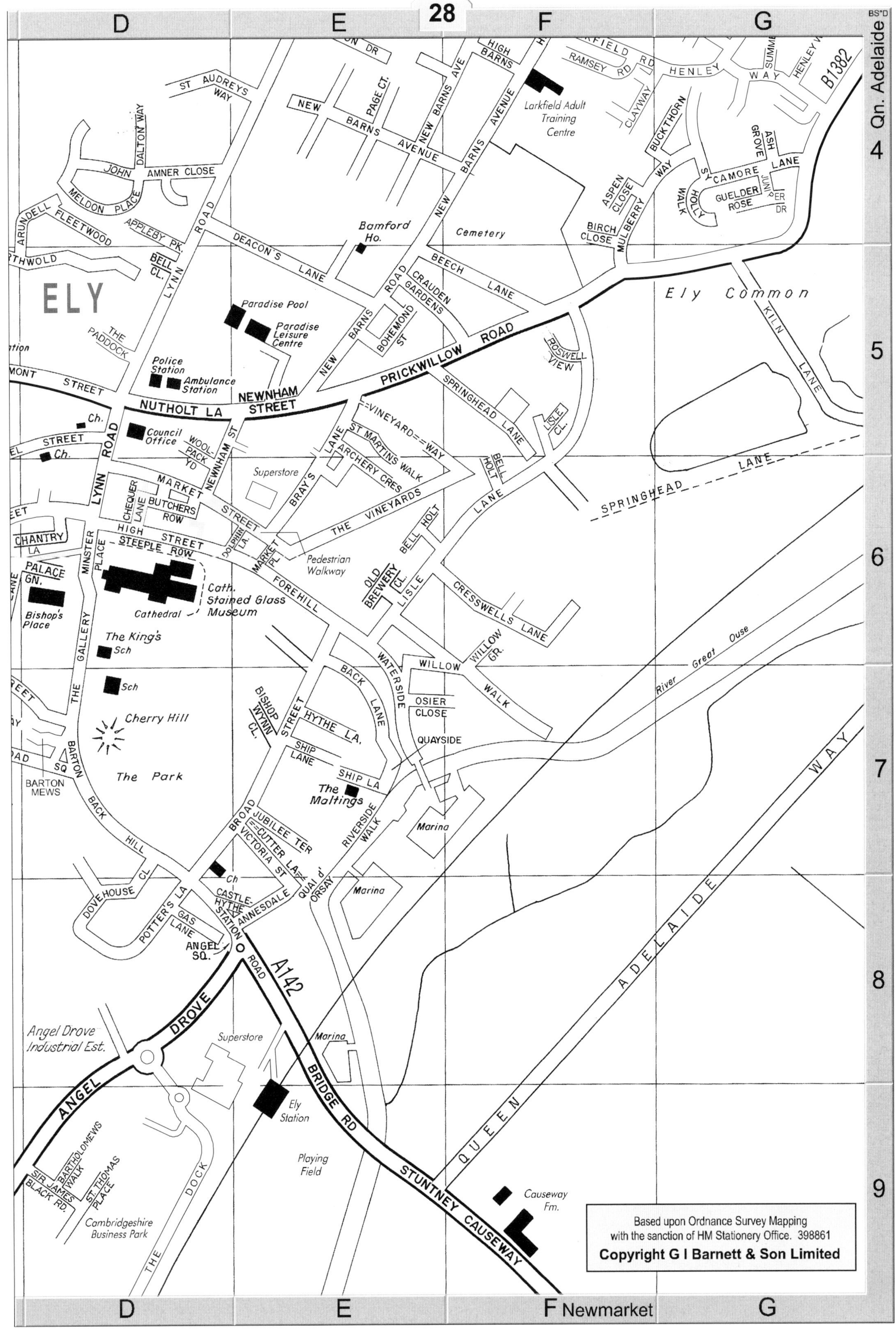

Based upon Ordnance Survey Mapping with the sanction of HM Stationery Office. 398861

Copyright G I Barnett & Son Limited

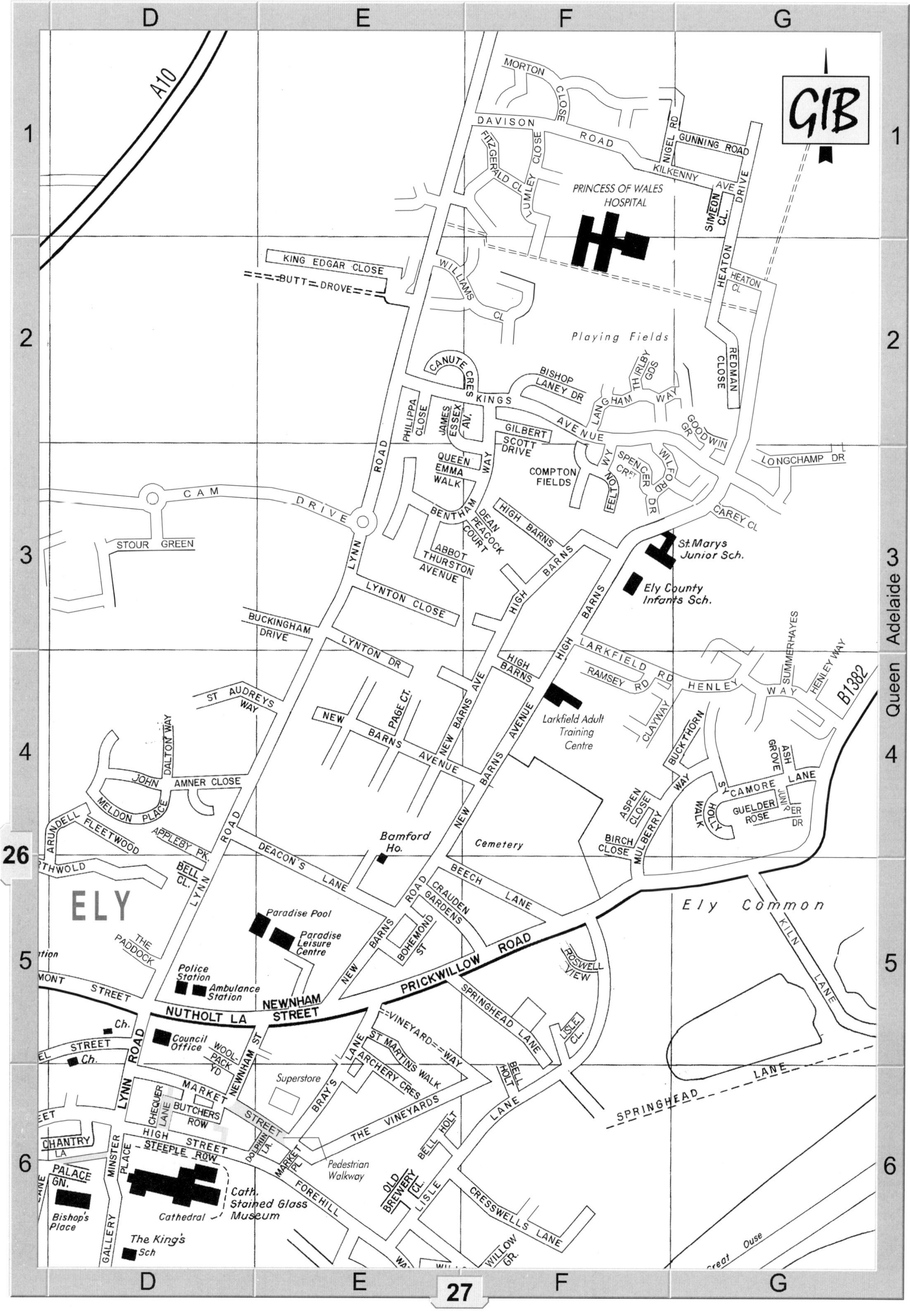
A10
GIB
MORTON CLOSE
DAVISON ROAD
NIGEL RD
GUNNING ROAD
FITZGERALD CL.
YUMLEY CLOSE
KILKENNY AVE
SIMEON CL.
HEATON DRIVE
HEATON CL
PRINCESS OF WALES HOSPITAL
KING EDGAR CLOSE
BUTT DROVE
WILLIAMS CL
REDMAN CLOSE
Playing Fields
CANUTE CRES
KINGS
BISHOP LANEY DR
THIRLBY GDS
LANGHAM WAY
GOODWIN GR
PHILIPPA CLOSE
JAMES
ESSEX AV.
GILBERT SCOTT DRIVE
AVENUE
SPENCER CRET
FELTON WY
WILFORD DR
LONGCHAMP DR
QUEEN EMMA WALK
COMPTON FIELDS
CAM DRIVE
CAREY CL.
STOUR GREEN
LYNN ROAD
BENTHAM WAY
DEAN
PEACOCK COURT
HIGH BARNS
St. Marys Junior Sch.
ABBOT THURSTON AVENUE
HIGH BARNS
Ely County Infants Sch.
LYNTON CLOSE
SUMMERHAYES
BUCKINGHAM DRIVE
LYNTON DR
HIGH BARNS
HIGH BARNS
LARKFIELD RD
RAMSEY RD
HENLEY WAY
HENLEY WAY
B1382
ST AUDREYS WAY
NEW BARNS
PAGE CT.
NEW BARNS AVENUE
NEW BARNS AVE
HIGH BARNS AVENUE
Larkfield Adult Training Centre
CLAYWAY
HENLEY WAY
Queen Adelaide
JOHN AMNER CLOSE
DALTON WAY
ASPEN CLOSE
BUCKTHORN WAY
GROVE
ASH LANE
MELDON PLACE
APPLEBY PK.
Bamford Ho.
NEW BARNS
CAMORE
JUNIPER DR
HOLLY WALK
ARUNDELL
FLEETWOOD
LYNN ROAD
DEACON'S LANE
Cemetery
MULBERRY
BIRCH CLOSE
GUELDER ROSE
ST.
NORTHWOLD
BELL CL.
THE PADDOCK
Paradise Pool
CRAUDEN GARDENS
BEECH LANE
Ely Common
KILN LANE
ELY
Paradise Leisure Centre
NEW BARNS ROAD
BOHEMOND ST
PRICKWILLOW ROAD
BOSWELL VIEW
Station
Police Station
Ambulance Station
NUTHOLT LA
NEWNHAM STREET
SPRINGHEAD LANE
LISLE CL.
MONT STREET
VINEYARD WAY
ST MARTINS WALK
SPRINGHEAD LANE
STREET
Ch.
Council Office
WOOL PACK YD
NEWNHAM ST
Superstore
LANE
ARCHERY CRES
BRAYS
BELL HOLT
LYNN ROAD
Ch.
MARKET
CHEQUER LANE
BUTCHERS ROW
STREET
DOLPHIN LA.
THE VINEYARDS
BELL HOLT
LANE
CRESSWELLS LANE
CHANTRY LA
PALACE GN.
MINSTER PLACE
HIGH STREET
STEEPLE ROW
MARKET PL.
Pedestrian Walkway
OLD BREWERY CL.
LISLE
Bishop's Place
Cath. Stained Glass Museum
Cathedral
FOREHILL
GALLERY
The King's Sch
WILLOW GR
WAY
Great Ouse

GIRTON INDEX TO STREETS

Cambridge Road C.5
Cherry Bounds Lane C.5
Church Lane B.5
Cockerton Road.......................C.4

Dodford Lane..........................B.3
Duck End B.5

Fairway B.3

Gifford's Close C.6
Girton Road C.6

Hicks Lane C.5
High Street............................B.5
Huntingdon Road....................A.7

Lawrence Close.......................B.5
Lees Way C.5

Manor Farm Road C.3
Marks Way.............................C.5
Mayfield Road.........................D.6
Michaels Close B.5

New Road B.1
Northfield B.3

Oakington Road.......................B.2
Orchard Close C.5

Pepys Way C.6

Red Gate Road C.5

St. Vincents Close B.6
Sterndale Close C.5

The Gowers B.5

Washpit Road A.5
Weavers Field C.7
Wellbrook Way.........................D.7
Whitegate Close C.5
Woodlands Park.......................B.5
Woody Green..........................B.6

BAR HILL INDEX TO STREETS

Acorn Avenue B.1
Almond Grove B.1
Appletrees B.2

Brookdale B.1

Chestnut Rise C.1
Crafts Way...............................B.1

Fieldview B.2
Foxhollow B.1

Hanover Close..........................B.1
Hillcrest C.1
Holytrees B.1

Industrial Estate........................A.1

Little Meadow B.2

Norman Park B.1

Oatlands Avenue A.2
Otter Close A.2
Otter Gardens A.2

Partridge Drive..........................A.2
Pheasant Rise A.2

Saxon Way A.1
Shopping Centre B.1
Stonefields...............................A.2

The Brambles C.1
The Fairway.............................C.1
The Spinney B.2
Thruffle Way C.2
Trafalgar Way A.1

Viking Way...............................A.1

Watermead B.2

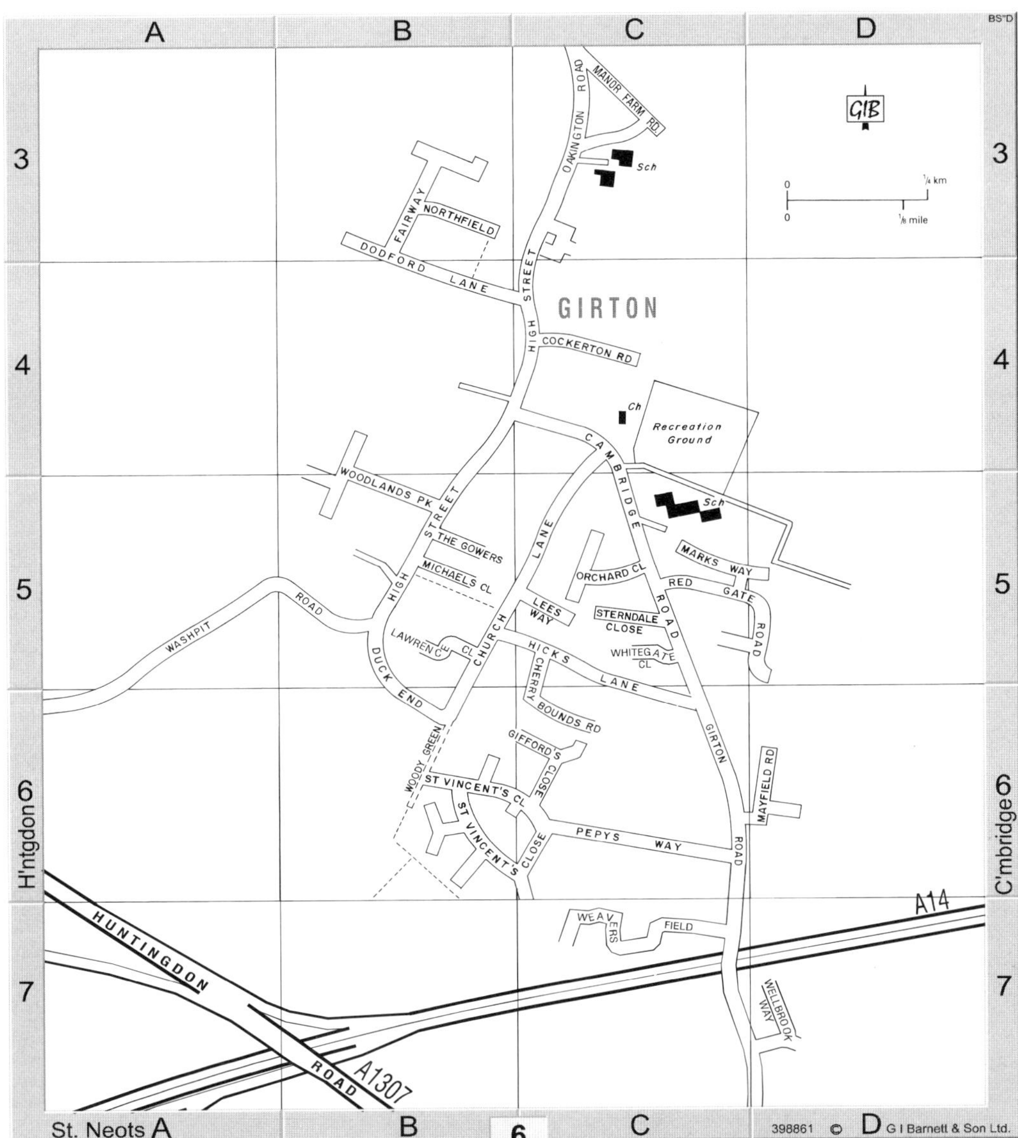

BAR HILL

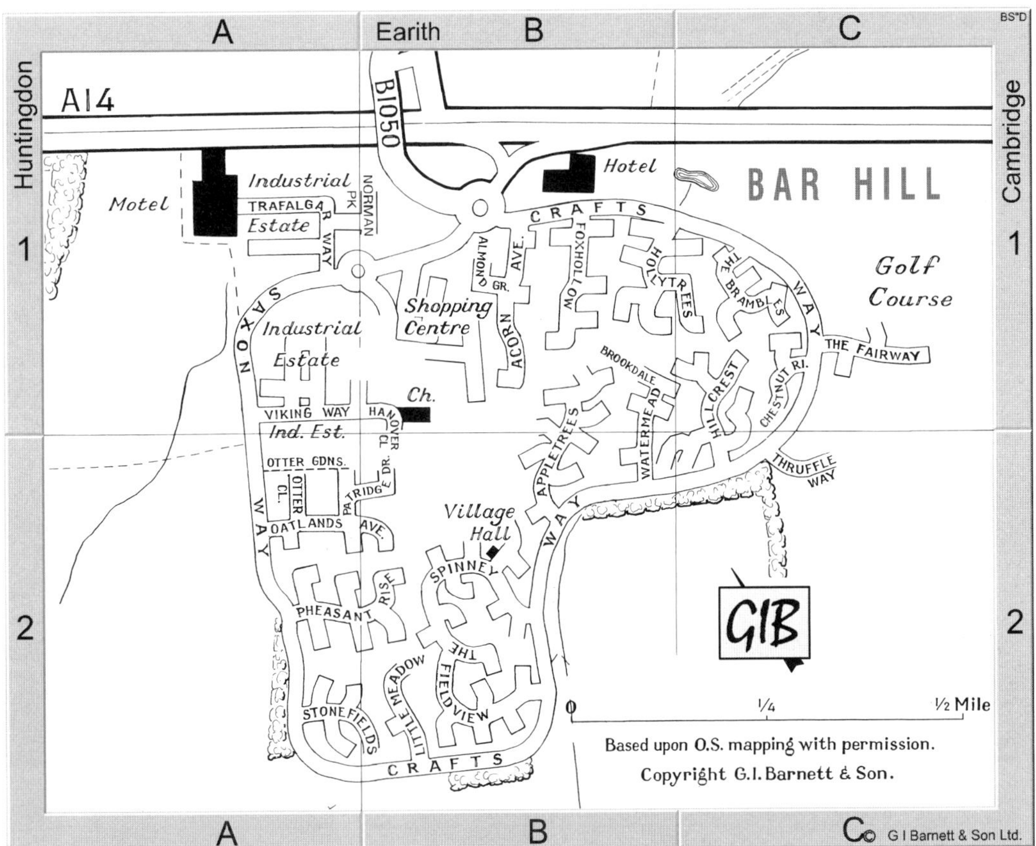

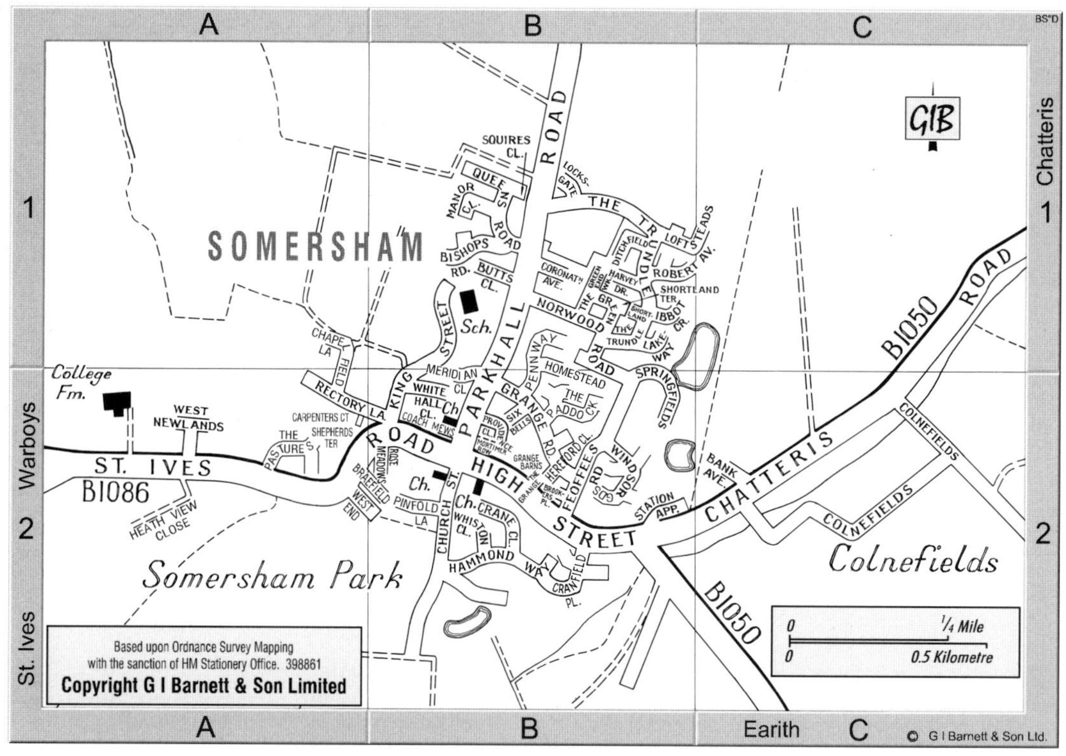

SOMERSHAM INDEX TO STREETS

Bank Avenue C.2
Bishops Road B.1
Braefield A.2
Brookers Place B.2
Butts Close B.1

Carpenters Court A.2
Chapel Field Lane.......A.1
Chatteris Road C.2
Church Street B.2
Coach Mews B.2
Colnefields C.2
Coronation Avenue B.1

Crane Close B.2
Cranfield Place B.2

Ditchfield B.1

Feoffees Road B.2

Grange Barns B.2
Grange Road B.2
Green End Walk B.1
Grove Gardens B.1

Hammond Way B.2

Harvey Drive B.1
Heath View Close A.2
Hereford Close B.2
High Street B.2
Homestead B.1

Ibbot Crescent B.1

King Street B.2

Lakeway B.1
Locks-Gate B.1
Loftsteads B.1

Manor Close B.1
Meridian Close B.2
Mortimer Row B.2

Norwood Road B.1

Parkhall Road B.2
Pennway B.2
Pinfold Lane B.2
Providence Close B.2

Queens Road B.1

Rectory Lane A.2
Robert Avenue B.1
Rose Meadows B.2
St. Ives Road A.2
Shepherds Terrace A.2
Shortland B.1
Shortland Terrace B.1
Six Bells B.2
Springfields B.2
Somersham Park A.2
Squires Close B.1
Station Approach B.2

The Grange B.2
The Green B.1
The Paddock B.2
The Pasture A.2
The Trundle B.1

Walton Close...........B.1
West End B.2
West Newlands A.2
Whiston Close B.2
Whitehall Close B.2
Windsors Gardens B.2

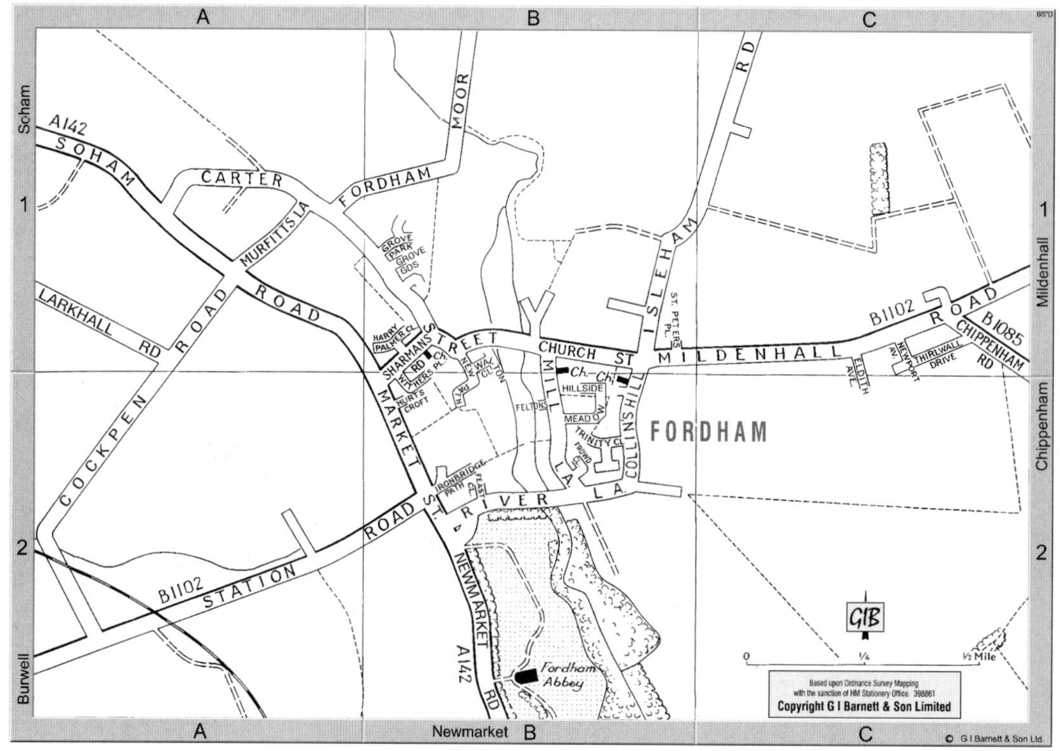

FORDHAM INDEX TO STREETS

Carter Street A.1
Chippenham Road C.1
Church Street B.1
Cockpen Road A.2
Collins Hill B.2

Eldith Avenue C.1

Feltons B.2
Fordham Abbey B.2
Fordham Moor A.1
Frowd Close B.2

Grove Gardens B.1
Grove Park B.1

Harry Palmer Close B.1
Hillside Meadow B.2
Hurt's Croft B.2

Ironbridge Path B.2
Isleham Road B.1

Larkhall Road A.1

Market Street B.2
Mildenhall Road B.1
Mill Lane B.1
Murfitts Lane A.1

New Path B.1

Newmarket Road B.2
Newport Avenue C.1

River Lane B.2

St. Peters Place B.1
Sharmans Road B.1
Soham Road A.1

Station Road A.2

Thirlwall Drive C.1
Trinity Close B.2

Walton Close..............B.1
Withers Place B.2

WILLINGHAM INDEX TO STREETS

Belland Field A.2
Belsars Close B.1
Berrycroft A.1
Brickhills B.1

Church Lane B.1
Church Street B.1

Earith Road B.1
Elm Way A.1

Fen End B.1

George Street B.1
Green Street B.1

Haden Way A.2
High Street A.1

Long Lane B.1
Lordship Close A.1

Meadow Road B.1
Mill Road B.2
Millfield A.2

Newington B.2

Osborn Close B.1
Over Road A.1

Pegler Court B.1
Priest Lane B.1
Pyrethrum Way B.1

Rampton End B.1
Rampton Road B.2
Rockmill End B.1
Rook Grove A.1

Schole Road B.1
Short Lane B.1
Silver Street B.1
Station Road A.2

Thodays Close B.1

West Fen Road...............A.1
West Meadow Close A.1
Wilford Furlong B.1
Willingham Road A.1

ISLEHAM INDEX TO STREETS

Aves Close A.2

Beck Road B.2
Beech Close A.2
Bowers Lane B.1

Chair Drove (Track) D.1
Church Lane A.1
Church Street A.2
Coates Drove A.1
Cornwell Close A.2
Croft Road B.2

Docking's Lane A.2

East Fen Road B.1
East Road B.1
Ellwoods Close A.1

Festival Road B.2
Fordham Road A.2

Goodchilds Gardens B.1

Hall Barn Road A.2
Houghtons Lane B.1

Isleham Marina B.1

Jubilee Close A.2
Kennedy Road B.2
Knaves Acres Drive A.1

Limestone Close A.2
Little London Drove A.2
Little London Lane A.2

Maltings Lane A.2
Mill Street A.2

Nursery Close A.2

Pound Lane A.1
Prickwillow Road A.1
Priory Gardens A.2

Robins Close A.2
Rudlands Close B.1

St. Andrews Close A.1
Sheldricks Road B.2
Sparks Close B.2
Station Road A.2
Sun Street A.2

Temple Road A.2
The Causeway B.2
The Pits B.2

Waterside B.1
West Street A.2

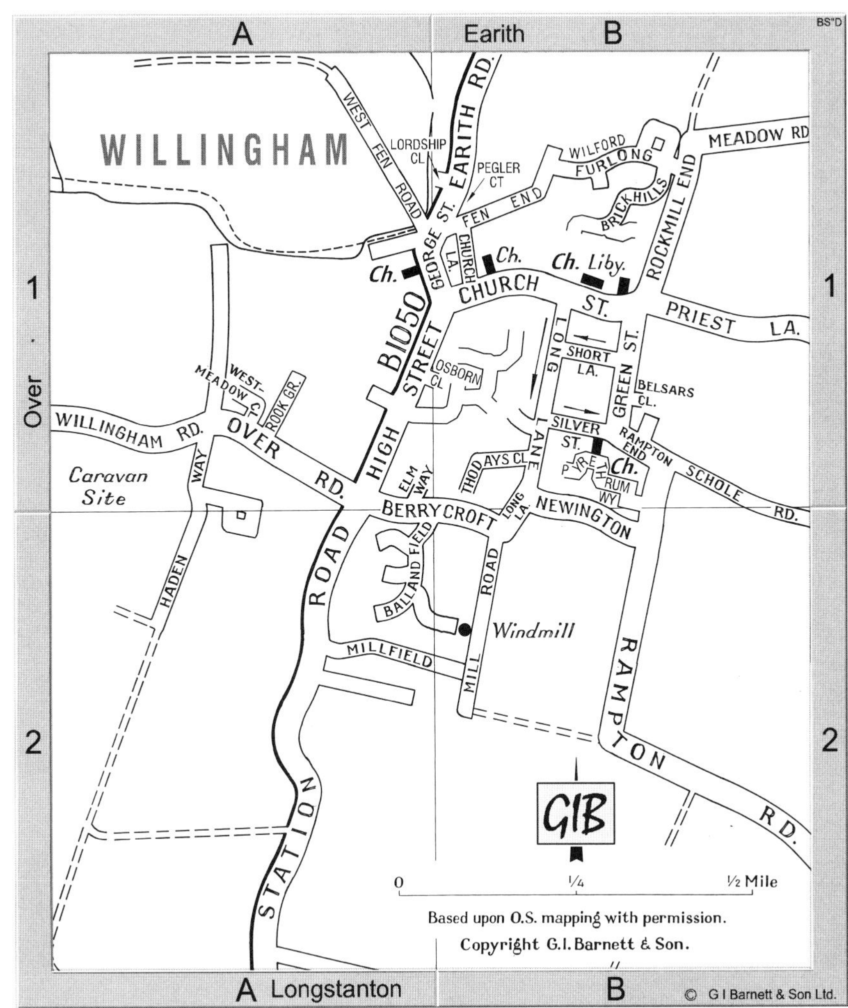

ISLEHAM

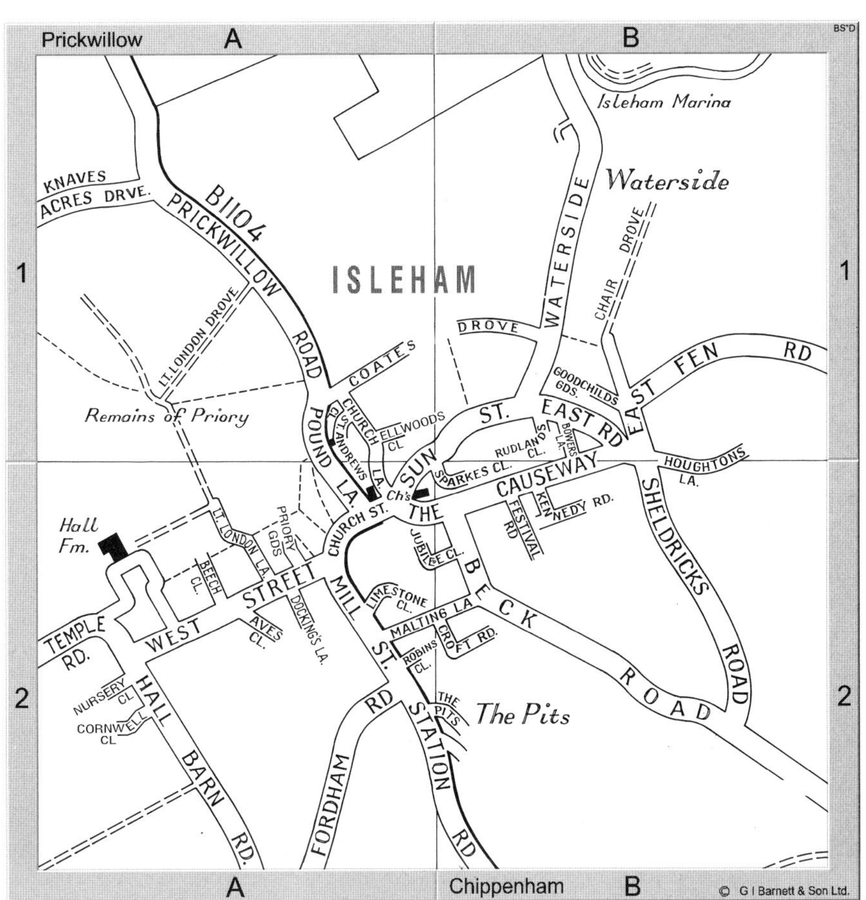

GREAT SHELFORD INDEX TO STREETS

Anvil Close D.3
Aschen Green B.2
Aylesford Way C.3

Bar Close D.3
Bar Lane D.3
Beech Close B.3
Birch Trees Road C.2
Bridge Close B.1
Bridge Lane B.3
Buristead Road B.2
Bury Road D.3

Cambridge Road B.1
Cambridge Road C.3-D.4
Chaston Road C.2
Cherry Trees B.1
Cherry Tree Avenue D.3
Chestnuts D.3
Church Street B.3
Collier Way D.3
Coppice Avenue C.1
Courtyards B.3
Coxs Close D.3
Crandal Way B.2

Davey Crescent................B.1

De Freville Road C.2
Dolphin Way C.3
Dukes Meadow D.2

Elms Avenue C.2

Finchs Close D.3
Forge End D.3

Garden Fields A.3
Gog Magog Way D.2
Grain Close C.2
Granhams Close C.2
Granhams Road C.2
Granta Terrace C.3
Greenfield Close D.3

Hauxton Road A.3
Hawthorne Road C.2
Headley Garens C.3
Heffer Close C.3
High Green C.2
High Street A.2
High Street A.3
High Street B.2
Hill Road D.3
Hills View.........................C.2

Hinton Way C.2

Joscelynes D.3

Kings Mill Lane B.3

Leeway Avenue................C.2
London Road C.3

Macauley Avenue C.2
Manor Road A.3
Marfleet Close B.1
Maris Green C.2
Mil Court C.2
Mingle Lane C.2
Moor Close A.3

Newton Road A.3

Orchard Road C.2

Peacocks B.3
Poplar Close C.2
Poplar Way.......................D.3
Priams Way......................C.3

St. Andrews Close.............C.3

Selwyn Close B.2
Shelford Park Avenue C.2
Shelford Road A.3
Spinney Drive C.3
Station Court C.2
Station Road C.2
Sternesway D.3
Stonehill Road..................B.1

The Hectare B.1
The Orchards C.1
The Terrace B.3
Tunwells Lane C.2

Vine Close.........................D.3

Walden Way B.1
Westfield Road B.1
Wheelers..........................C.1
Whittlesford Road B.3
Woodlands Close C.3
Woodlands Road...............C.3
Woollards Lane B.2

NEEDINGWORTH
INDEX TO
STREETS

Arnold Close B.3
Ashton Close C.3
Asplins Avenue B.2

Bedford Close C.2
Beldams C.2
Bluntisham Road C.1
Bramley Avenue C.4

Chapel Close C.3
Church Street B.3
Daintree D.2
Dales Way B.2

Fews Close C.2

Harris Crescent B.3
Hawkes Lane B.3
High Street B.2

Lowndes Drove A.2

Meeting Lane C.2

Old Farm Close C.2
Overcote Lane C.3

Park View B.3
Pound Hill Close A.2
Priory Close A.2
Priory Road B.2
Pyetts Row B.3

Ravens Court C.2
Russett Avenue C.4

St. John's Close C.3
Senescalls C.2
Silver Court C.2
Silver Lane C.2
Spinney Way D.2

The Furlongs C.3
The Maltings B.3
Townsend Road C.2

Willow Green C.2

STILTON/FOLKSWORTH
INDEX TO STREETS

STILTON / FOLKSWORTH

Apreece Road A.2
Apreece Way C.2
Ash Close B.2

Barn Close B.2
Bell Close C.2
Bishop Close B.3
Blackmans Road A.2

Caldecote Road A.3
Castel Way A.2
Cooper Thornhill
   Road B.2
Chapel Court C.3
Chervil Close A.2
Church Street, Stilton B.2
Elm Close B.2
Elm Road A.2
Ermine Court C.3

Fen Lane C.3
Fen Street C.3
Fishers Close B.3
Folksworth Road A.1
Fox Covert B.3

Gala Close C.2
George Street B.2
Glebe Road C.3

Harvest Close B.2
Hawthorn Road A.2
High Street C.3
Mallow Road A.2
Manor Road,
   Folksworth A.2

Manor Road,
   Stilton B.2
Maple Drive C.3
Meadow Close B.2
Mill Road C.2
Mondela Place C.3
Morborne Road A.1

Norman Cross B.1
Norman Drive B.2
North Street C.2

Oak Farm Close C.3
Oak Road C.3
Orchard Close C.3

Queen Eleanor Close
   ....C.2

Ravensdale B.3
Rectory Way B.3
Roman Way C.2

St. Mary's Road B.2

Talbot Close C.2
The Paddocks A.2
Townsend Way A.2
Turpin's Ride C.3
Walnut Way B.3
Washingley Road A.3
Willow Close B.2
Woburn Court C.3
Woodward Close C.2
Worthington Close C.2

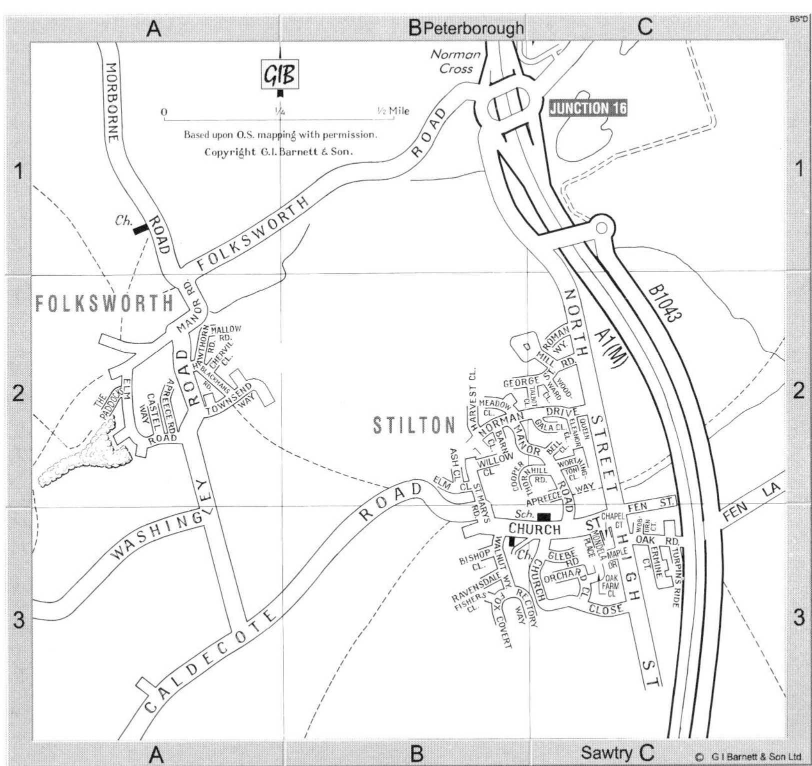

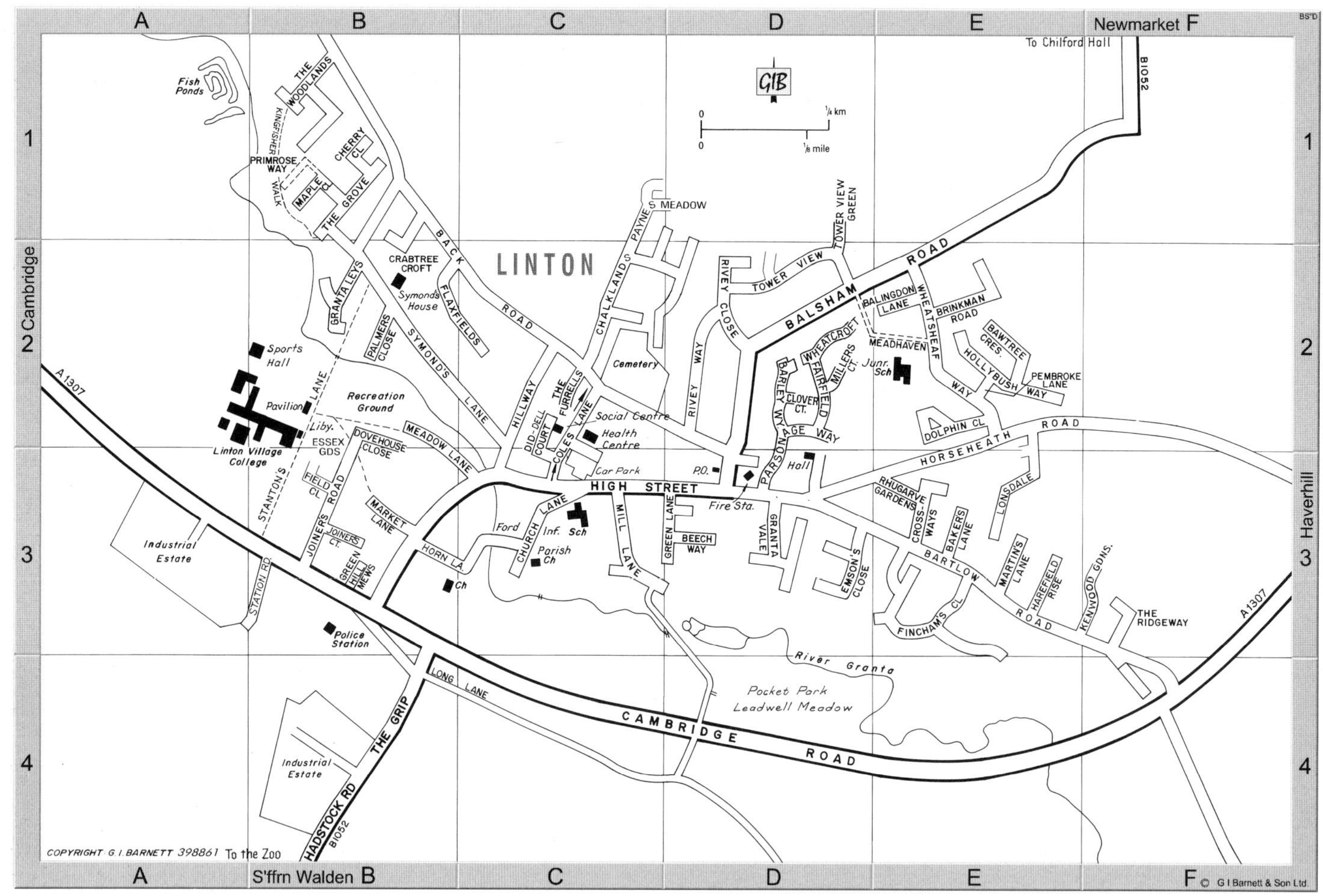

LINTON INDEX TO STREETS

Back Road B.2
Bakers Lane E.3
Balingdon Lane E.2
Balsham Road D.2
Barley Way D.2
Bartlow Road E.3
Bawtree Crescent E.2
Beech Lane D.3
Brinkman Road E.2

Cambridge Road C.4
Chalklands C.2
Cherry Close B.1
Church Lane C.3
Clover Court D.2
Coles Lane C.3
Crabtree Croft B.2
Crossways E.3

Did-Dell Court C.2
Dolphin Close E.2

Dovehouse Close B.2

Emson's Close D.3
Essex Gardens B.2

Fairfield D.2
Field Close B.3
Fincham's Close E.3
Flaxfields B.2

Granta Leys B.2
Granta Vale D.3
Green Hill Mews B.3
Green Lane C.3

Hadstock Road B.4
Harefield Rise E.3
High Street C.3
Hillway C.2
Hollybush Way E.2
Horn Lane B.3

Horseheath Road E.3
Joiners Court B.3
Joiners Road B.3

Kenwood Gardens F.3
Kingfisher Walk B.1

Long Lane B.4
Lonsdale E.3

Maple Close B.1
Market Lane B.3
Martins Lane E.3
Meadhaven E.2
Meadow Lane B.2
Mill Lane C.3
Millers Court D.2

Palmers Close B.2
Parsonage Way D.3
Paynes Meadow C.1

Pembroke Lane E.2
Primrose Way B.1

Rhugarve Gardens E.3
Rivey Close D.2
Rivey Way D.2

Stanton's Lane B.3
Station Road B.3
Symonds Lane B.2

The Furrells C.2
The Grip B.4
The Grove B.1
The Ridgeway F.3
The Woodlands B.1
Tower View D.2
Tower View Green D.1

Wheatcroft D.2
Wheatsheaf Way E.2

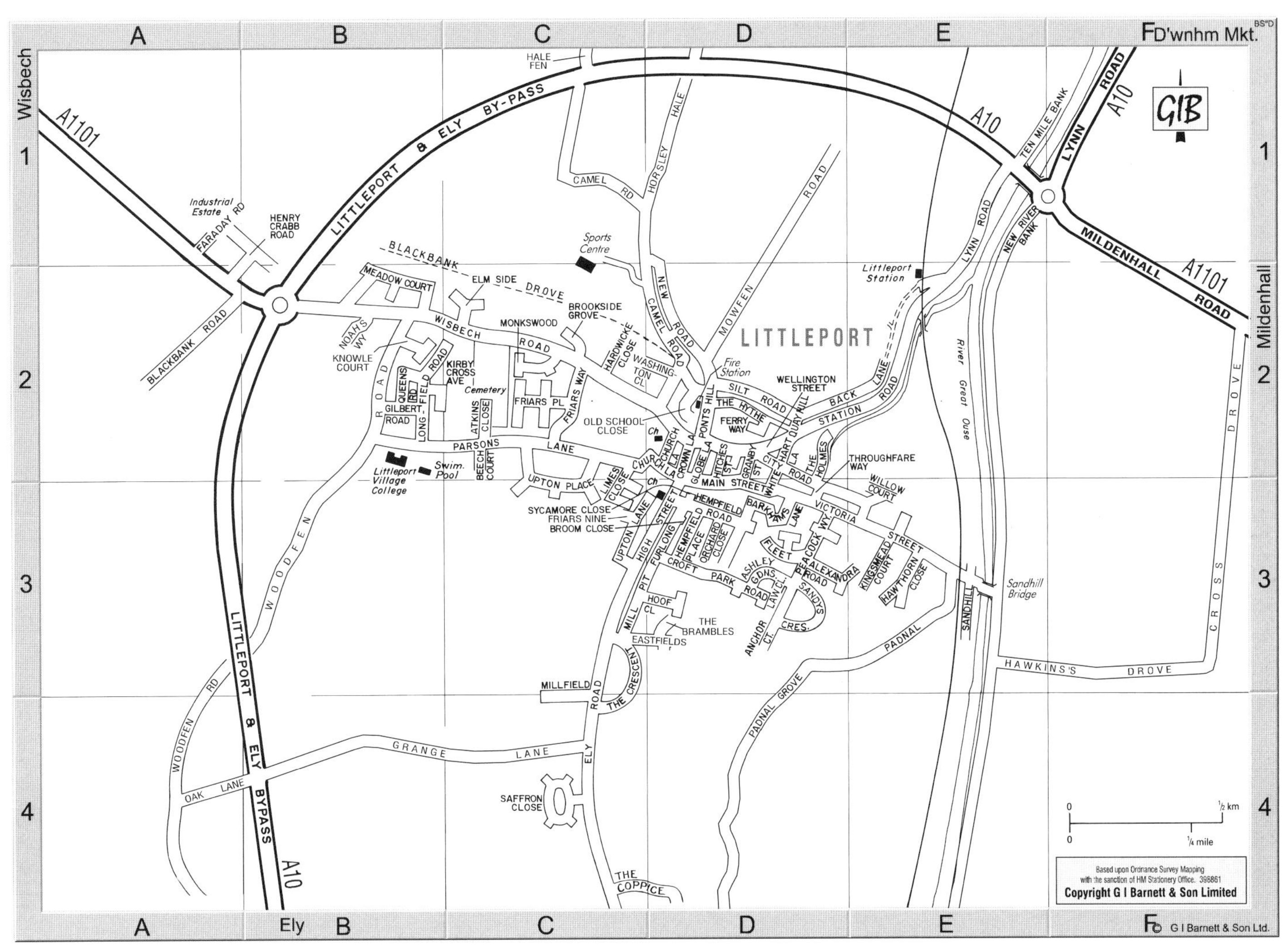

LITTLEPORT INDEX TO STREETS

Alexandra Road D.3
Anchor Court D.3
Ashley Gardens D.3
Atkins Close C.2

Back Lane D.2
Barkhams Lane D.3
Beech Court C.2
Blackbank Drove B.1
Blackbank Road A.2
Brookside Grove C.2
Broom Close C.3

Camel Road D.2
Church Lane...................D.2
City Road D.2
Croft Park Road D.3
Cross Drove F.3
Crown Lane D.2

Eastfields C.3
Elm Side........................C.2
Ely Road........................C.4

Faraday Road.................B.1
Ferry Way......................D.2
Fleet Close D.3
Friars Nine C.3

Friars Place C.2
Friars Way C.2

Gilbert Road B.2
Globe Lane....................D.2
Granby Street................D.2
Grange Lane B.4

Hale Fen........................C.1
Hardwicke Close C.2
Hawkins's Drove.............E.3
Hawthorn Close E.3
Hempfield Place D.3
Hempfield Road D.3
Henry Crabb Road B.1
High Street C.3
Hitches Street................D.2
Hoof Close D.3
Horsley Hale..................D.1

Kingsmead Court E.3
Kirby Cross Avenue C.2
Knowle Court B.2

Limes Close C.3
Littleport & Ely By-Pass ..B.1
Longfield Road B.2
Lynn Road E.1

Lynn Road.....................F.1

Main Street....................D.3
Meadow Court B.2
Mildenhall Road F.1
Mill Pit Furlong C.3
Millfield C.3
Monkswood C.2
Mowfen Road.................D.2

New River Bank E.1
New Road D.2
Noahs Way.....................B.2

Oak Lane A.1
Old School Close D.2
Orchard Close D.3

Padnal E.3
Padnal Grove D.4
Parsons Lane C.2
Peacock Way D.3
Ponts Hill D.2

Quay Hill........................D.2
Queens Road B.2

Saffron Close C.4

Sandhill..........................E.3
Sandys Crescent D.3
Silt Road........................D.2
Station Road D.2
Sycamore Close.............C.3

Ten Mile Bank.................E.1
The Brambles.................D.3
The Coppice C.4
The Crescent C.4
The Holmes D.2
The Hythe......................D.2
Throughfare Way D.3

Upton Lane.....................C.3
Upton Place C.3

Victoria Street.................D.3

Washington Close D.2
Wellington Street D.2
White Hart Lane D.2
Willow Court E.3
Wisbech Road C.2

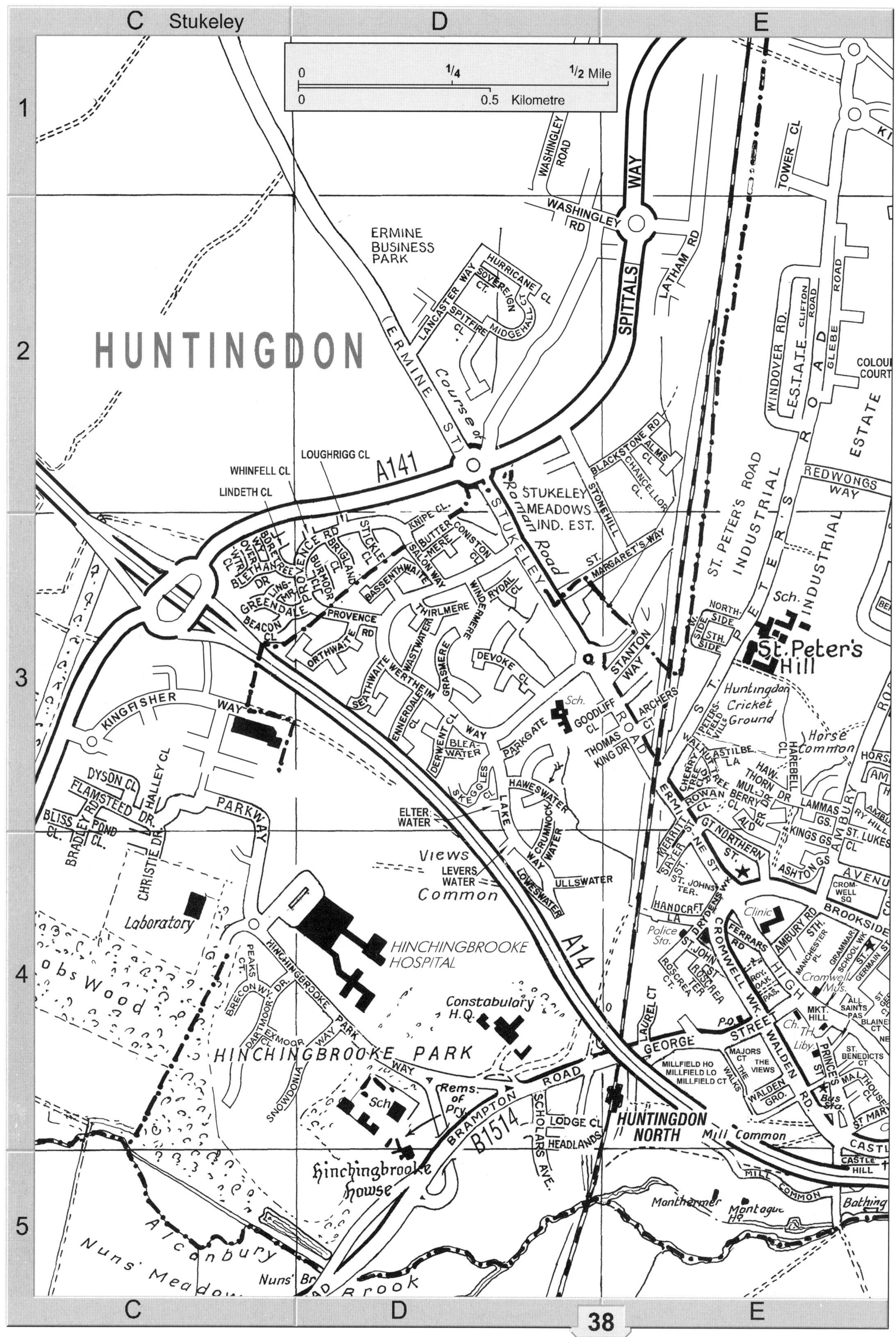
C
Stukeley
D
E
0   1/4   1/2 Mile
0   0.5   Kilometre
1
ERMINE BUSINESS PARK
HUNTINGDON
WASHINGLEY ROAD
WASHINGLEY RD
SPITTALS WAY
LATHAM RD
TOWER CL
K
2
LANCASTER WAY
SOVEREIGN CT.
HURRICANE CL
SPITFIRE CL
MIDGEHALL
Course of
ERMINE ST
Roman Road
STUKELEY MEADOWS IND. EST.
BLACKSTONE RD
ALMS CL
CHANCELLOR CL
STONEHILL
WINDOVER RD.
CLIFTON ROAD
L.E.S.T.A.T.E.
GLEBE ROAD
ROAD
COLOUR COURT
ESTATE
WHINFELL CL
LOUGHRIGG CL
LINDETH CL
A141
ST. PETER'S ROAD INDUSTRIAL
REDWONGS WAY
KNIPE CL
ST. MARGARET'S WAY
Sch.
St. Peter's Hill
INDUSTRIAL
3
KINGFISHER WAY
PROVENCE RD
BRIGLAND
STICKLE CL
BURMOOR
BUTTER-MERE
SALON WAY
CONISTON CL
WINDERMERE
RYDAL CL
STUKELEY Road
STANTON WAY
ARCHERS CT
NORTH SIDE
STH. SIDE
S.T. PETER'S FIELD WLKS
Huntingdon Cricket Ground
Horse Common
WHIN-WTR CL
OVERHANGER
BLETHAN
DR
LING-MR
GREENDALE
BEACON CL
PROVENCE RD
ORTHWAITE
BASSENTHWAITE
SEATHWAITE
WERTHEIM
WASTWATER
THIRLMERE
GRASMERE
DEVOKE CL
WAY
ENNERDALE
CL
DERWENT CL
BLEA-WATER
PARKGATE
GOODLIFF CL
THOMAS KING DR
Sch.
Q
CHERRY TREE
WALNUT
CASTILBE LA
HAWTHORN MUL-BERRY DR
ROWAN CL
HAREBELL
LAMMAS
KINGS GS
ASHTON GS
ST. LUKES CL
AVENUE
DYSON CL
HALLEY CL
FLAMSTEED RD
BRADLEY POND CL
BLISS CL
PARKWAY
SKEGGLES CL
HAWESWATER
ELTER WATER
CRUMMOCK WATER
LAKE
MERRITT
SAYER ST
GT NORTHERN ST
NE ST
ST. JOHNS TER.
CROM-WELL SQ
BROOKSIDE
CHRISTIE DR
Laboratory
PEAKS CT
BRECON WY.
DARTMOOR DR.
HINCHINGBROOKE PARK DR.
Views
LEVERS WATER
Common
ULLSWATER
LOWESWATER
A14
HANDCRFT LA
Police Sta.
DRYDENS CT
FERRARS RD
ST. JOHNS ST
ROSCREA CT
CROMWELL WK
AMBURY RD
MANCHESTER PL
STH. GRAMMAR SCHOOL WK
Clinic
Cromwell Mus.
4
Jobs Wood
EXMOOR WAY
DARTMOOR WAY
SNOWDONIA WAY
HINCHINGBROOKE WAY
HINCHINGBROOKE HOSPITAL
Constabulary H.Q.
HINCHINGBROOKE PARK
Rems. of Pry.
Sch
BRAMPTON ROAD
GEORGE STREET
MILLFIELD HO
MILLFIELD LO
MILLFIELD CT
MAJORS CT
THE WALKS
THE VIEWS
WALDEN GRO.
HIGH STREET
WALDEN RD.
PRINCES RD.
ROY. OAK PAS.
ST. JOHNS PAS.
P.O.
MKT. HILL
Ch. TH
Liby
ALL SAINTS PAS
BLAINE CT
ST. BENEDICTS CT
MALTHOUSE
ST. MARY
Hinchingbrooke House
Alconbury
Nuns' Meadow
Nuns' Br
Brook
LODGE CL
SCHOLARS AVE.
HEADLANDS
B1514
HUNTINGDON NORTH
Mill Common
Montagu Ho.
Monthermer
Bathing
MILL COMMON
CASTLE HILL
ST MARY
5

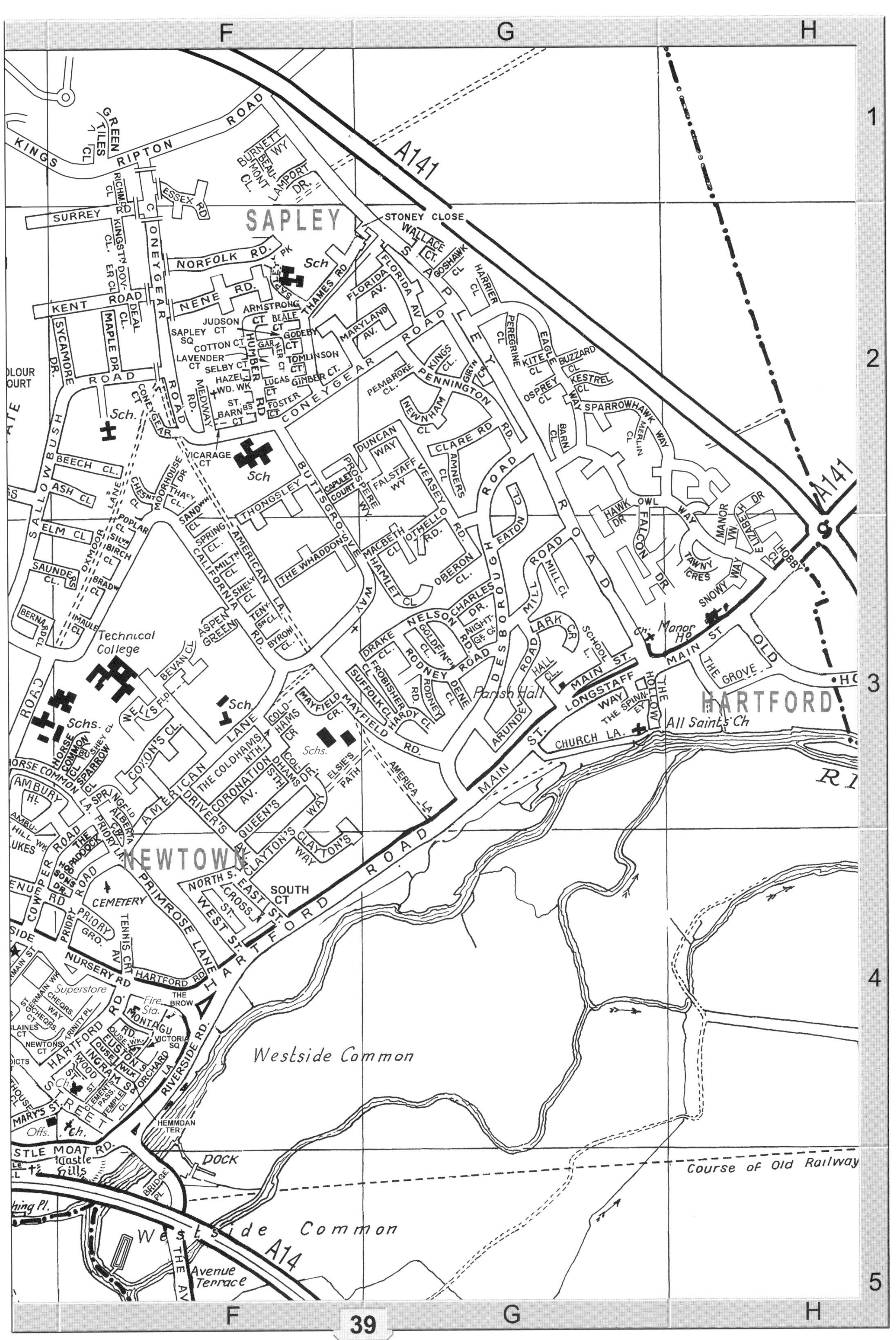
SAPLEY
HARTFORD
NEWTOWN
Westside Common
Westside Common
Technical College
Parish Hall
All Saints' Ch.
Course of Old Railway
A141
A14
KINGS
GREEN TILES CL.
RIPTON ROAD
SURREY RD.
RICHM'D RD.
KINGS'TY CL.
ER CL.
DOV-
DEAL CL.
CONEYGEAR
ESSEX RD.
BURNETT WY.
BEAU-MONT CL.
LAMPORT DR.
NORFOLK RD.
PK
Sch
STONEY CLOSE
WALLACE CT.
GOSHAWK CL.
HARRIER CL.
NENE RD.
THAMES RD.
FLORIDA AV.
FLORIDA AV.
SAPLEY ROAD
PEREGRINE CL.
EAGLE CL.
KITE CL.
OSPREY CL.
BUZZARD CL.
KESTREL WAY
KENT ROAD
MAPLE DR.
SYCAMORE DR.
SALLOWBUSH
COLOUR COURT
ARMSTRONG CT.
BEALE CT.
GODERY CT.
JUDSON CT.
SAPLEY SQ.
COTTON CT.
LAVENDER CT.
GAR-NER CT.
HUMBER RD.
SELBY CT.
TOMLINSON CT.
MARYLAND AV.
GIMBER CT.
LUCAS CT.
FOSTER CT.
HAZEL WD. WK.
ST. BARN'S CT.
MEDWAY RD.
CONEYGEAR ROAD
PEMBROKE CL.
NEWNHAM CL.
KINGS CL.
PENNINGTON
GIRTN
SPARROWHAWK WAY
MERLIN CL.
BARN CL.
HAWK DR.
OWL CL.
FALCON DR.
TAWNY CRES.
MANOR VW.
ELIZABETH DR.
HOBBY CL.
BEECH CL.
ASH CL.
ELM CL.
OXMOR BIRCH
BRAD-
SILVER
POPLAR
CHESNT
THACY CL.
MOORHOUSE LANE
SANDW'H
SPRING CL.
MILT'N
SHEL'Y
TENY'N
BYRON
VICARAGE CT.
Sch
THONGSLEY
AMERICAN LA.
CALIFORNIA RD.
BUTTSGROVE WAY
CAPULET
PROSPERO WY.
DUNCAN WAY
FALSTAFF WY.
CLARE RD.
VEASEY CL.
AMNERS
OTHELLO RD.
OBERON CL.
MACBETH CL.
HAMLET CL.
THE WHADDONS
DESBOROUGH ROAD
EATON CL.
MILL ROAD
MILL CL.
SNOWY WAY
MANOR HO.
SAUNDERS CL.
BERNARD CL.
MAULE CL.
CROFT
Technical College
BEVAN CL.
ASPEN
GREEN
Sch
WELLS FLD.
COXON'S CL.
Schs.
HORSE COMMON
SPARROW CL.
SHEY FLD.
MAYFIELD CR.
MAYFIELD CR.
COLD-HAMS CR.
COLD-HAMS NTH.
COLD'R
DR.
Schs.
ELSIE'S PATH
DRAKE CL.
GOLDFINCH CL.
ROBISHER CL.
RODNEY CL.
RODNET
NELSON DR.
NIGHT-GE
LARK CR.
SCHOOL CL.
SCHOOL ST.
MAIN ST.
CHARLES RD.
HARDY CL.
SUFFOLK CL.
RODNEY DENE
ARUNDEL ST.
HALL CL.
LONGSTAFF WAY
THE SPINNEY
THE HOLLOW
THE GROVE
MAIN ST.
OLD
CHURCH LA.
MAIN ROAD
AMBURY HT.
AMBU-HILL WK.
LUKES
CROWLEY
SPRINGFIELD
ALBERTA
PRIORY LA.
THE PADDOCK
HOB SONS DR.
PRIMROSE LANE
AMERICAN LA.
CORONATION AV.
DRIVER'S AV.
QUEEN'S
CLAYTON'S WAY
CLAYTON'S WAY
AMERICA LA.
HARTFORD ROAD
MAIN ROAD
COWPER RD.
AVENUE
PRIORY RD.
PRIORY GRO.
CEMETERY
TENNIS CRT.
HARTFORD RD.
NURSERY RD.
NORTH S.
WEST ST.
EAST ST.
SOUTH CT.
CROSS ST.
HARTFORD RD.
Superstore
STERMAN WK.
CHEORS WAY
CHEORS WAY
LAINES CT.
NEWTONS CT.
TRINITY PL.
THE BROW
Fire Sta.
MONTAGU RD.
QUSH WK.
VICTORIA SQ.
EUSTON WK.
INGRAM SQ.
WOOD ST.
ORCHARD LA.
CLEMENTS PASS.
TEMPLE CL.
HEMMDAN TER.
RIVERSIDE RD.
MARY'S ST.
Offs.
Ch.
STLE MOAT RD.
Castle Hills
DOCK
BRIDGE PL.
Westside Common
Avenue Terrace
THE AVE.
HARTFORD ROAD
DESBOROUGH ROAD

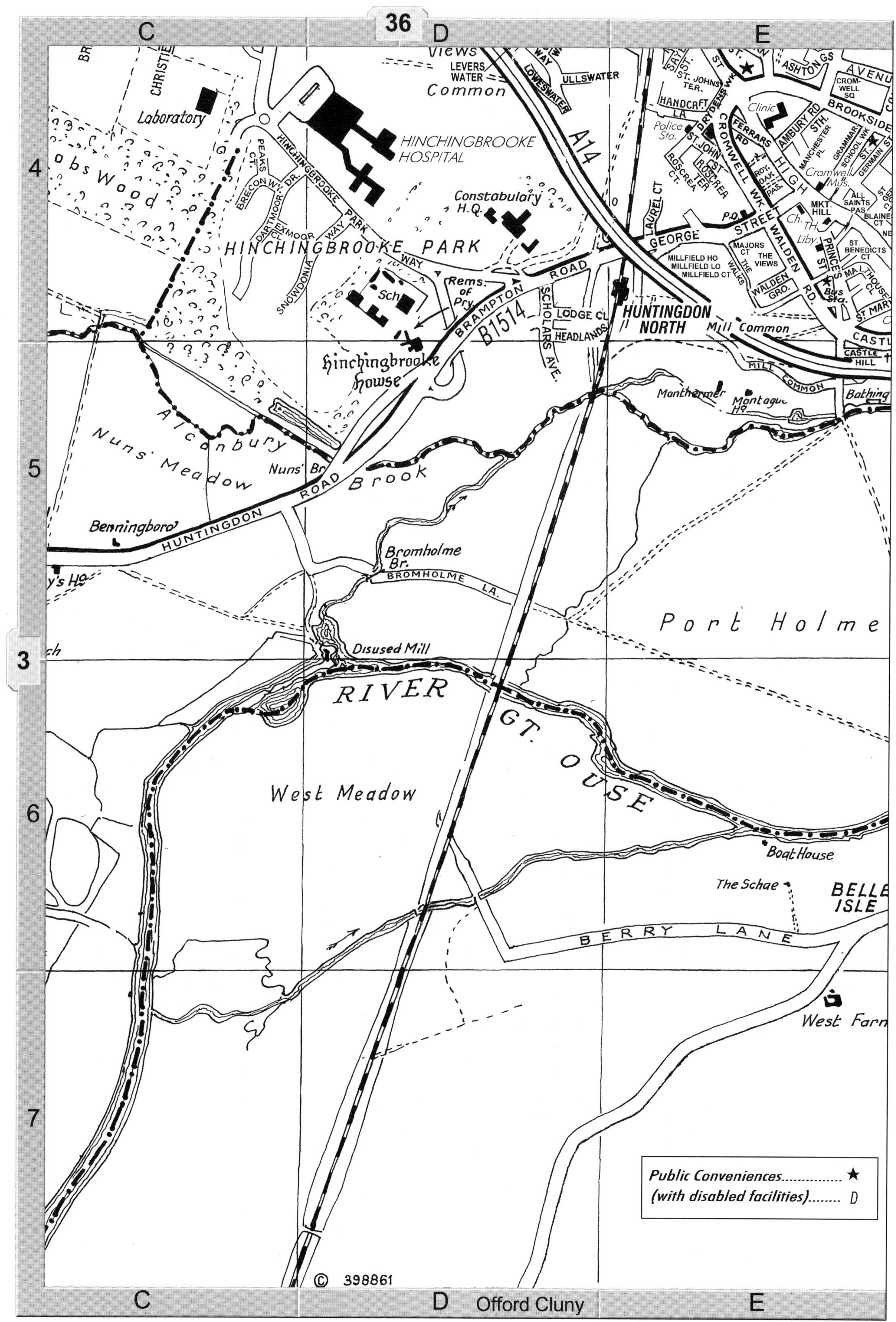
36
C
D
E
BR
CHRISTIE
Laboratory
VIEWS
LEVERS WATER
ULLSWATER
WAY
LOVESWATER
Common
A14
SAV. ST.
ST. JOHNS ST.
ST. JOHNS TER.
ASHTONGS
AVENUE
CROMWELL SQ.
BROOKSIDE
HANDCRFT LA
Police Sta.
DRYDENS
Clinic
AMBURY PL
STH.
GRAMMAR
SCHOOL WK
ST. GERMAIN ST.
obs Wood
PEAKS CT.
HINCHINGBROOKE PARK DR.
HINCHINGBROOKE HOSPITAL
FERRARS RD
CROMWELL RD
HIGH
MANCHESTER PL
Cromwell Mus.
4
BRECON WY.
DARTMOOR CL.
EXMOOR CL.
SNOWDONIA WAY
Constabulary H.Q.
LAUREL CT
ROSCREA CT.
ROY. OAK PAS.
STREET
MKT. HILL
ALL SAINTS PAS.
St. BLAINE CT.
ST. BENEDICTS CT.
HINCHINGBROOKE PARK
WAY
Sch.
Rems. of Pry.
GEORGE
P.O.
WALDEN
Ch. TH. Liby.
PRINCES ST.
MAL HOUSE CT.
Hinchingbrooke House
BRAMPTON
B1514
ROAD
SCHOLARS AVE.
LODGE CL
HEADLANDS
MILLFIELD HO
MILLFIELD LO
MILLFIELD CT.
HUNTINGDON NORTH
MAJORS CT
THE WALKS
WALDEN GRO.
THE VIEWS
RD.
Bus Sta.
ST. MAR
CASTLE
Alconbury
Nuns' Meadow
Nuns' Br.
HUNTINGDON
ROAD
Brook
Manthermer
Montagu Ho
Mill Common
MILL COMMON
CASTLE HILL
Bathing
5
Benningboro'
y's Ho
Bromholme Br.
BROMHOLME LA.
Port Holme
3
ch
Disused Mill
RIVER
West Meadow
GT. OUSE
6
Boat House
The Schae
BELLE ISLE
BERRY LANE
West Farm
7
© 398861
Public Conveniences............ ★
(with disabled facilities)........ D
C
D
Offord Cluny
E

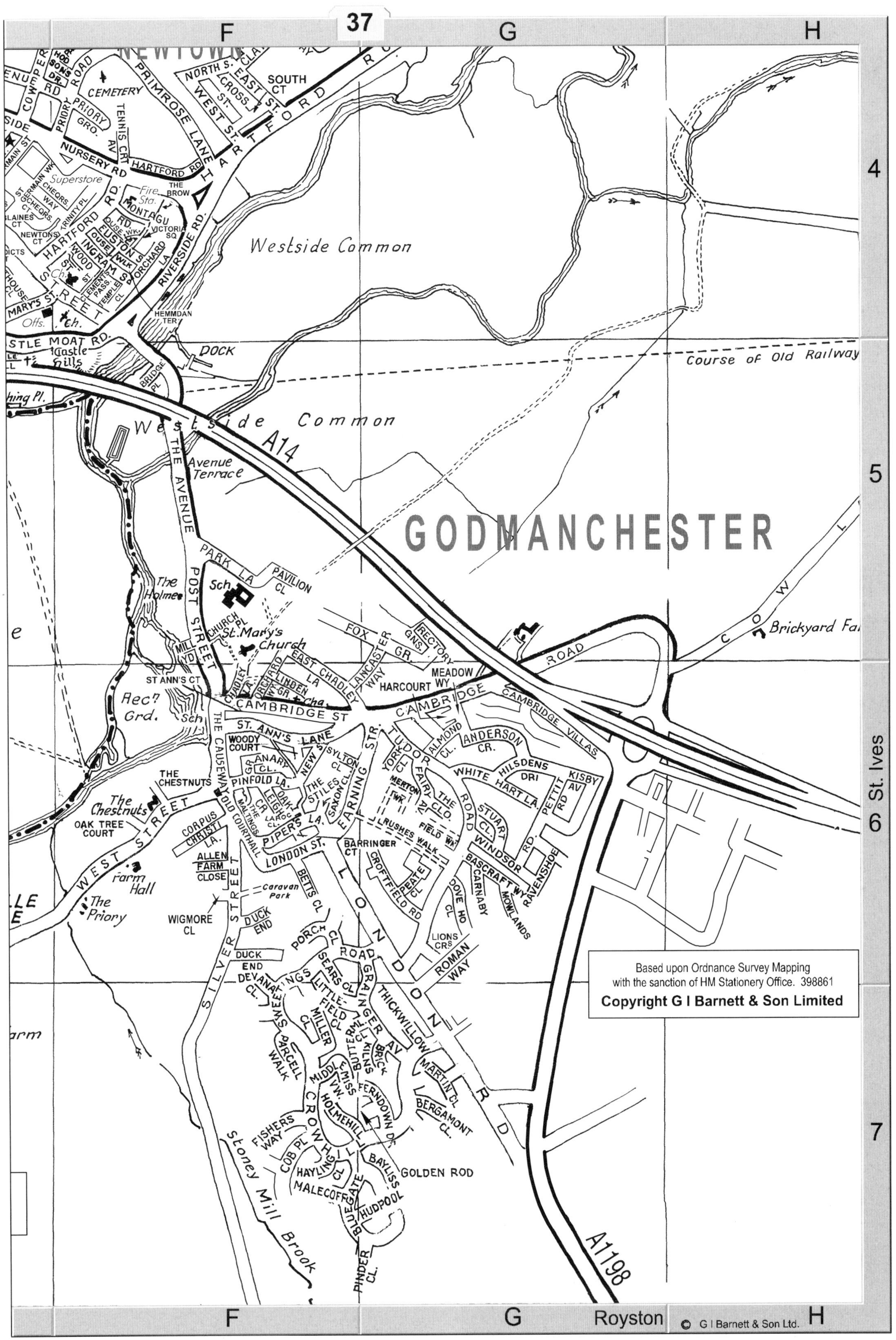
37
F
G
H
4
NEWTOWN
CLAY
COWPER
HOD SONS DR.
PRIORY RD.
PRIORY GRO.
CEMETERY
PRIMROSE LANE
NORTH S.
EAST S.
SOUTH CT.
CROSS ST.
WEST STR.
HARTFORD RD.
CLASS
HARTFORD RD.
TENNIS CRT.
THE BROW
NURSERY RD.
Superstore
Fire Sta.
MONTAGU
VICTORIA SQ.
ST GERMAIN WY
CHEQRS
TRINITY PL.
WAY
CHEQRS
NEWTONS CT.
BLAINES CT.
HARTFORD RD.
EUSTON HOUSE WLK
INGRAM S
ORCHARD
RIVERSIDE RD.
CLEMENTS PASS
TEMPLE CL.
WOOD ST.
DICTS
HOUSE
MARY'S
Offs.
Ch.
STREET
Ch.
HEMMDAN TER.
STLE MOAT RD.
Castle Hills
DOCK
BRIDGE PL.
hing Pl.
Westside Common
Course of Old Railway
Westside Common
A14
Avenue Terrace
THE AVENUE
POST STREET
PARK LA.
PAVILION CL.
Sch
The Holme
MILL YD.
Church PL.
St. Mary's Church
CHADLEY
ORCHARD
LINDEN
W. GR.
cha.
EAST CHADLEY LA.
FOX GR.
LANCASTER WY.
RECTORY GNS.
ROAD
GODMANCHESTER
Brickyard Fa
COW L
St Ann's CT.
Rec.d Grd.
Sch
CAMBRIDGE ST.
HARCOURT WY.
MEADOW WY.
CAMBRIDGE
CAMBRIDGE VILLAS
ST. ANN'S LANE
WOODY COURT
CANARY CL.
THE CHESTNUTS
PINFOLD LA.
NEW
SYLTON CL.
TUDOR
FAIRY PL.
ALMOND CL.
ANDERSON CR.
WHITE HART LA.
HILSDENS DRI
KISBY AV.
THE CHESTNUTS
LEIGH
OAK
THE STILES
SAXON CL.
YORK
MERTON WK
THE CLO.
FIELD WY.
PETTIT RD.
RAVENSHOE
The Chestnuts
OAK TREE COURT
CORPUS CHRISTI LA.
THE MALTINGS
OLD COURT HALL
PIPERS LA.
LONDON ST.
EARNING STR.
BARRINGER CT.
PEATE
ROAD
STUART CL.
WINDSOR
BASCRAFT WY.
CARNABY
MOWLANDS
WEST STREET
ALLEN FARM CLOSE
Farm Hall
The Priory
WIGMORE CL.
SILVER STREET
DUCK END
Caravan Park
BETTS CL.
PORCH CL.
CROFTFIELD RD.
DOVE HO CL.
LIONS CRS
ROMAN WAY
DUCK END
DEVANA CL.
SWEETINGS
SEARS CL.
GRAINGER
LITTLE FIELD
MILLER
BUTTERMEL
KILNS
THICKWILLOW AV.
LONDON ROAD
ROAD
PARCELL WALK
MIDDLE
VW.
BRICK
MARTIN CL.
CROWHILL
HOLMEHILL
MISS
FERNDOWN DR.
BERGAMONT CL.
FISHERS WAY
COB PL.
HAYLING CL.
BAYLISS
GOLDEN ROD
MALECOFFGATE
BLUEGATE
HUDPOOL
Stoney Mill Brook
PINDER CL.
A1198
Royston
F
G
H
St. Ives
4
5
6
7
Based upon Ordnance Survey Mapping
with the sanction of HM Stationery Office. 398861
Copyright G I Barnett & Son Limited
© G I Barnett & Son Ltd.

HUNTINGDON AND GODMANCHESTER INDEX TO STREETS

Alberta Crescent..........F.3
Alder Drive.................E.3
All Saints Passage......E.4
Allen Farm Close........F.6
Almond Close.............G.6
Alms Close................E.2
Ambury Hill...............E.3
Ambury Hill Walk........E.3
Ambury Road.............E.4
Ambury Road South....E.4
American Lane...........F.3
Amners Close............G.2
Anderson Crescent....G.6
Archers Place............E.3
Armstrong Court........F.2
Arundel Road.............G.3
Ash Close..................F.2
Ashton Gardens........E.4
Aspen Green.............F.3
Astible Lane...............E.3
Avenue Road.............E.4

Barn Close.................G.2
Barringer Court..........F.6
Bascraft Way.............G.6
Bassenthwaite...........D.3
Bayliss......................G.7
Beacon Close.............C.3
Beale Court...............C.3
Beaumont Close.........F.1
Beech Close...............F.2
Belle Isle...................E.6
Bergamont Close........G.7
Bernard Close............E.3
Berry Lane.................D.6
Betts Close................F.6
Bevan Close...............F.3
Blackstone Road........E.2
Blaines Court.............E.4
Bleawater..................D.3
Blethan Drive.............C.3
Bliss Close.................C.3
Bluegate...................F.7
Boretree Way.............C.3
Bradley Road.............C.4
Bradwell Close...........F.3
Brampton Road.........D.4
Brecon Way...............C.4
Brewery Yard.............E.4
Brick Kilns.................G.7
Bridge Place..............F.5
Brigland Close............D.3
Bromholme Lane........D.5
Brookside..................E.4
Burmoor Close...........D.3
Burnett Way..............F.1
Bushley Close............F.3
Buttermel Close.........G.7
Buttermere.................D.3
Buttsgrove Way..........F.2
Buzzard Close............G.2
Byron Close...............F.3

California Road...........F.3
Cambridge Road,
  Godmanchester......G.6
Cambridge Street.......F.6
Cambridge Villas........G.6
Capulet Course..........F.2
Carnaby....................G.6
Castle Hill..................E.5
Castle Moat Road......E.4
Chadley Lane............F.6
Chancellor Close........E.2
Charles Drive.............G.3
Chequers Court.........E.4
Chequers Way...........E.4
Cherry Tree Close......E.3
Chestnut Close,
  Sapley..................F.2
Christie Drive.............C.4
Church Lane...............G.3
Church Place..............F.5
Clare Road.................G.2
Claytons Way.............F.3
Clifton Road...............E.2
Cob Place..................F.7
Coldhams Crescent....F.3
Coldhams South.........F.3
Colour Court...............E.2
Coneygear Court........F.2
Coneygear Road........F.2
Coniston Close...........D.3
Coronation Avenue.....F.2
Corpus Christi Lane....F.6
Cotton Court...............F.2

County Hospital.........E.4
Cow Lane..................H.5
Cowper Road.............E.4
Coxon's Close............F.3
Croftfield Road...........G.6
Cromwell Square........F.4
Cromwell Walk...........E.4
Cross Street...............F.4
Crow Hill...................F.7
Crumnock Water........D.4

Dallington Court.........F.4
Dartmoor Court.........C.4
Deal Street................F.2
Dene Close................G.3
Derwent Close...........D.3
Desborough Road.......G.3
Devana Close.............F.6
Devoke Close.............D.3
Dove House Close......G.6
Dover Close...............F.2
Drake Close...............G.3
Driver's Avenue..........E.4
Drydens Walk.............E.4
Duck End..................F.6
Duncan Way...............G.2
Dyson Close...............C.3

Eagle Way..................G.2
Earning Street............F.6
East Chadley..............F.5
East Street.................F.4
Eaton Close................G.3
Elizabeth Drive...........H.3
Elm Close..................F.3
Elsie's Path................F.3
Elterwater..................D.3
Ennerdale Close.........D.3
Ermine Buisness
  Park.....................D.2
Ermine Street.............E.3
Essex Road................F.1
Euston Street.............F.4
Exmoor Close............C.4

Fairy Avenue.............G.6
Falcon Drive..............G.3
Falcon Way...............H.2
Falstaff Way..............G.2
Ferndown Drive.........G.7
Ferras Road...............E.4
Field Walk.................G.6
Fishers way...............F.7
Flamstead Drive.........C.3
Florida Avenue...........C.2
Foster Court...............F.2
Fox Grove..................F.5
Frobisher Close..........G.3

Garner Court..............F.2
George Street.............E.4
Gimber Court.............F.2
Girton Crescent..........G.2
Glebe Road,
  St. Peter's Hill........E.2
Godeby Court.............F.2
Godmanchester..........F.6
Goldenrod..................G.7
Goldfinch Close..........G.3
Goodlife Close............D.3
Goshalk Close............G.2
Grainger Avenue........G.6
Grammer
  School Walk...........E.4
Granary Close............F.6
Grasmere...................D.3
Great Northern
  Street...................E.4
Green Tiles Close.......F.1
Greendale..................C.3

Hall Close..................G.3
Halley Close...............C.3
Hamlet Close..............G.3
Handcroft Lane...........E.4
Harcourt....................G.6
Hardy Close...............G.3
Harebell Close............E.3
Harrier Close..............G.2
Hartford.....................H.3
Hartford Road.............F.4
Haweswater...............D.3
Hawk Drive................G.3
Hawthorn Drive..........E.3
Hayling Close.............F.7
Hazelwood Walk.........F.2

Headlands..................D.4
Hemmdan Terrace.....F.4
High Street
  Huntingdon.............E.4
Hilsdens Drive............G.6
Hinchingrooke
  Hospital.................D.4
Hinchingbrooke Park
  Way......................C.4
Hobby Close...............H.3
Hodsons Drive............F.4
Holmehill...................F.7
Horse Common
  Close....................F.3
Horse Common
  Lane.....................E.3
Hudpool....................G.7
Humber Road.............F.2
Huntingdon................F.4
Huntingdon Road........C.5
Hurricane Close..........D.2

Ingram Street.............F.4

Judson Court.............F.2

Kent Road..................F.2
Kestrel Close..............G.2
King Ripton Road........E.1
Kingfisher Way...........C.3
Kings Close................G.2
Kings Gardens...........E.4
Kingston Close...........F.1
Kisby Avenue.............G.2
Knipe Close................D.3

Lake Way...................D.3
Lammas Gardens......E.3
Lamport Drive............F.4
Lancaster Way...........D.2
Lancaster Way...........F.6
Lark Crescent............G.3
Laroc Close................F.6
Lathem Road..............E.2
Laurel Court...............E.4
Lavender Court...........F.2
Levers Water..............D.4
Lindeth Close.............C.3
Lindon Grove.............F.6
Lingmoor...................C.3
Lions Cross................G.6
Little Fields Cross.......F.7
Lodge Close...............D.4
London Road..............F.6
London Street............F.6
Longstaff Way............G.3
Loughrigg Close.........D.3
Lowewater.................D.4
Lucas Court...............F.2

Macbeth Close...........G.3
Main Street,
  Hartford.................G.3
Majors Court..............E.4
Malecoff...................F.7
Malthouse Close.........E.4
Manchester Place.......E.4
Manor View...............H.3
Maple Drive...............F.2
Market Hill.................E.4
Martin Close..............G.7
Maryland Avenue........F.2
Maule Close...............F.3
Mayfield Crescent.......F.3
Mayfield Road............F.3
Meadow Way.............G.6
Medway Road............F.2
Merlin Close...............G.2
Merritt Street.............E.4
Merton Walk..............G.6
Middlemiss View.........F.7
Midgehall Court..........D.2
Mill Close..................G.3
Mill Common.............E.5
Mill Road...................G.3
Mill Yard....................F.5
Miller Close................F.7
Millfield Court.............E.4
Millfield House...........E.4
Millfield Lodge............E.4
Milton Close...............F.3
Montagu Road............F.4
Moorhouse Drive........F.2
Mowlands..................G.6
Mulberry Close...........E.3

Nelson Road..............G.3
Nene Road.................F.2
New Street.................F.6
Newnham Close........G.2
Newtons Court...........E.4
Newtown...................F.4
Nightingale Close.......G.3
Norfolk Road..............F.2
North Street...............F.4
Northside...................E.3
Nursery Road.............F.4

Oak Tree Crescent.....F.6
Oakleigh Crescent.....F.6
Oberson Close...........G.3
Old Courthall..............F.6
Old Houghton Road....H.3
Orchard Lane,
  Huntingdon.............F.4
Orchard Way..............F.6
Orthwaite..................D.3
Othello Road..............G.3
Overwater Close.........C.3
Owl Way....................G.2
Oxmoor Lane.............F.3

Parcell Wall................F.7
Park Lane..................F.5
Parkgate....................D.3
Parkway....................C.3
Pavilion Close.............F.5
Peaks Court...............C.4
Peate Close................G.6
Pembroke Close.........G.2
Pennington Road........G.2
Peregrine Close..........G.2
Pettit Road.................G.6
Pinder Close...............G.7
Pinfold Lane...............F.6
Piper's Lane...............F.6
Pond Close.................C.3
Poplar Close...............F.3
Porch Close................F.6
Post Street.................F.5
Primrose Lane............F.4
Princes Street............E.4
Priory Grove...............F.9
Priory Lane.................F.3
Priory Road................F.4
Prospect Place...........G.3
Prospere Way............F.2
Provence Road...........D.3

Queen's Drive.............F.3

Ravenshoe.................G.6
Rectory Gardens........G.5
Redwongs Way...........E.2
Richmond Close..........F.1
Riverside Road............F.1
Rodney Road..............G.3
Roman Way................G.6
Roscrea Court.............E.4
Roscrea Terrace..........E.4
Rowan Close...............E.3
Royal Oak Passage.....E.4
Rushes Walk...............G.6
Rydal Close................D.3

St. Ann's Court...........F.6
St. Ann's Lane............F.6
St. Barnabas Court.....F.2
St. Benedicts Court.....E.4
St. Clements
  Passage.................F.4
St. Germain Close.......E.4
St. Germain Walk........E.4
St. John Street...........E.4
St. John's Terrace.......E.4
St. Luke's Close.........E.4
St. Margaret's Way.....D.3
St. Mary's Street.........E.4
St. Peter's Hill............E.3
St. Peter's Road.........E.3
St. Peter's Road
  Industrial Estate.....E.3
Salon Way..................D.3
Sallowbush Road........E.3
Sandown Close...........F.3
Sapley......................F.2
Sapley Park................F.2
Sapley Road...............G.2
Sapley Square............F.2
Saunders Close..........E.3
Saxon Close...............F.6
Sayer Street...............E.4

Scholars Avenue.........D.4
School Lane................G.3
Sears Close................F.6
Seathwaite.................D.3
Selby Court................F.2
Shelley Close..............F.3
Silver Birch Close........F.3
Silver Street...............F.7
Skeggles Close..........D.3
Snowdonia Way..........C.4
Snowy Way................H.3
South Street...............F.4
Southside...................E.3
Sovereign Court..........D.2
Sparrow Close............F.3
Sparrowhawk Way......G.2
Spitfire Close..............D.2
Spittals Way...............E.2
Spring Close...............F.3
Springfield.................F.3
Stanton Way...............E.3
Stickley Close.............D.3
Stonehill....................D.2
Stoney Close..............G.2
Stuart Close...............G.6
Stukeley Meadows
  Industrial Estate.....D.2
Stukeley Road............D.2
Suffolk Close..............G.3
Surrey Road...............F.2
Sweetings Road..........F.7
Sycamore Drive..........F.2
Sylton.......................F.6

Tawney Crescent........H.3
Temple Close..............F.4
Tenneyson Close........F.3
Tennis Court Avenue...F.4
Thakery Close.............F.2
Thames Road.............F.2
The Avenue................F.5
The Brow....................F.4
The Causway..............F.6
The Chestnuts............F.6
The Close...................G.6
The Coldhams North...F.3
The Grove..................H.3
The Hollow.................G.3
The Maltings...............F.6
The Paddock...............F.4
The Spinney...............G.3
The Spitals................D.2
The Stiles...................F.6
The Views...................E.4
The Walks North.........E.4
The Whaddons............F.3
Thick Willow...............G.7
Thirlmere...................D.3
Thomas King Drive.....E.3
Thongsley.................F.2
Tomlinson Court.........F.2
Tower Close................E.1
Trinity Place...............E.4
Tudor Road................G.6

Ullswater....................D.4

Veasey Road..............G.2
Vicarage Court............F.2
Victoria Square...........F.4

Walden Grove............E.4
Walden Road..............E.4
Wallace Court.............G.2
Walnut Tree Drive.......E.3
Washingley Road........D.2
Wastwater.................D.3
Wellsfield..................F.3
Wertern Way..............D.3
West Street,
  Huntingdon.............F.4
Westside....................E.3
Whinfell Close............D.3
White Hart Lane..........G.6
Wigmore Close...........F.6
Windermere...............D.3
Windover Road...........E.2
Windsor Road.............G.6
Wood Street...............F.4
Woodly Court..............F.6

York Close..................G.6

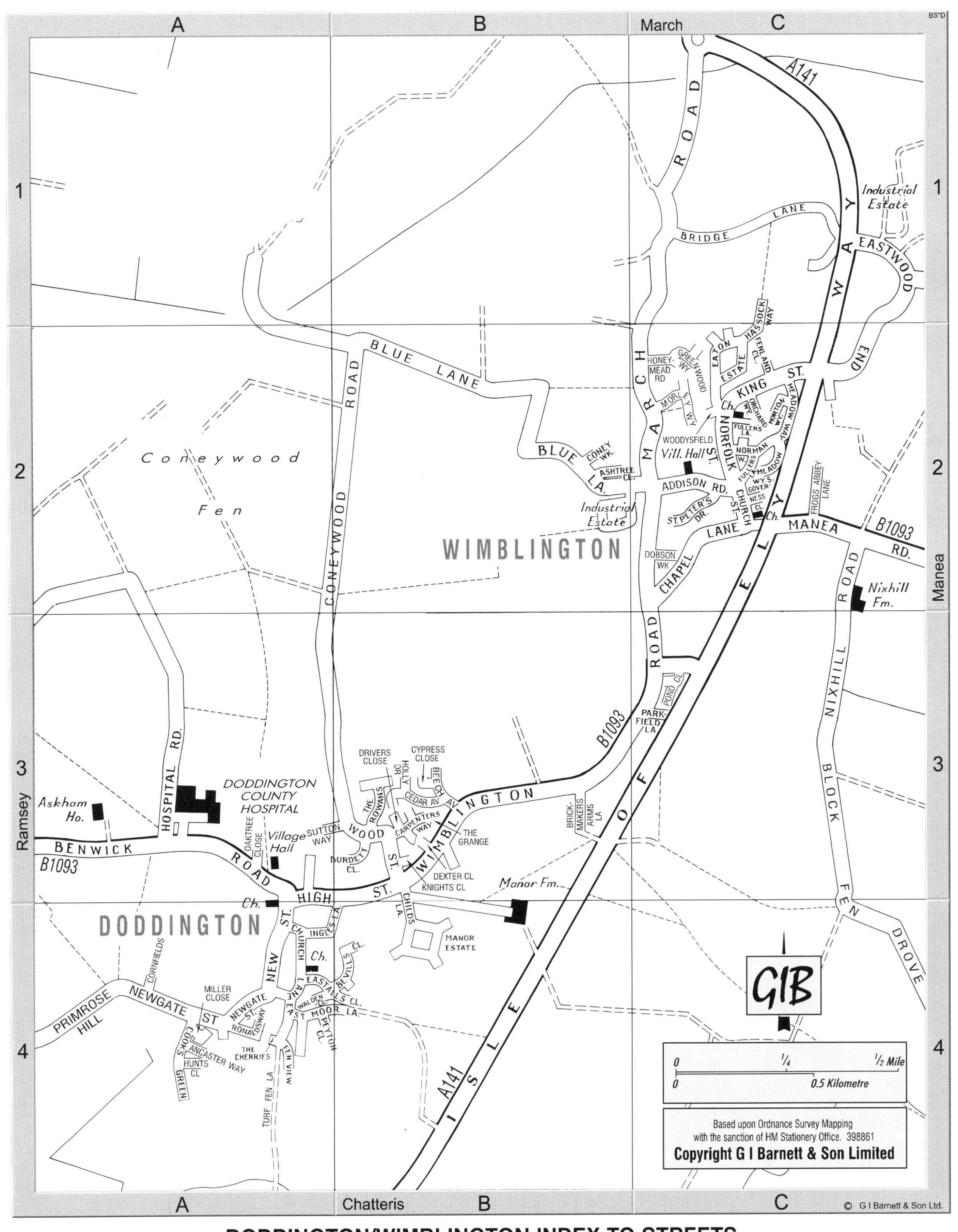

DODDINGTON/WIMBLINGTON INDEX TO STREETS

Addison Road C2
Ancaster Way A4
Ashtree Close......................B2

Beech Avenue B3
Benwick Road A3
Bevills Close.......................B4
Block Fen Drove C3
Blue Lane B2
Brickmakers Arms Lane B3
Bridge Lane C1
Burdett Close B3

Carpenters Way B3
Cedar Avenue B3
Chapel Lane C2

Childs Lane B3
Church Lane.......................A4
Church Street (Wimblington) C2
Coney Walk B2
Coneywood Road................A2
Cooks Green A4
Cornfields A4
Cypress Close B3

Dexter Close B3
Dobson Walk C2
DODDINGTON......................A4
Drivers Close B3

East Moor Lane A4
Eastalls Close A4

Eastwood End C1
Eaton Estate C2

Fen View A4
Fenland Close C2
Frogs Abbey Lane C2
Fullers Lane C2

Governess Close C2
Greenwood Way C.2

Hassock Way C2
High Street A3
Holly Drive B3
Honeymead Road................C.2
Hospital Road.....................A3

Hunts Close A4

Ingles Lane A4
Isle of Ely Way B4-C1

King Street C2
Knights Close B3

Manea Road C2
Manor Estate B4
March Road C2
Meadow Way C2
Meadow Way South C2
Miller Close A4
Morley Way C2
Morton Way C2

New Street A4
Newgate Street A4
Nixhill Road C3
Norfolk Street C2
Norman Way C2

Oaktree Close A3
Orchard Way C2

Parkfield Lane C3
Peyton Close A4
Pond Close C3
Primrose Hill A4
Ronaldsway A4

St Peter's Drive C2

Sutton Way........................A3
The Cherries A4
The Grange B3
The Rowans B3
Turf Fen Lane.....................A4

Walden Close A4
WIMBLINGTON B2
Wimblington Road...............B3
Wood Street B3
Woodysfield C2

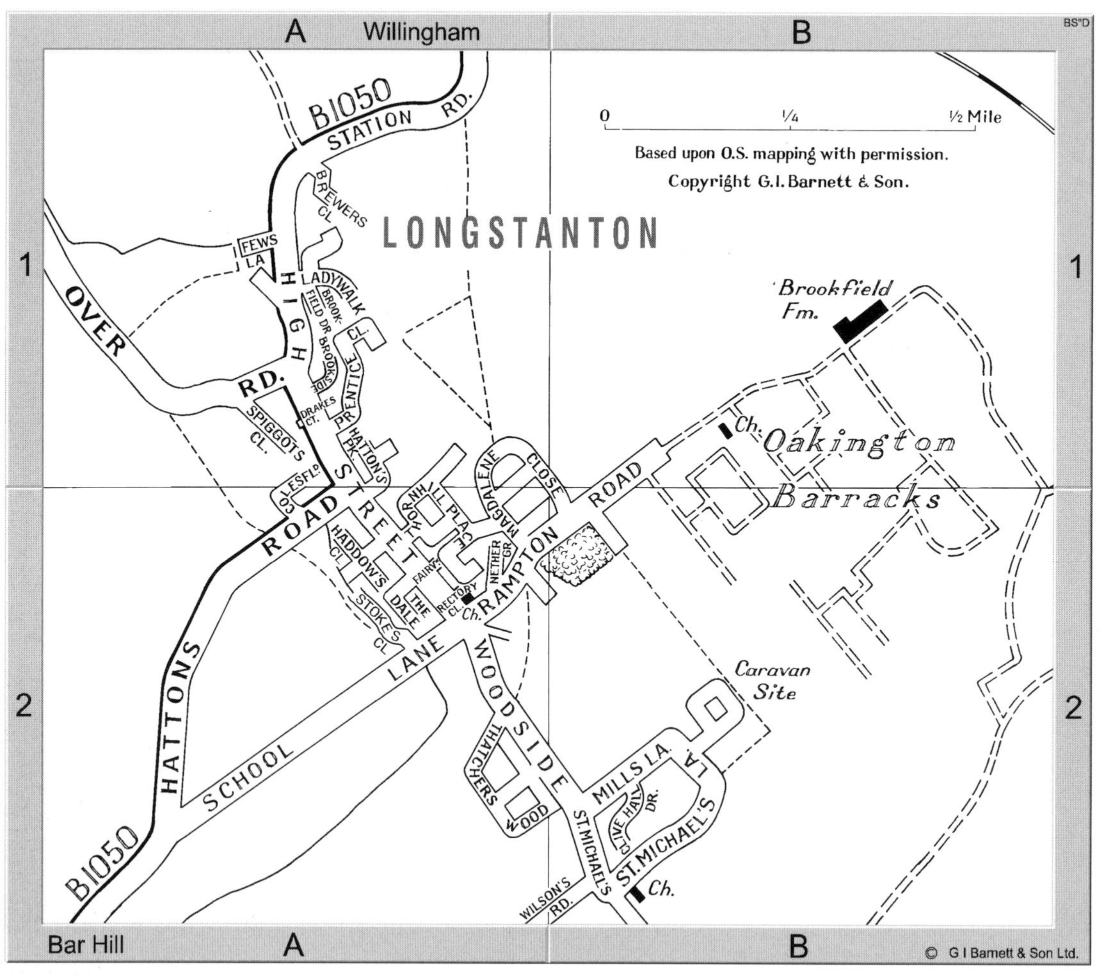

LONGSTANTON INDEX TO STREETS

Brewers Close A.1
Brookfield Drive A.1
Brookside A.1

Clive Hall Drive B.2
Colesfield A.2

Drakes Court A.1

Fairview A.2
Fews Lane A.1
Haddow's Close A.2
Hatton's Park A.1
Hattons Road A.2
High Street A.1

Lady Walk A.1

Magdalene Close A.2
Mills Lane B.2

Nether Green A.2

Oakington
    Barracks B.1
Over Road A.1

Prentice Close A.1
Rampton Road A.2
Rectory Close A.2

St. Michael's Lane B.2
School Lane A.2
Spiggots Close A.1
Station Road A.1
Stokes Close A.2

Thatchers Wood A.2
The Dale A.2
Thornhill Place A.2

Wilson's Road A.2
Woodside A.2

STRETHAM

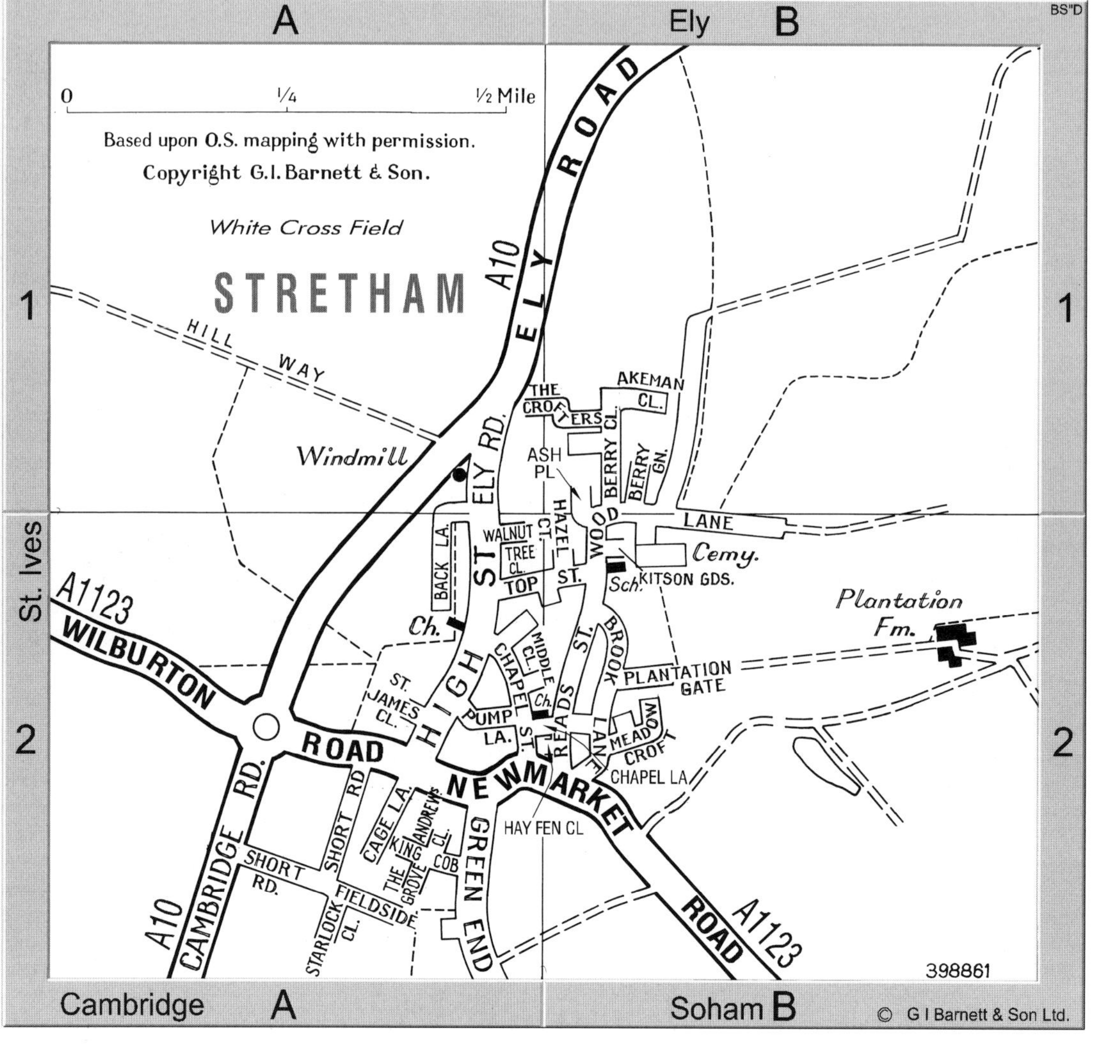

STRETHAM INDEX TO STREETS

Akeman Close B.1
Andrews Close A.2
Ash Place B.1

Back Lane A.2
Berry Close B.1
Berry Green B.1
Brook Lane B.2

Cage Lane A.2
Cambridge Road A.2
Chapel Lane A.2
Chapel Street A.2

Ely Road A.1
Fieldside A.2

Green End A.2

Hazel Court B.2
Hey Fen Close B.2
High Street A.2
Hill Way A.1

King Cob A.2
Kitson Gardens B.2

Meadow Croft B.2
Middle Close A.2

Newmarket Road A.2

Plantation Gate B.2
Pump Lane A.2

Reads Street B.2

St. James Close A.2
Short Road A.2
Starlock Close A.2

The Crofters B.1
The Grove A.2
Top Street A.2

Walnut Tree Close A.2
Wilburton Road A.2
Wood Lane B.2

FENSTANTON INDEX TO STREETS

Bell Lane A1
Bourdillon Close B1

Cambridge Road B2
Chequer Street A1
Chequers Close A1
Cherry Tree Way A1
Church Lane B1
Church Leys B1
Church Street B1
Connington Road A2

Dove Close B1

Four Acres B1

Hall Green Lane A1
Hampton Close B1
Headlands B1
High Street A1
Hilton Road A1
Honey Hill B1

Lancelot Way B1
Leechcroft B1
Little Moor B1
Low Road A1

Manor Drive A1

Oaklands B2
Orchard Gardens A1

Pear Tree Close A2
Pitfield Close B2

Rookery Place B1
Rookery Way B2

Sallows B1
School Lane B1
Scorney B1
Simmer Piece B2
Swan Gardens B1
Swan Road A1

Tall's Lane A1
The Fen B1
The Gables A2
Tythe Piece B2

Walnut Tree Crescent B1
West End Road A2

HOUGHTON INDEX TO STREETS

Ansley Road B2

Brookside B2

Chapel Lane A2

Green Lane A2

Hill Estate B2
Home Farm Road B2
Houghton Hill Road B2
Huntingdon Road A2

Laughton's Lane B2
Leslie Green Road B2
Love Lane B2
Loxley Green A2

Manor Close A2
Mere Way B1
Mill Street B2

Rectory Lane A2
Rhymers Gate A2
Ruddles Lane A1

Splash Lane A1
St Ives Road B2
St Margarets Road A1

The Lanes B2
Thicket Road B2
Townsend Close A2

Victoria Crescent A2

Ward Close B2
Ware Lane A2
Warren Close A1
Wessell B2

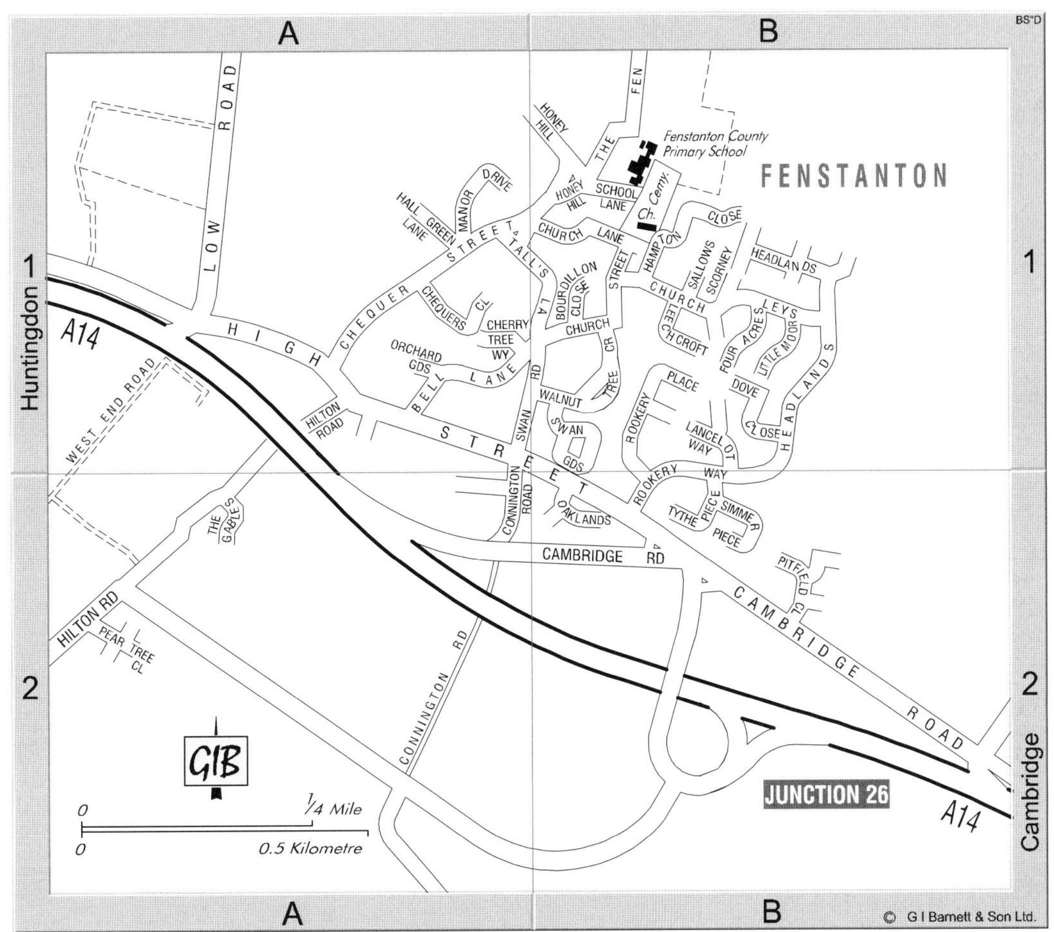

HOUGHTON

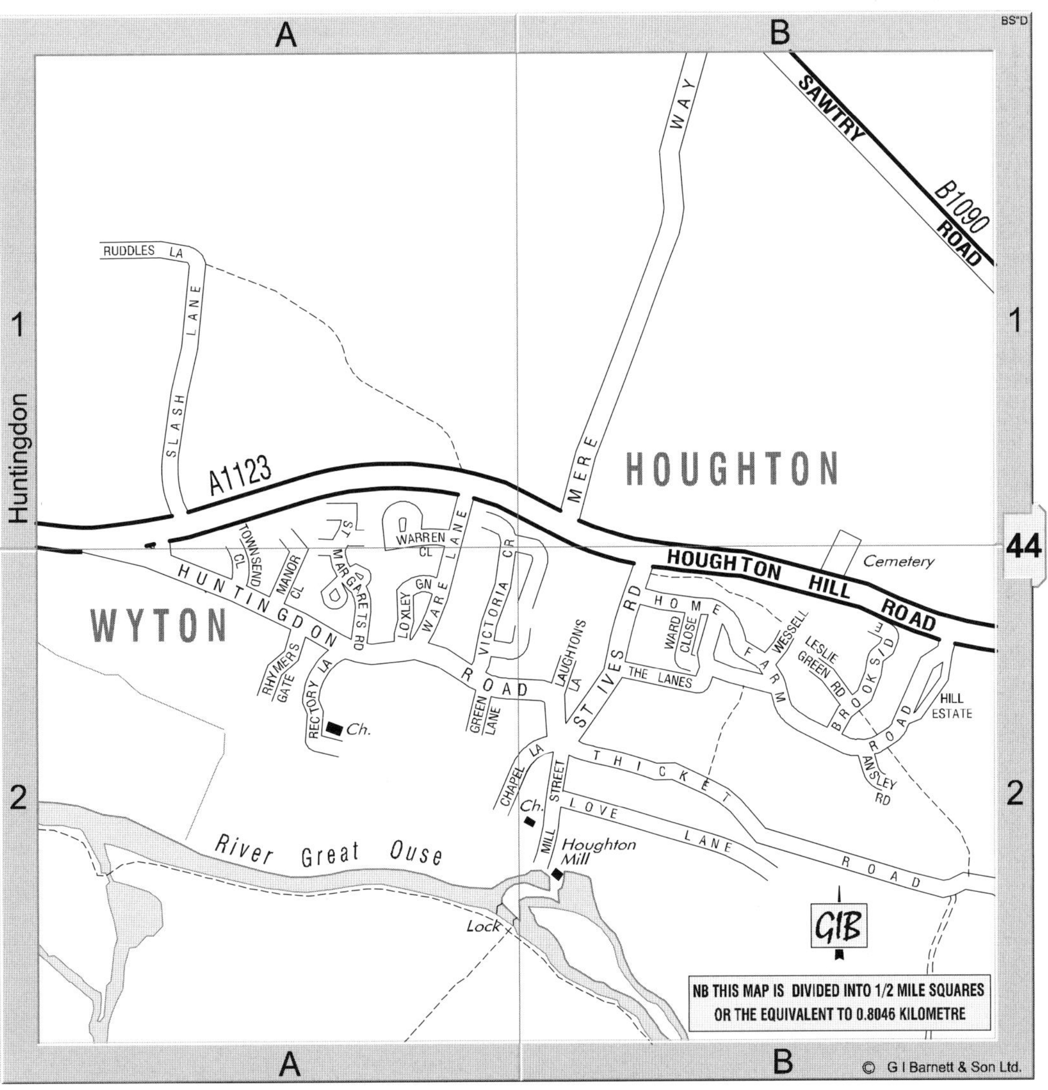

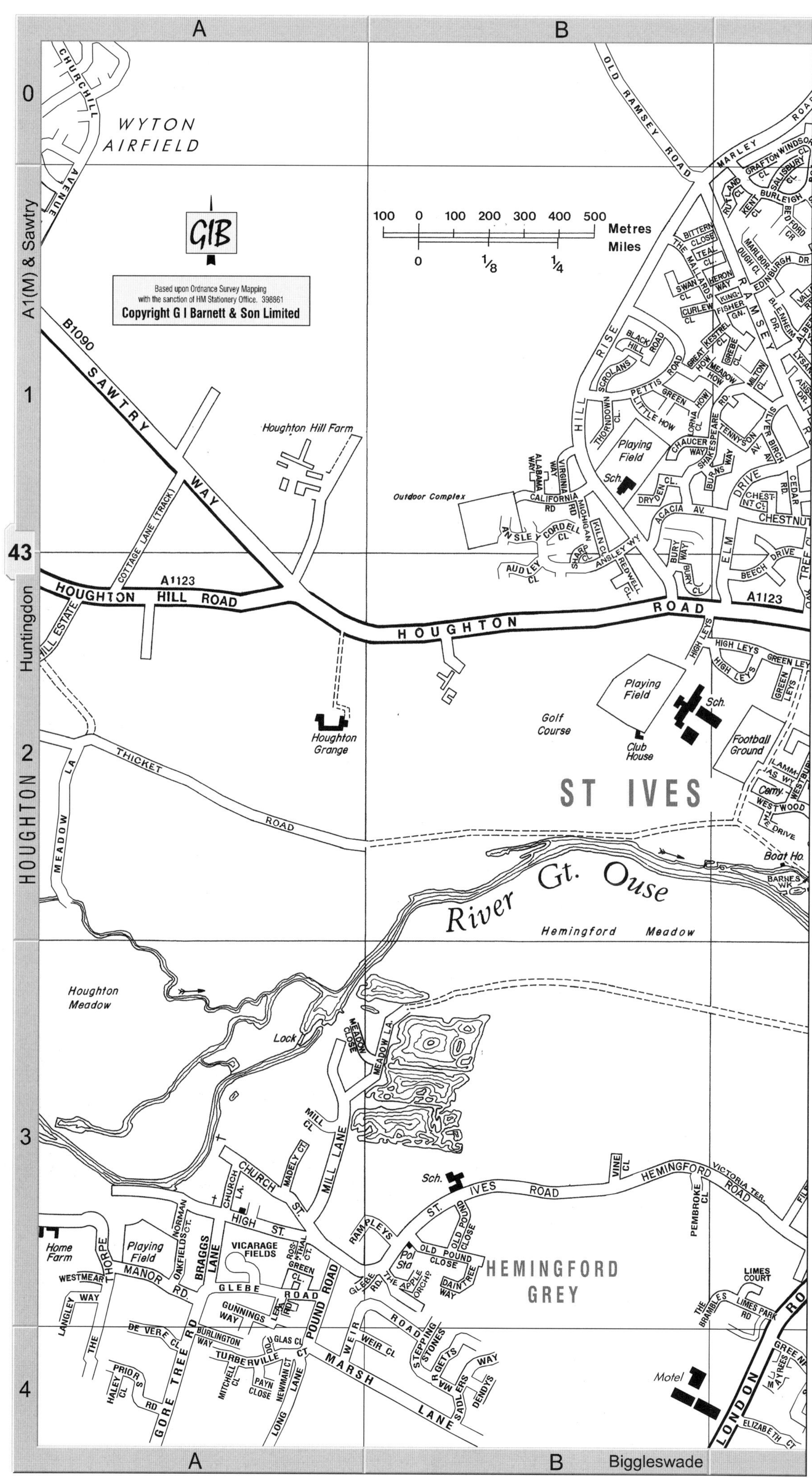
A
B
0
1
43
2
3
4
A
B
A1(M) & Sawtry
Huntingdon
WYTON AIRFIELD
CHURCHILL AVENUE
B1090
SAWTRY WAY
Houghton Hill Farm
GIB
Based upon Ordnance Survey Mapping
with the sanction of HM Stationery Office. 398861
Copyright G I Barnett & Son Limited
100   0   100 200 300 400 500
Metres
Miles
0   1/8   1/4
OLD RAMSEY ROAD
MARLEY LANE
RUTLAND
KENT CL.
BURLEIGH
GRAFTON CL.
WINDSOR
SALISBURY
BEDFORD CR.
THE MALL
BITTERN CL.
TEAL CL.
DUGH CL.
MARLBOROUGH DR.
BLENHEIM
SWAN CL.
CURLEW CL.
HERON WAY
MEADOW WAY
KING CL.
FISHER GN.
EDINBURGH
VALE
ALB
AB
ALDE
DR.
RIVER
BIRCH
RISE
HILL
SCROLANS
BLACK HILL
GREAT HOW
KESTREL
GREBE
MILTON
TENNYSON AV.
THORNDOWN CL.
PETTIS ROAD
LITTLE HOW
CALIFORNIA HOW
CL.
GREEN
CHAUCER WAY
SHAKESPEARE WAY
BURNS WAY
DRIVE
Playing Field
Sch.
ALABAMA WAY
VIRGINIA ROAD
MICHIGAN CL.
DRYDEN CL.
ACACIA AV.
CHESTNUT CT.
CEDAR
CHESTNUT
Outdoor Complex
CALIFORNIA RD.
ANSLEY
CORDELL CL.
SHARP
KILN CL.
ANSLEY WY.
REDWELL CL.
BURY WAY
BURY CL.
ELM
BEECH
TREE DRIVE
OAK
AUDLEY CL.
A1123
ROAD
HOUGHTON HILL ROAD
A1123
COTTAGE LANE (TRACK)
MILL ESTATE
HOUGHTON
Huntingdon
HOUGHTON ROAD
HIGH LEYS
HIGH LEYS
GREEN LEY
HIGH LEY
GREEN LEYS
Playing Field
Sch.
Club House
Golf Course
Football Ground
ILAMM
AS WY.
WESTBUR
Carry.
WESTWOOD DRIVE
ST IVES
HOUGHTON LA.
THICKET
MEADOW LA.
ROAD
Houghton Grange
Boat Ho.
BARNES WK.
River Gt. Ouse
Hemingford Meadow
Houghton Meadow
Lock
MEADOW CLOSE
MILL CL.
MILL LANE
Sch.
ST. IVES ROAD
VINE CL.
HEMINGFORD ROAD
VICTORIA TER.
FILB
CHURCH LA.
CHURCH ST.
MADELY CT.
RAMPLEYS
OLD POUND CLOSE
OLD POUND CLOSE
DAIN TREE
PEMBROKE CL.
HEMINGFORD GREY
LIMES COURT
LIMES PARK RD.
THE BRAMBLES
Home Farm
Playing Field
HIGH ST.
ROSS GREEN CL.
BETHAL CT.
INGRAM CT.
OAKFIELDS
BRAGGS LANE
VICARAGE FIELDS
GLEBE RD.
THE APPLE ORCHD.
Pol Sta
ST. IVES
GLEBE RD.
LONDON RD.
GREEN N
MAYTHES CT.
WESTMEAR
HORPE
MANOR RD.
GUNNINGS WAY
LEA
POUND ROAD
WEIR ROAD
STEPPING STONES
GETS
WAY
LANGLEY WAY
THE CT.
DE VERE CL.
BURLINGTON WAY
TURBERVILLE WAY
GLAS CL.
NEWMAN CT.
LONG LANE
MARSH LANE
SADLERS
MA
DENDYS
GORE TREE RD.
PRIORS RD.
HALEY CL.
MITCHELL CL.
PAYN CLOSE
WEIR CL.
Motel
ELIZABETH CT.
Biggleswade

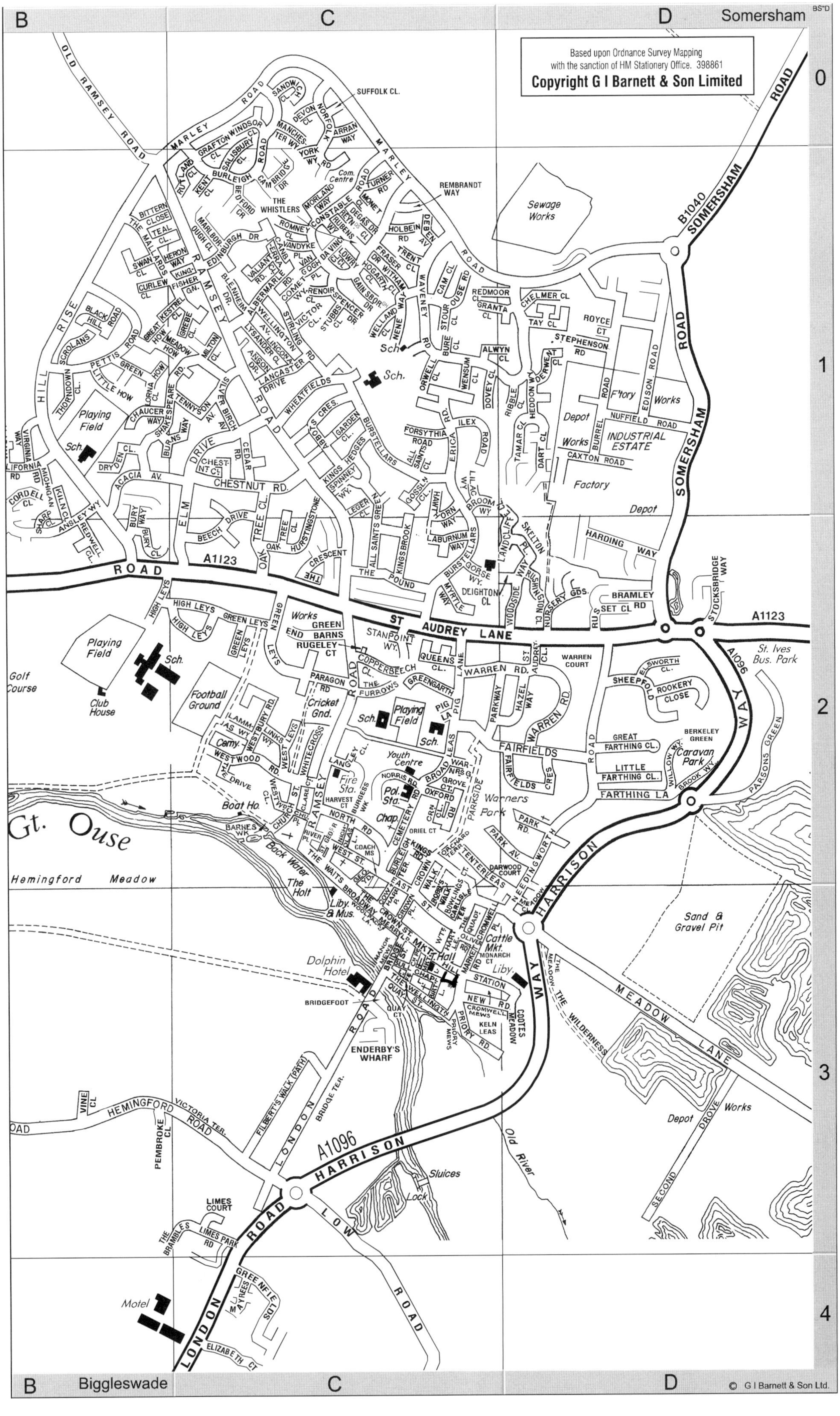
B
C
D
Somersham
0
1
2
3
4
Based upon Ordnance Survey Mapping
with the sanction of HM Stationery Office. 398861
Copyright G I Barnett & Son Limited
OLD RAMSEY ROAD
MARLEY ROAD
SUFFOLK CL.
REMBRANDT WAY
Sewage Works
B1040 SOMERSHAM ROAD
SOMERSHAM ROAD
RAMSEY ROAD
HILL RISE
Playing Field
Sch.
CHESTNUT RD.
ACACIA AV.
ROAD
A1123
ST AUDREY LANE
A1123
St. Ives Bus. Park
A1096 WAY
HARRISON WAY
INDUSTRIAL ESTATE
Factory
Depot
Works
F'tory
NUFFIELD ROAD
CAXTON ROAD
EDISON ROAD
STEPHENSON RD
ROYCE CT
CHELMER CL
HARDING WAY
BRAMLEY RD
SET CL
STOCKSBRIDGE WAY
HIGH LEYS
GREEN LEYS
Playing Field
Golf Course
Club House
Football Ground
Cricket Gnd.
Works
GREEN END BARNS
RUGELEY CT
STANPOINT WY.
COPPERBEECH CL.
THE FURROWS
GREENGARTH
QUEENS CL.
WARREN RD.
WARREN COURT
SHEEPFOLD
ROOKERY CLOSE
ELSWORTH CL.
BERKELEY GREEN
GREAT FARTHING CL.
LITTLE FARTHING CL.
FARTHING LA
Caravan Park
PARSONS GREEN
FAIRFIELDS
Warners Park
Youth Centre
Fire Sta.
Pol. Sta.
Chap.
Gt. Ouse
Hemingford Meadow
Boat Ho.
Back Water
The Holt
Liby. & Mus.
Dolphin Hotel
BRIDGEFOOT
ENDERBY'S WHARF
Cattle Mkt.
Liby.
STATION RD
NEW RD
Sand & Gravel Pit
MEADOW LANE
THE MEADOW
THE WILDERNESS
Depot
Works
SECOND DROVE
Old River
Sluices
Lock
HEMINGFORD ROAD
VICTORIA TER.
PEMBROKE CL
VINE CL
FILBERT'S WALK (PATH)
LONDON ROAD
BRIDGE TER.
A1096 HARRISON WAY
LOW ROAD
LIMES COURT
LIMES PARK RD
THE BRAMBLES
GREENFIELDS
MAYRES
ELIZABETH CT
Motel
LONDON ROAD
B
Biggleswade
C
D
© G I Barnett & Son Ltd.

ST. IVES INDEX TO STREETS

Abbots Crescent C.1
Acacia Avenue B.1
Alabama Way..................B.1
Albermarle Road C.1
All Saints Close C.1
All Saints Green..............C.2
Alwyn Close C.1
Ansley Way B.2
Anson Drive C.1
Arran Way C.0
Audley Close B.2

Barnes Walk...................C.2
Bedford Crescent............C.1
Beech Drive C.2
Berkeley Green D.2
Birt Lane C.3
Bittern Close B.1
Black Hill Road...............B.1
Blenheim Drive C.1
Bowlings Court...............C.3
Braggs Lane...................A.3
Bramley Road D.1
Bridge Street C.3
Bridge Terrace C.3
Bridgefoot......................C.3
Broad Leas C.2
Brook Way D.2
Broomway......................C.1
Bull Lane C.3
Burgess Walk.................C.2
Burleigh Road C.1
Burleigh Terrace.............C.2
Burlington Way...............A.4
Burns Way C.1
Burrel Road D.1
Burstellars C.2
Bury Way B.1

California Road B.1
Cam Close......................C.1
Cambridge Drive C.1
Canberra Close C.1
Carlisle Terrace C.3
Caxton Road D.1
Cedar Road C.1
Cemetery Road C.2
Chapel Lane C.3
Chaucer Way B.1
Chelmer Close D.1
Chestnut Close C.1
Chestnut Road................C.1
Church Lane A.3
Church Place C.2
Churchill Avenue A.0
Clare Court C.2
Coach Mews C.2
Comet Way C.1
Constable Road C.1
Copperbeech Close........C.2
Cordell Close B.1
Cottage Lane A.2
Cowhare Place C.3
Cromwell Mews C.3
Cromwell Place C.3
Crown Close C.2
Crown Place C.3
Crown Street C.3
Crown Walk C.2
Curlew Close B.1

Da Vinci Close C.1
Daintree Way B.3
Dart Close D.1
Darwood Court...............C.2
De Vere Close A.4
Deben Avenue C.1
Degas Close C.1
Deighton Close D.2
Dendys..........................B.4
Derwent Close D.1
Devon Close C.0
Douglas Close A.4
Dovey Close C.1
Dryden Close B.1

East Street.....................C.2
Edinburgh Drive.............C.1
Edison Road D.1
Elizabeth Court C.4

Elm Drive C.2
Elsworth Close................D.2
Enderby's Wharf C.3
Erica Road C.1

Fairfields D.2
Fairfields Crescent.........D.2
Farthing Lane.................D.2
Filbert's Walk C.3
Forsythia Road C.1
Fraser Drive C.1
Free Church Passage C.3

Gainsborough Drive........C.1
Garden Close..................C.1
George yard....................C.2
Glebe Road A.3
Gore Tree Road A.4
Gorse Way C.2
Gosslan Close C.1
Grafton Close..................C.1
Granta Close D.1
Great Farthing Close D.2
Grebe Close....................C.1
Green Close....................A.3
Green End Barns............C.2
Green How......................B.1
Green Leys C.2
Greenfields.....................C.4
Greengarth.....................C.2
Grove Court C.2
Gunnings Way A.3

Haley Close A.4
Harding Way D.1
Harrison Way C.3
Harvest Court.................C.2
Hawthorn Way C.1
Hazel Way D.2
Heddon Way D.1
HEMINGFORD GREY B.3
Hemingford Road............B.3
Heron Way......................C.1
High Leys C.2
High Street A.3
Hill Estate......................A.2
Hill Rise B.1
Hogarth Close C.1
Holbein Road..................C.1
Houghton A.2
Houghton Road B.2
Hurstingstone.................C.2

Ilex Road C.1

Keln Leas.......................C.3
Kent Close C.1
Kestrel Close C.1
Kiln Close.......................B.1
Kingfisher Green C.1
Kings Hedges C.1
Kings Road C.2
Kingsbrook.....................C.2

Laburnum Way...............C.2
Lammas Way..................C.2
Lancaster Drive C.1
Landcliffe Close D.2
Langley Close C.2
Langley Way A.3
Law Road.......................A.3
Lea Road A.3
Leger Close C.1
Lilac Way C.1
Limes Court C.3
Limes Park Road C.3
Lincoln Avenue C.1
Links Way C.2
Little Farthing Close........D.2
Little How B.1
London Road C.3
Long Lane A.4
Lorna Close B.1
Low Road.......................C.3
Lowry Close....................C.1
Lysander Close C.1

Madely Court A.3
Manchester Way C.0
Manor Mews C.3

Manor Road A.3
Margetts B.4
Market Lane...................C.3
Market Road C.3
Marlbough Close C.1
Marley Road C.0
Marsh Lane A.4
Maytrees C.4
Meadow Close B.3
Meadow Close D.3
Meadow How C.1
Meadow Lane A.2
Meadow Lane,
    Hemingford Grey B.3
Merryland Hill.................C.3
Michigan Road................B.1
Mill Close A.3
Mill Lane A.3
Milton Close C.1
Mitchell Close.................A.4
Monarch Court C.3
Monet Close...................C.1
Morland Way C.1
Myrtle Way C.2

Needingworth Road........D.3
Nene Way C.1
New Road C.3
Newman Court A.4
Nicholas Lane C.2
Norfolk Road C.0
Norman Close A.3
Norman court A.3
Norris Road C.2
North Road C.2
Nuffield Road D.1
Nursery Gardens D.2

Oak Tree Close C.2
Oakfields A.3
Old Pound Close B.3
Old Ramsey Road B.0
Oliver Road C.3
Orchard Terrace.............C.2
Oriel Court C.2
Orwell Close C.1
Ouse Road.....................C.1
Oxford Road C.2

Paragon Road C.2
Park Avenue C.2
Park Road D.2
Parkside.........................C.2
Parkway.........................C.2
Parsons Green...............D.2
Payn Close.....................A.4
Pembroke Close B.3
Pettis Road B.1
Pig Lane.........................C.2
Pound Road...................A.3
Priors Road A.4
Priory Mews C.3
Priory Road C.3

Quay Court C.3
Queens Close C.2

Rampleys A.3
Ramsey Road C.2
Redmoor Close D.1
Redwell Close B.2
Rembrandt Way..............C.1
Renoir Close C.1
Reynold C.1
Ribble Close D.1
River Place C.2
Robb's Walk...................C.2
Romney Close C.1
Rookery Close D.2
Rosenthal court A.3
Royce Court...................D.1
Rubens Way C.1
Rugeley Court C.2
Rushington Close D.2
Russet Close D.2
Rutland Close C.1

St. Audrey Close D.2
St. Audrey Lane..............C.2
St. George's Road C.2

St. Ives Road B.3
Sadlers Way...................B.4
Salisbury Close C.1
Sandwich Close.............C.0
Sawtry Way A.1
Second Drive D.3
Shakespeare Road B.1
Sharp Close B.2
Sheepfold.......................D.2
Silver Birch Avenue C.1
Skelton Place.................D.2
Somersham Road D.1
Spencer Drive C.1
Spinney Way C.1
Stanpoint Way C.2
Station Road C.3
Stephenson Road D.1
Stepping Stones.............B.4
Stirling Road C.1
Stocksbridge Way D.2
Stour Close C.1
Stubbs Close C.1
Suffolk Close C.0
Swan Close B.1

Tamar close D.1
Tay Close D.1
Teal Close B.1
Tennyson Avenue C.1
Tente Leas C.2
The Apple Orchard.........B.3
The Brambles C.3
The Broadway C.3
The Crescent C.2
The Drive C.2
The Furrows...................C.2
The Mallards B.1
The Meadow D.3
The Pound C.2
The Quadrant..................C.3
The Quay........................C.3
The Thorpe A.4
The Waits C.2
The Whistlers C.1
The Wilderness D.3
Thicket Road A.2
Thorndown Close...........B.1
Trent Close C.1
Turberville Court.............A.4
Turner Road....................C.1

Valiant Road C.1
Van Gogh Place.............C.1
Vandyke Place C.1
Vicarage Fields A.3
Victor Close C.1
Victoria Terrace C.3
Vine Close B.3
Virginia Way B.1

Warners Gardens...........C.2
Warners Park.................C.2
Warren Court D.2
Warren Road D.2
Waveney Road C.2
Weir Close B.4
Weir Road A.4
Welland Close C.1
Wellington Avenue C.1
Wellington Street C.3
Wensum Close C.1
West Leys C.2
West Street C.2
Westbury Road C.2
Westmear.......................A.3
Westwood Close C.2
Westwood Road C.2
Wheatfields C.1
White Hart Lane..............C.3
Whitecross C.2
Willow Way D.2
Windsor Close C.0
Witham Close C.1
Woodside Way D.2
Woolpack Lane C.3

York Way C.1

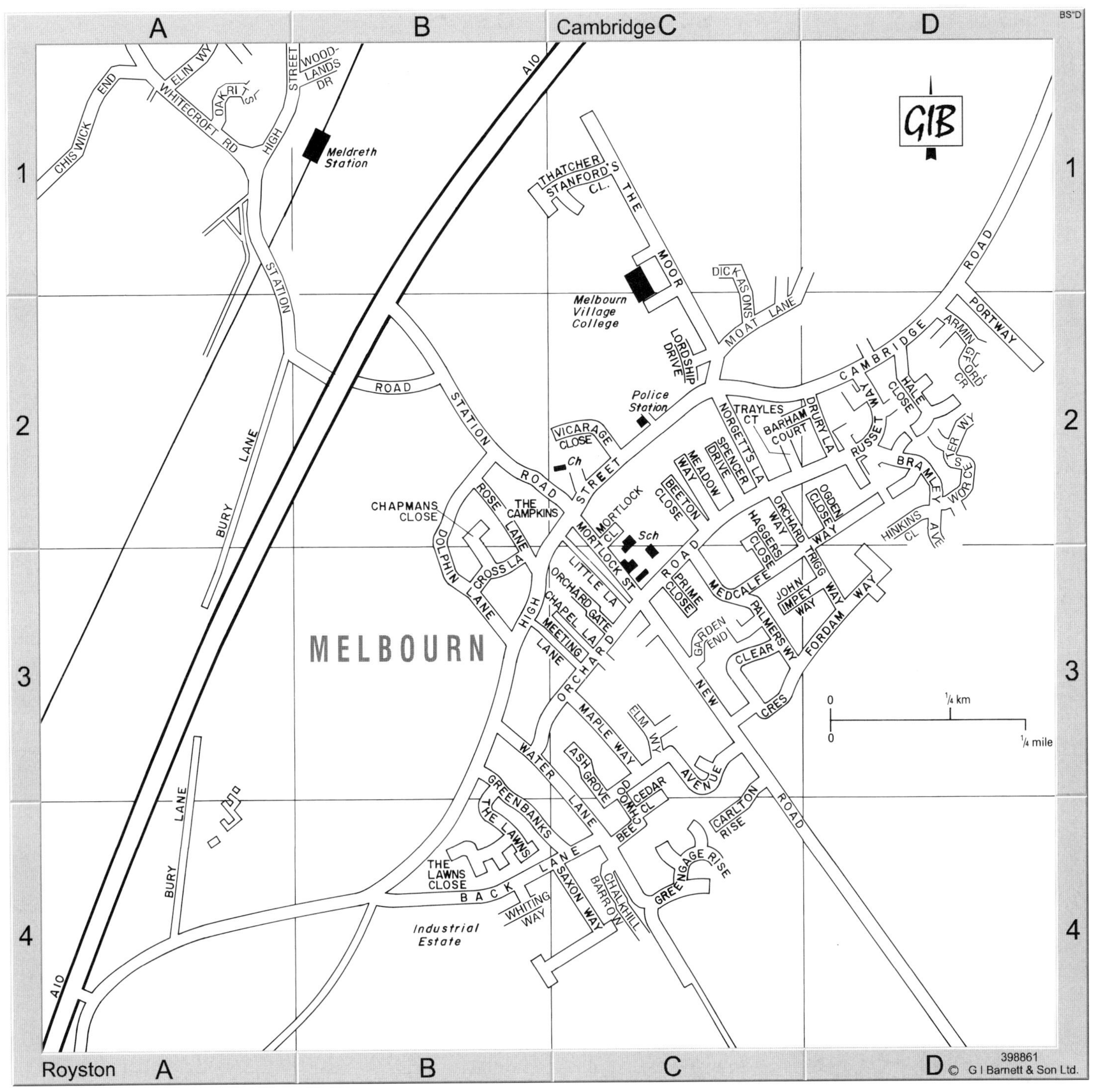

MELBOURN INDEX TO STREETS

Armingford Crescent ..D.2
Ash Grove C.3

Back Lane B.4
Barham Court C.2
Beechwood Avenue C.4
Beeton Close C.2
Bramley Avenue D.2
Bury Lane A.2

Cambridge Road D.2
Carlton Rise C.4
Cedar Close C.3
Chalkhill Barrow C.4
Chapel Lane C.3
Chapmans Close B.2
Chiswick End A.1
Clear Crescent C.3
Cross Lane B.3

Dickasons C.1
Dolphin Lane B.3

Drury Lane D.2

Elin Way A.1
Elm Way C.3

Fordam Way D.3

Garden End C.3
Greenbanks B.4
Greengage Rise C.4

Haggers Close C.2
Hale Close D.2
High Street A.1
High Street B.3
Hinkins Close D.2

John Impey Way C.3

Little Lane C.3
Lordship Drive C.2

Maple Way C.3
Meadow Way C.2
Medcalfe Way C.3
Meeting Lane C.3
Moat Lane C.2
Mortlock Close C.2
Mortlock Street C.2

New Road C.3
Norgett's Lane C.2

Oakrits A.1
Ogden Close D.2
Orchard Gate C.3
Orchard Road C.3
Orchard Way C.2

Palmers Way C.3
Portway D.2
Prime Close C.3

Rose Lane B.2

Russet Way D.2

Saxon Way C.4
Spencer Drive C.2
Station Road B.2

Thatcher Stanford's
Close C.1
The Campkins B.2
The Lawns B.4
The Lawns Close B.4
The Moor C.1
Trayles Court C.2
Trigg Way D.3

Vicarage Close C.2

Water Lane B.3
Whitecroft Road A.1
Whiting Way B.4
Woodlands Drive B.1
Worcester Way D.2

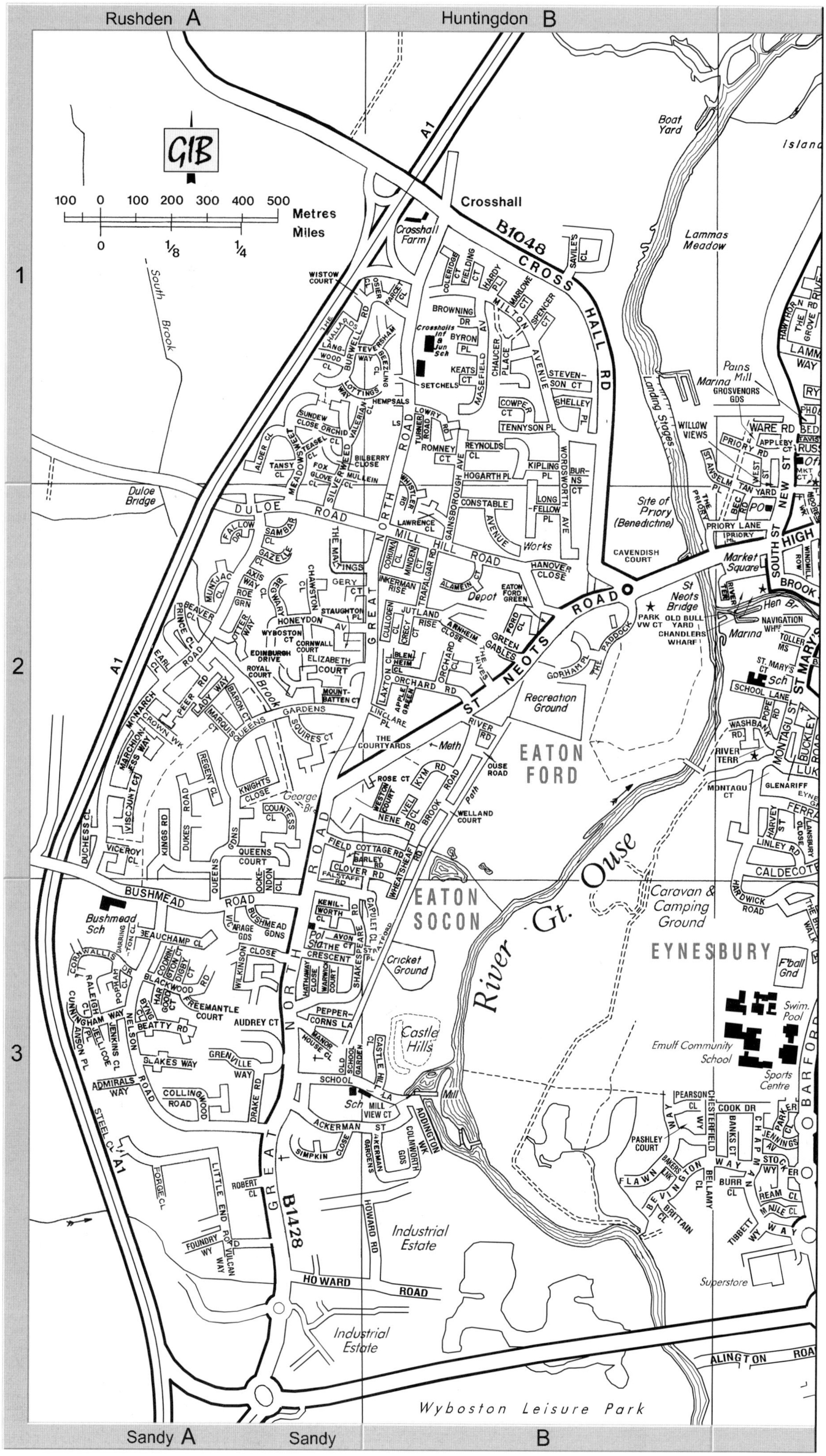

Rushden A
Huntingdon B
GIB
100 0 100 200 300 400 500 Metres
0 1/8 1/4 Miles
South Brook
Boat Yard
Island
Crosshall
B1048
CROSS HALL RD
SAVILE'S CL
Crosshall Farm
Lammas Meadow
WISTOW COURT
COLERIDGE CT
FIELDING CT
HARDY PL
MARLOWE CT
SPENCER CT
MILTON AVENUE
Pains Mill
Marina
GROSVENORS GDS
HAWTHORN
THE GROVE
LAMMAS WAY
BROWNING DR
BYRON PL
CHAUCER PL
STEVENSON CT
SHELLEY PL
WILLOW VIEWS
WARE RD
APPLEBY
RY
PHO
BED
Crosshalls Inf & Jun Sch
KEATS CT
MASEFIELD CT
COWPER CT
TENNYSON PL
Site of Priory (Benedictine)
ST ANSELM
WEST ST
PRIORY
TAN YARD
BEC
RUSS
Of
MKT
THE HALLARDS
BURWELL
OSIER
FAICE
TEVERSHAM WAY
LANG CL
WOOD CL
LOFTINGS
HEMPSALS
ALERIAN
TURNED
LOWRY ROAD
ROMNEY CT
REYNOLDS CT
KIPLING PL
WORDSWORTH AVE
BURNS CT
LONG-FELLOW PL
THE PRIORY
PRIORY LANE
PRIORY
PO
BROOK
NEW ST
SOUTH ST
HIGH ST
SUNDEW CLOSE
ORCHID
TEASEL WAY
FOX
SILVERWEED
MULLEIN
BILBERRY CLOSE
GLOVE CL
LAWRENCE CL
WHISTLER RD
GAINSBOROUGH AVE
HOGARTH PL
CONSTABLE
Works
HANOVER CLOSE
Market Square
RIVER TERR
ST MARY'S
ALDER CL
TANSY CL
MEADOWSWEET
NORTH ROAD
MILL HILL ROAD
ST. MARY'S CT
Sch
SCHOOL LANE
Duloe Bridge
DULOE ROAD
FALLOW DR
SAMBAR CL
GAZELLE CL
THE MAYINGS
GERY
CORBIN
MINDEN
TRAFALGAR RD
ALAMEIN
EATON FORD GREEN
Depot
CAVENDISH COURT
St Neots Bridge
St Neots Bridge
NAVIGATION WHF
TOLLER MS
WASHBANK RD
MONTAGU ST
BUCKLEY
LUK
FERR
MUNTJAC CL
AXIS WAY
ROE GRN
REG WAY
CHAWSTON
INKERMAN RISE
JUTLAND
CRECY RISE
ARNHEM CLOSE
FORD CL
GREEN GABLES
Park VW CT
Old Bull Yard
CHANDLERS WHARF
Marina
Hen Br.
MONTAGU CT
GLENARIFF
EYNE
BEAVER
PRINCE CL
OTTER WAY
HONEYDON
STAUGHTON AV
WYBOSTON CT
CORNWALL COURT
ELIZABETH COURT
CULLODEN CL
BLEN HEIM CL
ORCHARD GREEN
APPLE GREEN
ORCHARD RD
ST NEOTS ROAD
Recreation Ground
GORHAM PL
THE PADDOCK
RIVER TERR
HARVEY CL
LINLEY RD
CALDECOTE
EARL CL
DEER RD
LADY WAY
BARON CL
MARQUIS CT
ROYAL COURT
MOUNT-BATTEN CT
LAXTON CL
INCLARE
THE COURTYARDS
RIVER RD
Meth
EATON FORD
EDINBURGH DRIVE
MONARCH
MARCHION CL
VISCOUNT CT
ESS WAY
CROWN WK
REGENT CL
KNIGHTS CLOSE
COUNTESS CL
GONS
SQUIRES CT
George Br.
ROSE CT
WESTON CL
KYM RD
YVELI
RIVER RD
OUSE ROAD
Path
WELLAND COURT
River Gt. Ouse
EATON SOCON
Caravan & Camping Ground
EYNESBURY
F'ball Gnd
DUCHESS CL
VICEROY CL
KINGS RD
DUKES RD
QUEENS COURT
QUEENS ROAD
OCKENDON
FIELD
BARLEY RD
COTTAGE RD
FALSTAFF RD
CLOVER RD
NENE RD
WHEATSHEAF RD
BROOK RD
Swim. Pool
BUSHMEAD
Bushmead Sch
BEAUCHAMP CL
DARRING
TON CL
ARAGE GDS
BUSHMEAD GDNS
VIA
KENIL-WORTH CL
Pol Sta
AVON CT
CRESCENT
SHAKESPEARE RD
Cricket Ground
Emulf Community School
Sports Centre
BARFORD
CORNWALLIS
RALEIGH
STEELE CL
DIGBY
BLACKWOOD
CUNNINGHAM WAY
JENKINS CL
ANSON PL
LAYWOOD
BYNG
HARDY RD
CORNWALL
GOODWIN CL
FREEMANTLE COURT
WILKINSON CLOSE
HATHAWAY CLOSE
WARWICK COURT
PEPPER-CORNS LA
MANOR HOUSE CL
NELSON ROAD
BEATTY RD
AUDREY CT
GRENVILLE WAY
DRAKE RD
COLLINGWOOD ROAD
BLAKES WAY
ADMIRALS WAY
SCHOOL
SCHOOL GARDEN
Sch
MILL VIEW CT
Castle Hills
CASTLE TH
Mill
ACKERMAN
ST
ACKERMAN GARDENS
COLMWORTH GDS
ADDINGTON
PEARSON CL
COOK DR
PARKER
CHESTERFIELD WY
BANKS CT
CHAPMAN AV
STOC
PASHLEY COURT
FLAWN
BAKERS WK
JENNINGS
BEVINGTON
BELLAMY
BURR CL
BRITTAIN CL
M NILE CL
REAM CL
TIBBETT WY
WAY
STEEL CL
A1
SIMPKIN CL
ROBERT CL
LITTLE END RD
VULCAN WAY
FORGE CL
FOUNDRY WY
GREAT NORTH ROAD
B1428
HOWARD RD
Industrial Estate
HOWARD ROAD
Industrial Estate
Superstore
ALINGTON ROAD
Wyboston Leisure Park
Sandy A
Sandy
B
A1
A1
Duloe Bridge

Sandy A
Sandy
B

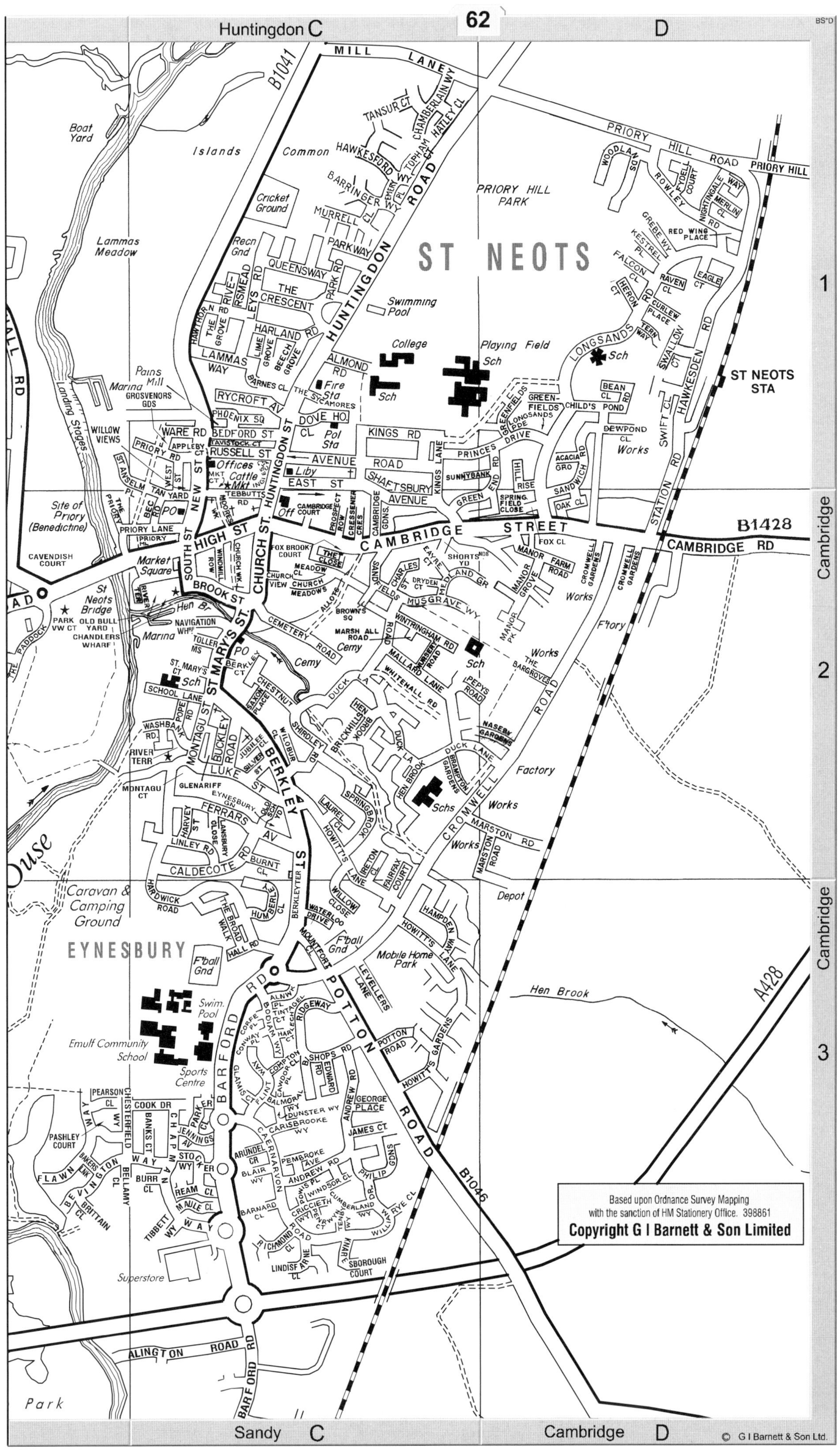
ST NEOTS
EYNESBURY
Huntingdon C
62
D
Sandy C
Cambridge D
Priory Hill
St Neots Sta
B1428
Cambridge Rd
Based upon Ordnance Survey Mapping
with the sanction of HM Stationery Office. 398861
Copyright G I Barnett & Son Limited
© G I Barnett & Son Ltd.

ST. NEOTS INDEX TO STREETS

Acacia Grove D.1
Ackerman Gardens B.3
Ackerman Street A.3
Addington Walk B.3
Alamein Court B.2
Alder Close A.1
Alington Road C.3
Allots C.2
Almond Road C.1
Alnwick Place C.3
Andrew Road C.3
Anson Place A.3
Apple Green B.2
Appleby Court C.1
Arnhem Close B.2
Arundel Crescent C.3
Audrey Court A.3
Avenue Road C.1
Avon Court A.3
Axis Way A.2

Bakers Link B.3
Balmoral Way C.3
Banks Court C.3
Barford Road C.3
Barley Road A.2
Barnard Close C.3
Barnes Close C.1
Baron Court A.2
Barringer Way C.1
Bean Close D.1
Beatty Road A.3
Beauchamp Close A.3
Beaver Close A.2
Bec Road C.2
Bedford Street C.1
Beech Grove C.1
Beezling Way B.1
Bellamy Close B.3
Berkley Court C.2
Berkley Street C.2
Berkley Terrace C.2
Bevington Way B.3
Bilberry Close A.1
Bishops Road C.3
Blackwood Road A.3
Blair Way C.3
Blakes Way A.3
Blenheim close B.2
Bodiam Way C.3
Brampton Gardens C.2
Brickhills C.2
Brittain Close B.3
Brook Road B.2
Brook Street C.2
Browning Drive B.1
Browns Square C.2
Buckley Road C.2
Burns Court B.1
Burnt Close C.3
Burr Close C.3
Burwell Road A.1
Bushmead Gardens A.3
Bushmead Road A.3
Byng Close A.3
Byron Place B.1

Caernarvon Road C.3
Caldecote Road C.2
Cambridge Court C.2
Cambridge Gardens C.2
Cambridge Road D.2
Cambridge Street C.2
Capulet Close B.3
Carisbrooke Way A.3
Castle Hill Close B.3
Cavendish Court B.2
Cemetery Road C.2
Chamberlain Way C.1
Chandlers Wharf C.2
Chapman Way C.3
Charles Street C.2
Chaucer Place B.1
Chesterfield Way B.3
Chestnut Grove C.2
Child's Pond Road D.1
Church Meadows C.2
Church Street C.2
Church View C.2
Church Walk C.1
Clover Road A.2
Codrington Court A.3
Coleridge Court B.1
Collingwood Road A.3
Colmworth Gardens B.3
Compton Close C.2
Constable Avenue B.2
Conway Place C.3
Cook Drive C.1
Corfe Place C.3
Cornwall Court A.2
Cornwallis Drive A.3
Coruna Close B.2
Countess Close A.2
Cowper Court B.1
Crecy Court B.2
Cressener Crescent C.2
Criccieth Way C.3
Cromwell Gardens D.2
Cromwell Road C.2
Crosshall B.1

Crosshall Road B.1
Crown Walk A.2
Culloden Close B.2
Cumberland Way C.3
Cunningham Way A.3
Curlew Place D.1

Darlington Close A.3
Dewpond Close D.1
Digby Court A.3
Dove House Close C.1
Drake Road A.3
Dryden Court C.2
Duchess Close A.2
Duck Lane c.2
Dukes Road A.2
Duloe Road A.2
Dunster Way C.3

Eagle Court D.1
Earl Close A.2
Earye Court C.2
East Street C.1
Eaton Ford B.2
Eaton Ford Green B.2
Eaton Socon A.3
Eaton Socon B.3
Edinburgh Drive A.2
Edward Road C.3
Elizabeth Court A.2
Elizabeth Way A.2
Emery Place C.1
Eynesbury C.3
Eynesbury Green C.2

Fairfax Court C.3
Falcon Close D.1
Fallow Drive A.2
Falstaff Road A.2
Farcet Close B.1
Ferrars Avenue C.2
Field Cottage Road A.2
Fielding Court B.1
Flawn Way B.3
Flint Way C.3
Ford Close B.2
Forge Close A.3
Foundry Way A.3
Fox Brook Court C.2
Fox Close D.2
Fox Grove Close A.1
Freemantle Court A.3
Fydell Court D.1

Gainsborough Avenue B.2
Gazelle Close A.2
George Place C.3
Gery Court A.2
Glamis Court C.3
Glenariff C.2
Gorham Place B.2
Great North Road B.2
Grebe Way D.1
Green End Road C.2
Green Gables B.2
Greenfields D.1
Grenville Way A.3
Grosvenors Gardens C.1

Hall Road C.3
Hampden Way C.3
Hanover Close B.2
Hardwick Road C.3
Hardy Place B.1
Hargood Court A.3
Harland Road C.1
Harlech Court C.3
Harvey Street C.2
Hathaway Close C.3
Hatley Close C.1
Hawkesden Road D.1
Hawkesford Way C.1
Haqwthorn Road C.1
Hempsals B.1
Hen Brook C.2
Heron Court D.1
Hewitts Gardens C.3
High Street C.2
Hill Rise D.1
Hogarth Place B.1
Howard Road B.3
Howitt's Gardens C.3
Howitt's Lane C.3
Humberley Close C.3
Huntingdon Road C.1
Huntingdon Street C.2

Ingles Court C.2
Inkerman Rise B.2
Ireton close C.2
Ivel Close B.2

James Court C.3
Jellicoe Place A.3
Jenkins Close A.3
Jennings Avenue C.3
Jubilee Close C.2
Jutland Rise B.2

Keats Court B.1
Kenilworth Close A.3

Kestrel Place D.1
King's Lane C.1
Kings Road A.2
Kipling Place B.1
Knaresborough Court C.3
Knights Close A.2
Kym Road B.2

Lady Way A.2
Lammas Way C.1
Langwood Close A.1
Lansbury Close C.2
Laurel Close C.2
Lawrence Close B.2
Laxton Close B.2
Levellers Lane C.3
Leys Road C.1
Lime Grove C.1
Linclare Place B.2
Lindisfarne Close C.3
Linley Road C.2
Longfellow Place B.2
Longsands Parade D.1
Longsands Road D.1
Lottings Way A.1
Lowry Road B.1
Luke Street C.2

Mallard Lane C.2
Manor Farm Road D.2
Manor Grove D.2
Manor House Close A.3
Manor Park D.2
Marchioness Way A.2
Market Court C.2
Market Square C.2
Marlowe Court B.1
Marquis Court A.2
Marshall Road C.2
Marston Road D.2
Masefield Avenue B.1
Maule Close C.3
Meadow Close C.2
Meadowsweet A.1
Medland Grove C.2
Merlin Close D.1
Mill Hill Road B.2
Mill Lane C.1
Mill View Court B.3
Milton Avenue B.1
Minden Court B.1
Monarch Road A.2
Montagu Court C.2
Montagu Street C.2
Moores Walk C.1
Mountbatten Court A.2
Mountfort Close C.3
Mulllein Close A.1
Muntjac Close A.2
Murrell Close C.1
Musgrave Way C.2

Naseby Gardens D.2
Navigation Wharf C.2
Nelson Road A.3
Nene Road B.2
New Street C.2
Nightingale Way D.1
Nursery Road C.2

Oak Close D.2
Ockendon Close A.3
Old Bull Yard C.2
Old School Gardens A.3
Old School Yard C.2
Orchard Close B.2
Orchard Road B.2
Orchid Close A.1
Osier Close B.1
Otter Way A.2
Ouse Road B.2

Park Road C.1
Park View Court B.2
Parker Close C.3
Parkway C.1
Pashley Court B.3
Pearson Close B.3
Peer Road A.2
Pembroke Avenue C.3
Penrwyn Court C.3
Peppercorns Lane A.3
Pepys Road C.2
Philip Gardens C.3
Phoenix Square C.1
Pope Road C.2
Popham Way A.3
Potton Road C.3
Powis Road C.3
Prince Close A.2
Princes Drive C.1
Priory Hill D.1
Priory Hill Road D.1
Priory Lane C.2
Priory Mall C.2
Priory Road C.1
Prospect Row C.2
Putton Road C.3

Queens Court A.2
Queens Gardens A.3

Queensway C.1

Raleigh Close A.3
Raven Close D.1
Ream Close C.3
Red Wing Place D.1
Regent Close A.2
Reynolds close B.1
Richmond Close C.3
Ridgeway C.3
River Road B.2
River Terrace C.2
River Terrace (Eynesbury) C.2
Riversmead C.1
Roe Green A.2
Romney Court B.1
Rose Court B.2
Rowley Road D.1
Royal Court A.2
Russell Street C.1
Rycroft Avenue C.1
Rye Close C.3

St. Anselm Place B.1
St. Mary's Street C.2
St. Neots Road B.2
Sambar Close A.2
Sandfields Road C.2
Sandwich Road D.1
Sandyfields Road C.2
Savin's Close B.1
Saxon Place C.2
School Lane, Eaton Secon A.3
School Lane, St. Neots C.2
Setchels B.1
Shaftesbury Avenue C.1
Shakespeare Road A.3
Shelley Place B.1
Shirdley Road C.2
Shortsands Yard C.2
Silver Street C.2
Silverweed A.1
Simpkin Close A.3
South Street C.2
Spencer Court B.1
Springbrook C.2
Springfield Close D.2
Squires Court A.2
Station Road D.2
Steel Close A.3
Stevenson Court B.1
Stocker Way C.3
Stratford Place B.3
Sundew Close A.1
Sunnybank D.1
Swallow Court D.1
Swift Close D.1

Tan Yard C.2
Tansey Close A.1
Tansur Court C.1
Tavistock Court C.2
Teasel Close A.1
Tebbutts Road C.2
Tenby Way C.3
Tennyson Place B.1
Tern Way D.1
Teversham Way B.1
The Bargroves D.2
The Broad Walk C.3
The Close C.2
The Crescent C.1
The Grove C.1
The Hallards A.1
The Hives B.2
The Maltings A.2
The Paddock B.2
The Priory B.2
The Sycamores C.1
Tibbett Way C.3
Tintagel Court C.3
Toller Mews C.2
Topham Court C.1
Trafalgar Road B.2
Turner Road B.1

Valerian Close A.1
Vicarage Gardens A.3
Viceroy Close A.2
Viscount Court A.2
Vulcan Road A.3

Ware Road C.1
Warwick Court A.3
Washbank Road C.2
Waterloo Drive C.2
Welland Court B.2
West Street C.1
Weston Court B.3
Whistler Road B.2
Whitehall Walk C.2
Widbur Close C.2
Wilkinson Close A.3
William Drive C.3
Willow Close C.3
Windmill Row C.2
Windsor Close C.3
Wintringham Road C.2
Wistow Court A.1
Woodlands D.1
Wordsworth Avenue B.1

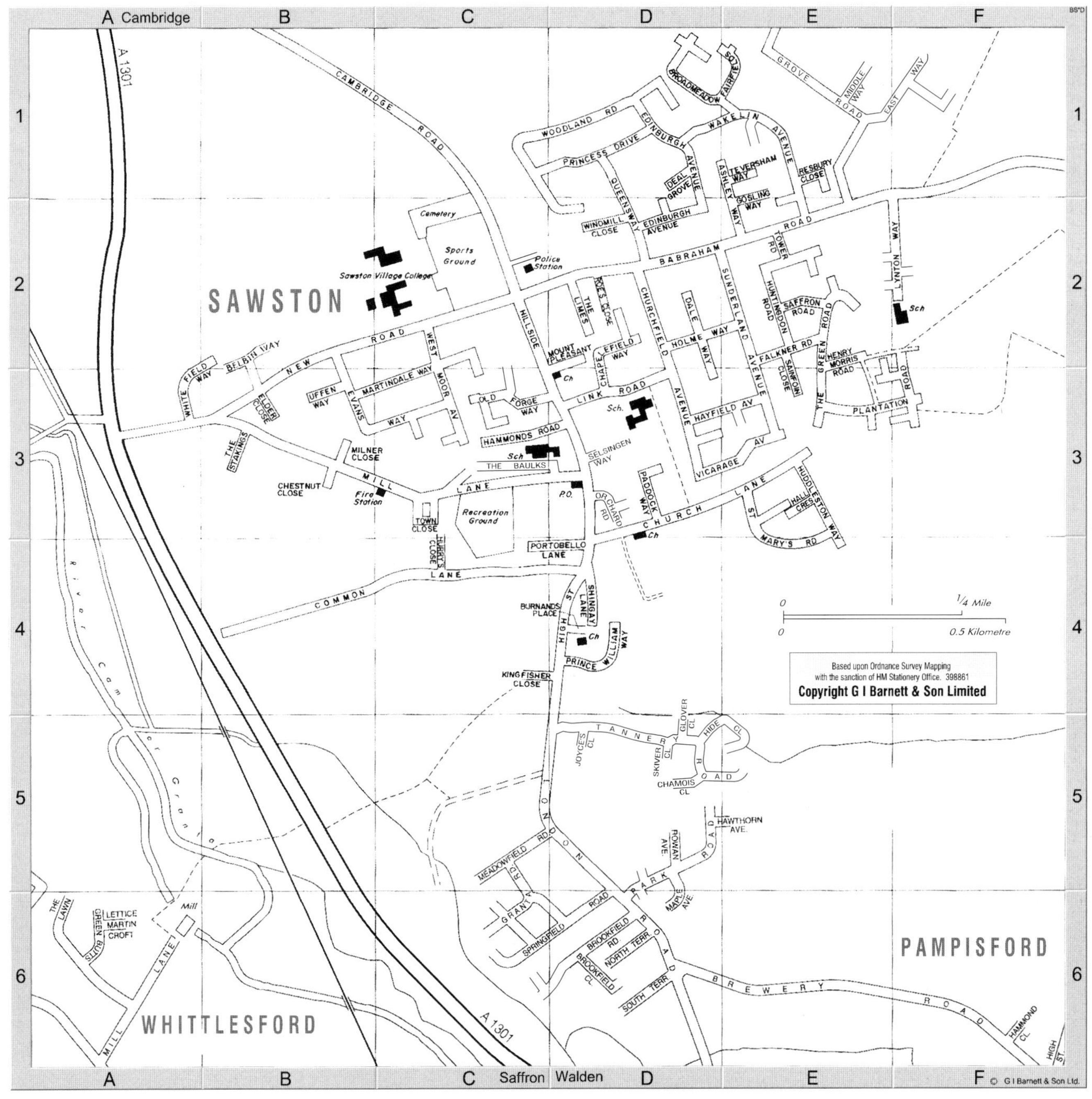

SAWSTON INDEX TO STREETS

Ashley Way E.1

Babraham Road D.2
Belbin Way B.2
Brewery Road D.6
Broadmeadow D.1
Brookfield Close D.6
Brookfield Road D.6
Burnands Place C.4

Cambridge Road B.1
Chamois Close....................D.5
Chapelfield Way D.3
Chestnut Close B.3
Church Lane D.3
Churchfield Avenue D.2
Common Lane B.4

Dale Way D.2
Deal Grove D.1

East Way E.1
Edinburgh Avenue D.1
Elder Close B.3
Evans Way B.3

Fairfields E.1
Falkner Road E.2

Glover Close D.5
Gosling Way E.2
Granta Road C.6
Green Butts A.6
Grove Road E.1

Hall Crescent E.3
Hammond Close F.6
Hammonds Road C.3
Hawthorn Avenue D.5
Hayfield Avenue D.3
Henry Morris Road E.2
Hide Close D.5
High Street D.4
High Street (Pampisford) F.6
Hillside C.2
Holme Way D.2
Huddleston Road E.3
Huntingdon Road E.2
Hurry's Close C.4

Joyce's Close D.5

Kingfisher Close D.4

Lettice Martin Croft A.6
Link Road D.3
London Road C.5
Lynton Way F.2

Maple Avenue D.6
Martindale Way B.3
Meadowfield Road C.5
Middle Way.........................E.1
Mill Lane C.3
Mill Lane A.6
Milner Close B.3
Mount Pleasant D.2

New Road B.2
North Terrace D.6

Old Forge Way C.3
Orchard Road D.3

Paddock Way D.3
Park Road D.5
Plantation Road E.3
Porobello Road C.4
Prince William Way D.4
Princess Drive D.1

Queensway D.1

Resbury Close E.1
Roe's Close D.2
Rowan Avenue D.5

Saffron Road E.2

Sainfoin Road E.2
St. Mary's Road E.3
Selsingen Way D.3
Shingay Lane D.4
Skiver Close.......................D.5
South Terrace D.6
Springfield Road C.6
Sunderland Avenue E.2

Tannery Road......................D.5
Teversham Way E.1
The BaulksThe Green Road ..E.3
The Lawn A.6
The Limes D.2
The Stakings B.3
Tower Road E.2
Town Close C.3

Uffen Way B.3

Vicarage Avenue D.3

Wakelin Avenue D.1
West Moor Avenue C.2
White Field Way A.3
Windmill Close D.2
Woodland Road D.1

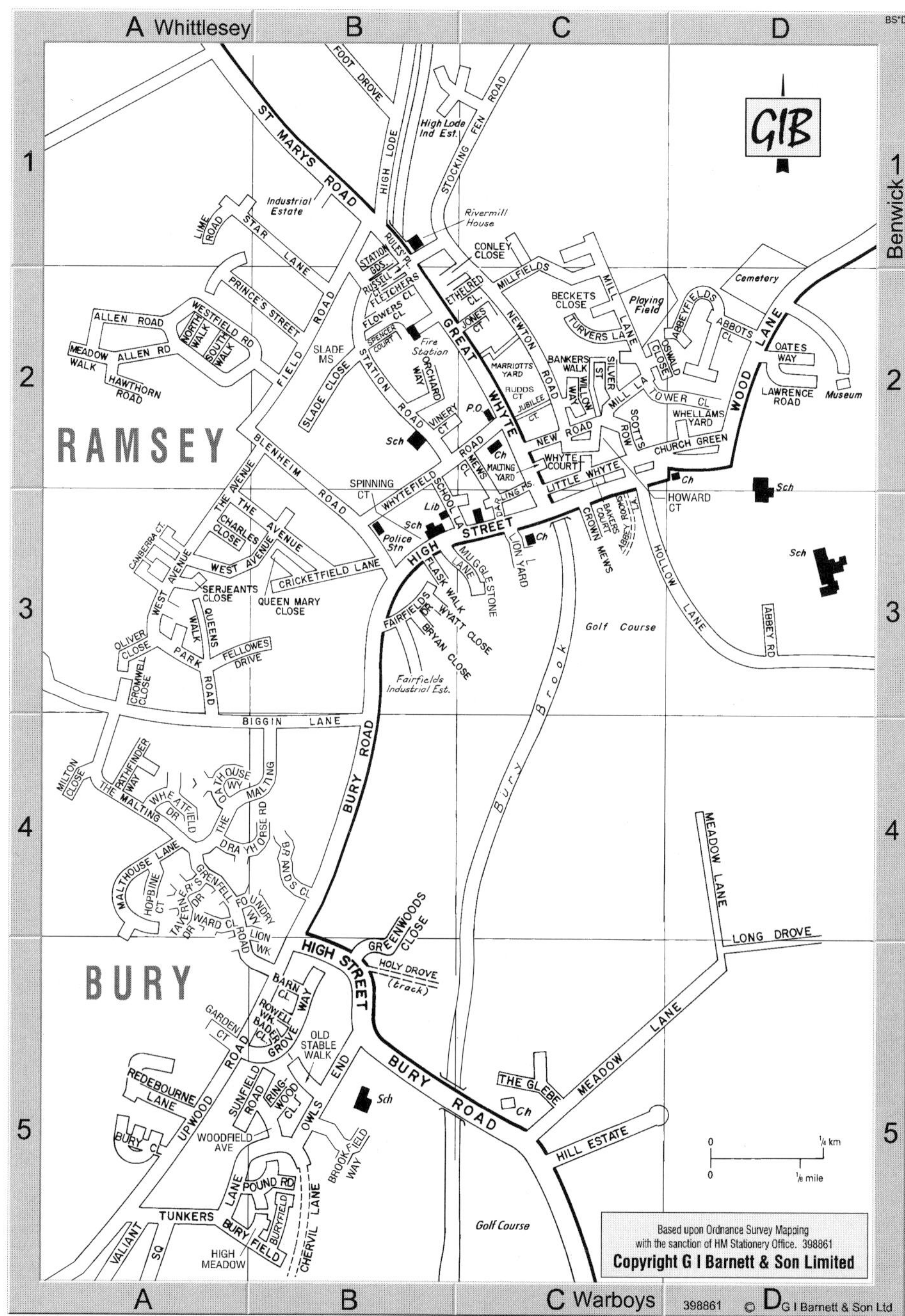

RAMSEY INDEX TO STREETS

Abbey Road D.3
Abbey Rooms Lane C.3
Abbeyfields D.2
Abbots Close D.2
Allen Road A.2

Bader Close B.5
Bakers Court C.2
Bankers Walk C.2
Barn Close B.5
Becketts Close C.2
Biggin Lane B.4
Blenheim Road B.2
Brand's Close B.4
Brookfield Way B.5
Bryan Close B.3
Bury...A.5
Bury Close A.5
Bury Road B.4
Buryfield A.5

Canberra Court A.3
Charles Close A.3
Chervil Lane B.5
Church Green D.2
Colney Close B.2
Conley Close C.2
Cricketfield Lane B.3
Cromwell Close A.3
Crown Mews C.3

Darling Mews C.3
Drayhorse Lane A.4

Etheired Close C.2

Fairfields Drive B.3
Fellowes Drive A.3

Field Road B.2
Flash Walk B.3
Fletchers Close B.2
Flowers Close B.2
Foot Drove B.1
Foundry Way A.4

Garden Court A.5
Great Whyte C.2
Greenwoods Close B.5
Grenfell Road A.4
Grove Way B.5

Hawthorn Road..............................A.2
High Lode B.1
High Meadow B.5
High Street (Bury) B.5
High Street B.3
Hill Estate C.5
Hollow Lane C.3
Holy Drove B.5
Hopbine Court A.4
Howard Court C.2

Jones Court C.2
Jubilee Court...................................C.2
Judds Court C.2

Lawrence Road...............................D.2
Lime Road A.1
Lion Walk...B.4
Lion Yard..C.3
Little Whyte C.2
Long Drove D.5

Malthouse Lane A.4
Malting Yard C.2
Marriots Yard..................................C.2

Meadow Lane C.5
Meadow Walk A.2
Mill Lane C.2
Millfields C.2
Milton Close A.4
Mugglestonelane...........................C.3

New Road C.2
Newton Road C.2
North Walk A.2

Oasthouse Way...............................A.4
Oates Way D.2
Old Stable Walk B.5
Oliver Close A.3
Orchard Way B.2
Oswald Close C.2
Owls End B.5

Park Road A.3
Pathfinder Way A.4
Pound Road B.5
Princes Street A.2

Queen Mary Street B.3
Queens Walk A.3

Redebourne Lane A.5
Ringwood Close B.5
Rowell Walk B.5
Rule's Place B.2
Russell Court B.2

St. Marys Road B.1
School Lane B.3
Scotts Row C.2
Serjeants Close A.3
Silver Street C.2

Slade Close B.2
Slade Mews B.2
South Walk A.2
Spinning Court B.3
Spender Court................................B.2
Star Lake B.1
Station Gardens B.2
Station Road B.2
Stocking Fen Road B.1
Sunfield Road B.5

Taverner's Drive A.4
The Avenue A.3
The Glebe C.5
The Malting B.4
Tower Close C.2
Tunkers Lane B.5
Turvers Lane C.2

Upwood Road B.5

Valiant Square.................................A.5
Vinery Court B.2

Ward Close A.4
West Avenue A.3
Westfield Road A.2
Wheatfield Drive A.4
Whellams Yard D.2
Whyte Court C.2
Whytefield Road B.3
Willow Way C.2
Wood Lane D.2
Woodfield Avenue B.5
Wyatt Close B.3

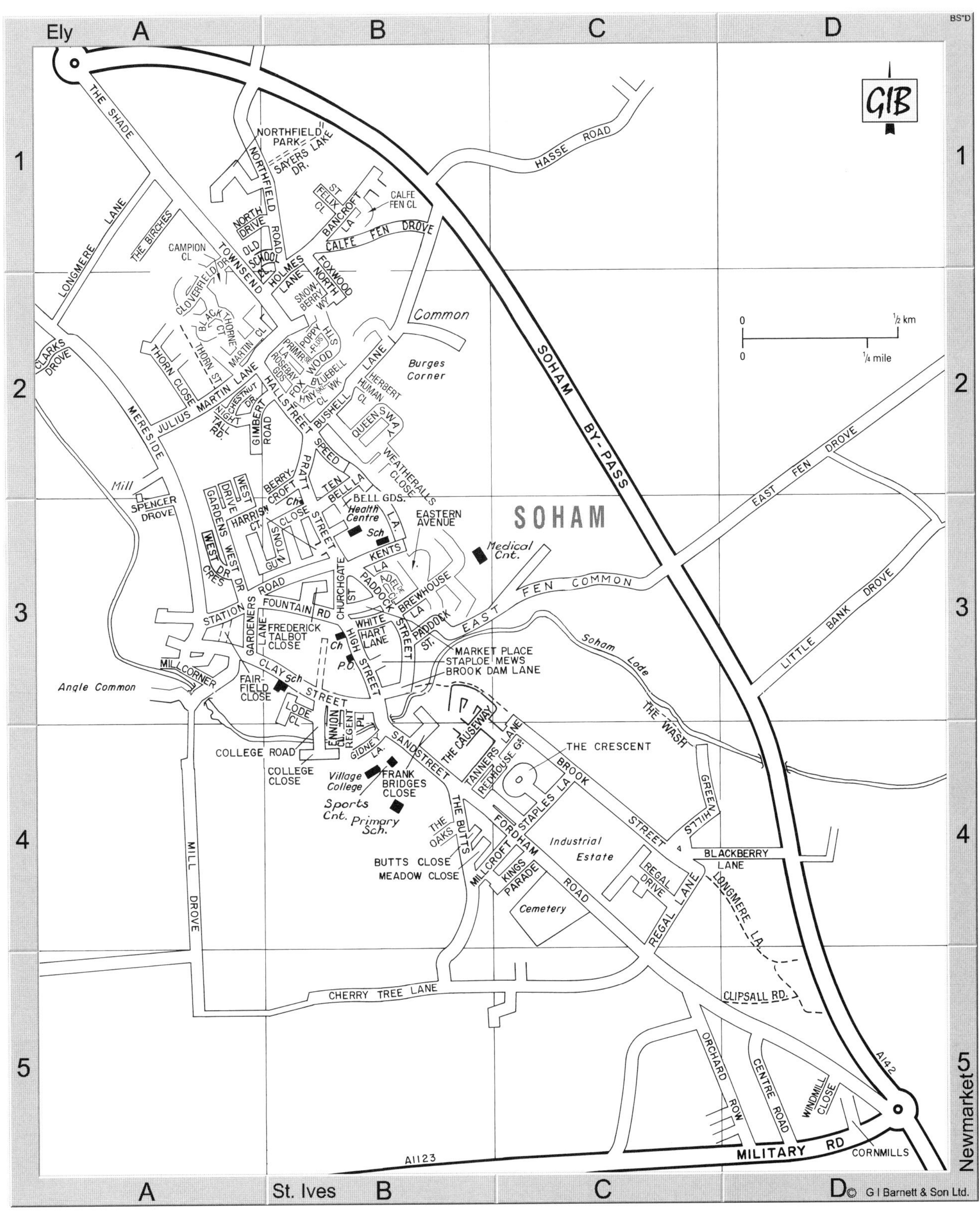

SOHAM INDEX TO STREETS

Adelaide Close B.3

Bancroft Lane B.1
Bell Gardens B.3
Berrycroft B.2
Blackberry Lane C.4
Blackthorne Court A.2
Bluebell Walk B.2
Brewhouse Lane B.3
Brook Dam Lane B.3
Brook Street C.4
Bushell Lane B.2
Butts Close B.4

Calfe Fen Close B.1
Calfe Fen Drive B.1
Campion Close A.2
Causeway B.3
Centre Road D.5
Cherry Tree Lane B.5
Chestnut Drive A.2
Churchgate Street B.3
Clarks Drove A.2
Clay Street B.3
Clipsall Road (Track) D.5

Cloverfield Drive A.2
College Close B.4
College Road B.4
Cornmills D.5

East Fen Common B.3
East Fen Drove D.2
Eastern Avenue B.3
Ennion Close B.4

Fairfield Close A.3
Fordham Road C.4
Fountain Road B.3
Foxwood North B.1
Foxwood South B.2
Frank Bridges Close B.4
Frederick Talbot Close B.3

Gardeners Lane A.3
Gidney Lane B.4
Gimbert Road A.2
Greenhills C.4
Guntons Close B.3

Hall Street B.2

Harrison Court B.3
Hasse Road C.1
Herbert Human Close B.2
High Street B.3
Holmes Lane B.2
Honeysuckle Close B.2

Julius Martin Lane A.2

Kents Lane B.3
Kings Parade C.4

Little Bank Drove D.3
Lode Close B.3
Longmere Lane A.1
Longmere Lane
  (Track) D.4

Market Place B.3
Martin Close A.2
Meadow Close B.4
Mereside A.2
Military Road D.5
Mill Drove A.4
Mill Corner A.3

Millcroft B.4

Night Tall Road A.2
Northfield Park A.1
Northfield Road B.1
Norton Drive A.1

Old School Close B.1
Orchard Row C.5
Poppyfields B.2
Pratt Street B.2
Primrose Lane B.2

Queensway B.2

Redhouse Gardens B.4
Regal Drive C.4
Regal Lane C.4
Regent Place B.4
Rosebay Gardens B.2

St. Felix Close B.1
Sandstreet B.4
Sayers Lake Drive B.1
Snowberry Way B.2

Soham By-Pass C.2
Speed Lane B.2
Spencer Drove A.3
Staples Lane C.4
Staploe Mews B.3
Station Road A.3

Tanners Lane B.4
Ten Bell Lane B.2
The Birches A.1
The Butts B.4
The Crescent C.4
The Oaks B.4
The Shade A.1
The Wash (Track) C.3
Thorn Close A.2
Thorn Street A.2
Townsend A.1

Weatheralls Close B.2
West Drive A.3
West Drive Crescent A.3
West Drive Gardens A.3
White Hart Lane B.3
Windmill Close D.5

© G I Barnett & Son Ltd.

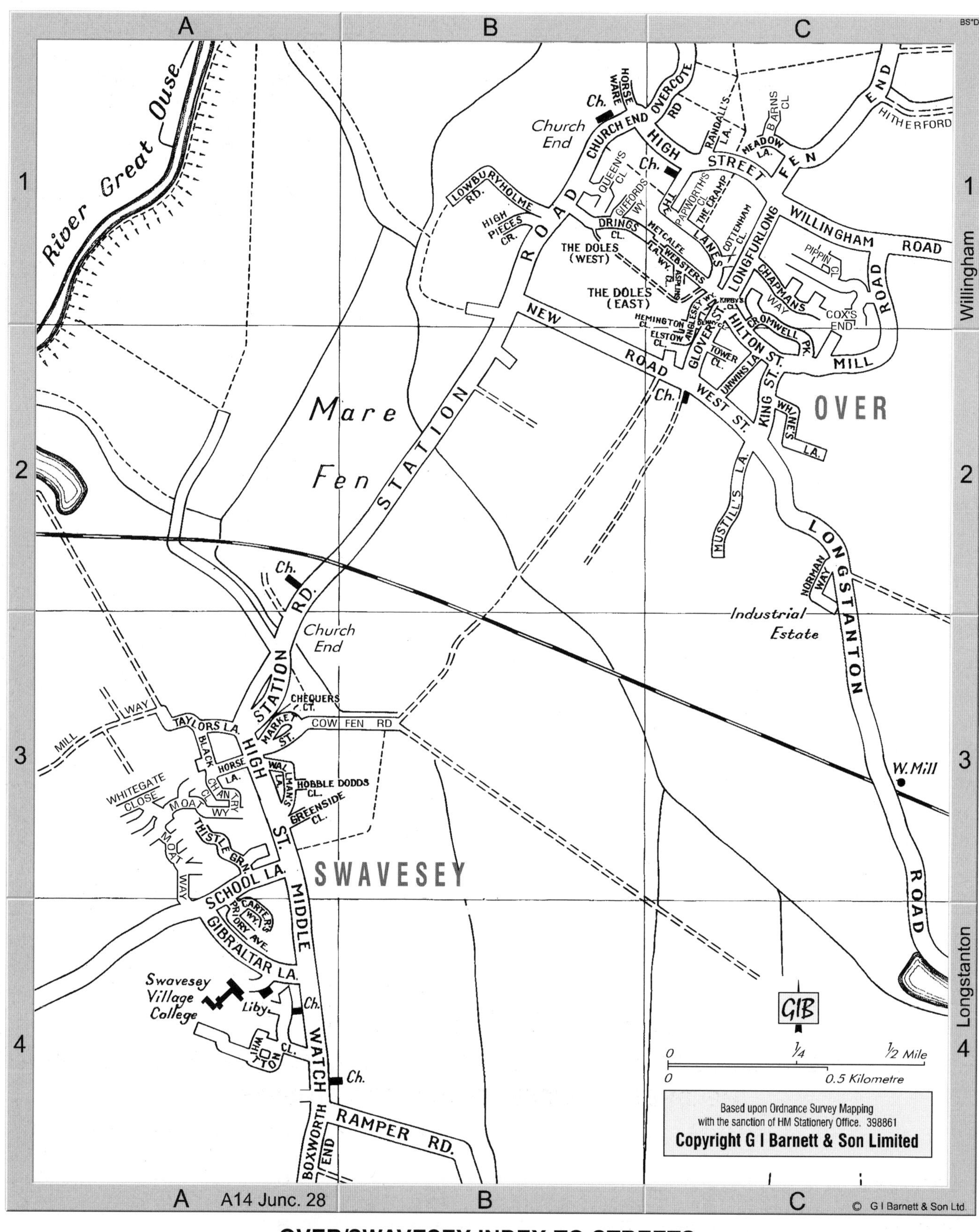

OVER/SWAVESEY INDEX TO STREETS

Anglesey Way C.2
Asplins Close....................C.1

Barns Close C.1
Black Horse Lane A.3
Boxworth End A.4

Carter's Way A.4
Chantry Close A.3
Chapmans Way C.1
Chequers Court A.3
Church End, Over B.1
Church End, Swavesey A.3
Cottenham Close C.1
Cow Fen Road..................A.3
Cox's End C.1
Cromwell Park C.1

Denny Close C.1

Drings Close B.1

Elstow Close C.2

Fen End C.1

Gibraltar Lane A.4
Giffords Way B.1
Glover Street C.2
Greenside Close A.3

Hemington Close C.1
High Pieces Crescent B.1
High Street, Over C.1
High Street, Swavesey A.3
Hilton Street....................C.2
Hitherford C.1
Hobble Dodds Close A.3
Horse Ware B.1

King Street........................C.2
Kirby's Close C.1

Longfurlong C.1
Longstanton Road C.2
Lowburyholme
   Road............................B.1

Market Street A.3
Meadow Lane C.1
Metcalfe Lane C.1
Middle Watch A.4
Mill Road C.2
Mill way A.3
Moat Way A.3
Mustill's Lane C.2

New Road B.1

Norman Way C.2

Overcote Road C.1

Papworth's Close..............C.1
Pippin Close C.1
Priory Avenue..................A.4

Queen's Close B.1
Ramper Road B.4
Randall's Lane C.1

School Lane......................A.3
Station Road, Over B.2
Station Road, Swavesey A.3
Swavesey Village College A.4

Taylors Lane A.3

The Cramp........................C.1
The Doles (East) B.1
The Doles (Wes) B.1
The Lane C.1
Thistle Green A.3
Tower Close C.2

Unwins Lane C.2

Wallman's Lane A.3
Websters Way C.1
West Street........................C.2
Whine's Lane....................C.2
Whitegate Close A.3
Whitton Close A.4
Willingham Road C.1

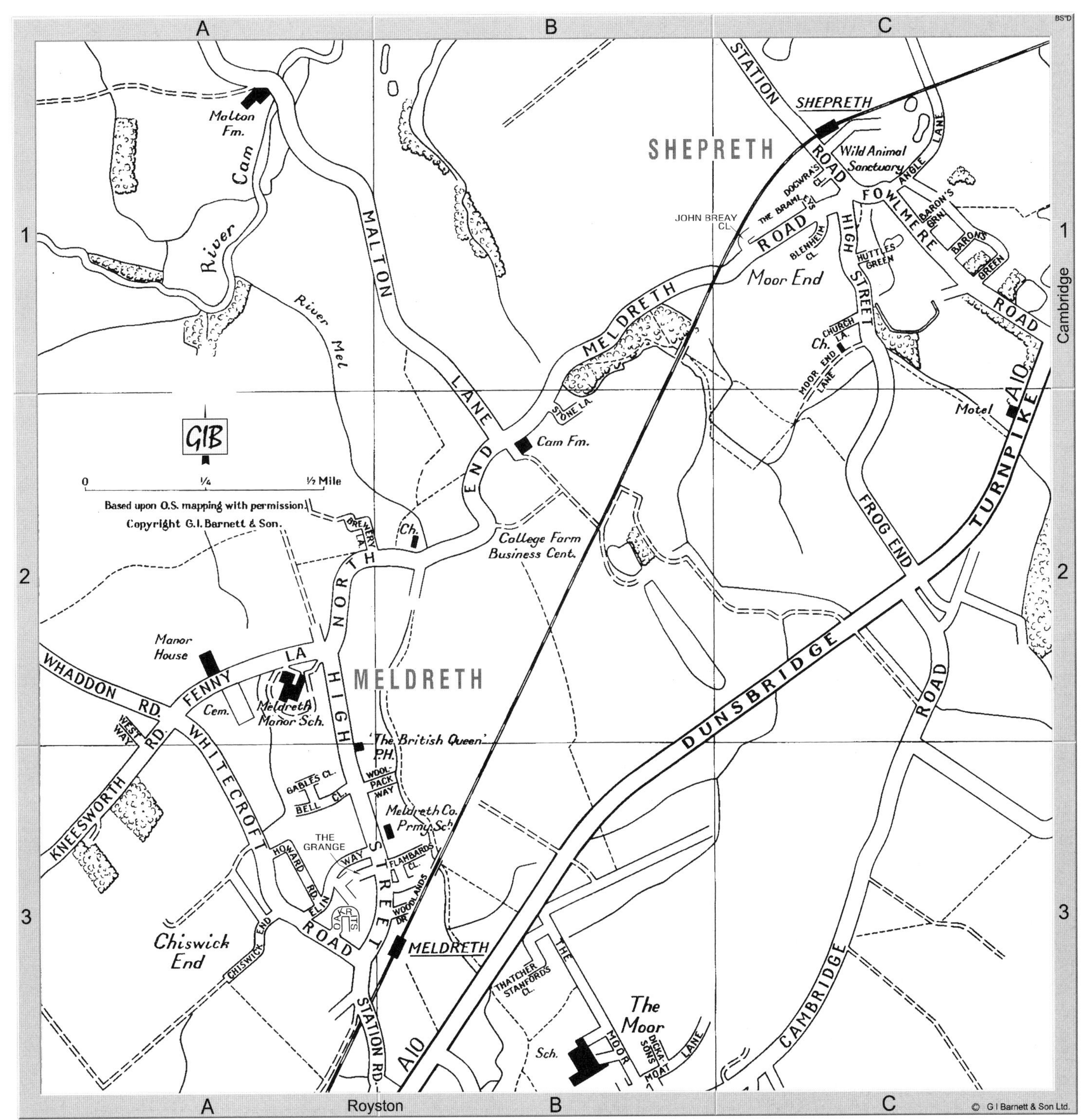

MELDRETH & SHEPRETH INDEX TO STREETS

Angle Lane C.1

Baron's Green..............C.1
Bell Close A.3
Blenheim Close............C.1
Brewery Lane A.2

Cambridge Road..........C.3
Chiswick End A.3
Church Lane C.1
College Farm,
   Business Centre B.2

Dickasons B.3
Docwra's Close............C.1
Dunsbridge Turnpike....C.2

Elin Way A.3
Fenny Lane.................A.2
Flambards Close..........B.3
Fowlmere Road C.1
Frog End....................C.2

Gables Close A.3
Grange A.3

John Breay Close C.1

High Street, Meldreth ..A.2
High Street, Shepreth ..C.1
Howard Road A.3
Huttles Green C.1

Kneesworth Road A.3

Malton Lane B.1
Meldreth Road B.1
Moat Lane..................B.3
Moor End Lane............C.1

North End A.2

Oakrits.......................A.3

Station Road, Meldreth A.3
Station Road,
   Shepreth C.1
Stone Lane B.2

Thatcher Stanford's
   Close B.3
The Bramley C.1
The Moor....................B.3

West Way A.2
Whaddon Road...........A.2
Whitecroft Road A.3
Wild Animal Sanctuary C.1
Woodlands Drive..........B.3
Woolpack Way A.3

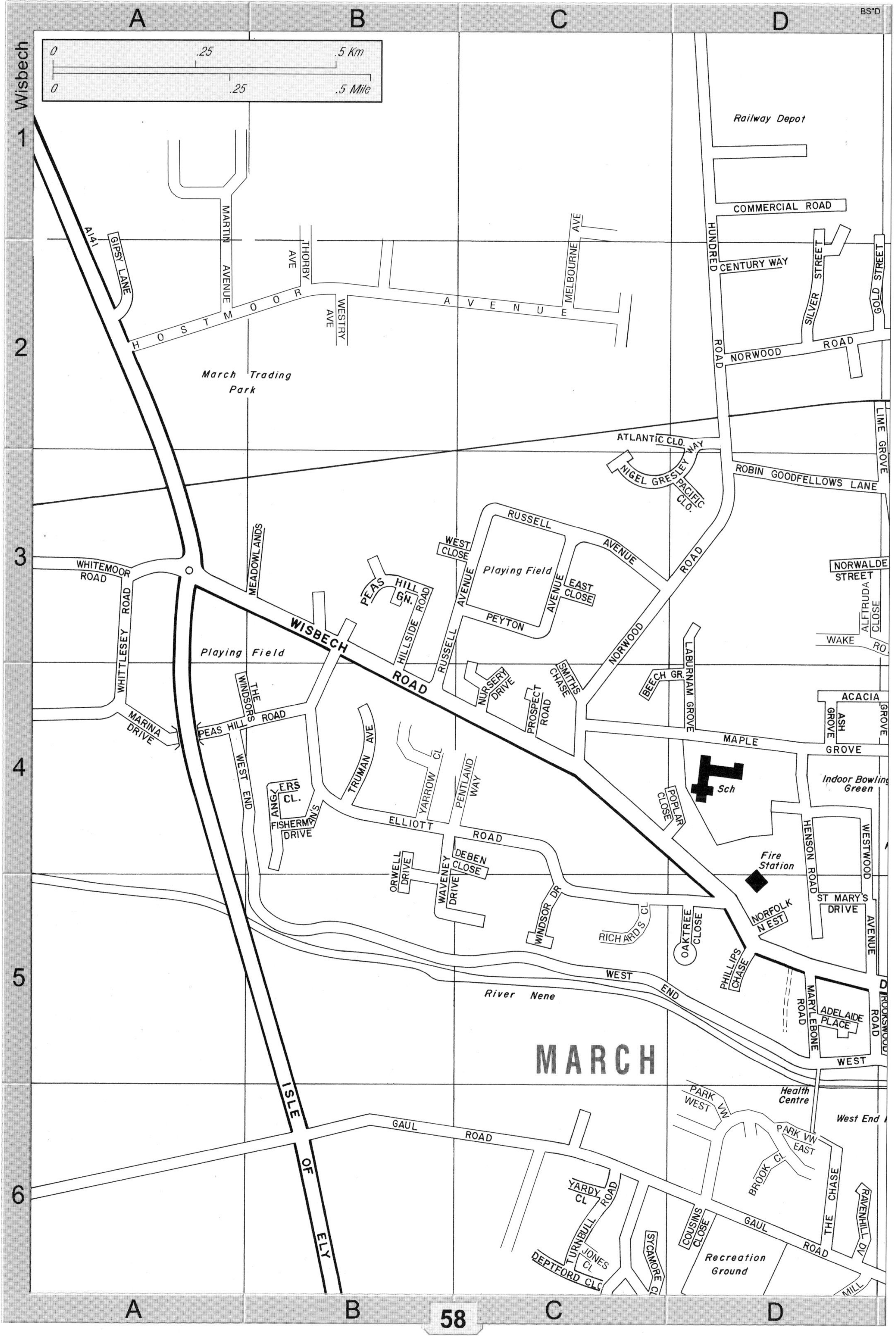

Wisbech
BS"D
A
B
C
D
0
.25
.5 Km
0
.25
.5 Mile
Railway Depot
COMMERCIAL ROAD
MARTIN AVENUE
THORBY AVE
MELBOURNE AVE
HUNDRED ROAD
CENTURY WAY
SILVER STREET
GOLD STREET
A141
GIPSY LANE
HOSTMOOR
WESTRY AVE
AVENUE
NORWOOD ROAD
LIME GROVE
March Trading Park
ATLANTIC CLO.
NIGEL GRESLEY WAY
PACIFIC CLO.
ROBIN GOODFELLOWS LANE
NORWALDE STREET
ALFTRUDA CLOSE
WHITEMOOR ROAD
MEADOWLANDS
WEST CLOSE
RUSSELL
AVENUE
Playing Field
EAST CLOSE
NORWOOD ROAD
WAKE RO
WHITTLESEY ROAD
PEAS HILL GN.
HILLSIDE ROAD
RUSSELL AVENUE
PEYTON
SMITHS CHASE
BEECH GR.
LABURNAM GROVE
ACACIA GROVE
ASH GROVE
GROVE
WISBECH ROAD
Playing Field
Marina Drive
THE WINDSORS
ROAD
PEAS HILL
WEST END
TRUMAN AVE
YARROW CL.
PENTLAND WAY
NURSERY DRIVE
PROSPECT ROAD
MAPLE GROVE
Sch
Indoor Bowling Green
ANGLERS CL.
FISHERMAN'S DRIVE
ELLIOTT ROAD
POPLAR CLOSE
HENSON ROAD
WESTWOOD AVENUE
ORWELL DRIVE
WAVENEY DRIVE
DEBEN CLOSE
WINDSOR DR.
RICHARDS CL.
OAKTREE CLOSE
Fire Station
NORFOLK N EST
ST MARY'S DRIVE
WEST END
River Nene
PHILLIPS CHASE
MARYLEBONE ROAD
ADELAIDE PLACE
BROOKSWOOD ROAD
WEST
MARCH
Health Centre
PARK VW WEST
PARK VW EAST
West End
GAUL ROAD
YARDY CL.
TURNBULL ROAD
BROOK CL.
COUSINS CLOSE
GAUL ROAD
THE CHASE
RAVENHILL DV.
JONES CL.
DEPTFORD CLO.
SYCAMORE CL.
Recreation Ground
MILL

© G I Barnett & Son Ltd.

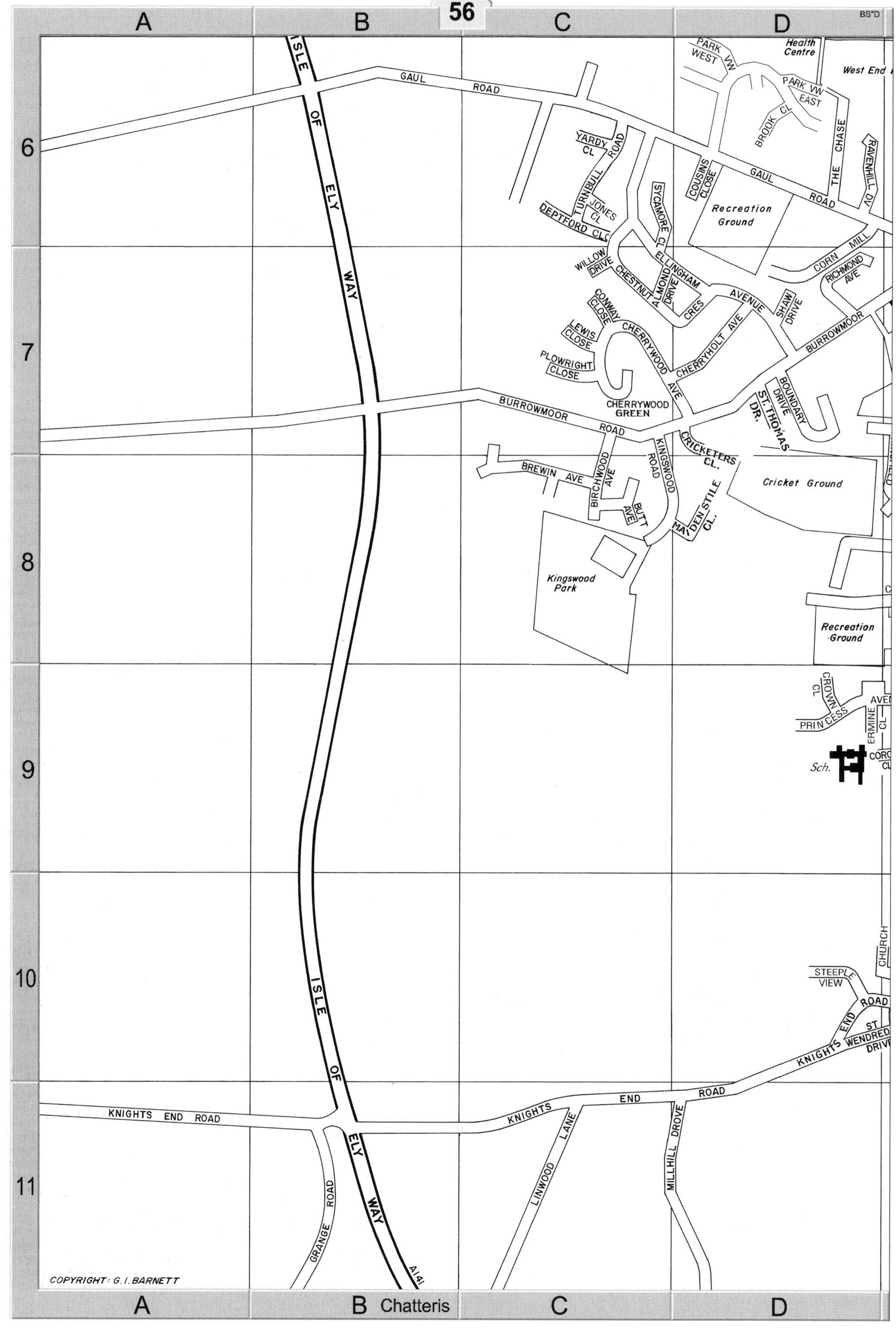
56
A
B
C
D
BS*D
Health Centre
PARK VW WEST
West End
PARK VW EAST
BROOK CL
THE CHASE
RAVENHILL DV
GAUL ROAD
YARDY CL
TURNBULL ROAD
JONES CL
DEPTFORD CL
SYCAMORE CL
ELLINGHAM
COUSINS CLOSE
Recreation Ground
GAUL ROAD
CORN MILL
RICHMOND AVE
WILLOW DRIVE
CHESTNUT A
MOON
CRES
SHAW DRIVE
AVENUE
CONWAY CLOSE
LEWIS CLOSE
CHERRYWOOD
CHERRYHOLT AVE
BURROWMOOR
PLOWRIGHT CLOSE
CHERRYWOOD AVE
CHERRYWOOD GREEN
ST. THOMAS DR.
BOUNDARY DRIVE
BURROWMOOR ROAD
BREWIN AVE
BIRCHWOOD AVE
KINGSWOOD ROAD
CRICKETERS CL.
BUTT AVE
MAIDEN STILE CL.
Cricket Ground
ISLE OF ELY WAY
Kingswood Park
Recreation Ground
CROWN CL
PRINCESS
ERMINE CL
AVE
CORO CL
Sch.
CHURCH
STEEPLE VIEW
ROAD
KNIGHTS END
WENDRED DRIVE
ST
ISLE OF ELY WAY
KNIGHTS END ROAD
KNIGHTS END ROAD
LINWOOD LANE
MILLHILL DROVE
GRANGE ROAD
A141
COPYRIGHT: G.I. BARNETT
A
B Chatteris
C
D
6
7
8
9
10
11

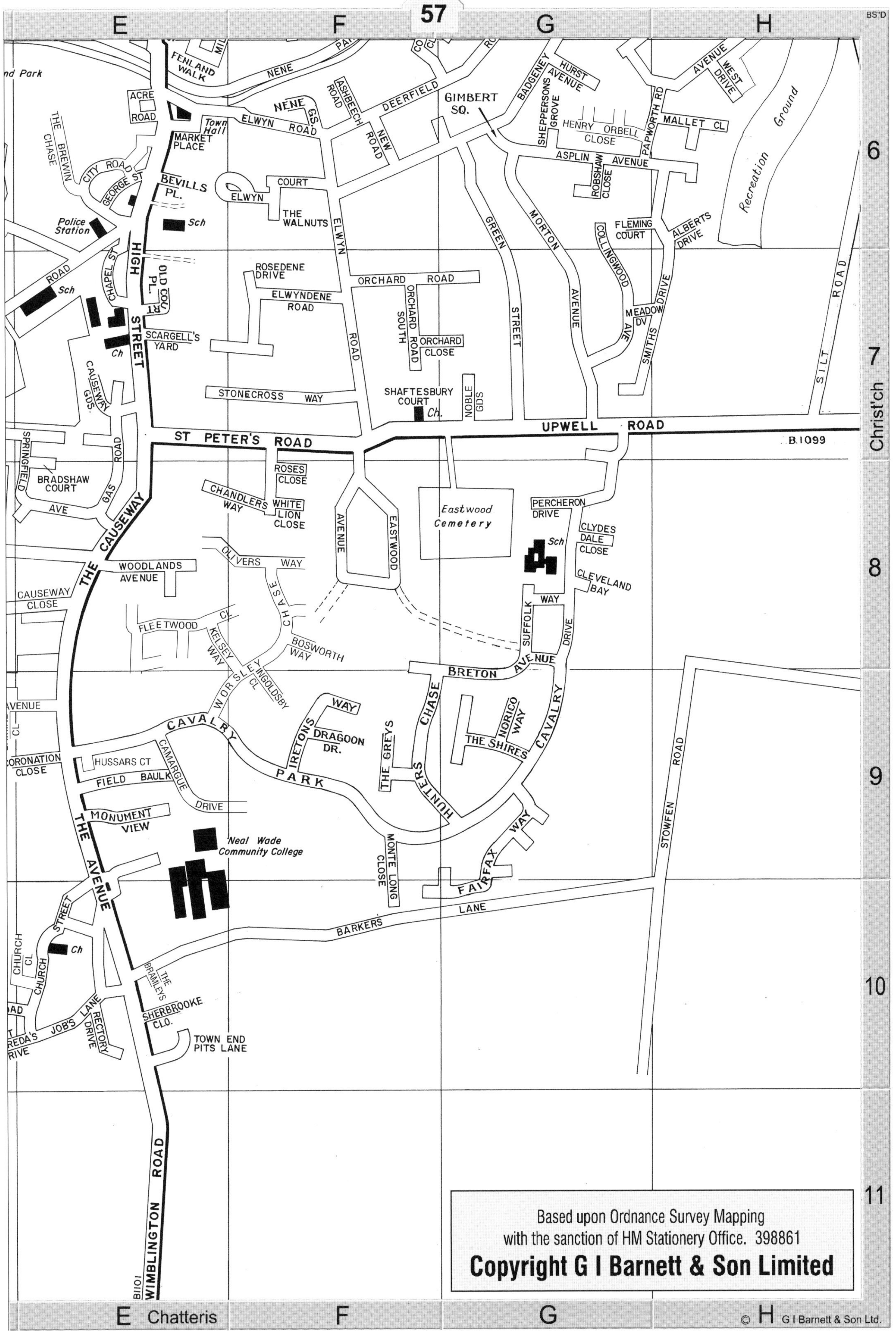

Based upon Ordnance Survey Mapping
with the sanction of HM Stationery Office. 398861
Copyright G I Barnett & Son Limited

MARCH INDEX TO STREETS

Acacia Grove D.4
Acre Road E.6
Adelaide Place..................D.5
Alberts Drive H.6
Alftruda Close D.3
Almond Drive C.7
Alpha Street....................E.4
Anglers Close B.4
Ash Grove D.4
Ashbeech Road F.6
Asplin Close G.6
Atlantic Close..................C.2

Badgeney Road...............G.6
Barkers Lane F.10
Beech Grove C.4
Belmont Road..................F.5
Berryfield F.1
Bevills Place E.6
Birchwood Avenue...........C.8
Bittern Way H.5
Bosworth Way F.8
Boundary Drive D.7
Bradshaw Court...............D.8
Bramble Walk F.1
Breton Avenue.................G.8
Brewin Avenue.................C.8
Broad Street....................E.5
Brook Close D.6
Brooks Road E.5
Burn Street.....................E.4
Burnet Gardens...............G.1
Burrowmoor Road C.7
Butt Avenue C.8

Camargue Drive...............E.9
Camargue Drive...............E.9
Causeway Close E.8
Causeway Gardens E.7
Cavalry Drive...................G.9
Cavalry Park E.10
Cawood Close.................G.2
Cedar Close F.4
Century Way D.2
Chandlers Way D.8
Chapel Street..................E.7
Cherryholt Avenue...........D.7
Cherrywood Avenue C.7
Cherrywood Green C.7
Chesnut Crescent C.7
Church Close.................D.10
Church Street.................E.10
City Road E.6
Cleveland Bay G.8
Clydesdale Close G.8
College Gardens F.2
Collingwood Avenue G.6
Commercial Road D.1
Conway Close C.7
Corn Mill D.7
Coronation Close.............E.9
Cotswold Close F.6
County Road E.3
Cousins Close D.6
Creek Fen H.2
Creek Road G.4
Cricketers Close D.7
Cromwell Road E.4
Crown Close D.9

Dagless Way E.1
Dartford Road E.5
Darthill Road E.5
Deben Close C.4
Deerfield Road F.6
Depford Close C.6

Dragoon Drive F.9

East Close C.3
East Drive H.5
Eastwood Avenue............F.8
Ellingham Avenue C.7
Elliot Road B.4
Elm Close F.2
Elm Road F.2
Elwyn Court F.6
Elwyn Road F.6
Elwyndene Road F.7
Ermine Close...................D.9
Estover Road...................G.2

Fairfax Way G.9
Fairfax Way G.10
Fenland Walk..................E.6
Field Baulk E.9
Fisherman's Drive B.4
Flaggrass Hill Road.........H.1
Fleetwood Close E.8
Fleming Court G.6

Gas Road D.8
Gaul Road B.6
George Street E.6
Gimbert Square...............G.6
Gipsy Lane.....................A.2
Gold Street D.2
Gordon Avenue E.5
Grange Road B.11
Grays Lane E.5
Green Street G.6
Grounds Avenue H.5

Hansart Court E.5
Hawthorne Grove.............E.4
Hazelhurst Close H.5
Heathcote Close H.5
Henford Gardens.............E.5
Henry Orbell Close G.6
Henson Road..................D.4
Hereward Street..............E.4
Heron.............................H.4
High School Close F.3
High Street.....................E.7
Highfield Road E.2
Hillside Road B.3
Hobart Court E.5
Hostmoor Avenue A.2
Hundred Road.................D.1
Hunters Chase F.9
Hurst Avenue..................G.6
Hussars Court E.9

Ingoldsby Close F.9
Iretons Way F.9
Isle of Ely Way................B.6

Jim Hocking Court E.5
Job's Lane E.10
Jones Close...................C.6

Kelsey Way E.9
Kingfisher Close G.4
Kingsley Street................F.4
Kingswood Road C.7
Knights End Road A.11

Laburnam Grove D.3
Lambs Place...................F.5
Landau Way G.3
Lewis Close C.7
Lime Grove D.2
Linwood Lane C.11

Maiden Stile Close D.8
Mallard Way....................H.4
Mallet Close....................H.6
Maple Grove D.4
Marina Drive A.4
Market Place E.6
Marsh Close H.3
Martin Avenue A.1
Marwick Road..................F.1
Marylebone Road D.5
Mayors Close F.1
Meadow Drive G.7
Meadowlands...................B.3
Melbourne Avenue...........C.2
Millhill Drove D.11
Milner Close F.5
Monte Long Close F.9
Monument View...............E.9
Morton Avenue G.6

Nene Gardens F.6
Nene Parade F.6
New Park.........................G.4
Newlands Avenue............F.4
Nigel Gresley Way...........C.3
Nightall Drive E.1
Noble Gardens G.7
Norfolk Court F.5
Norfolk Nest....................D.5
Norico Bay......................G.9
North Drive G.5
North Street E.4
Norwalde Street...............D.3
Norwood Avenue E.5
Norwood Crescent...........E.2
Norwood Road.................D.2
Nursery Drive..................C.4

Oaktree Close D.5
Old Court Place E.7
Olivers Way F.8
Orchard Close F.7
Orchard Road...................F.7
Orchard Road South F.7
Orwell Drive B.5

Pacific Close D.3
Papworth Road G.6
Park View East D.6
Park View West D.6
Peas Hill Green B.3
Peas Hill Road.................A.4
Pentland Way C.4
Percheron Drive G.8
Peter House Crescent F.2
Peyton Avenue C.3
Phillips Chase D.5
Plover Drive.....................H.4
Plowright Close C.7
Poplar Close D.4
Princes Walk E.5
Princess Avenue D.9
Prospect Road.................C.4

Queens Street F.3
Queens Street Close E.3

Ravenhill Drive D.6
Rectory Drive..................E.10
Regent Avenue E.4
Richards Close C.5
Richmond Avenue............D.7
River Drive......................G.5
Robin Goodfellows Lane ..E.4
Robshaw Close G.6

Roman Way.....................G.2
Rookswood Road E.5
Rosedene Drive F.7
Roses Close F.8
Russell Avenue B.3

Scargell's Yard.................E.7
Shaftesbury Avenue G.4
Shaw Drive D.7
Shepperson's Grove G.6
Sherbrooke Close E.10
Silt Road H.7
Silver Street....................D.2
Smiths Chase C.4
Smiths Drive H.7
South Drive G.5
Springfield Avenue...........E.7
St. John's Road..............F.4
St. John's Chase F.4
St. Mary's Drive D.5
St. Peter's Road E.7
St. Thomas Drive.............D.7
St. Wendreda's Drive......D.10
Station Approach F.3
Station Road....................F.4
Steeple View D.10
Stevens Way E.3
Stonecross Way...............E.7
Stowfen Road H.9
Suffolk Way G.8
Swallow Way H.4
Swan Close F.2
Swanton Close.................E.1
Swift Drive H.5
Sycamore Close C.6

The Brewin Chase...........E.6
The Bramleys E.10
The Cause Way...............D.8
The Chase D.6
The Greys.......................F.9
The Hollies G.1
The Laurels F.1
The Shires G.9
The Walnuts F.6
The Windsors..................B.4
Thorby Avenue................B.2
Thornton Road F.3
Town End Pits Lane........E.10
Truman Avenue B.4
Turnbull Road C.6

Upwell Road G.7

Vardy Close C.6

Wake Road D.3
Waterside Gardens G.4
Waveney Drive B.5
West Close B.3
West Drive H.6
West End A.4
Westry Avenue................B.2
Westwood Avenue...........D.4
White Lion Close F.8
Whitemoor Road A.3
Whittlesey Road A.4
Wigstones Road...............F.5
Wilkinson Close F.4
Wilkinson Close F.4
Willow Drive....................C.7
Wimblington Road E.11
Windsor Drive C.5
Wisbech Road B.3
Woodlands Avenue D.8
Worsley Chase E.9

YAXLEY INDEX TO STREETS

Abbott Way A.3
Allard Close....................A.2
Alvis Drive A.2
Appletree Close...............D.2
Ashridge Walk C.2
Askews Lane....................B.3
Austin Court.....................A.1
Azalea Court C.1

Back Lane B.3
Badger Close C.2
Baird Close A.2
Beatons Close.................B.3
Beauvoir Place B.3
Bentley Avenue A.2
Birch Close C.2
Blenheim Way B.3
Bramble Close.................C.3
Broad Drove....................D.3
Broadway C.2
Brunel Drive.....................A.2

Carysfort Close A.3
Chapel Street A.3
Cherry Tree Walk C.2
Church Street A.3
Church Walk A.3
Cock Close Road A.2
Cookson Close A.4

Cookson Walk A.4
Crane Avenue B.2
Crocus Way.....................C.1

Daimler Avenue B.1
Dovecote Lane A.3
Dundee Crest C.2

Edison Drive A.2
Elm Close C.1

Faraday Close..................A.1
Ferndale A.2
Field Rise A.3
Flemming Close A.2
Ford Close B.1
Freesia Way C.1

Great Drove......................C.2
Green Lane A.2

Hawthorn Road C.2
Highfields Walk C.2
Hillcrest Avenue...............B.2
Hillside Walk C.2
Hod Fen Drove B.4
Hog Fen Drove D.3
Humber Drive B.1

Jasmine Way....................C.1
Kingfisher Close A.2

Laburnum Avenue C.2
Lancaster Court................C.2
Lancaster Way C.2
Lansdowne Road B.2
Larch Close C.1
Laurel Close B.3
Lavender Close.................C.2
Lawn Close B.3
Leading Drove B.3
Lee Road...........................A.3
Limetree Close B.1
Litchfield Close B.2
London Road.....................A.2

Main Street B.3
Malting Square B.2
Manor Close A.3
Maple Court......................C.1
Marconi Drive A.2
Marlborough Close B.2
Meadow Walk C.2
Mere Drove B.3
Mere View C.2
Middletons Road B.2
Mile Drove........................D.3
Morgan Close B.2

Morris Court......................A.2
Mountbatten Avenue A.2
Mulberry Close C.2

Nightingale Drive..............A.2

Orchard Walk C.2
Orchid Close C.1
Owl End.............................A.2
Owl End Walk A.2

Park Close.........................B.2
Partridge Close A.2
Peartree Walk C.2
Pheasant Way A.2
Pooley Way A.2
Primrose Drive C.1
Proby Close......................A.3

Queen Street....................B.2
Quickest Drove C.4

Riley Close A.2
Rolls Close B.1
Rosewood Close B.3
Royce Close B.2

Seaton Close....................A.2
Silverwood Walk C.2

Southdown B.2
Speechley Road B.2
Spring Field Road C.2
St. Peter's Walk C.2
Station Road D.1
Stephenson Close............A.2
Stonehouse Road B.3

Telford Drive A.2
The Green B.3
The Rookery A.2

Vicarage Way A.3
Violet Way C.1
Vixen Close......................C.2

Westfield Close A.3
Westfield Road A.3
Willow Road C.2
Windsor Road C.2
Wisteria Road A.3
Wolseley Close A.2
Wykes Road A.3

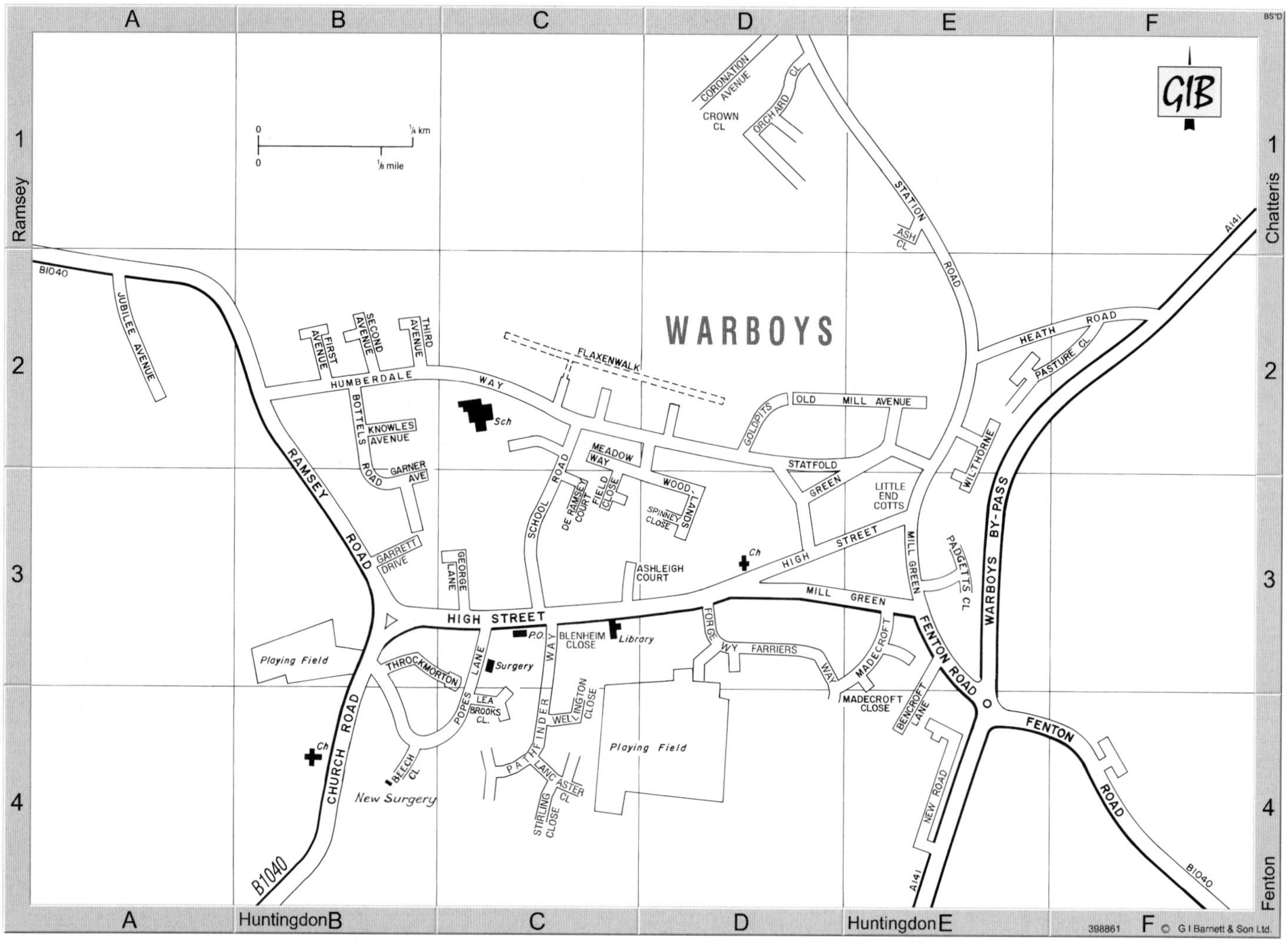

GREAT & LITTLE PAXTON

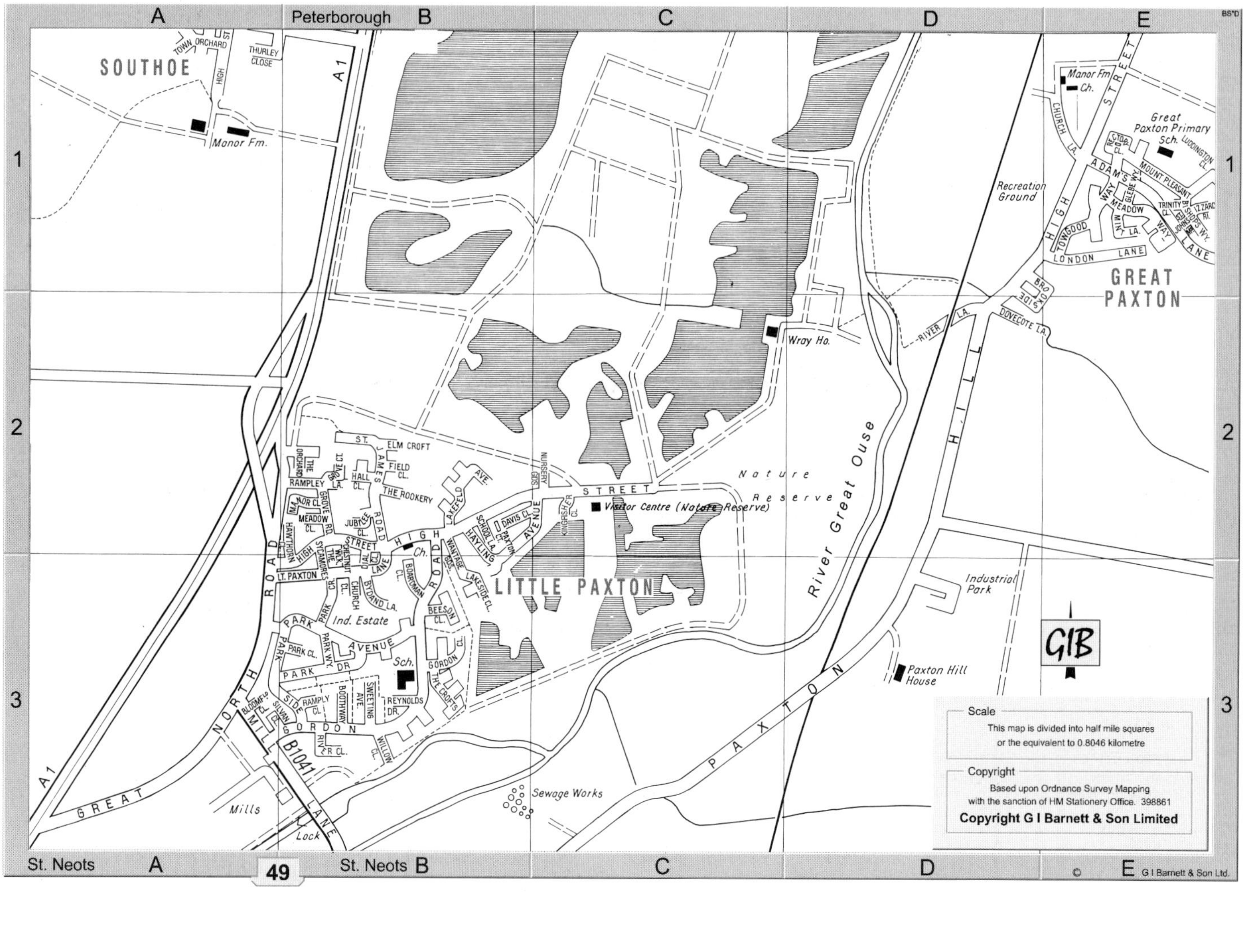

Scale

This map is divided into half mile squares or the equivalent to 0.8046 kilometre

Copyright

Based upon Ordnance Survey Mapping with the sanction of HM Stationery Office. 398861

WARBOYS INDEX TO STREETS

Ash Close E.1
Ashleigh Court C.3

Beech Close B.4
Bencroft Lane E.4
Blenheim Close C.3
Bottles Road B.2

Church Road B.4
Coronation Avenue D.1
Crown Close D.1

De Ramesy Court C.3

Farriers Way............................D.3
Fenton Road E.3
Field Close C.3
First Avenue B.2

Flaxenwalk C.2
Forge Way D.3

Garner Avenue B.3
Garrett Drive B.3
George Lane C.3
Goldpits D.2

Heath Road E.2
High Street C.3
Humberdale Way B.2

Jubilee Avenue A.2

Knowles Avenue B.2

Lancaster Close C.4
Lee Brookes Close C.4

Little End Cottages E.3

Madecroft E.3
Madecroft Close E.4
Meadow Way C.2
Mill Green D.3
Mill Green E.3

New Road E.4

Old Mill Avenue D.2
Orchard Close D.1

Padgetts Close E.3
Pasture Close E.2
Pathfinder Way C.4
Popes Lane C.4
Ramsey Road B.3

School Road C.3
Second Avenue B.2
Spinney Close D.3
Statfold Green D.2
Station Road E.1
Stirling Close C.4

Third Avenue B.2
Throckmorton B.3

Warboys By-Pass E.3
Wellington Close C.4
Wilthorne E.2
Woodlands D.3

GREAT & LITTLE PAXTON INDEX TO STREETS

Adam's Lane............E.1

Beeson Close B.3
Bishops Way............E.1
Bloomfield Close......A.3
Boardman Close......B.3
Boothway B.3
Brookside D.1
Bydand Lane B.3

Chestnut Walk B.2
Church Close B.3
Church Lane E.1

Davis Close B.2
Dial Close B.3

Dovecote Lane D.2
Elm Croft.................B.2

Field Close B.2

Glebe Way E.1
Gordon Close B.3
Gordon Road B.3
Great North Road A.3
GREAT PAXTON E.1
Grove Court B.2
Grove Road B.2

Hall Close B.2
Hawthorn Close B.2
Hayling Avenue.......B.2

High Street B.2
High Street E.1
High Street A.1

Izzard Risa E.1

Jubilee Close B.2

Kingfisher Close C.2

Lakefield Avenue B.2
Lakeside Close.......B.3
LITTLE PAXTON B.3
Little Paxton Lane....B.3
London Lane...........E.1
Luddington Close E.1

Manor Close B.2
Meadow Close B.2
Meadow Way E.1
Mill Lane A.3
Mint Lane E.1
Mount Pleasant......E.1

Nursery Gardens C.2

Park Avenue B.3
Park Close B.3
Park Crescent.........B.3
Park Drive..............B.3
Park Side B.3
Park Way B.3
Paxton Court...........B.2

Paxton Hill C.3-D.2

Rampley Close B.3
Rampley Lane B.2
Rectory Close E.1
Reynolds.................B.3
River Close B.3
River Lane D.2

School Lane B.2
Silvan Close A.3
SOUTHOE A.1
St. James Road B.2
St. John's Mews E.1
Sweeting Avenue B.3

The Crofts...............B.3
The Orchard B.2
The Rookery B.2
The Sycamores B.3
Thurley Close A.1
Towgood Way E.1
Town Orchard A.1
Trinity Close E.1

Wantage Gardens....B.2
Willow Close B.3

COLNE/EARITH/BLUNTISHAM INDEX TO STREETS

Adelaide Walk D.2

BLUNTISHAM A.3
Blacksmiths End A.2
Bluntisham Road
   (Colne) B.2
Bramley Green B.3
Bridge End C.3

Chapel Lane C.3
Chapel Road C.3
COLNE B.2
Colne Road (Earith) C.2
Colne Road
   (Bluntisham) B.3
Cooks Drove D.2

Darford C.2
Drury Lane B.1
Dunholt Way B.1

EARITH C.2
Earith Fen Drove D.1
Earith Road
   (Colne) B.1
East Street,
   Bluntisham A.3
East Street, Colne ..B.2
Edwards Walk C.3
Elizabeth Way B.1

Frogs Hall B.3

Greenfields C.2

Hereward D.2
Hermitage Road D.2
High Street
   (Bluntisham) A.3
High Street (Colne) ..B.1
High Street (Earith) ..C.3
Hollidays Road B.3
Holme Fen Drove C.1

Kingfisher Court........C.3

Laxton Grange B.3

Maple Close A.2

Meadow Drove D.2
Meadow Lane C.2
Meadow Way D.2
Meggs Close B.3
Mill Lane B.3

Nobles Lane A.3

Old Church Lane B.1
Old Farm Court A.2
Orchard Crescent ...C.2
Orchard End A.3
Osier Halt B.1

Parrens Road C.2
Presses Close A.3

Rectory Road A.3

St. Mary's D.2
St. Mary's Close B.3
St. Mary's Road B.3
Sayers Court A.3
School Road C.3
Short Drove C.2
Short Lane A.3
Station Road A.3
Sumerling Way B.3

The Bulwark D.2
The Fairway A.2
The Hawthorns A.2
The Hermitage D.3

The Poplars A.2
The Rhees B.2
The Shires A.3
The Quadrangle B.1
The Sycamores A.2
The Vineyard B.1
The Waterhaven C.3

Vermuyden D.2

Westview Marina C.3
Wheatley Crescent ..A.2
Whybrows Lane C.3
Wood End A.2

SUTTON/MEPAL/WITCHAM INDEX TO STREETS

Astley Close B.3

Bellairs B.3
Brangehill Lane B.1
Brick Lane B.1
Bridge Road B.1
Brookside B.3
Bury Lane A.2

Cherry Rise A.3
Chestnut Way..........................B.1
Churchill Close B.3
Church Lane C.3
Cromwell Road B.3

Eastwood Close C.3
Elizabeth Court B.3

Fairfield B.3
Field Gate B.3

Garden Close C.3

Headley's Lane D.2

High Street, Mepal B.1
High Street, Sutton B.3
High Street, Witcham D.2
Hillside A.3
Hive Road D.1

Laurel Close B.1
Lawn Lane C.3
Link Lane B.3
Longview B.3

Market Way D.2
Markfield Rise B.3
Marins Lane D.2
Meadow Way B.1
MEPAL B.1
Mepal Road, Sutton B.2
Mepal Road, Witcham C.1
Mill Field B.2
Mostyn Close B.3

New Road B.1
Nunns Way B.3

Oates Lane C.3
Painters Lane B.3
Park Road C.3
Pound Lane B.3
Priors Court B.3

Rectory Fields B.1
Red Lion Lane B.3
Red Lion Walk B.3
River Close B.1
Rosemary Lane A.3

Saffron Piece B.3
School Lane B.1
Scott Court B.3
Silver Street D.2
Station Road C.3
Stewards Close B.3
Stewards Lane B.3
SUTTON B.3
Sutton Court C.3
Sutton Park C.3

The America A.3

The Brook B.3
The Close B.3
The Orchards, Sutton B.3
The Orchard, Witcham D.2
The Row A.3
The Southerns B.3
Tower Road C.3
Tramar Drive C.3

Vermuyden Gardens B.3
Victoria Place B.3

WITCHAM D.2
West Lodge Lane A.3
Westway Place D.2
Wilton Gardens B.1
Windmill Lane B.3
Windmill Walk B.3
Witcham Road, Mepal B.1
Witcham Road, Witcham D.3

York Road A.3

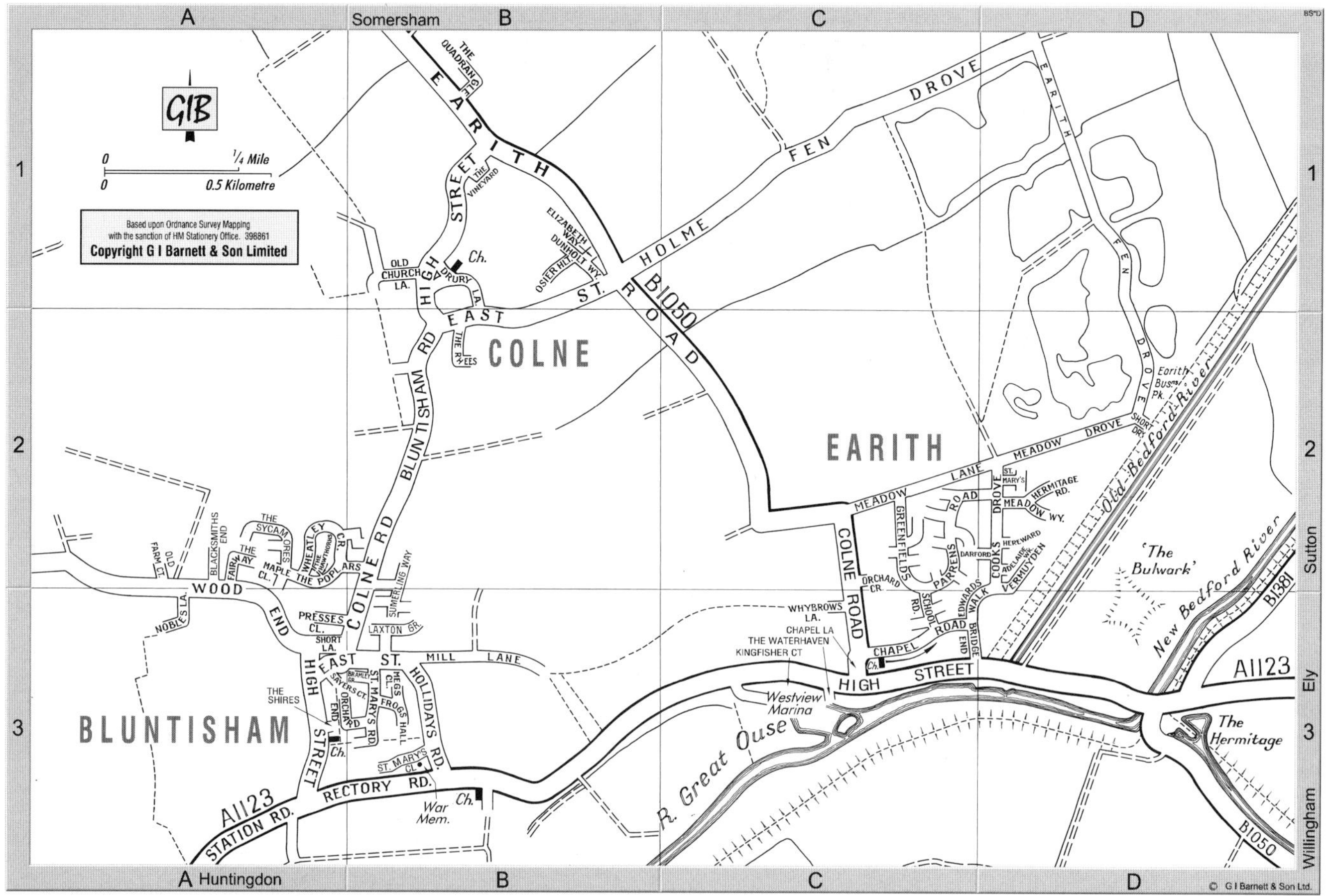

SUTTON/MEPAL/WITCHAM

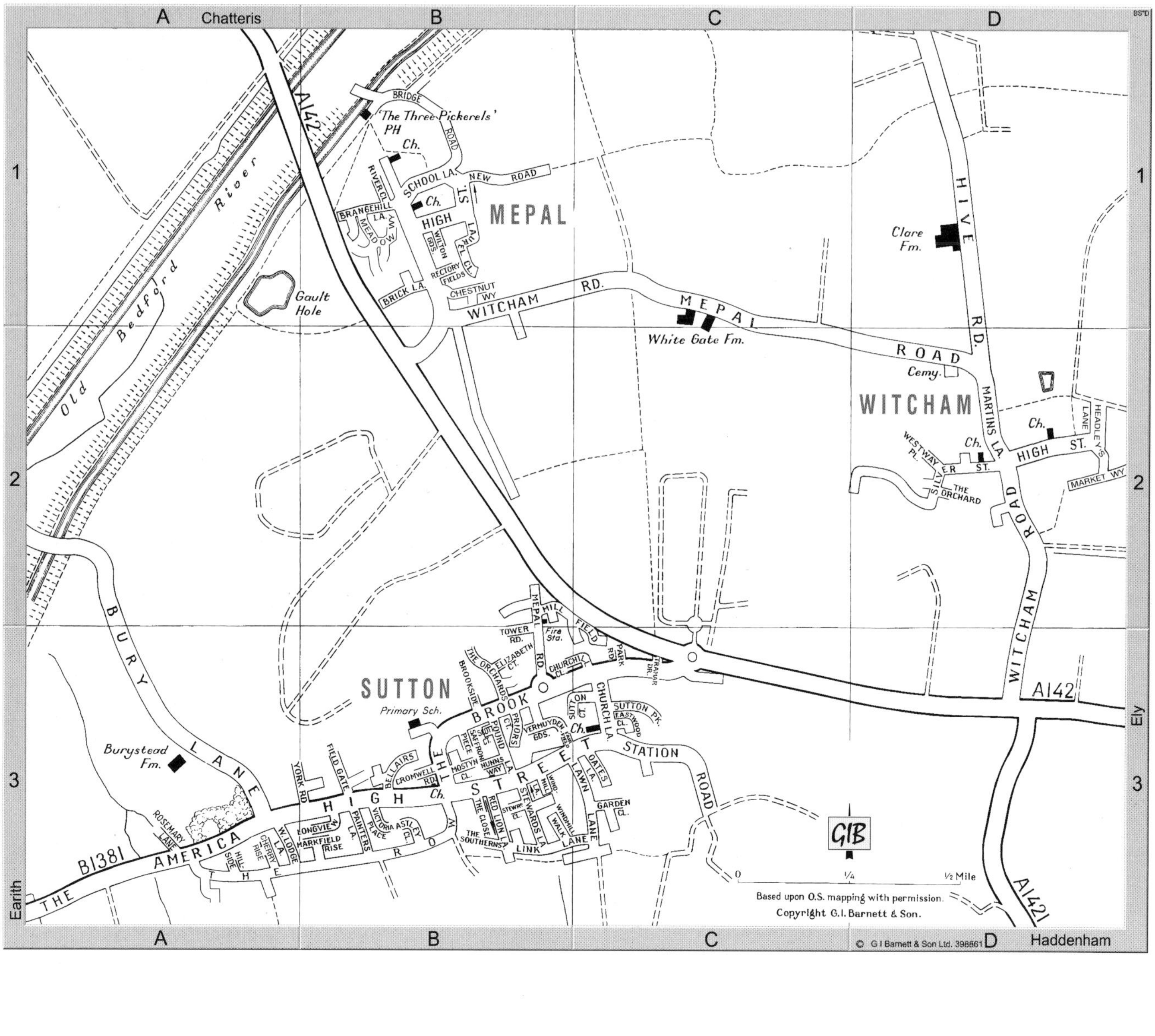

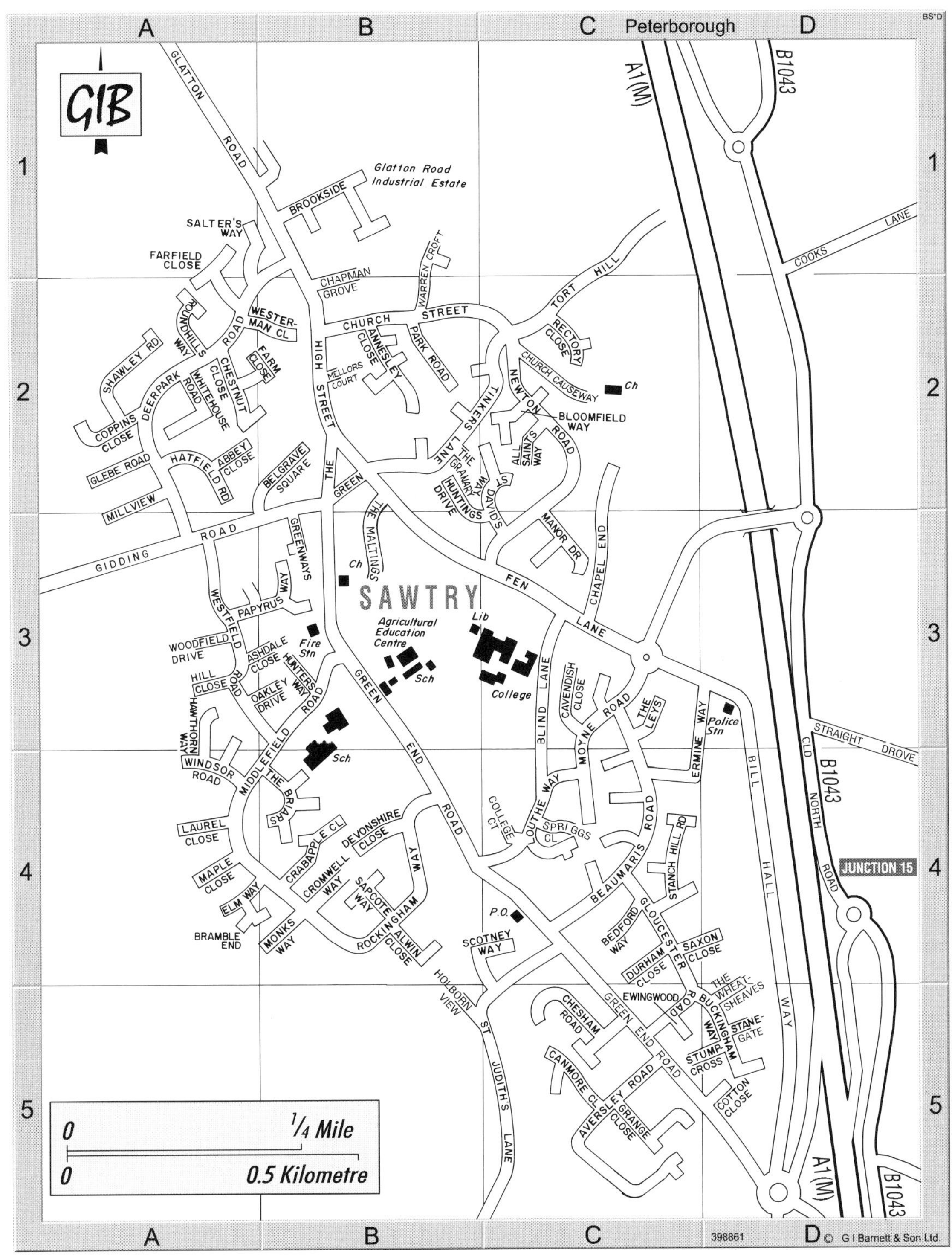

SAWTRY INDEX TO STREETS

Abbey Close A.2
All Saints Way C.2
Alwin Close B.4
Annesley Close B.2
Ashdale Close B.3
Aversley Road C.5

Beaumaris Road C.4
Bedford Way C.4
Belgrave Square B.2
Bill Hall Way D.4
Blind Lane C.3
Bloomfield Way C.2
Bramble End A.4
Brookside B.1
Buckingham Way D.5

Canmore Close C.5
Cavendish Close C.3
Chapel End C.3
Chapman Grove B.1
Chesham Road C.5
Chestnut Close A.2
Church Causeway C.2
Church Street B.2
College Court C.4
Cooks Lane D.1
Coppins Close A.2

Cotton Close D.5
Crabapple Close B.4
Cromwell Way B.4

Deerpark Road A.2
Devonshire Close B.4
Durham Close C.4

Elm Way A.4
Ermine Way C.3
Ewingswood C.5

Fairfield Close A.1
Farm Close B.2
Fen Lane C.3

Gidding Road A.3
Glatton Road A.1
Glebe Road A.2
Gloucester Road C.4
Grange Close C.5
Green End Road B.3
Greenways B.3

Hatfield Road A.2
Hawthorn Way A.3
High Street B.2
Hill Close A.3

Holborn View B.5
Hunters Way B.3
Huntings Drive B.2

Laurel Close A.4
Louthe Way C.4

Manor Drive C.3
Maple Close A.4
Mellors Court B.2
Middlefield Road A.4
Millview A.2
Monks Way B.4
Moyne Road C.3

Newton Road C.2

Oakley Drive B.3
Old North Road D.3

Papyrus Way A.3
Park Road B.2

Rectory Close C.2
Rockingham Way B.4
Roundhills Way A.2

St. David's Way C.2

St. Judith's Lane C.5
Salters Way A.1
Sapcote Way B.4
Saxon Close C.4
Scotney Way B.4
Shawley Road A.2
Spriggs Close C.4
Stanch Hill Road C.4
Stanegate D.5
Straight Drove D.3
Stump Cross D.5

The Briars B.4
The Granary B.2
The Green B.2
The Leys C.3
The Maltings B.3
The Wheatsheaves D.5
Tinkers Lane B.2
Tort Hill C.2

Warren Croft B.2
Westerman Close B.2
Westfield Road A.3
Whitehouse Road A.2
Windsor Road A.4
Woodfield Drive A.3

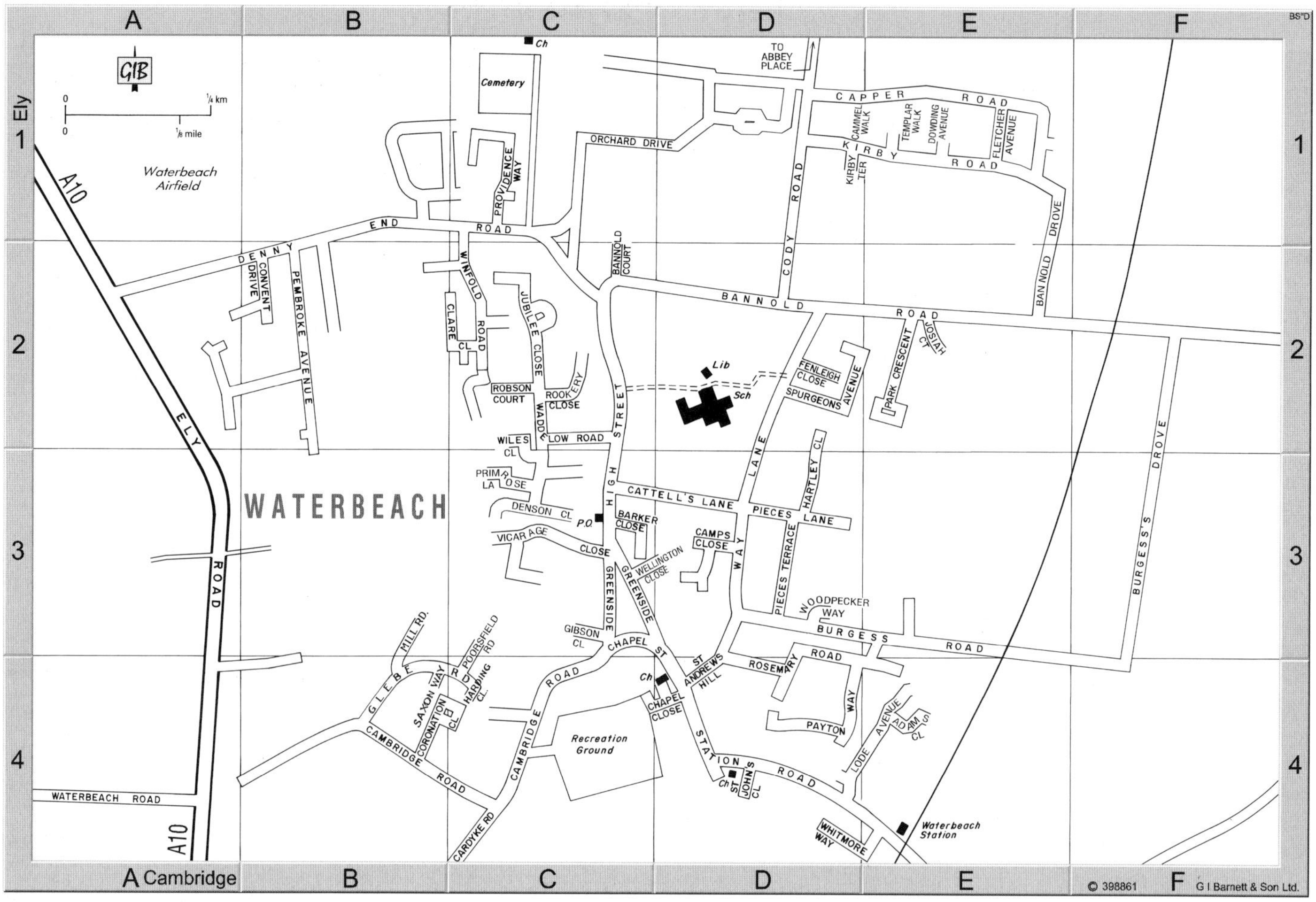

HADDENHAM/WILBURTON

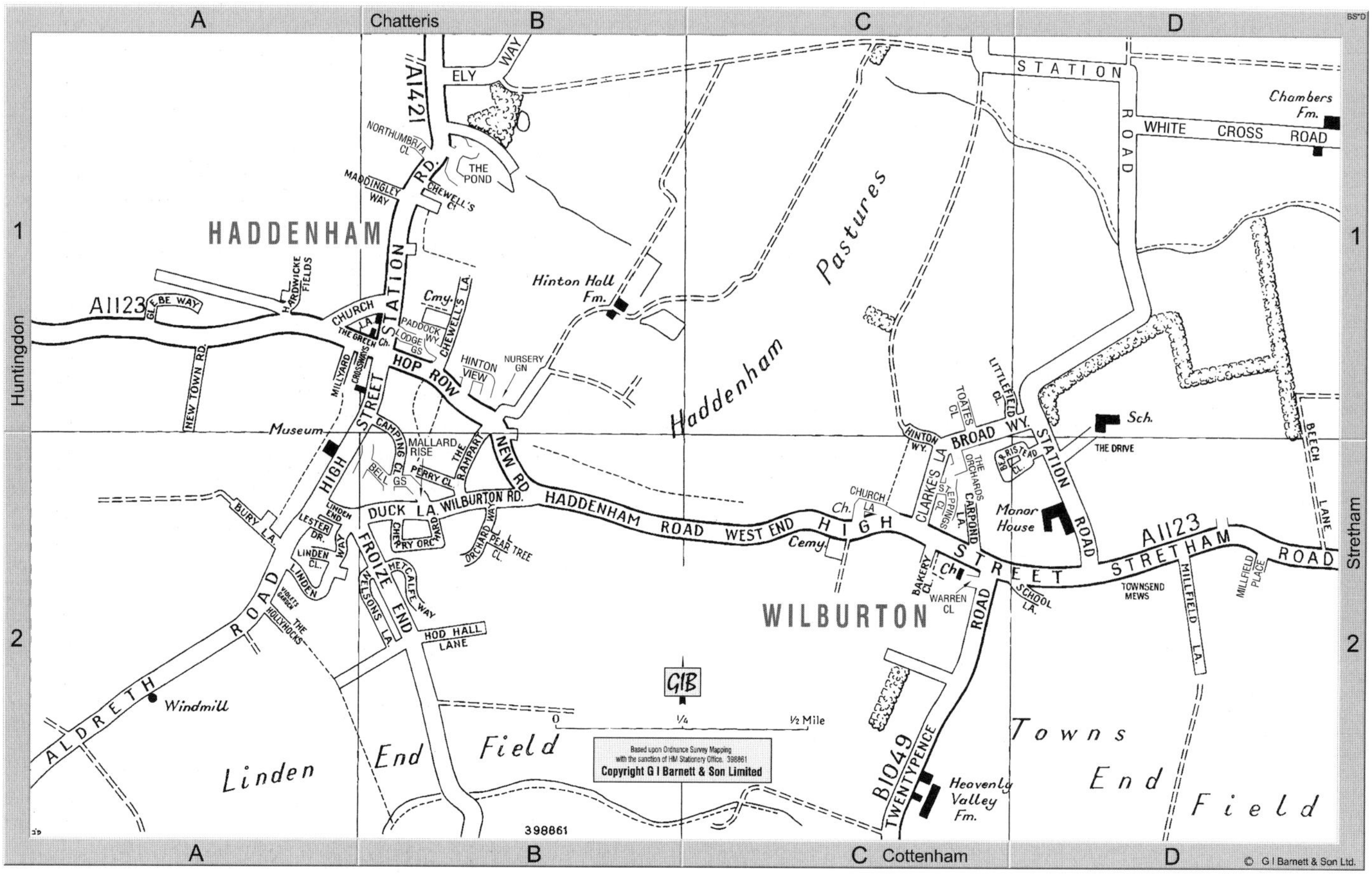

WATERBEACH INDEX TO STREETS

Abbey Place..............................D.1
Adams Court E.4

Bannold Court C.2
Bannold Drove E.2
Bannold Road D.2
Barker Close C.3
Burgess Drove F.3
Burgess Road D.3

Cambridge Road B.4
Cammel Walk D.1
Camps Close D.3
Capper Road D.1
Cardyke Road C.4
Cattell's Lane C.3
Chapel Close D.4
Chapel Street C.3
Clare Close C.2
Cody Road D.2
Convent Drive B.2

Coronation Close B.4

Denny End B.2
Denson Close C.3
Dowding Avenue E.1

Ely Road A.2

Fenleigh Close D.2
Fletcher Avenue E.1

Gibson Close C.3
Glebe Road B.4
Greenside C.3

Harding Close C.4
Hartley Close D.3
High Street C.3

Josiah Court E.2
Jubilee Close C.2

Kirby Road D.1
Kirby Terrace D.1

Lode Avenue D.4

Mill Road B.3

Orchard Drive C.1

Park Crescent E.2
Payton Way D.4
Pembroke Avenue B.2
Pieces Lane D.3
Pieces Terrace D.3
Poorsfield Road C.4
Primrose Lane C.3
Providence Way C.1

Robson Court C.2
Rookery Close C.2
Rosemary Road D.4

St. Andrews Hill D.4
St. Johns Close D.4
Saxon Way B.4
Spurgeons Avenue D.2
Station Road D.4

Templar Walk E.1

Vicarage Close C.3

Waddelow Road C.2
Waterbeach Road A.4
Way Lane D.3
Wellington Close C.3
Whitmore Way D.4
Wiles Close C.2
Winfold Road C.2
Woodpecker Way.....................D.3

HADDENHAM/WILBURTON INDEX TO STREETS

Aldreth Road A.2

Bakery Close C.2
Bell Gardens B.2
Berristead Close C.2
Broad Way C.1
Bury Lane A.2

Camping Close B.1
Carpond Lane C.2
Cherry Orchard B.2
Chewell's Close B.1
Chewell's Lane B.1
Church Lane, Haddenham A.1
Church Lane, Wilburton C.2
Clarke's Lane C.2
Crossways A.1

Duck Lane B.2

Ely Way B.1

Froize End B.2

Glebe Way A.1

Haddenham Road B.2
Hardwicke Fields A.1
High Street,
   Haddenham A.2
High Street,
   Wilburton C.2
Hinton View B.1
Hinton Way C.1
Hod Hall Lane B.2
Hop Row B.1

Lester Drive A.2
Linden Close A.2
Linden End A.2
Linden Way A.2
Littlefield Close C.1
Lodge Gardens B.1

Maddingley Way B.1
Mallard Rise B.2
Manor House D.2
Metcalfe Way B.2
Millfield Lane D.2
Millfield Place D.2
Millyard A.1

Nelsons Lane B.2
New Road B.2
New Town Road A.1
Northumbria Close B.1
Nursery Green B.1

Orchard Way B.2

Paddock Way B.1
Pear Tree Close B.2
Perry Close B.2

School Lane D.2
Station Road, Haddenham B.1

Station Road, Wilburton D.2
Steppings Close C.2
Stretham Road D.2

The Drive D.2
The Green A.1
The Hollyhocks A.2
The Orchards C.2
The Pond B.1
The Rampart B.2
Toates Close C.1
Townsend Mews D.2
Twenty Pence Road C.2

Violets Garden A.2

Warren Close C.2
West End C.2
White Cross Road D.1
Wilburton Road B.2

BUCKDEN INDEX TO STREETS

Aragon Close B.2

Beaufort Drive A.1
Bishops Way B.2
Burberry Road B.2

Church Street A.2
Copes Close B.2
Cranfield Way B.3

Falcon Way B.2
Field Close A.2

George Lane A.2
Glebe Lane A.3
Greenway B.2

High Street A.2
Hoo Close B.2
Hunts End B.2

Ivelbury Close A.2

King George Court A.1

Lark End B.2
Lincoln Close A.1
Lucks Lane A.3

Manor Close A.3
Manor Gardens A.2
Mayfield A.3
Mill Road B.2
Monk's Cottages B.2
Morris Close A.3

Park Road B.2
Perry Road A.3

St. Hughs Road A.2
School Lane B.2
Silver Street A.1
Smith's Drive B.3
Springfield Close A.3
Stirloe Lane A.3
Swan End B.2

Taylors Lane A.2
The Barns B.2
The Grove A.2
The Osiers A.3

Village Hall B.3
Vineyard Way B.2

Weir Close A.3
Wolsey Gardens A.2

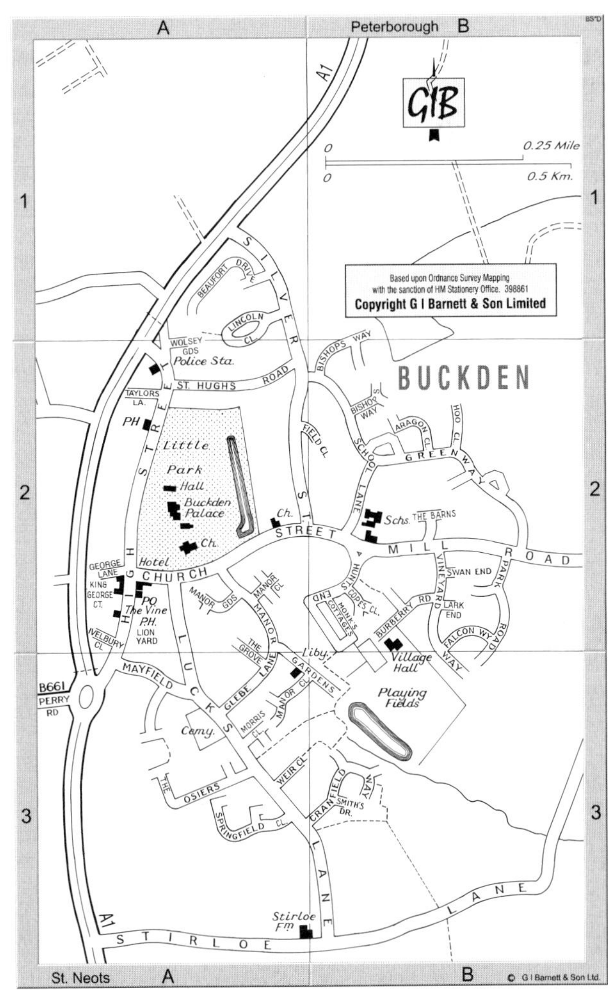

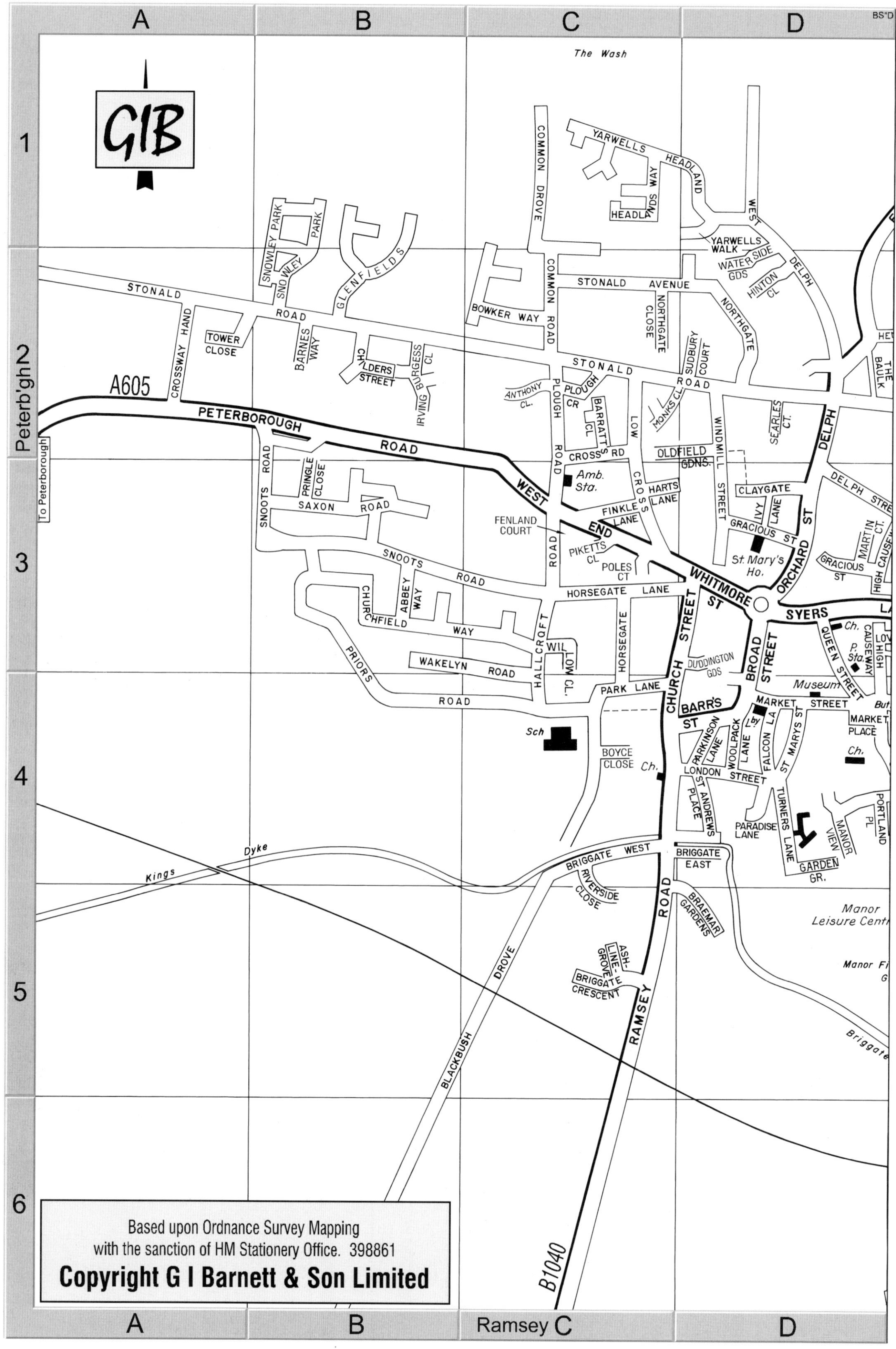
GIB
A
B
C
D
The Wash
BS"D
1
Common Drove
Yarwells Headland
Headlands Way
Headla
West
Yarwells Walk
Water Side Gds
Hinton Cl
Delph
The Baulk
HE
Peterb'gh2
Snowley Park
Snowley Park
Glenfields
Stonald
Crossway Hand
Tower Close
Road
Barnes Way
Childers Street
Irving Burgess Cl
Bowker Way
Common Road
Stonald Avenue
Northgate Close
Sudbury Court
Northgate
Searles Ct.
Delph
Delph Stree
To Peterborough
A605
PETERBOROUGH ROAD
Stonald Road
Anthony Cl.
Plough CR
Plough Road
Barratt's Cl
Low
Monks Cl.
Windmill Street
Oldfield Gdns.
Claygate
Ivy Lane St
Martin Ct.
Gracious St
High Causewa
WEST END
Snoots Road
Pringle Close
Saxon Road
Cross's Rd
Harts Lane
Cross Lane
Finkle Lane
Gracious St
Amb. Sta.
St. Mary's Ho.
Claygate
3
Fenland Court
Road
Piketts Cl
Poles Ct
WHITMORE ST
Orchard St
Syers La
Snoots Road
Abbey Way
Churchfield Way
Horsegate Lane
Horsegate
Hallcroft
Wil Low Cl.
Park Lane
Church Street
Duddington Gds
Broad Street
Queen Street
Museum
Ch. P. Sta.
Lov High
Priors Road
Wakelyn Road
Barr's St
Parkinson Lane
Woolpack Lane
Falcon La
Lby
Market St Marys St Street
Market Place
Ch.
But
4
Sch
Boyce Close
Ch.
London St
St Andrews Place
Paradise Lane
Turners Lane
Garden Gr.
Manor View
Portland Pl
Dyke
Kings
Briggate West
Riverside Close
Briggate East
Braemar Gardens
Manor Leisure Cent
Manor Fi G
5
Blackbush Drove
Ash-Line-Grove
Briggate Crescent
Ramsey Road
Briggate
6
B1040
Ramsey
Based upon Ordnance Survey Mapping
with the sanction of HM Stationery Office. 398861
Copyright G I Barnett & Son Limited

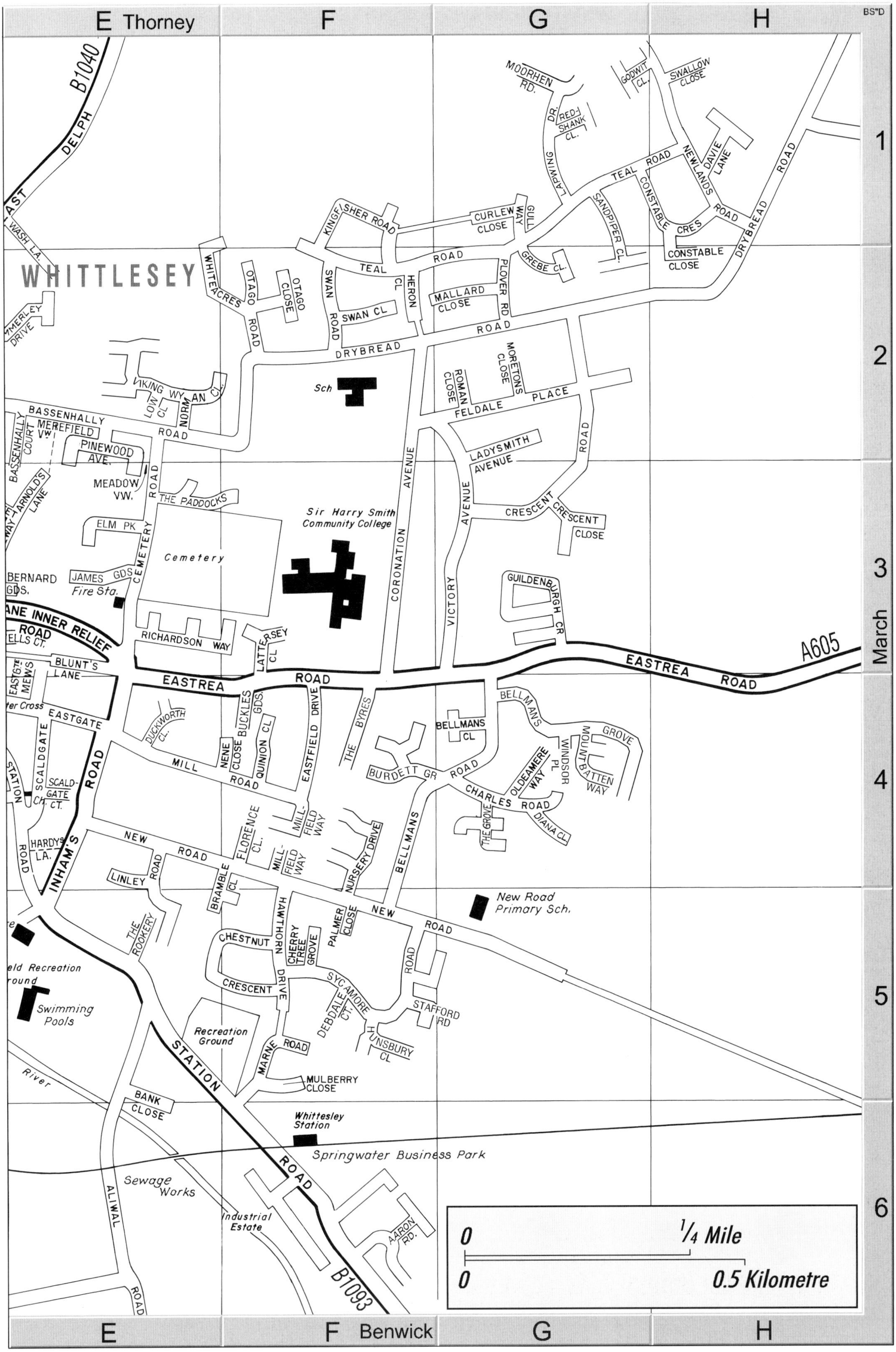

BS"D
E Thorney
F
G
H
WHITTLESEY
B1040
DELPH
LAST
WASH LA.
YMERLEY DRIVE
WHITEACRES
OTAGO ROAD
OTAGO CLOSE
KINGFISHER ROAD
SWAN ROAD
SWAN CL.
TEAL CL.
HERON
CURLEW CLOSE
ROAD
MALLARD CLOSE
PLOVER RD.
GULL WAY
GREBE CL.
LAPWING
DR.
REDSHANK CL.
MOORHEN RD.
SANDPIPER CL.
TEAL ROAD
CONSTABLE
CRES
GODWIT CL.
SWALLOW CLOSE
NEWLANDS ROAD
DAVIE LANE
DRYBREAD ROAD
CONSTABLE CLOSE
1
DRYBREAD
ROAD
ROMAN CLOSE
FELDALE
MORETONS CLOSE
PLACE
ROAD
2
VIKING WY
SWAN CL.
LOW CL.
NORMAN CL.
Sch
ROAD
LADYSMITH AVENUE
BASSENHALLY
BASSENHALLY COURT
MEREFIELD VW.
PINEWOOD AVE.
MEADOW VW.
ROAD
CEMETERY ROAD
THE PADDOCKS
ELM PK
CORONATION AVENUE
Sir Harry Smith Community College
VICTORY AVENUE
CRESCENT
CRESCENT CLOSE
WAY
ARNOLD'S LANE
BASSENHALLY
BERNARD GDS.
JAMES GDS.
Fire Sta.
Cemetery
RICHARDSON WAY
LATTERSEY CL.
GUILDENBURGH CR.
3
LANE INNER RELIEF
ROAD
WELLS CT.
EASTGATE MEWS
BLUNT'S LANE
ter Cross
EASTGATE
SCALDGATE
EASTREA
ROAD
DUCKWORTH CL.
NENE CLOSE
BUCKLES GDS.
QUINION CL.
EASTFIELD DRIVE
THE BYRES
BURDETT GR.
ROAD
BELLMANS CL.
BELLMAN'S ROAD
OLDEAMERE WAY
CHARLES ROAD
THE GROVE
DIANA CL.
WINDSOR PL.
MOUNTBATTEN WAY
GROVE
EASTREA
ROAD
A605
March
STATION ROAD
SCALDGATE CT.
Ch.
HARDY'S LA.
INHAM'S ROAD
MILL ROAD
FLORENCE CL.
MILLFIELD WAY
MILLFIELD WAY
NURSERY DRIVE
BELLMANS
4
NEW ROAD
LINLEY
THE ROOKERY
BRAMBLE CL.
HAWTHORN DRIVE
CHESTNUT
CRESCENT
CHERRY TREE GROVE
PALMER CLOSE
SYCAMORE CT.
DEBDALE CT.
HUNSBURY CL.
NEW ROAD
New Road Primary Sch.
STAFFORD RD.
e
eld Recreation Ground
Swimming Pools
River
STATION
Recreation Ground
MARNE ROAD
MULBERRY CLOSE
5
BANK CLOSE
Whittlesey Station
Springwater Business Park
Sewage Works
ALIWAL
Industrial Estate
AARON RD.
ROAD
B1093
0   1/4 Mile
0   0.5 Kilometre
6
E
F Benwick
G
H

WHITTLESEY INDEX TO STREETS

Aaron Road F.6
Abbey Way B.3
Aliwal Road E.6
Anthony Close...............C.2
Arnold's Lane E.3
Ashline Grove C.5

Bank Close E.5
Barnes Way..................B.2
Barr's Street D.4
Barratt's Close C.2
Bassenhally Road E.2
Bellmans Close.............G.4
Bellmans Grove G.4
Bellmans Road F.4
Bernard Gardens D.3
Blackbush Drove...........B.5
Blunt's Lane E.3
Bowker Way C.2
Boyce Close C.4
Braemar Gardens D.5
Bramble Close..............E.4
Briggate Crescent C.5
Briggate East D.4
Briggate West C.4
Broad Street D.3
Buckles Gardens F.4
Burdett Grove F.4

Cemetery Road.............E.3
Charles Road G.4
Cherry Tree Grove.........F.5
Chestnut Crescent.........F.5
Childers Street B.2
Church Street C.4
Churchfield Way B.3
Claygate D.3
Common Drove.............C.1
Common Road C.2
Constable Close H.2
Constable Crescent H.1
Coronation Avenue F.3
Crescent Close G.3
Crescent Road G.3
Cross Road..................C.2
Crossway Hand.............A.2
Curlew Close G.1

Davie Lane H.1
Debdale Court F.5
Delph..........................D.2
Delph Street D.3
Diana Close G.4

Drybread Road F.2
Duckworth Close...........E.4
Duddington Gardens......D.3

East Delph....................E.1
Eastfield Drive F.4
Eastgate E.4
Eastgate Mews E.4
Eastrea Road G.3
Elm Park E.3

Falcon Lane D.4
Feldale Place G.2
Fenland Court C.3
Finkle Lane C.3
Florence Close..............F.4

Garden Grove D.4
Glenfields B.2
Godwit Close G.1
Gracious Street.............D.3
Guildenburgh
    Crescent G.3
Gull Way G.1

Hallcroft Road C.3
Hardys Lane E.4
Harts Lane C.3
Hawthorn Drive F.5
Headlands Way..............C.1
Hemmerley Drive D.2
Heron Close..................F.2
High Causeway..............D.3
Hinton Close D.2
Horsegate C.3
Horsegate Lane C.3
Hunsbury Close F.5

Inham's Road E.4
Inner Relief Road E.3
Irving Burgess Close......B.2
Ivy Lane D.3

James Gardens.............E.3

Kingfisher Road F.1

Ladysmith Avenue G.2
Lapwing Drive...............G.1
Lattersey Close F.3
Linely Road E.4
London Street D.4
Lovells Court.................D.3

Low Close E.2
Low Cross C.2

Mallard Close G.2
Manor View D.4
Market Place D.4
Market Street D.4
Marne Road F.5
Martin Court D.3
Meadow View E.3
Merefield View...............E.2
Mill Road E.4
Millfield Way.................F.4
Monks Close C.2
Moorhen Road G.1
Moretons Close.............G.2
Mountbatten Way G.4
Mulberry Close F.5

Nene Close F.4
New Road E.4
Newlands Road..............H.1
Norman Close E.2
Northgate D.2
Northgate Close C.2
Nursery Drive.................F.4

Oldeamere Way G.4
Oldfield Gardens............C.2
Orchard Street D.3
Otago Close...................F.2
Otago Road F.2

Palmer Close F.5
Paradise Lane................D.4
Park Lane C.4
Parkinson Lane..............D.4
Peterborough
    Road A.2
Piketts Close C.3
Pinewood Avenue E.2
Plough Crescent C.2
Plough Road C.2
Plover Road G.2
Poles Court C.3
Portland Place...............D.4
Pringle Close.................B.3
Priors Road B.3

Queen Street.................D.3
Quinon Close.................F.4

Ramsey Road C.5

Redshank Close G.1
Richardson Way E.3
Riverside Close.............C.4
Roman Close G.2

Sandpiper Close G.1
Saxon Road B.3
Scaldgate E.4
Scaldgate Court E.4
Searles Court D.2
Snoots Road B.3
Snowley Park B.2
St. Andrews Place.........D.4
St. Marys Street D.4
Stafford Road................F.5
Station Road E.4
Stonald Avenue.............C.2
Stonald Road A.2
Sudbury Court...............D.2
Swallow Close...............H.1
Swan Close F.2
Swan Road F.2
Sycamore Road.............F.5
Syers Lane D.3

Teal Road.....................F.2
Teal Road G.1
The Baulk D.2
The Byres F.4
The Grove....................G.4
The Paddocks E.3
The Rookery E.5
Tower Close A.2
Turners Lane.................D.4

Victory Avenue G.3
Viking Way E.2

Wakelyn Road...............B.3
Waterside Gardens D.2
West Delph D.1
West End C.3
Whiteacres Road............E.2
Whitmore Street D.3
Willow Close C.3
Windmill Street D.2
Windsor Place...............G.4
Woolpack Lane D.4

Yarwells Headland C.1
Yarwells Walk D.1

WISBECH INDEX TO STREETS

Acacia Avenue D.2
Admirals Drive D.2
Albany Road D.3
Albert Court D.4
Alexandra Road C.4
Algores Way.................C.5
All Saints Avenue F.2
Anderson Close C.2
Apeldoorn Walk E.2
Ardleigh Close E.3
Arles Avenue E.5
Armada Close D.2
Artillery Street D.4
Ashdale Park B.4

Baldwin Close D.4
Balmoral Close.................E.2
Bank Drive C.2
Bannister Row C.2
Barton Road B.4
Bath Road D.2
Baxter Close.................E.3
Beatrice Road D.2
Bedford Street D.3
Beechwood Close D.2
Beechwood Road D.2
Black Bear Lane.................E.2
Blackfriars Road.................D.4
Blenheim Way E.5
Boleness Road.................D.5
Borough Close D.5
Bowthorpe Hall Gardens D.3
Bowthorpe Road D.3
Boyce's Road E.4
Boydon Court.................D.4
Braeburn Avenue D.2
Bramley Road D.2
Brampton Close B.4
Brancaster Court E.3
Bridge Street C.4
Brigstock Road.................C.2
Brittania Way C.5
Broadend Road F.4
Buckingham Walk E.2
Burcroft Road.................C.3
Burdett Road C.4
Burrett Gardens F.3
Burrett Gate Road F.4
Burrett Road F.2
Bush Lane E.4

Cambridge Drive B.3
Canal Street.................D.3
Cannon Street D.4
Cannon Terrace D.4
Carmargue Place E.5
Castle Square D.4
Catherine Terrace D.4
Chapel Road C.4
Chapel Street.................D.4
Chapnall Close F.3
Chapnall Road E.3
Charles Street D.4
Chase Street D.3
Cherry Road.................D.2
Chestnut Road.................D.4
Christopher Drive.................C.2
Church Mews.................D.4
Church Road E.3
Church Terrace D.4
Churchill Road D.3
Claremont Road.................E.4
Clarence Road.................D.3
Clarkson Avenue D.3
Clarkson Court.................D.3
Clayton Close.................E.3
Clarkson Court.................D.3
Coalwharf Road C.4
Cocketts Drive E.4
Coldhorn Crescent E.2
Colvile Road.................E.3
Conference Way D.2
Coppins Court E.5
Cordon Street.................D.4
Cornhill.................C.4
Corporation Road.................D.5
Council Road E.3
Crab Marsh C.2
Cricketers Way.................C.3
Cromwell Road C.4

DeHavilland Court D.3
DeHavilland Road D.3
Discovery Walk E.5
Dowgate Road B.2
Duke Street D.4

East Place D.3
East Street.................D.3
Eastfield Road E.2
Eastfield Way D.3
Edinburgh Drive D.2
Eighth Avenue E.4

Elizabeth Terrace D.4
Elm High Road.................D.5
Elm Low Road D.5
Elm Road D.4
Ely Place D.4
Enterprise Way.................B.5
Europa Way C.5
Exchange Square C.3

Falcon Road.................D.4
Falklands Drive E.5
Fardell Road D.4
Felsted Avenue E.3
Fen Close E.3
Fenland Road E.3
Fifth Avenue E.4
First Avenue E.4
Fourth Avenue E.4
Freedom Bridge D.3
Frinton Way E.4
Fundrey Road E.3

Gaol Street.................D.4
Gloucester Court D.2
Goddard Crescent D.2
Godwin Road D.2
Golding Place.................D.4
Grange Road B.2
Great Eastern Road.................C.4
Green Lane.................F.4
Grimmers Road E.3
Grosvenor Road.................D.2
Guild Road E.3

Haley Close D.2
Halfpenny Lane D.5
Halstead Close.................E.3
Hampden Road D.3
Hanchant Court D.4
Harecroft Road.................C.3
Harolds Drive F.3
Hawkins Drive E.3
Hawthorn Avenue.................C.2
Hazel Gardens D.4
Hedgelands D.2
Heney Street D.3
Henson Close D.2
Hereward Road D.4
Heron Road D.5
High Street.................C.4
Hill Street D.3
Hillburn Road C.4
Hogherd's Lane D.4
Holmes Drive E.3
Horsefair D.3
Horseshoe Terrace.................C.2
Howletts Hill D.4
Hunchback Lane E.1

Jasmin Close E.2
Jeffery Avenue E.2
John F. Kennedy Court D.4
John Thompson Road D.4
Jubilee Walk.................E.2

Keillers Close C.2
Kenlan Road D.3
Kestrel Drive D.5
Kinderley Road D.2
King Street D.4
King's Road C.4
King's Walk D.4
Kings Way F.2
Kingsfiisher Drive.................D.5
Kingsley Avenue C.4
Kirkgate Street E.2
Kooreman Avenue D.2

Laburnum Close.................E.2
Lake Court D.4
Larkfield F.1
Lebanon Drive F.2
Legge Bourke Court F.3
Lerowe Road E.3
Lesbaux Place E.5
Leverington Road.................C.3
Lickings Drove B.5
Lilac Close E.2
Lime Avenue D.2
Little Church Street D.4
Little Dowgate B.2
Lonsdale Terrace D.4
Love Lane D.4
Lucombe Drive F.2
Lynn Road D.3

Magazine Close B.4
Magazine Lane B.4
Maldon Road E.4
Malt Drive.................C.5
Manor Gardens B.4
Mansell Road.................D.5

Maple Avenue D.2
Market Mews D.4
Market Place D.4
Market Street D.4
Marlborough Court.................C.4
Mayflower Road.................E.4
Meadowgate Lane E.5
Medway Close E.4
Mill Close D.3
Milner Road D.4
Money Bank E.4
Mount Drive D.4
Mount Pleasant Road D.2
Mountbatten Drive B.2
Museum Square.................D.4
Musicott Place F.3
Myles Way D.2

Napier Court.................D.4
Nelson Gardens.................D.3
Nene Court.................D.4
Nene Parade C.2
Nene Quay.................C.4
New Common Bridge.................D.5
New Drove D.5
Norfolk Street.................D.4
North Brink B.5
North End.................C.3
North Street C.3
North Terrace C.3
Norwich Road D.4
Nursery Drive E.2

Oaklands Drive F.2
Oakley Close E.4
Oakroyd Crescent D.3
Octagon Drive C.3
Octavia Close.................E.3
Odom Street.................D.3
Oil Mill Lane C.3
Old Lynn Road E.2
Old Market C.3
Oldfield Lane C.4
Ollard Avenue.................E.2
Onyx Court.................D.4
Opportune Road D.3
Orange Grove D.4
Orchard Drive E.4
Osborne Park.................D.1
Osborne Road C.2
Oxburgh Close B.2

Park Avenue.................D.3
Park Road D.4
Park Street.................D.4
Payne Avenue D.2
Peatlings Lane B.2
Peckover Drive.................D.4
Pedley Lane C.3
Peldon Drive.................E.4
Pendula Road E.2
Penrose Gardens E.4
Petts Close E.2
Pickards Way B.2
Pippin Place E.5
Port Quay.................C.2
Post Office Lane C.4
Prince of Wales Close E.2
Prince Street D.4
Princes Road D.4
Prins Avenue D.2
Prospect Place.................D.4
Prosperous Place E.4
Provence Place E.5
Purbeck Close B.4

Quaker Lane E.4
Queen Elizabeth Drive.................D.5
Queen Street D.3
Queen's Road C.4

Railway Road D.5
Ramnoth Road.................D.4
Raymond Street D.4
Rectory Gardens E.3
Redwing Drive D.5
Regal Road C.5
Rhone Place E.5
Richard Young Close D.1
Richmond Court.................C.4
Rigg Close C.5
River Terrace C.2
Riverside Way C.4
Robin Mews D.5
Rochford Walk E.4
Rose Walk B.3
Rowan Close E.2
Royal Road D.4
Ruby Street D.3
Russell Street.................D.3
Russett Close.................E.5

Salcott Drive.................E.3
Salters Way B.5
Sandall Road C.5
Sandown Road C.5
Sandringham Avenue.................E.3
Sandy Lane E.4
Sandyland Street C.3
Savory Road C.2
School Lane D.3
Seabank Road E.3
Second Avenue D.4
Sefton Avenue E.3
Seventh Avenue E.4
Sherwood Avenue D.2
Silver Street D.3
Sixth Avenue E.4
Sleights Drive F.3
Small Lane F.3
Somers Road C.4
South Brink.................B.5
Southwell Road D.2
Sovereign Close B.3
Sparrowgate Road F.3
Spartan Close E.5
St. Augustincs Road D.3
St. Martins Road E.2
St. Michael's Avenue D.2
St. Paul's Close D.4
St. Peter's Road D.4
Stafford Street D.4
Staithe Road E.3
Station Drive C.4
Stermyn Street D.4
Storbeck Road D.2
Stow Gardens E.4
Stow Lane E.4
Stow Road E.3
Strawberry Close B.3
Sturmer Field E.5
Summerfield Close.................C.3
Sunset Gardens E.5
Sutton Meadows B.2
Sutton Road B.2
Sybil Road D.3
Sylvden Drive F.3

Tavistock Road.................D.3
The Chase, Spittle Field C.2
The Chase, Wisbech C.3
The Crescent D.4
The Lawns C.3
The Water Gardens B.4
Third Avenue E.4
Tindall Close D.2
Tinker's Drove D.2
Townshend Road D.3
Trafford Park E.3
Trafford Road E.3
Trinity Road E.3
Turnpike Close E.3

Union Place D.4
Union Street.................D.4

Verdun Road D.3
Victoria Place D.4
Victoria Road D.4
Victory Road C.4

Walsingham Court C.2
WALSOKEN F.2
Walton Road E.2
Waterlees Road D.1
Weasenham Lane C.5
Wedgewood Court D.4
Wedgewood Drive D.4
Welbech Road E.4
West Parade C.2
West Street D.4
Westfield Road E.2
Westmead Avenue.................D.5
Weston Road D.4
Westonmiller Drive.................C.2
Westry Close F.3
Whitby Street D.3
Whitecross Lane F.5
Wilberforce Road D.4
William Road D.4
Willow Way D.5
Windmill Gardens.................E.2
Windsor Drive E.2
Wistaria Road.................E.2
Wood Street.................C.3
Woodcoote Park.................B.4
Woodcote Park C.4
Woodlands Court E.2
Worcester Road.................D.2

York Gardens D.3
York Road D.3
York Row D.4

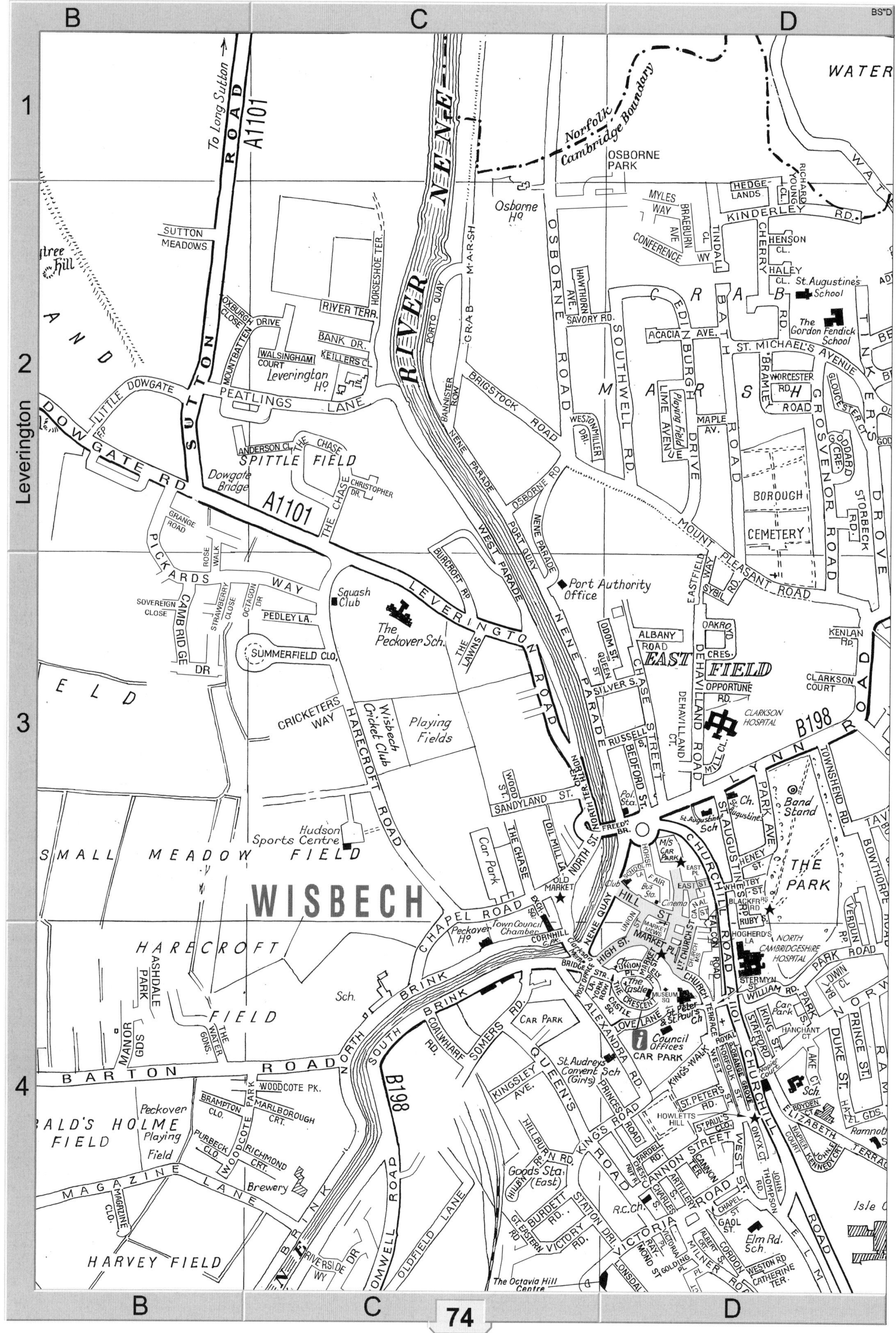
B
C
D
BS*D
WATER
1
To Long Sutton
A1101
ROAD
RIVER NENE
Norfolk Cambridge Boundary
Osborne Park
OSBORNE
PARK
RICHARD
YOUNG
RD.
WAT
SUTTON MEADOWS
Osborne Ho.
MYLES
WAY
HEDGE-
LANDS
KINDERLEY
CL.
Tree Hill
HAWTHORN AVE.
CONFERENCE
BRAEBURN AVE.
TINDAL
CHERRY
HENSON CL.
St. Augustine's School
HALEY CL.
River Terr.
PORTO QUAY
GRAB MARSH
SAVORY RD.
EDIZBURGH AVE.
ACACIA AVE.
CRA
B
St. Michael's Avenue
The Gordon Fendick School
OXBURGH CLOSE
MOUNTBATTEN DRIVE
RIVER TERR.
BANK DR.
KEILLERS CL.
HORSESHOE TER.
BRIGSTOCK ROAD
WESTONMILLER DRI.
SOUTHWELL RD.
LIME AVEN.
M
A
WORCESTER RD.
BRAMLEY
H
WALSINGHAM COURT
Leverington Ho.
Playing Fields
MAPLE AV.
GLOUCESTER RD.
GODDARD CRE.
LAND
AND
LITTLE DOWGATE
DOWGATE RD.
SUTTON ROAD
PEATLINGS
Leverington LANE
ANDERSON CL.
THE CHASE
SPITTLE FIELD
BANNISTER ROW
NENE PARADE
OSBORNE RD.
QUEEN ST.
BOROUGH CEMETERY
STORBECK RD.
DROVE
A1101
Dowgate Bridge
THE CHASE
CHRISTOPHER DR.
WEST PARADE
PORT QUAY
NENE PARADE
MOUNT PLEASANT ROAD
LYNN ROAD
GRANGE ROAD
ROSE WALK
BURCROFT RD.
LEVERINGTON ROAD
EASTFIELD RD.
SYBIL RD.
PICKARDS WAY
CAMBRIDGE DR.
SOVEREIGN CLOSE
STRAWBERRY CLOSE
OCTAGON DR.
PEDLEY LA.
Squash Club
THE LAWNS
Port Authority Office
ALBANY ROAD
OAKROYD CRES.
KENLAN RD.
SUMMERFIELD CLO.
The Peckover Sch.
ODDM ST.
QUEEN ST.
SILVER S.
EAST
FIELD
DEHAVILLAND ROAD
Opportune RD.
CLARKSON COURT
FIELD
CRICKETERS WAY
HARECROFT ROAD
Wisbech Cricket Club
Playing Fields
CHASE STREET
RUSSELL S.
BEDFORD ST.
Clarkson Hospital
B198
3
SMALL MEADOW FIELD
Sports Centre
Hudson Field
WOOD ST.
SANDYLAND ST.
NORTH ST.
TITHE ST.
Pol. Sta.
FREED BR.
PARK AVE.
Band Stand
TOWNSHEND RD.
TAV
BOWTHORPE ROAD
Ch.
St. Augustine's Sch
St. Augustine's
HENEY ST.
WHITBY ST.
THE PARK
VERDUN RD.
WISBECH
Car Park
THE CHASE
OIL MILL LA.
HORSE FAIR
M/S CAR PARK
SCHOOL
CHURCH ROAD
EAST ST.
BLACKFRIARS RD.
RUBY ST.
HARECROFT
ASHDALE PARK
Sch.
CHAPEL ROAD
Peckover Ho.
CORNHILL
Town Council Chamber
NENE QUAY
HILL ST.
Bus Sta.
Cinema
MARKET MEWS
MARKET PL.
CHURCH TERRACE
FALCON ROAD
HOGHERD'S LA.
North Cambridgeshire Hospital
WILLIAM RD.
PARK RD.
FIELD
THE WATER GDNS.
MANOR SQ.
BRINK
SOUTH BRINK
Sch.
BRIDGE ST.
HIGH ST.
UNION PL.
CHURCH STR.
UNION ST.
THE CRESCENT
The Castle
Museum Sq.
ST. PETER'S RD.
STERMYN ST.
KING ST.
STAFFORD RD.
HANCHANT CT.
PRINCE ST.
DUKE ST.
4
BARTON ROAD
NORTH BRINK
B198
WOODCOTE PK.
WOODCOTE PARK
MARLBOROUGH CRT.
RICHMOND CRT.
COALWHARF RD.
SOMERS RD.
Car Park
QUEEN'S ROAD
ALEXANDRA RD.
St. Audreys Convent Sch (Girl's)
Council Offices CAR PARK
LOVE LANE
St. Peter & St. Paul's Ch
KING'S WALK
ROYAL ORANGE GROVE
NORFOLK ST.
Car Park
CHURCH ST.
LAKE RD.
NAPIER COURT
JOHN THOMPSON RD.
ELIZABETH TERRACE
Sch.
BOYDEN RD.
ONYX CL.
BALD'S HOLME FIELD
Peckover Playing Field
BRAMPTON CLO.
PURBECK CLO.
MARLBOROUGH CRT.
Brewery
KINGSLEY AVE.
QUEEN'S ROAD
PRINCESS ROAD
KINGS ROAD
HILLBURN RD.
ST. PETERS RD.
HOWLETTS HILL
ST. PAUL'S CLO.
FARDELL RD.
CHARLES ST.
CANNON STREET
ARTILLERY ROAD
WEST ST.
CHAPEL RD.
GAOL ST.
Sch.
RAYMOND ST.
GOLDING
JOHN ST.
KENNEDY CRE.
MAGAZINE LANE
MAGAZINE CLO.
HARVEY FIELD
RIVERSIDE WY.
RIVERSIDE DR.
CROMWELL ROAD
OLDFIELD LANE
Goods Sta. (East)
BURDETT RD.
STATION DRI.
VICTORY RD.
R.C. Ch.
VICTORIA ROAD
LONSDALE
MILNER RD.
GORDON RD.
ELM RD. Sch.
WESTON RD.
CATHERINE TER.
ELM ROAD
Isle of
The Octavia Hill Centre
B
C
74
D

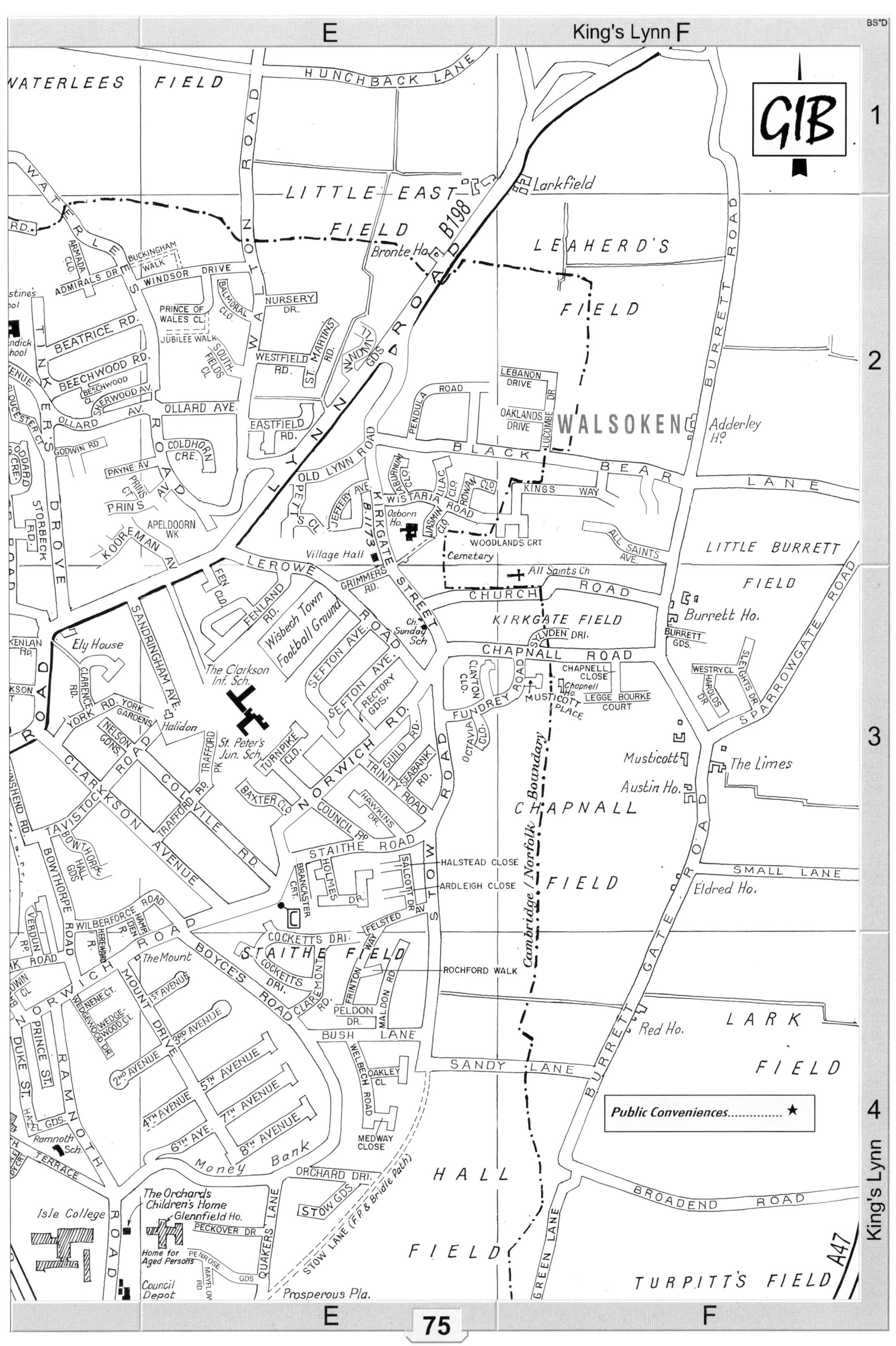
E
King's Lynn F
BS"D
GIB
1
WATERLEES FIELD
HUNCHBACK LANE
LITTLE EAST
FIELD
Larkfield
B198
LEAHERD'S
Bronte Ho.
ROAD
FIELD
BURRETT ROAD
2
ARMADA CLO.
ADMIRALS DR.
BUCKINGHAM WALK
WINDSOR DRIVE
NURSERY DR.
istine's hool
TINKER'S
PRINCE OF WALES CL.
BALMORAL CLO.
JUBILEE WALK
BEATRICE RD.
BEECHWOOD RD.
BEECHWOOD AV.
SHERWOOD AV.
OLLARD AVE.
SOUTH FIELDS CL.
WESTFIELD RD.
ST. MARTINS
VINDA
GDS.
LEBANON DRIVE
OAKLANDS DRIVE
LUCOMBE DR.
WALSOKEN
Adderley Ho.
ndick hool
GLOUCESTER CT.
OLLARD AV.
EASTFIELD RD.
BLACK
BEAR
LANE
GODDARD CRE.
GODWIN RD.
COLDHORN CRE.
PAYNE AV.
PRINS CT.
PRINS
ROAD
OLD LYNN ROAD
PENDULA ROAD
PETT'S CL.
JEFFERY AVE.
LABURNUM CLO.
WISTARIA ROAD
LILAC CLO.
ROWAN CLO.
KINGS WAY
ALL SAINTS AVE.
LITTLE BURRETT
FIELD
STORBECK RD.
DROVE
APELDOORN WK.
KOOREMAN AV.
LEROWE
B.1173
KIRKGATE STREET
Osborn Ho.
JASMIN CLO.
WOODLANDS CRT.
Cemetery
All Saints Ch.
BURRETT HO.
SPARROWGATE ROAD
Village Hall
FEN CLO.
FENLAND RD.
Wisbech Town Football Ground
GRIMMERS RD.
CHURCH ROAD
KIRKGATE FIELD
BURRETT GDS.
3
KENLAN RD.
Ely House
SANDRINGHAM AVE.
The Clarkson Inf. Sch.
SEFTON AVE.
SEFTON AVE.
Ch. Sunday Sch.
NORWICH ROAD
RECTORY GDS.
SYLDEN DRI.
CHAPNALL ROAD
CHAPNELL CLOSE
Chapnell Ho.
MUSTICOTT PLACE
LEGGE BOURKE COURT
WESTRY CL.
HAROLDS DR.
SLEIGHTS DR.
ROAD
CLARENCE RD.
RD. YORK GARDENS
YORK
NELSON GDNS.
Halidon
TRAFFORD RD.
St. Peter's Jun. Sch.
TURNPIKE CLO.
RECTORY RD.
GUILD RD.
TRINITY ROAD
SEABANK RD.
CLAYTON CLO.
OCTAVIA CLO.
FUNDREY ROAD
Musticott
Austin Ho.
The Limes
CLARKSON ROAD
TAVISTOCK RD.
TOWNSHEND RD.
COLVILLE RD.
TRAFFORD RD.
BAXTER CLO.
COUNCIL RD.
HAWKINS DR.
CHAPNALL
FIELD
SMALL LANE
Eldred Ho.
ROAD
BOWTHORPE HALL GDS.
CLARKSON AVENUE
STAITHE ROAD
HOLMES DR.
BRANCASTER CRT.
SALCOTT DR.
HALSTEAD CLOSE
ARDLEIGH CLOSE
STOW ROAD
Cambridge / Norfolk Boundary
BOWTHORPE ROAD
VERDUN RD.
WILBERFORCE ROAD
HAMPDEN R.
HEREWARD R.
FELSTED RD.
4
ORWICH ROAD
Boundary
COCKETTS DRI.
STAITHE FIELD
Cocketts Dri.
CLAREMONT RD.
FRINTON RD.
ROCHFORD WALK
BURRETT GATE ROAD
LARK
FIELD
BAWDWIN ROAD
MOUNT DRIVE
The Mount
1ST AVENUE
2ND AVENUE
3RD AVENUE
WEDGE WOOD DR.
ENE CT.
WEDGWOOD CT.
PELDON DR.
MALDON RD.
BUSH LANE
Red Ho.
Public Conveniences.............. ★
HAZEL GDS.
PRINCE ST.
DUKE ST.
RAMNOTH ROAD
4TH AVENUE
5TH AVENUE
7TH AVENUE
8TH AVENUE
WELBECH ROAD
OAKLEY CL.
SANDY LANE
GREEN LANE
DEWED
TERRACE
Ramnoth Sch.
6TH AVE.
Money Bank
MEDWAY CLOSE
ORCHARD DRI.
STOW GDS.
HALL FIELD
BROADEND ROAD
King's Lynn
Isle College
The Orchard's Children's Home
Glennfield Ho.
PECKOVER DR.
QUAKERS LANE
STOW LANE (F.P. & Bridle Path)
Home for Aged Persons
PENROSE GDS.
MAYFLOW GDS.
Council Depot
Prosperous Pla.
TURPITT'S FIELD
A47
E
F

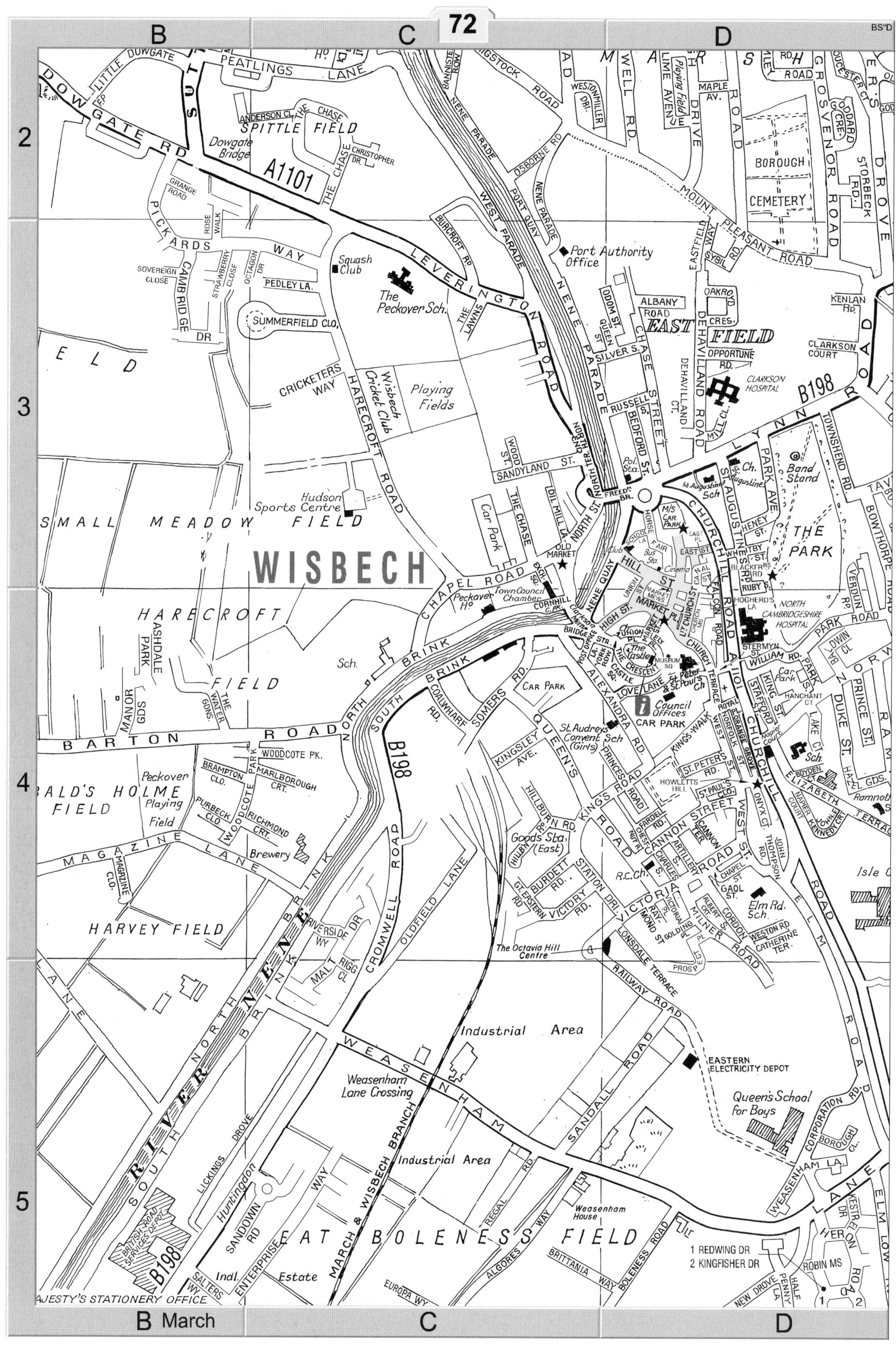
72
B
C
D
BS"D
DOWGATE RD
LITTLE DOWGATE
FP
PEATLINGS LANE
HO.
THE CHASE
BANNISTER ROW
KINGSTOCK ROAD
MA
OR
RD
H
ROAD
GROSVENOR ROAD
STORBECK
ERS CT
GODDARD
CRE
GOD
DROVE
GOD
ANDERSON CL
SPITTLE FIELD
CHRISTOPHER DR
NENE PARADE
WESTON
MILLER
DRI
OSBORNE RD
PLAYING FIELD
LIME AVEN
MAPLE AV
BOROUGH CEMETERY
KENLAN RD.
2
Dowgate Bridge
A1101
THE CHASE
PORT QUAY
WEST PARADE
WELL RD
DRIVE
SYBIL
PICKARDS
GRANGE ROAD
ROSE WALK
WAY
BURCROFT RD.
LEVERINGTON ROAD
NENE PARADE
Port Authority Office
EASTFIELD
ODOM ST
ALBANY ROAD
OAKROYD
DEHAVILLAND ROAD
CRES
CLARKSON RD
CAMBRIDGE DR
SOVEREIGN CLOSE
STRAWBERRY CLOSE
OCTAGON DR
PEDLEY LA.
Squash Club
THE LAWNS
QUEEN ST
SILVER S.
EAST FIELD
OPPORTUNE RD.
CLARKSON COURT
B198
LYNN ROAD
ELD
SUMMERFIELD CLO.
The Peckover Sch.
CRICKETERS WAY
Wisbech Cricket Club
Playing Fields
RUSSELL ST
BEDFORD ST
CHASE STREET
Clarkson Hospital
DEHAVILLAND CT.
MILL CL
TOWNSHEND RD
3
FIELD
HARECROFT ROAD
WOOD ST
SANDYLAND ST.
NORTH TER.
ON ST
NORTH ST
DIL MILL ST
POL. STA.
FREED'N BR.
St. Augustine Sch
Ch. St. Augustine
PARK AVE.
Band Stand
HENEY ST
BOWTHORPE RD
TAV
SMALL MEADOW FIELD
Hudson Sports Centre
THE CHASE
Car Park
OLD MARKET
Old Market
HORSE FAIR
M/S Car Park
CHURCHILL ROAD
EAST PL
EAST ST
STBY ST
THE PARK
WISBECH
CHAPEL ROAD
SOUTH BRINK
NORTH BRINK
Sch.
Peckover Ho.
Town Council Chambers
CORNHILL
BRIDGE
NENE QUAY
HILL ST
SCHOOL LA
BUS. STA.
UNION PL
HIGH ST.
Cinema
MARKET PL
FALCON RD
EAST ST
BLACKFRS RD
RUBY S
HOGHERD'S LA
NORTH CAMBRIDGESHIRE HOSPITAL
VERDUN RD.
PARK ROAD
HARECROFT
HASHDALE PARK
THE WATER GDNS.
MANOR
SDG
FIELD
EXCH.
BRIDGE
POST OFFICE
YORK
ROW
THE CRESCENT
The Castle
MUSEUM
UNION PL
LOVE LANE
St. Peter & St. Paul's Ch
St Paul's Ch
CHURCH TERRACE
STERMYN ST
WILLIAM RD.
KING ST
Car Park
DWIN CL
PRINCE ST
BARTON ROAD
WOODCOTE PK.
BRAMPTON CLO.
MARLBOROUGH CRT.
WOODCOTE PARK
B198
COALWHARF RD.
SOMERS RD.
Car Park
St. Audrey's Convent Sch (Girls)
ALEXANDRA RD
Council Offices Car Park
KINGS WALK
ST. PETERS RD.
ROYAL
GRANGE
NORFOLK ST
STAFFORD RD
Napier Court
HANCHANT CT.
DUKE ST
Isle
4
BALD'S HOLME FIELD
Peckover Playing Field
PURBECK CLO.
RICHMOND CRT.
Brewery
KINGSLEY AVE.
QUEEN'S
KINGS ROAD
PRINCESS ROAD
HILLBURN RD.
Goods Sta. (East)
BURDETT RD.
ST. PETERS RD.
HOWLETTS HILL
CHARLES ST
ST CHARLES
CANNON STREET
ARTILLERY
WEST ST
JOHN THOMPSON RD.
GAOL ST.
CHAPEL ST.
ELIZABETH TERRACE
BOYDEN
HAZEL GDS.
Sch
Ramnoth
MAGAZINE LANE
MAGAZINE CLO.
HARVEY FIELD
CROMWELL ROAD
OLDFIELD LANE
RIVERSIDE DR
RIGG CL
MALT
VICTORY RD.
STATION DRI.
R.C. Ch.
VICTORIA ROAD
CANNON STREET
MILNER ROAD
WESTON RD
CATHERINE TER.
Elm Rd. Sch
CORDIN
GOLDING
ROBERT S
ELM ROAD
Isle C
NORTHERN RINK
RIVER NENE
SOUTH BRINK
BRENK
RIVERSIDE WY
The Octavia Hill Centre
G. EASTERN
BRITTANIA WAY
LONSDALE TERRACE
RAILWAY ROAD
Eastern Electricity Depot
Queen's School for Boys
CORPORATION RD.
WEASENHAM
Industrial Area
SANDALL ROAD
WEASENHAM
LANE
ELM LOW RD
Weasenham Lane Crossing
MARCH & WISBECH BRANCH
Industrial Area
Weasenham House
ROAD
5
SOUTHERN RINK
B198
BRITISH ROAD SERVICES DEPOT
LICKINGS DROVE
Huntingdon
SANDOWN RD
ENTERPRISE WAY
SALTERS WY
Indl. Estate
EAT BOLENESS FIELD
EUROPA WY
ALGORES WAY
REGAL RD
BOLENESS ROAD
Weasenham Ho.
WESTFIELD
DR
HERON RD
1 REDWING DR
2 KINGFISHER DR
WEASENHAM LA.
NEW DROVE
PENNY LA
HALF
ROBIN MS
MAJESTY'S STATIONERY OFFICE
B March
C
D

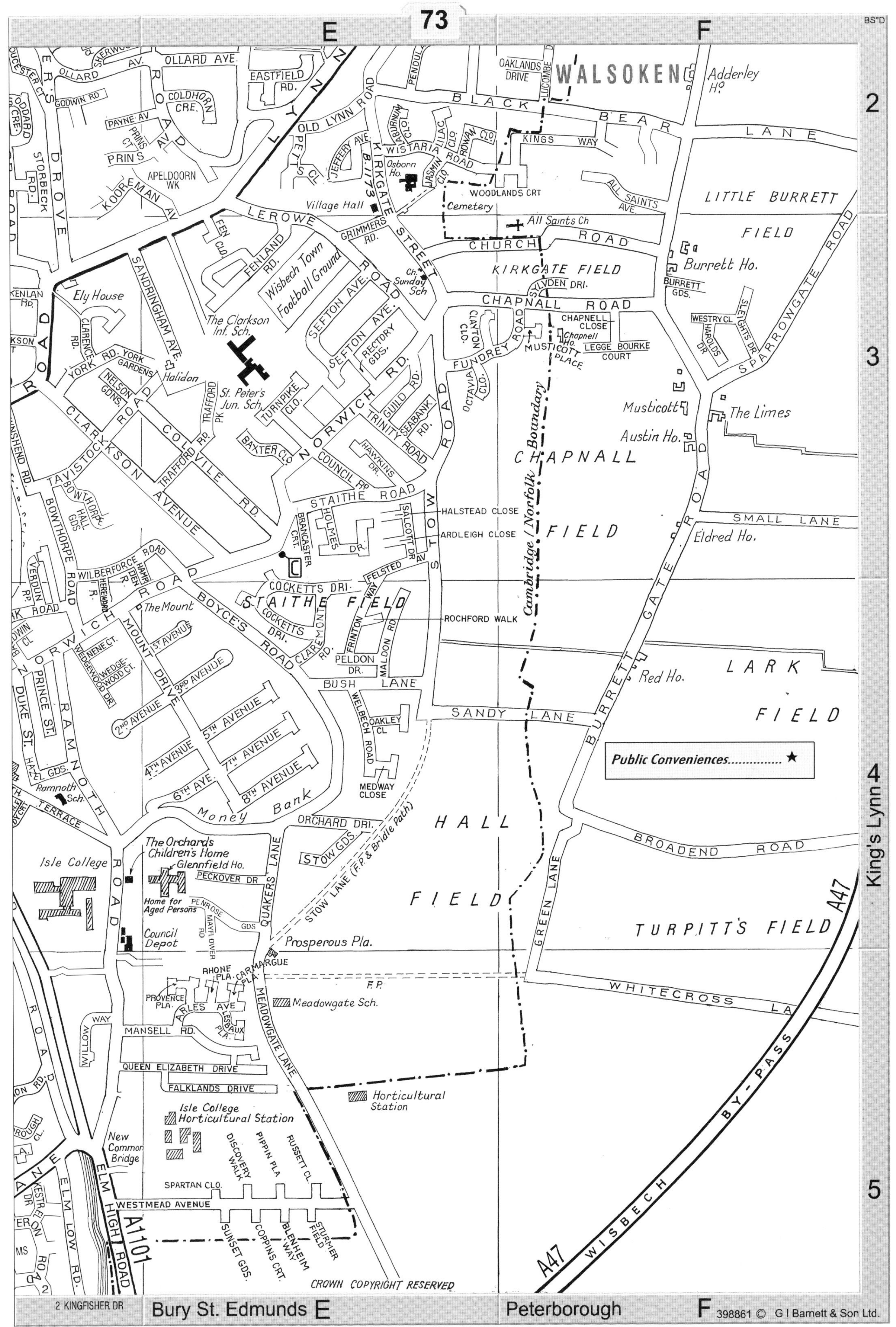
73
E
F
BS"D
WALSOKEN
OAKLANDS DRIVE
LUCOMBE D
Adderley Ho.
BLACK
BEAR
LANE
2
KINGS WAY
ALL SAINTS AVE.
LITTLE BURRETT
FIELD
SHERWOOD AV.
OLLARD AVE.
EASTFIELD RD.
OLD LYNN ROAD
PENDULA
WOODLANDS CRT
Cemetery
All Saints Ch
CHURCH ROAD
BURRETT HO.
BURRETT GDS.
SPARROWGATE ROAD
OLLARD
GODWIN RD.
PAYNE AV.
COLDHORN CRE.
PRINS CL.
PRINS
KIRKGATE STREET
WISTARIA ROAD
LABURNUM CLO.
JASMIN LILAC CLO.
Osborn Ho.
Village Hall
KIRKGATE FIELD
SLYDEN DRI.
CHAPNALL ROAD
WESTRY CL.
HAROLDS DR.
SLEIGHTS DR
STORBECK RD.
APELDOORN WK
KOOREMAN AV.
LEROWE
FEN CLO.
FENLAND RD.
Wisbech Town Football Ground
GRIMMERS RD.
SEFTON AVE.
Ch. Sunday Sch.
CHAPNELL CLOSE
Chapnell Ho.
LEGGE BOURKE COURT
MUSTICOTT PLACE
The Limes
3
ELY HOUSE
CLARENCE RD.
RD. YORK GARDENS
NELSON GDNS.
TRAFFORD RD.
The Clarkson Inf. Sch.
SEFTON AVE.
RECTORY GDS.
NORWICH RD.
St. Peter's Jun. Sch.
TURNPIKE CLO.
GUILD RD.
TRINITY ROAD
SEABANK RD.
STOW ROAD
FUNDREY ROAD
OCTAVIA CLO.
CLAYTON CLO.
Musticott
Austin Ho.
CHAPNALL
FIELD
Cambridge / Norfolk Boundary
SANDRINGHAM AVE.
YORK RD.
COLVILLE RD.
Halidon
TRAFFORD PK.
BAXTER CLO.
HAWKINS DR.
STAITHE ROAD
Ch. Sunday Sch.
TAVISTOCK RD.
CLARKSON AVENUE
BOWTHORPE HALL GDS.
BOWTHORPE ROAD
WILBERFORCE ROAD
HEREWARD R.
HAMPDEN R.
BRANCASTER CRT.
HOLMES DR.
SALCOTT DR.
HALSTEAD CLOSE
ARDLEIGH CLOSE
SMALL LANE
Eldred Ho.
VERDUN RD.
The Mount
BOYCE'S ROAD
MOUNT DRIVE
CLAREMONT RD.
COCKETTS DRI.
COCKETTS DRI.
FELSTED WAY
FRINTON WAY
MALDON RD.
PELDON DR.
STAITHE FIELD
ROCHFORD WALK
LARK
FIELD
NORWICH ROAD
PRINCE ST.
DUKE ST.
HAZEL GDS.
RAMNOTH ROAD
MENE CT.
WEDGEWOOD CT.
WELBERWOOD DR.
1st AVENUE
2nd AVENUE
3rd AVENUE
4th AVENUE
5th AVENUE
6th AVE.
7th AVENUE
8th AVENUE
BUSH LANE
WELBECH ROAD
OAKLEY CL.
Money Bank
SANDY LANE
Red Ho.
BURRETT GATE ROAD
BROADEND ROAD
King's Lynn
4
Ramnoth Sch.
TERRACE
MEDWAY CLOSE
ORCHARD DRI.
STOW GDS.
STOW LANE (F.P. & Bridle Path)
HALL
FIELD
GREEN LANE
Isle College
The Orchards Children's Home
Glennfield Ho.
PECKOVER DR.
QUAKERS LANE
PENROSE RD.
MAYFLOWER RD.
GDS.
Prosperous Pla.
Home for Aged Persons
Council Depot
RHONE PLA.
CARMARGUE PLA.
PROVENCE PLA.
ARLES AVE.
LES BAUX PLA.
MEADOWGATE LANE
F.P.
Meadowgate Sch.
TURPITT'S FIELD
WHITECROSS LA.
A47
WISBECH BY-PASS
MANSELL RD.
WILLOW WAY
QUEEN ELIZABETH DRIVE
FALKLANDS DRIVE
Horticultural Station
New Common Bridge
Isle College Horticultural Station
DISCOVERY WALK
PIPPIN PLA.
RUSSETT CL.
STURMER FIELD
BLENHEIM WAY
SPARTAN CLO.
COPPINS CRT.
SUNSET GDS.
WESTMEAD AVENUE
ELM HIGH ROAD
ELM LOW RD.
A1101
ROAD
Public Conveniences.............. ★
5
2 KINGFISHER DR
Bury St. Edmunds E
Peterborough
F
CROWN COPYRIGHT RESERVED
398861 © G I Barnett & Son Ltd.

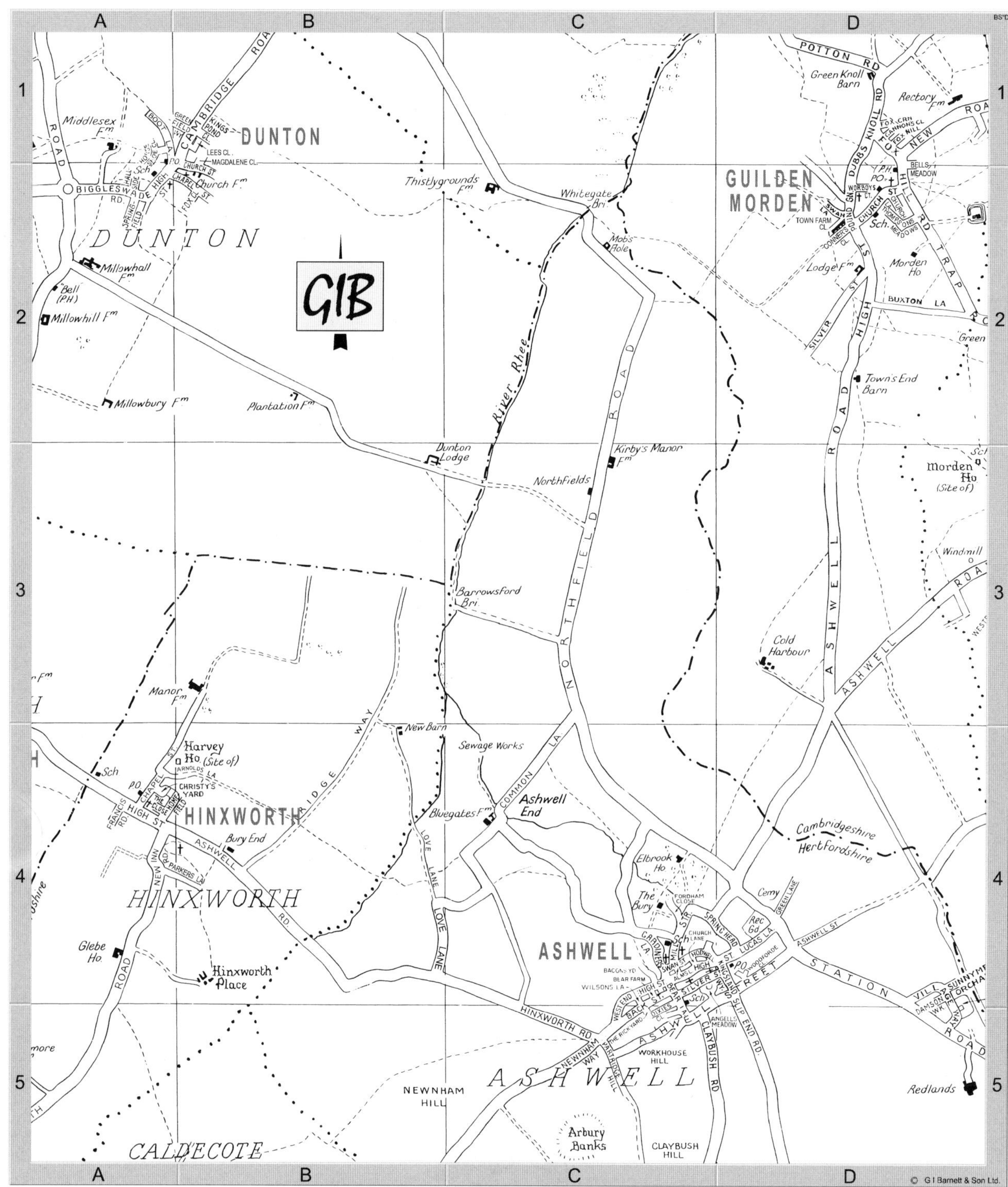

ASHWELL INDEX TO STREETS

Alms Lane C.4
Angeus Meadow C.5
Arnolds Lane B.4
Ashwell End C.4
Ashwell Road D.3
Ashwell Road,
  Hinxworth B.4
Ashwell Street C.5

Back Street C.5
Bacons Yard C.4
Bear Farm C.4
Bear Lane C.4
Biggleswade Road A.2
Boot Lane A.1
Buxton Lane D.2

Cambridge Road B.1
Cannons Close D.1
Chapel Street, Dunton B.2
Chapel Street,
  Hinxworth A.4
Church Lane, Ashwell C.4
Church Lane,
  Guilden Morden D.2

Church Street, Dunton B.2
Church Street,
  Guilden Morden D.2
Cold Harbour D.3
Common Lane C.4
Conner's Close D.2

Dixies Close C.5
Dubbs Knoll Road D.2
DUNTON A.2

Fordham Close C.4
Fox Close B.2
Fox Green D.1
Fox Hill D.1
Fox Hill Road D.1
Francis Road A.4

Gardiners Lane C.4
Green Field Way B.1
Green Lane D.4
GUILDEN MORDEN D.4

Hall-Side A.2
High Street, Ashwell C.4

High Street, Dunton A.2
High Street,
  Guilden Morden D.2
High Street, Hinxworth A.4
HINXWORTH A.4
Hinxworth Road C.5
Hodwell C.4
Horse Shoe Close A.1

Kings Pond Close B.1
Kingsland Way D.4

Lees Close B.2
Lucas Lane D.4

Magdalene Close B.1
Mill Street C.4

New Inn Road A.4
Newnham Way C.5
Northfield Road C.3

Partridge Hill C.5
Potton Road D.1
Pound Green D.2

Ridge Way B.4

Silver Street, Ashwell C.4
Silver Street,
  Guilden Morden D.2
Slip End Road D.5
Spring Head C.4
Springfield A.2
Station Road D.4
Swan Lane D.2
Swan Street C.4

The Close A.4
The Rick Yard C.5
Town Farm Close D.2

West End C.5
Wilsons Lane C.4
Woodforde Close D.4
Workhouse Hill C.5

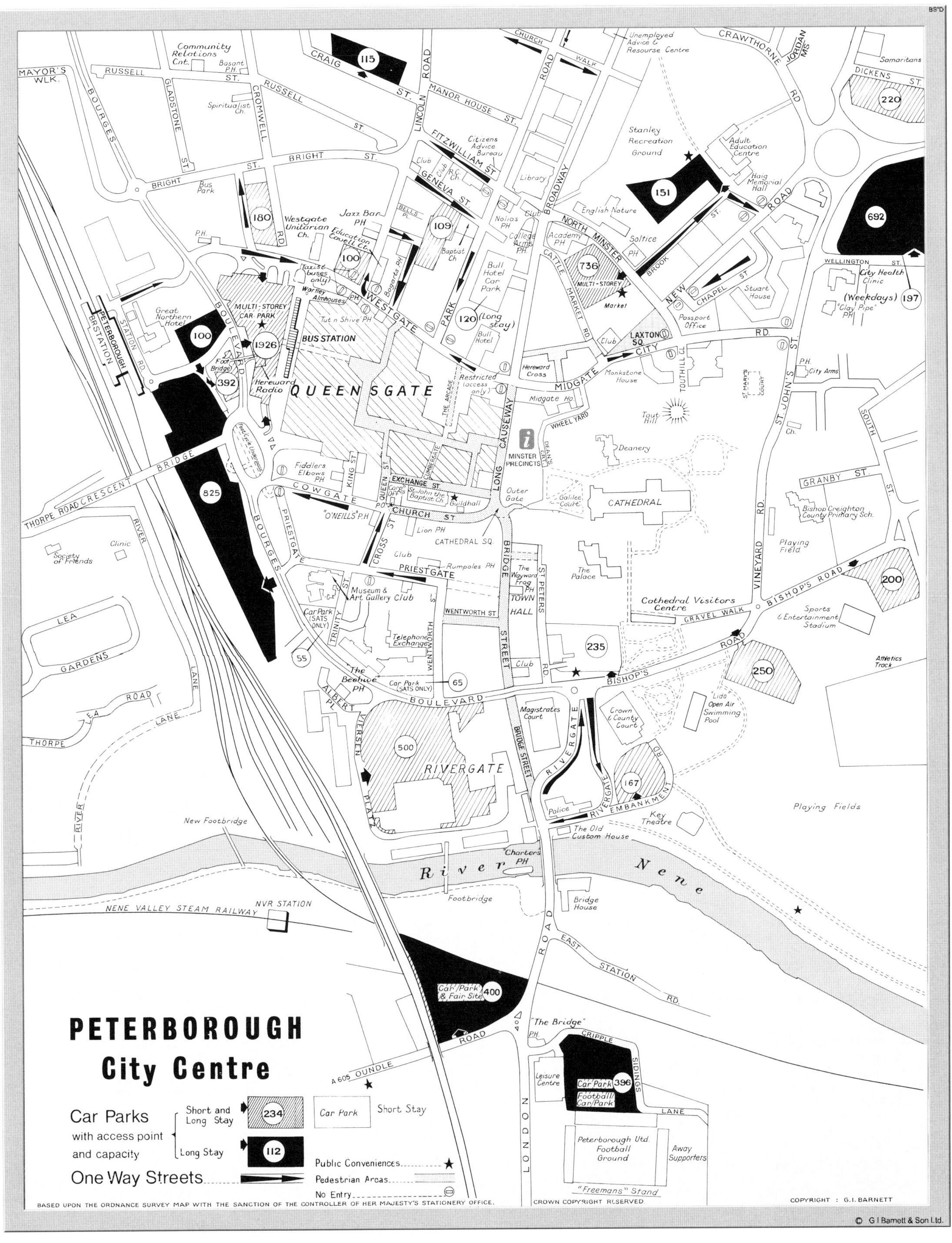
PETERBOROUGH
City Centre
Car Parks
with access point
and capacity
Short and Long Stay
234
Long Stay
112
One Way Streets
Car Park
Short Stay
Public Conveniences
Pedestrian Areas
No Entry
BASED UPON THE ORDNANCE SURVEY MAP WITH THE SANCTION OF THE CONTROLLER OF HER MAJESTY'S STATIONERY OFFICE.
CROWN COPYRIGHT RESERVED
COPYRIGHT : G.I. BARNETT
© G I Barnett & Son Ltd.
MAYOR'S WLK.
RUSSELL ST.
Community Relations Cnt.
Basant P.H.
Spiritualist Ch.
BOURGES
GLADSTONE ST.
CROMWELL
RUSSELL ST.
BRIGHT ST.
CRAIG ST.
115
LINCOLN ROAD
MANOR HOUSE ST.
CHURCH WALK
CRAWTHORNE
JORDAN MS.
Samaritans
DICKENS ST.
220
BRIGHT
Bus Park
FITZWILLIAM ST.
Citizens Advice Bureau
Library
Unemployed Advice & Resourse Centre
Stanley Recreation Ground
Adult Education Centre
Haig Memorial Hall
BROADWAY
WELLINGTON ST.
692
P.H.
180
GENEVA ST.
Club
R.C. Ch.
151
English Nature
NORTH MINSTER
Soltice
NEW
CHAPEL ST.
City Health Clinic
(Weekdays)
"Clay Pipe" P.H.
197
Westgate Unitarian Ch.
Jazz Bar P.H.
Education Cavell Ct.
109
100
Baptist Ch.
Bossars Rd.
Nolios P.H.
College Arms P.H.
Academy P.H.
736
MULTI-STOREY
Market
BROOK
Stuart House
Passport Office
ST. MARY'S COURT
P.H.
City Arms
Great Northern Hotel
PETERBOROUGH STATION
STATION RD.
100
MULTI-STOREY CAR PARK
1926
BOULEVARD
Tourist buses only
Warner Almhouses
Tut n Shive P.H.
Fair Bridge
392
Hereward Radio
BUS STATION
WESTGATE
PARK
120 (Long stay)
Bull Hotel Car Park
Bull Hotel
Hereward Cross
MIDGATE
Midgate Ho.
LAXTON SQ.
CITY
Monkstone House
TOUTHILL CT.
Tout Hill
Deanery
ST. JOHN'S RD.
GRANBY ST.
SOUTH ST.
Bishop Creighton County Primary Sch.
THORPE ROAD
CRESCENT
BRIDGE
RIVER
LEA
LANE
825
QUEENSGATE
Restricted (access only)
THE ARCADE
LONG CAUSEWAY
Wheel Yard
MINSTER PRECINCTS
Outer Gate
DEAN'S
Galilee Court
CATHEDRAL
Playing Field
VINEYARD RD.
BISHOP'S ROAD
200
Society of Friends
Clinic
Fiddlers Elbows P.H.
KING ST.
EXCHANGE ST.
QUEEN ST.
Corp. St. John the Baptist Ch.
Guildhall
Cathedral Visitors Centre
GRAVEL WALK
Sports & Entertainment Stadium
250
Athletics Track
COWGATE
"O'NEILLS" P.H.
PRIESTGATE
CROSS ST.
CHURCH ST.
Lion P.H.
CATHEDRAL SQ.
Rumpoles P.H.
Club
The Palace
ROAD
LEA GARDENS
LEA ROAD
THORPE
PRIESTGATE
Museum & Art Gallery
Club
Car Park (SATS ONLY)
55
TRINITY ST.
WENTWORTH ST.
WENTWORTH
ST. PETERS RD.
TOWN HALL
The Wayward Frog P.H.
235
Crown & County Court
"Lido" Open Air Swimming Pool
Playing Fields
Telephone Exchange
The Beehive P.H.
65
Car Park (SATS ONLY)
BOULEVARD
Club
Bishop's
ROAD
167
Key Theatre
EMBANKMENT
ALBERT PL.
PATERSON
500
RIVERGATE
BRIDGE STREET
Magistrates Court
RIVERGATE
RIVERGATE
Police
The Old Custom House
River Nene
New Footbridge
Charters P.H.
Footbridge
Bridge House
NENE VALLEY STEAM RAILWAY
NVR STATION
RIVER
ROAD
EAST STATION RD.
Car Park & Fair Site
400
"The Bridge" P.H.
A 605 OUNDLE
ROAD
CRIPPLE
SIDINGS
Leisure Centre
Car Park Football Car Park
396
LONDON
Peterborough Utd. Football Ground
Away Supporters
LANE
"Freemans" Stand

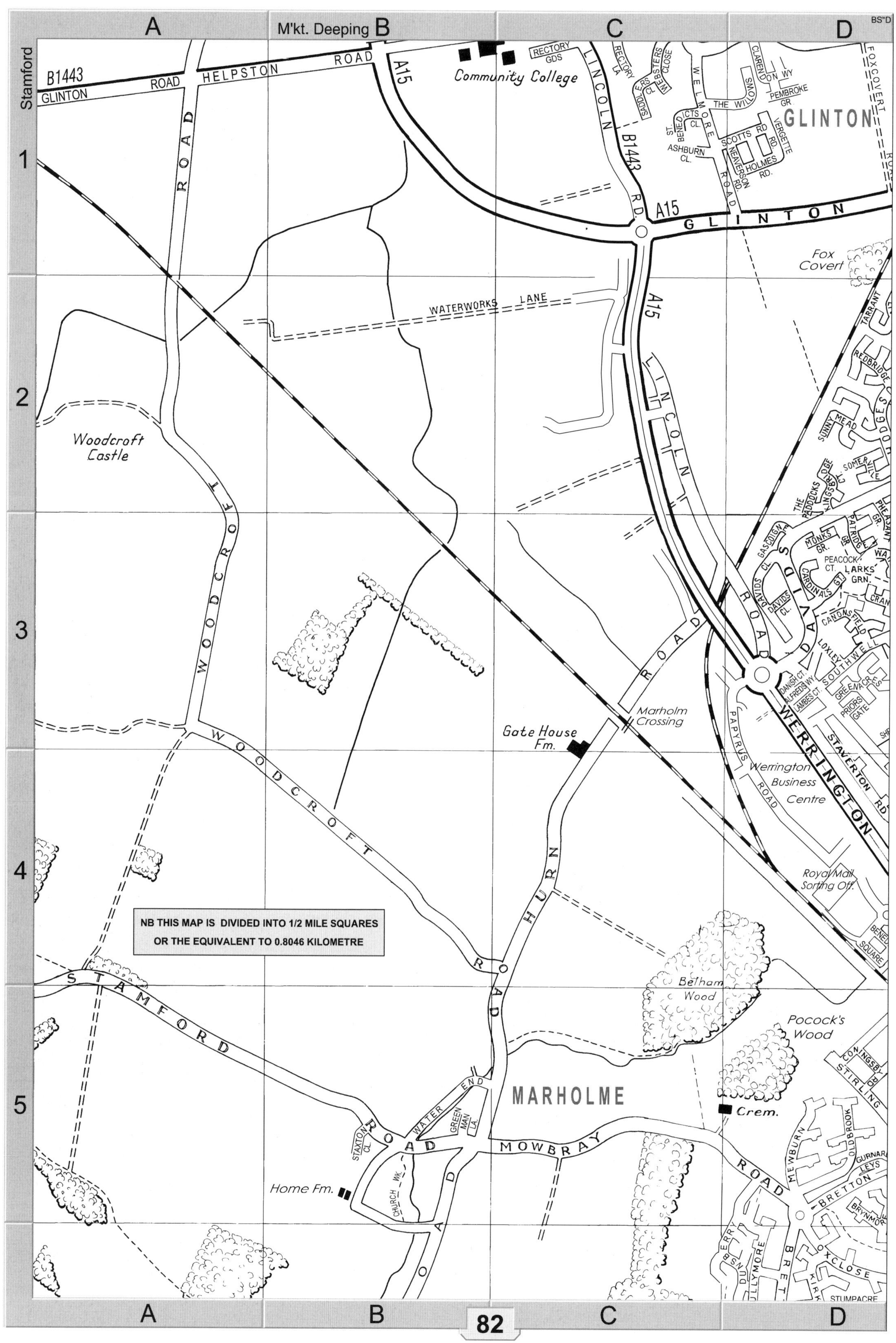
A
M'kt. Deeping B
C
D
BS"D
Stamford
B1443
GLINTON
ROAD
HELPSTON
ROAD
A15
RECTORY
GDS
Community College
LINCOLN
RECTORY LA
B1443
WEBSTERS CLOSE
TODDS
WELMORE
CLAREN ON WY
FOX COVERT
THE WI
SMOL
PEMBROKE GR.
ST
BENED
CTS
CL.
SCOTTS RD.
VERGETTE
GLINTON
ASHBURN CL.
NEAVERSON
HOLMES RD.
RD.
ROAD
A15
RD.
A15
GLINTON
Fox Covert
1
WATERWORKS LANE
LINCOLN
TARRANT
REDBRIDGE
SUNNY MEAD
DGES
SOMER VILLE
2
Woodcroft Castle
WOODCROFT
THE PADDOCKS
KINGSSEE
PLEASANT GR.
PATRIDG
WA
GASCOIGH
MONKS GR.
PEACOCK CT.
LARKS GRN.
CRAM
CARDINALS GT.
CARDINSFIELD
DAVIDS CL.
LOXLEY
SOUTHWELL
GREENACRE
ROAD
3
WOODCROFT
Marholm Crossing
Gate House Fm.
DAVIDS ROAD
DANISH CT
ALFREDS WY
JAMES CT.
GREENACRE
PRIORS GATE
SHR
PAPYRUS
WERRINGTON
Werrington Business Centre
STAVERTON RD.
WOODCROFT
HURN
4
NB THIS MAP IS DIVIDED INTO 1/2 MILE SQUARES
OR THE EQUIVALENT TO 0.8046 KILOMETRE
ROAD
Royal Mail Sorting Off.
Betham Wood
Pocock's Wood
BENE
SQUARE
STAMFORD
ROAD
HURN
ROAD
CONINGSBY
STIRLING
5
END
WATER
GREEN MAN LA
MARHOLME
Crem.
MEYBURN
OLDBROOK
ROAD
STAXTON CL.
CHURCH WK.
MOWBRAY
LEYS
GURNAR
BRETTON
Home Fm.
ROAD
BERRY
DUNS
LLYMORE
BRETT
KIRK
BRYNMOR
CLOSE
STUMPACRE
A
B
C
D

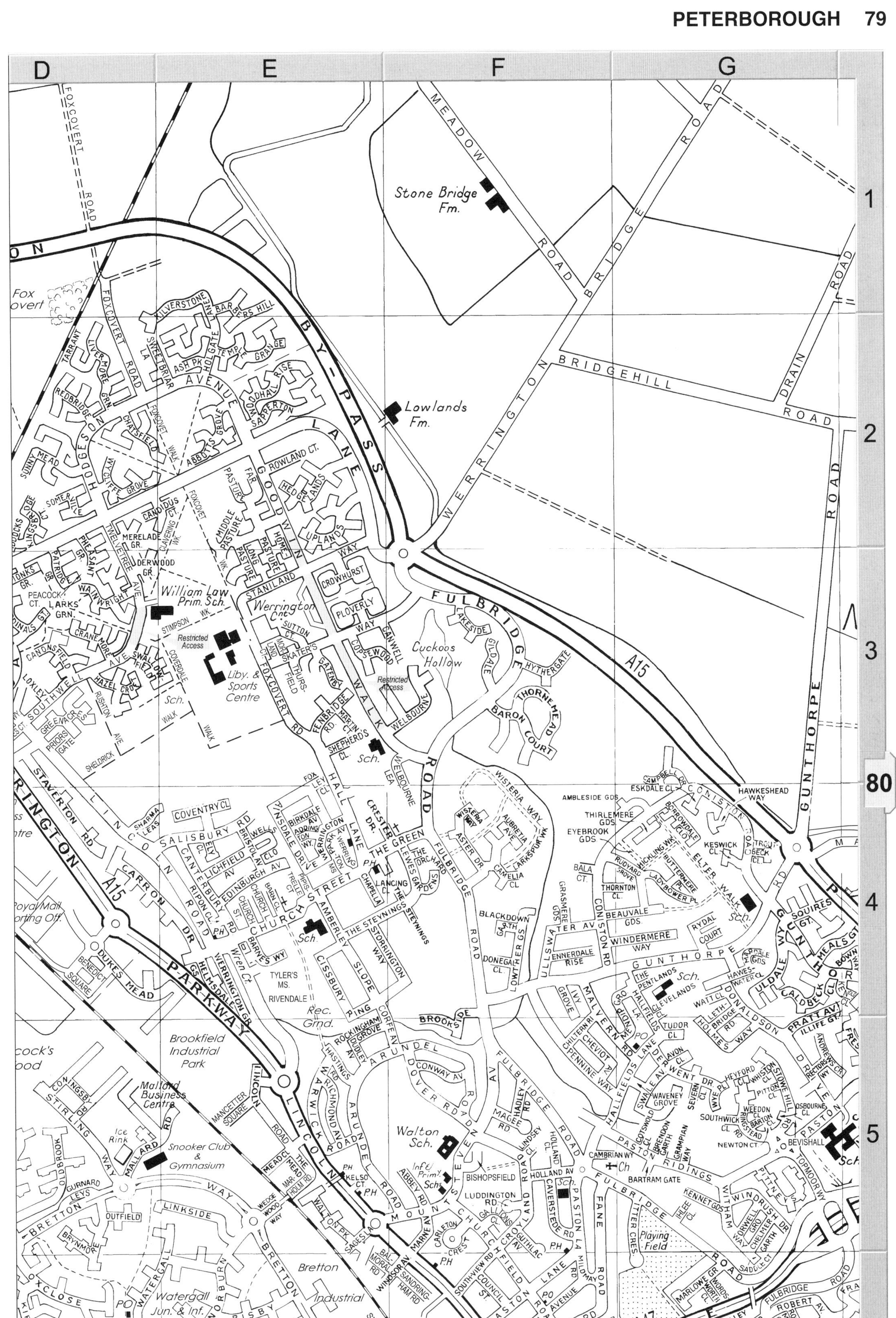

D
E
F
G
MEADOW
Stone Bridge Fm.
1
BY-PASS LANE
Fox Covert
Fox covert
FOX COVERT ROAD
SILVERSTONE
BARS HILL
BRS HILL
TARRANT
LIVERMORE GRN.
STREETBRIAR
HOLGATE
TEMPLE
GRANGE
REDBRIDGE GRN.
HODGESON ROAD
CHAPSFIELD
FOXCOVET WALK
ASP PK.
SUNNY MEAD
SOMERVILLE
WYCLIFFE GROVE
ABBOTS GROVE
SAPPERTON
GOODHALL RISE
ROWLAND CT.
FARR
HEDGELANDS
MIDDLE PASTURE
WERRINGTON
BRIDGEHILL
ROAD
DRAIN
GUNTHORPE ROAD
ROAD
Lowlands Fm.
2
KINGSBURY
PATRIDGE
DERWOOD GR.
MERELADE GR.
CLAVERING CT.
FOXCOVET
LONG PASTURE
STANILAND
UPLANDS
CANOLDUS GR.
PLEASANT
TWELVETREE AVE.
WAINWRIGHT
LARKS GRN.
PEACOCK CT.
CANONSFIELD
CRANEMORE
HAZEL CROS.
RUSTON AVE.
GREENACRES
PRIORS GATE
SHELDRICK
William Law Prim. Sch.
Werrington Cnt.
SUTTON CT.
SKATER'S FIELD
THURSBY
GATEWAY
FENBRIDGE
RD.
MARTIN'S
SHEPHERD'S CL.
Sch.
Restricted Access
Liby. & Sports Centre
STIMPSON
COVERDALE
SWALLOW WK.
FOXCOVERT RD.
WALK
CROWHURST
PLOVERLY WAY
CANWELL
COPSEWOOD
WELBOURN
Cuckoos Hollow
Restricted Access
LAKESIDE
GILDALE
HYTHERGATE
THORNEMEAD
BARON COURT
FULBRIDGE
A15
3
80
STAVERTON RD.
LINCOLN ROAD
A15
CARRON DR.
SHARMA LEAS
COVENTRY CL.
SALISBURY RD.
WELLS
BIRKDALE AV.
ADDINGTON WY.
WERRINGTON
FOX LEY CL.
HALL LANE
CRESTER DR.
THE GREEN
WELBOURNE
LEA
WISTERIA WAY
ASTER DR.
WISTERIA
AUBRETIA AVE.
LARKSPUR WK.
CAMELIA CL.
AMBLESIDE GDS.
THIRLEMERE GDS.
EYEBROOK GDS.
CAMPBELL DR.
ESKDALE CL.
CONISTON
SCROWDALE
HAWKESHEAD WAY
KESWICK CL.
ELTER WALK
TROUTBECK
LICHFIELD AV.
ELY CL.
BRISTOL AV.
CANTERBURY
EDINBURGH AV.
RIPON CL.
CHURCH ST.
THE ORCHARD
LEWES GDN.
LANCING CL.
FULBRIDGE ROAD
BLACKDOWN
GARTH
DONEGAL CL.
LOWTHER GDS.
GRASMERE GDS.
ULLSWATER AV.
ENNERDALE RISE
RUDYARD GROVE
BALA CT.
THORNTON CL.
BEAUVALE GDS.
WINDERMERE WAY
CONISTON RD.
RYDAL COURT
HAWESWATER
ELY GDS.
LEY
SCH.
STANWICK
4
Royal Mail Sorting Off.
DUKES MEAD
BENEDICT SQUARE
HELMSDALE GR.
WREN CT.
AMBERLEY SLOPE
CISSBURY RING
CHURCH STREET
BARN CL.
ST. BARNES WY.
Sch.
TYLER'S MS.
RIVENDALE
Rec. Grnd.
THE STEVNINGS
STORRINGTON WAY
ROCKINGHAM
DUDLEY
CORFEA
BROOKSIDE
GUNTHORPE
MALVERN LA.
HALLFIELDS LA.
THE PENTLANDS
CLEVELANDS
WATT CL.
TUDOR CL.
IVY GROVE
CHILTERN RD.
CHEVIOT CL.
LETH BRIDGE RD.
HOLMES WAY
DONALDSON
UDALE WY.
GT. N
CALDBECK CLO.
MEALS GT.
PRATT AV.
ILLIFE GT.
5
Brookfield Industrial Park
Mallard Business Centre
Ice Rink
Snooker Club & Gymnasium
CONINGSBY
STIRLING
GURNARD
LEYS
MALLARD RD.
MANCETTER SQUARE
LINCOLN ROAD
MEADOW
THE ROOM RD.
WEDGEWOOD
KELSO CT.
Walton Sch.
Inf. & Prim. Sch.
ABBEY RD.
MAGEE RD.
LINDSEY RD.
HADLEY RD.
HOLLAND
BISHOPSFIELD
LUDDINGTON RD.
GALLIONS CL.
GUTHLAC
CROYLAND
CAVENSTEDE AV.
HOLLAND AV.
CAMBRIAN WY.
PASTON LANE
BARTRAM GATE
FULBRIDGE ROAD
COTSWOLD
BRENDON
GRAMPIAN
PENNINE WAY
SWALE AV.
SEVERN DR.
WAVENEY GROVE
WENT DR.
WYE PL.
WHISTON RD.
WEEDON CL.
SOUTHWICK CL.
NEWTON CT.
HEYFORD
PITTON RD.
STONE HILL
RINGSTEAD
BARTON
OSBOURNE CL.
BEVISHALL Sch.
RIDINGS
KENNET GDS.
FULBRITTER CRES.
Playing Field
WINDRUSH DR.
TORMORE WY.
PASTON LA.
MILDMAY RD.
BRETTON
BRYNMOR
OLDBROOK
WATERGALL WAY
LINKSIDE
OUTFIELD
NORBURN
RISBY
BRETTON Industrial Area
Bretton
WATERGALL Jun. & Inf. School
KIRK
STUMPACRE
FOXCLOSE
MORAL.
WINDSOR AV.
SANDRING. HAM RD.
MARKHAM
CARLETON
CRES.
SOUTHVIEW RD.
COUNCIL ST.
PASTON
CHURCHFIELD ROAD
PASTON AVENUE
ST. GUTHLAC
CH.
FULBRIDGE ROAD
A47
MARLOWE
CHELTER GARTH
ROBERT AV.
D
E
83
F
G

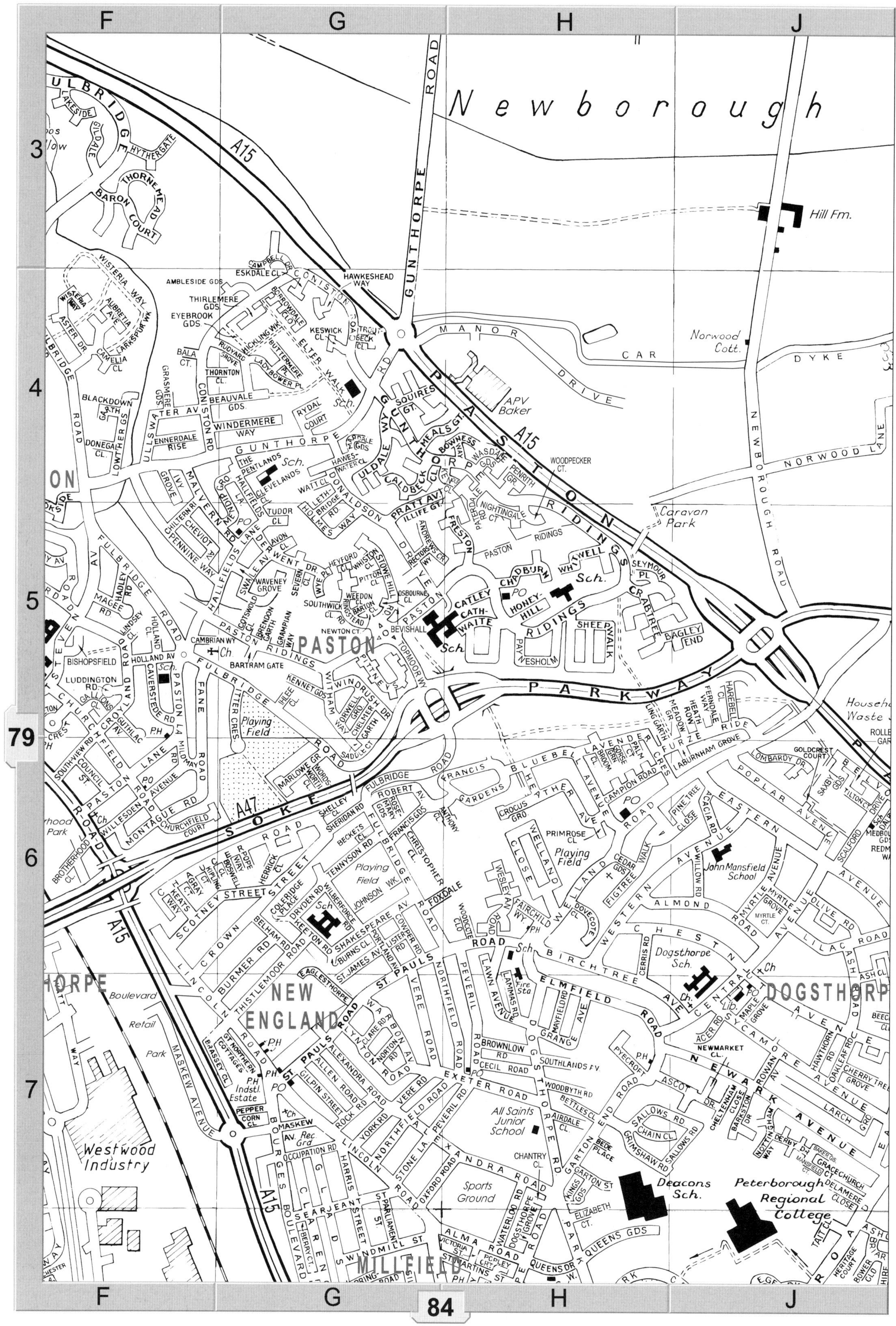
Newborough
Hill Fm.
Norwood Cott.
CAR
DYKE
NORWOOD LANE
NEWBOROUGH ROAD
GUNTHORPE ROAD
MANOR DRIVE
A15
FULBRIDGE
LAKESIDE
GILDALE
HYTHEGATE
THORNEMEAD
BARON COURT
WISTERIA WAY
AUBRETIA LANE
CAMELIA CL
ASTER DR
LARKSPUR WK
CAMPELL CL
ESKDALE CL
CONISTON
HAWKESHEAD WAY
AMBLESIDE GDS
THIRLMERE GDS
EYEBROOK GDS
BROMDALE
KICKLING WK
KESWICK CL
TROUT BECK CL
BALA CT
RUDYARD GROVE
BUTTERMERE
ELTER WALK
LADYBOWER PL
THORNTON CL
BEAUVALE GDS
BLACKDOWN
DONEGAL CL
GRASMERE GDS
ULLSWATER AV
ENNERDALE RISE
CONISTON RD
WINDERMERE WAY
RYDAL COURT
GUNTHORPE
GUNTHORPE WY
SQUIRES GT
MEALS GT
ULDALE WY
CALOBECK
BOWNESS
WASDALE GDS
PENRITH GDS
APV Baker
WOODPECKER CT
THE PENTLANDS
CLEVELANDS
WATT CL
LETH BRIDGE
HANESWATER CL
MALVERN RD
IVY GROVE
CHILTERN RI
CHEVIOT AV
PENNINE WAY
TUDOR CL
WENT DR
SWALE AV
WAVENEY GROVE
SEVERN
HEYFORD CL
WINSTON
STONE HILL
PITTON
OSBOURNE CL
PRATT AV
ILLIFE GT
RECTORS DR
ANDREWS GT
PRESTON
NIGHTINGALE CT
PASTON RIDINGS
CHADBURN
WHITWELL
SEYMOUR PL
CRABTREE
CATLEY CATHWAITE
HONEY HILL
Sch
PAYNESHOLM
SHEEPWALK
BAGLEY END
Caravan Park
RIDINGS
PARKWAY
Household Waste
GOLDCREST COURT
LOMBARDY DR
SAXBY GDS
TILTON CT
MEDBOURNE GDS
PASTON
CAMBRIAN WY
BARTRAM GATE
KENNET GDS
WITHAM
WINDRUSH DR
MARLOWE GR
FULBRIDGE ROAD
ITTER CRES
MILDMAY RD
FANE RD
PASTON LA
CAVERSTEDE RD
HOLLAND AV
BISHOPSFIELD
LUDDINGTON RD
GALLOWS
CHURCHFIELD
PASTON ROAD
MAGEE RD
LINDSEY CL
HADLEY RD
FULBRIDGE ROAD
Playing Field
SOKE
A47
Playing Field
FRANCIS GARDENS
BLUEBELL
CROCUS GRO
WELLAND
PRIMROSE CL
LAVENDER
CAMPION ROAD
PO
PINE TREE CLOSE
ACACIA DUE
POPLAR AVENUE
EASTERN AVENUE
John Mansfield School
SHELLEY
SHERIDAN RD
BECKETS
ROBERT AV
ROSE GDS
FRANCIS GDS
CHRISTOPHER CL
FOXDALE
ANTHONY
TENNYSON RD
FULBRIDGE ROAD
Playing Field
JOHNSON WK
COWPER RD
LUSTER RD
SHAKESPEARE AV
ST JAMES AV
BURNS CL
ST PAULS ROAD
VERE RD
NORTHFIELD ROAD
PEVERIL ROAD
LAWN AVENUE
FAIRCHILD WY
DOVECOTE CL
CEDAR GDS
FIGTREE WALK
LLAND
WILLOW RD
WESTERN AVENUE
ALMOND RD
CHESTNUT
CERRIS RD
BIRCHTREE
Dogsthorpe Sch
MYRTLE ROAD
MYRTLE GROVE
OLIVE RD
LILAC RD
ASH RD
NEW ENGLAND
EAGLESTHORPE
CLYNTON
CLARE RD
NORTON AV
ELMFIELD AVENUE
MAYFIELD RD
GRANGE
BROWNLOW RD
CECIL ROAD
SOUTHLANDS FV
PYECROFT
NEWMARKET CL
ACER RD
MAPLE GROVE
SYCAMORE
HAWTHORN AV
CHERRY TREE GROVE
OAKLEAF RD
BEECH
Dogsthorpe
CROWN STREET
BURMER RD
THISTLEMOOR RD
KEETON RD
BELHAM RD
LINCOLN ROAD
GT NORTHERN COTTAGES
BARNSLEY CL
PO
GILPIN STREET
ROCK RD
YORK RD
ALEXANDRA ROAD
ALLEN ROAD
STONE LA
OXFORD ROAD
EXETER ROAD
PEVERIL RD
WOODBYTH RD
BETTLES CL
AIRDALE RD
All Saints Junior School
CHANTRY RD
KINGS GDS
GARTON ST
BECK PLACE
SALLOWS RD
CHAIN CL
GRIMSHAW RD
CHELTENHAM CLOSE
BARKSTON CLOSE
NOTTINGHAM AV
DERBY DR
MANSFIELD
GRACECHURCH RD
DELAMERE CLOSE
Deacons Sch.
Peterborough Regional College
Westwood Industry
MASKEW AVENUE
Boulevard
Retail Park
A15
LINCOLN ROAD
CLARENCE RD
FERRY RD
BOULEVARD
JEANT ST
PARLIAMENT ST
WINDMILL ST
MILLFIELD
Sports Ground
QUEENS GDS
QUEENS RD
ELIZABETH CT
ALMA RD
VICTORIA RD
ST MARTINS ST
SPRING RD
MASKEW AV
PEPPERCORN CL
Indstl. Estate
Rec Grd
OCCUPATION RD
HARRIS RD
NEW ENGLAND
PASTON
THORPE
MILTON
BROTHERHOOD
NEWTON CT
BEVISHALL
TOPMOOR WY
PINEY
SADDLER
CHELMER
WARWELL
MORRIS
DRYDEN RD
WILBERFORCE
COLERIDGE PLACE
SCOTNEY ST
HERRICK ST
POPE WY
BOSWELL
GRAY
KEATS
KIPLING
CLAY
POTT
AVENUE
MONTAGUE RD
CHURCHFIELD COURT
WILLESDEN AV
SOUTHVIEW RD
COUNCIL ST
CREST
ROSLYN

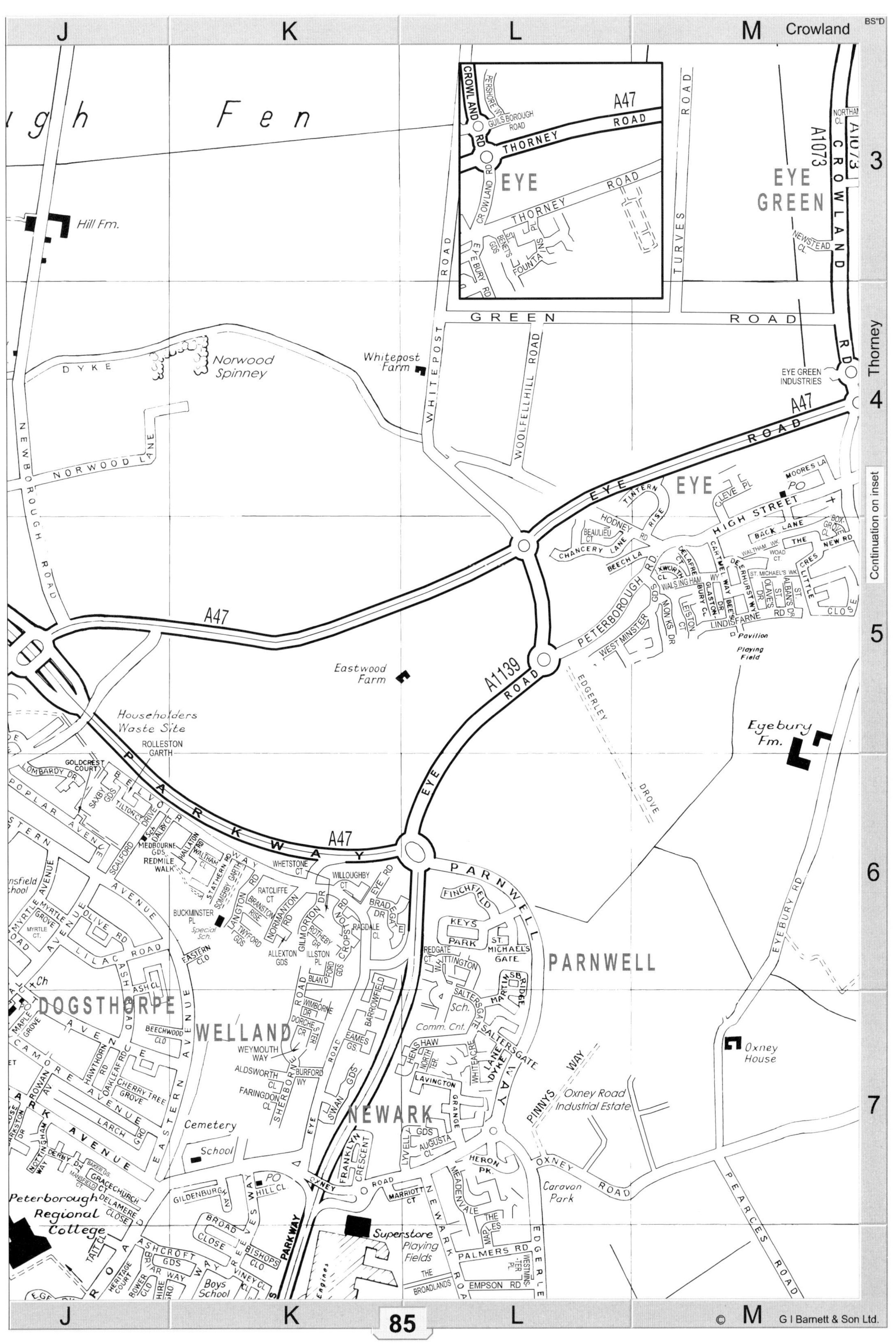
J
K
L
M   Crowland
BS"D
ough   Fen
CROWLAND RD
PERSHORE WK
GUILSBOROUGH ROAD
A47
THORNEY   ROAD
CROWLAND RD
EYE
CROWOLD RD
BENET'S GDS
FOUNTAINS
EYEBURY RD
THORNEY   ROAD
NORTHAM CL
A1073
A1073 CROWLAND RD
NEWSTEAD CL
A1073
EYE GREEN
3
ROAD
TURVES   ROAD
Hill Fm.
Thorney
DYKE
Norwood Spinney
Whitepost Farm
WHITEPOST ROAD
GREEN   ROAD   ROAD
WOOLFELLHILL ROAD
EYE GREEN INDUSTRIES
A47
4
NEWBOROUGH ROAD
NORWOOD LANE
EYE   ROAD
TIMTERN RISE
HODNEY CT
BEAULIEU CT
CHANCERY LANE
BEECH LA
HIGH STREET
BACK LANE
CLEVE PL
MOORES LA
PO
BOX GR CL
NEW RD
A47
EYE
WALSINGHAM
KWORTH CL
KELAFRE DR
CANTWEL WAY
WALTHAM WK
THE CRES
WOAD CT
NEW RD
ST OLAVE'S RD
ST ALBAN'S RD
LITTLE CLOSE
PETERBOROUGH RD
GLASTON CL
BEESTON
LEISTON
LINDISFARNE
ST MICHAEL'S WK
Pavilion
Continuation on inset
5
WEST MINSTER
MONKS DR
Playing Field
A1139   ROAD
EDGERLEY
Eastwood Farm
Egebury Fm.
Householders Waste Site
ROLLESTON GARTH
GOLDCREST COURT
DROVE
PARKWAY
A47
EYE
6
LOMBARDY DR
POPLAR AVENUE
STERN
MANSFIELD SCHOOL
MYRTLE AVENUE
MYRTLE GROVE
MYRTLE CT
OLIVE RD
LILAC ROAD
ASH ROAD
SAXBY GDS
TILTON CT
SCALFORD
DALBY RD
MEDBOURNE GDS
REDMILE WALK
MALLARD
WALTHAM
SOMERBY GARTH
STATHERN RD
LANGTON RD
TWYFORD GDS
RATCLIFFE CT
BRANSTON RISE
NORMANTON RD
BUCKMINSTER PL Special Sch.
EASTERN CLO
ALLEXTON GDS
ILLSTON PL
GILMORTON DR
ROTHERBY GR
CROP STON RD
FORD
BLAND
WHETSTONE CT
WILLOUGHBY CT
EYE RD
BRAD GATE
RAGDALE CL
EYE GDS
EASTERN AVENUE
WELLAND
Ch
DOGSTHORPE
PO
MAPLE GROVE
SYCAMORE
BEECHWOOD CLO
HAWTHORN RD
OAKLEAF RD
CHERRY TREE GROVE
WEYMOUTH WAY
ALDSWORTH CL
FARINGDON CL
WIMBORNE DR
DORCHESTER CR
EAMES GDS
BARROWFIELD
BURFORD WY
SHERBORNE RD
EYE GDS
SWAN GDS
NEWARK
Cemetery
School
ROWAN AVENUE
LARCH AVENUE
PARK AVENUE
NOTTINGHAM WAY
DERBY DR
MANSFIELD CT
BARKERS GDS
GRACECHURCH
DELAMERE CLOSE
GILDENBURGH WAY
HILL CL
PO
REEVES WAY
FRANKLYN CRESCENT
OXNEY ROAD
MARRIOTT CT
NEWARK ROAD
Peterborough Regional College
TATTLE
HERITAGE COURT
ROWER CLO
ASHCROFT GDS
BROAD CLOSE
BISHOPS CLO
VINEYARD
PARKWAY
Engines
Superstore Playing Fields
THE BROADLANDS
HERON PK
LYVELL GDS
AUGUSTA CL
MEADENVALE
THE LES CHW
PALMERS RD
WESTMINSTER
EMPSON RD
EDGERLE ROAD
FINCHFIELD DR
KEYS PARK
ST MICHAEL'S GATE
REDGATE CT
WHITTINGTON
PARNWELL WAY
MARTINSBRIDGE
SALTERSGATE SCH.
HENSHAW
NORTH TER
WHITEACRE
LAVINGTON GRANGE
SALTERSGATE
LATTERSEY DYKE
Comm. Cnt.
PARNWELL
PINNYS WAY
Oxney Road Industrial Estate
Caravon Park
OXNEY ROAD
Oxney House
EYEBURY RD
PEARCES ROAD
7
J
K
85
L
M
© G I Barnett & Son Ltd.

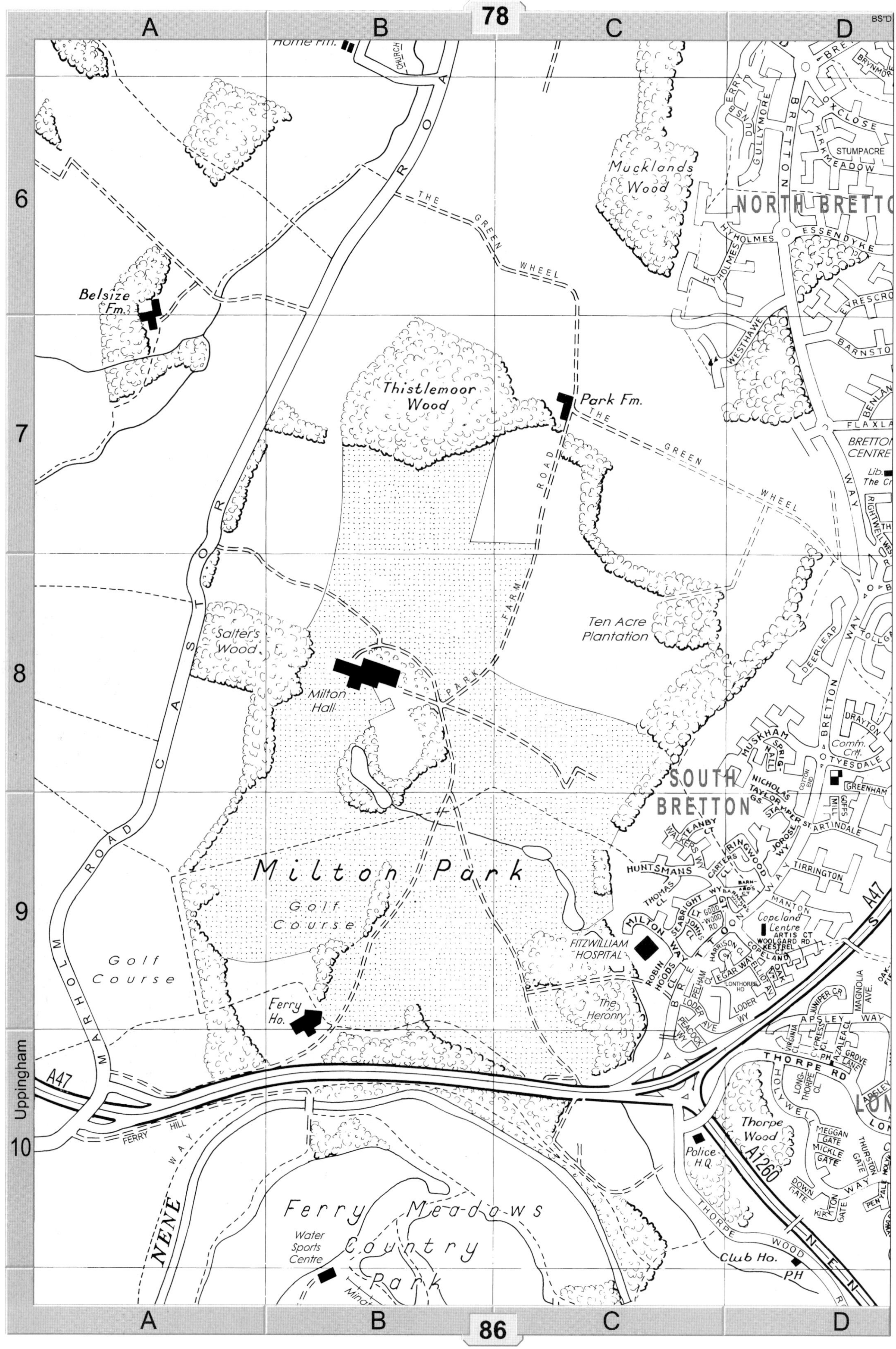
78
A
B
C
D
BS"D
Home Fm.
CHURCH
Mucklands
Wood
NORTH BRETTO
BRETTON CENTRE
BERRY
GULLYMORE
DRY
BRETTON
OXCLOSE
KIRKMEADOW
STUMPACRE
ESSENDYKE
HYHOLMES
HYHOLMES
EVRESCRO
WESTHAWE
BARNSTO
BENLAN
FLAXLA
6
THE GREEN WHEEL
Belsize Fm.
Thistlemoor Wood
Park Fm.
THE GREEN WHEEL
Lib.
The Cr
WAY
RIGHTWELWE
7
R OOR
CASS R
OY
Ten Acre
Plantation
DEERLEAP WAY
TOLLG
WA
BENLAN
8
Salter's Wood
Milton Hall
PARK ROAD
FARM ROAD
SOUTH BRETTON
MUSKHAM
SPRIG
HILL
TYESDALE
DRAYTON
Comn.
Cntl.
GREENHAM
NICHOLAS
TAYLOR
STAMPER
MARTINDALE
COTTON END
HILL
JOROSE WY
TIRRINGTON
LEANBY CT
WALKERS WY
CARTERS CL
RINGWOOD
HUNTSMANS
THOMAS CL
BARN CLO
KARESTOS
9
Milton Park
Golf Course
Golf Course
MILTON WAY
ROBIN HOODS CL
STABRIGHT
ST JOHN'S CL
LT GODD
GOOD WOOD RD
FITZWILLIAM HOSPITAL
MANTON
Copeland Centre
ARTIS CT
WOOLGARD RD
WESTREL CTRE
COPELAND
HARRISON CL
PELHAM CL
EGAR WAY
LONTHORPE RD
BRETTON
A47
MARHOLM ROAD
Ferry Ho.
The Heronry
LODER AV
PEACOCK
LODER WY
APSLEY WAY
VIRGINIA CL
CYPRESS WY
PH
AZALEAC
GROVE
MAGNOLIA AVE.
OAK
JUNIPER CR
Uppingham
A47
FERRY HILL
NENE WAY
THORPE RD
LONG THORPE CL
HOLYWELL
APSLEY LON
10
Ferry Meadows
Water Sports Centre
Country Park
Mino
Police H.Q.
A1260
Thorpe Wood
MEGGAN GATE
MICKLE GATE
THURSTON GATE
KIRKTON GATE
PENYALE
DOWN GATE
NENE
THORPE WOOD
Club Ho.
PH
A
B
C
D
86

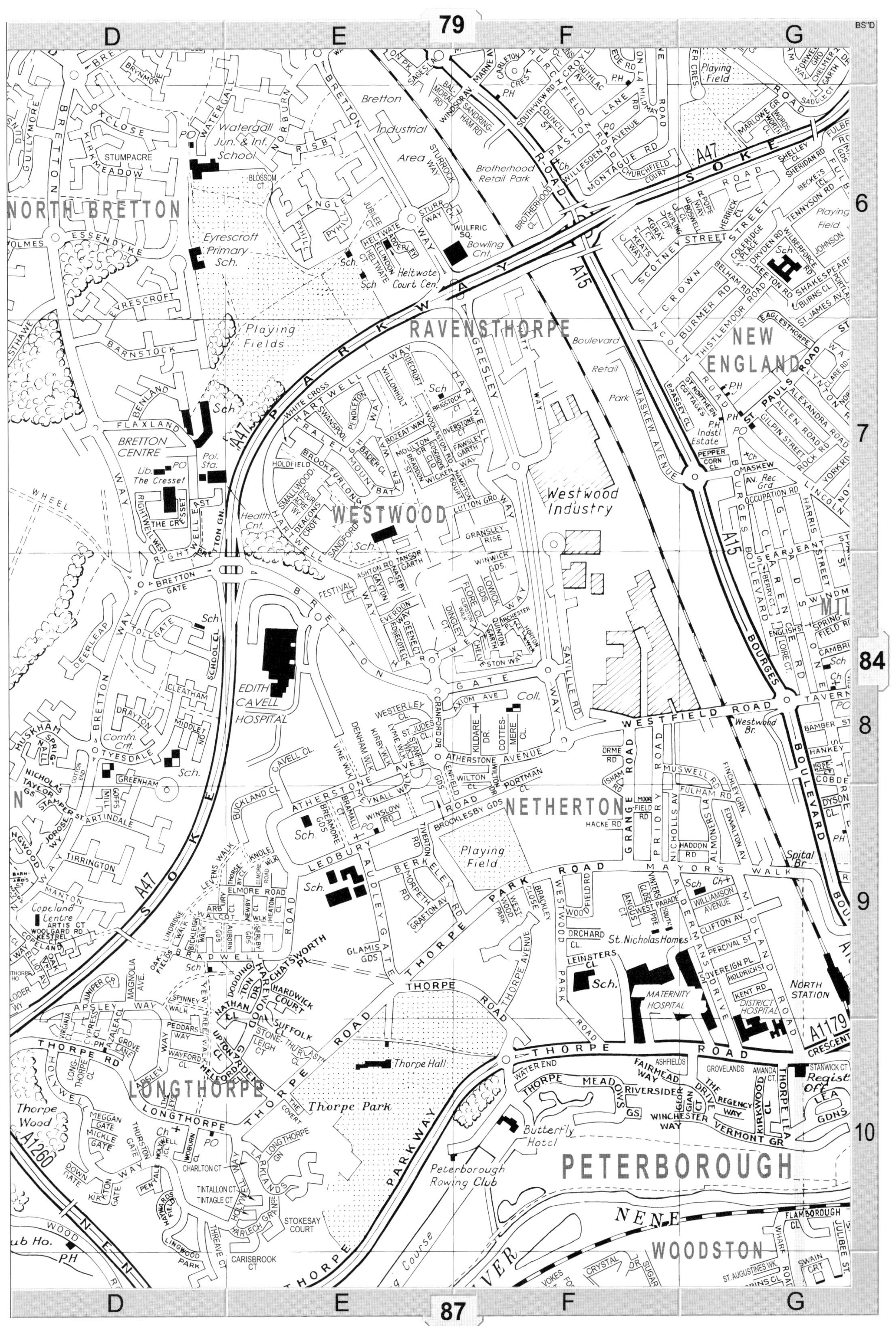

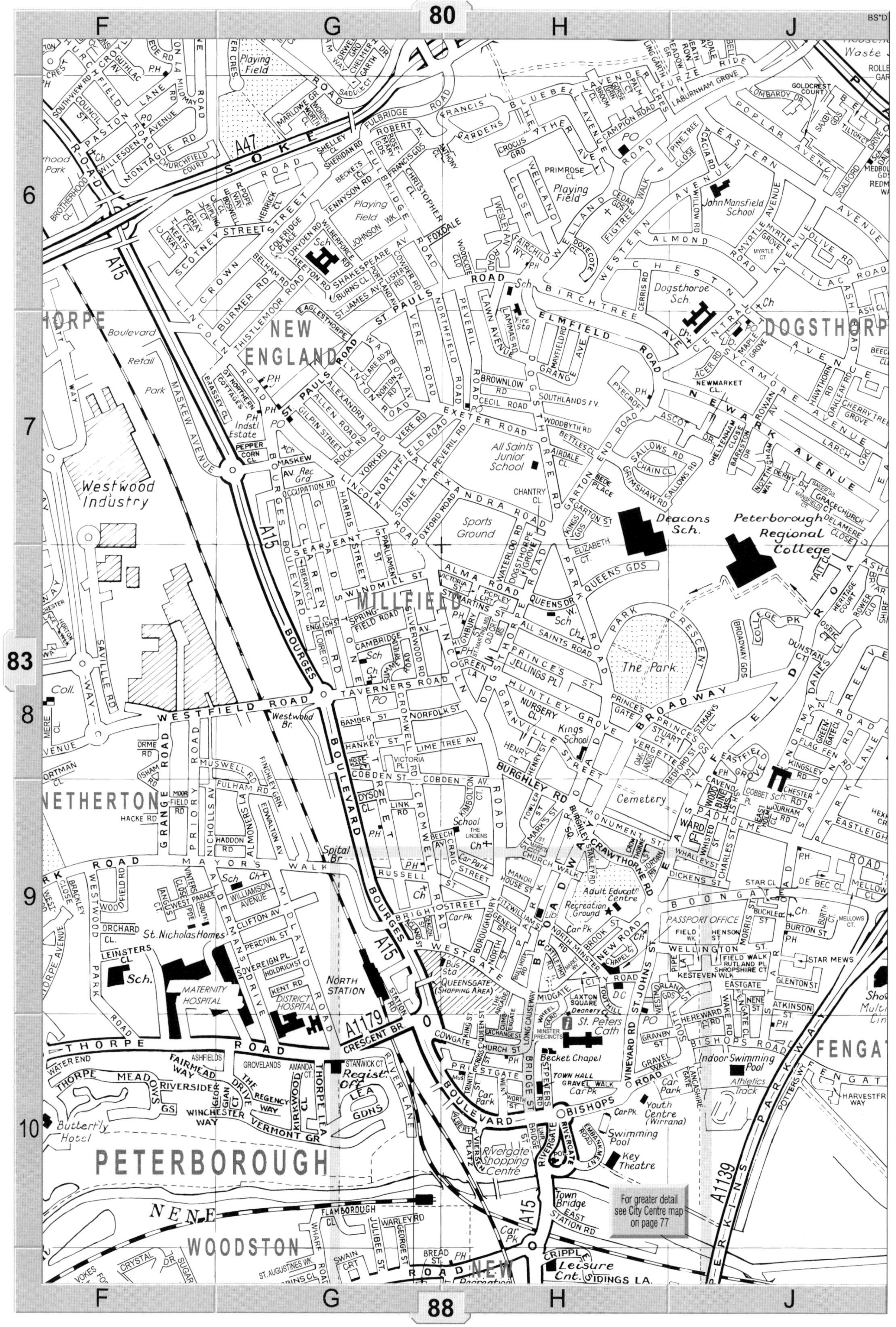

For greater detail
see City Centre map
on page 77

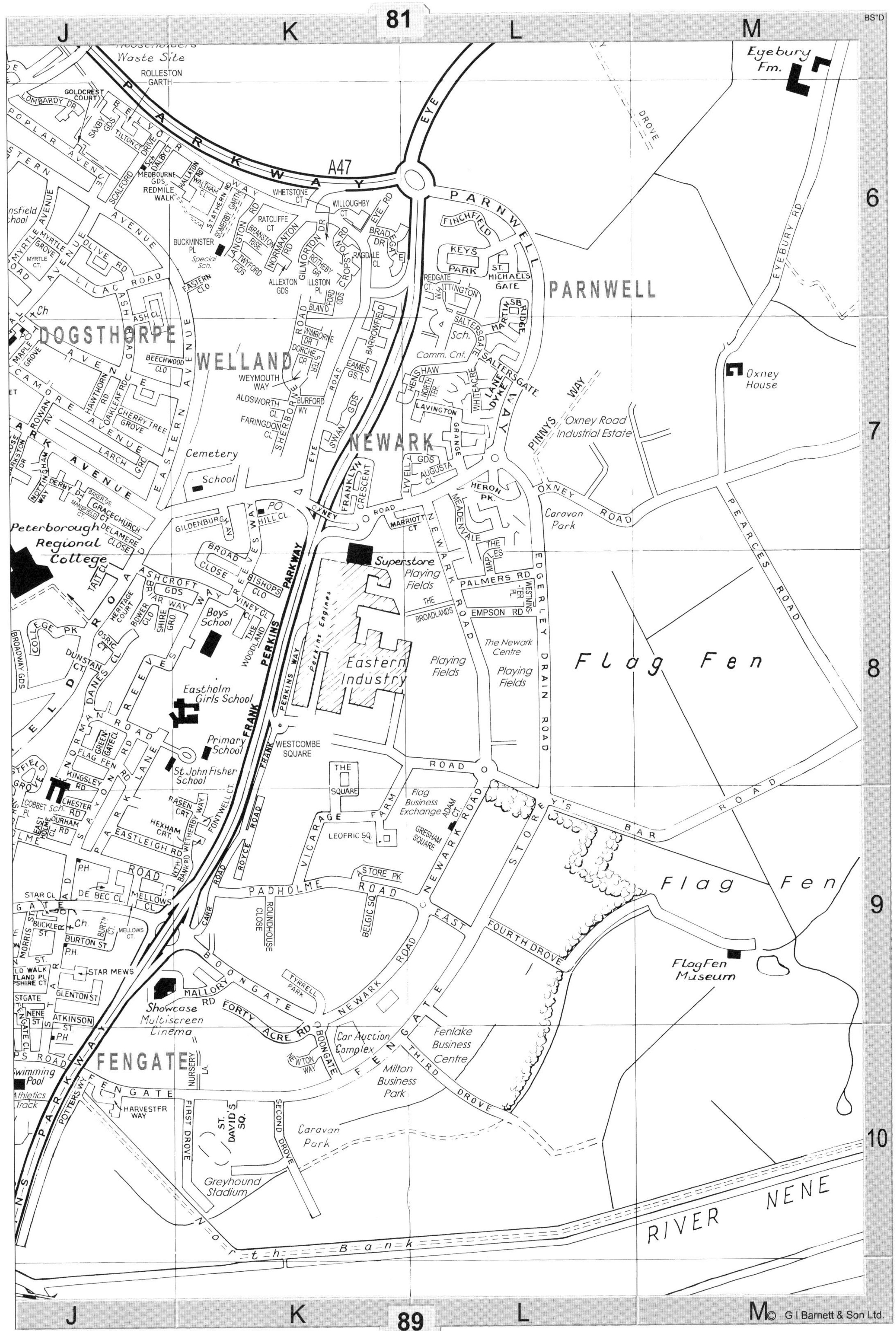

81
89
J
K
L
M
BS"D
Householders Waste Site
ROLLESTON GARTH
GOLDCREST COURT
LOMBARDY DR
POPLAR AVENUE
EASTERN AVENUE
SAXBY GDS
TILTON CT
BELVOIR DRIVE
TALBOT
SCALFORD
MEDBOURNE GDS
REDMILE WALK
WALTHAM
HALLATON
STATHERN RD
SOMERBY GARTH
WHETSTONE CT
WILLOUGHBY CT
EYE RD
BRADEGATE
WILLOUGHBY CT
PARKWAY
A47
EYE
PARNWELL
Eyebury Fm.
DROVE
EYEBURY RD
6
PARNWELL
FINCHFIELD
KEYS PARK
ST. MICHAEL'S GATE
REDGATE CT
WHITTINGTON
SALTERSGATE
MARTIN
SB
Sch.
BRIDGE
WAY
Oxney House
Myrtle AVENUE
MYRTLE GROVE
OLIVE RD
MYRTLE CT.
LILAC AVENUE
ASH RD
ASH CL
BUCKMINSTER PL
Special Sch.
LANGTON
TWYFORD GDS
RATCLIFFE CT
BRANSTON RISE
NORMANTON RD
ALLEXTON GDS
EASTERN CLO
GILMORTON DR
ROTHBY
CROPSTON
ILLSTON PL
BLAND
WIMBORNE DR
DORCHESTER CR
ROAD
BARROWFIELD
EAMES GS
BURFORD
RAGDALE CL
Comm. Cnt.
HENSHAW
NORTH TIER
WHITEACRE
LAVINGTON
SALTERSGATE
LANE
DYKE
GRANGE
MEADENVALE
HERON PK.
OXNEY ROAD
Oxney Road Industrial Estate
PINNYS WAY
Caravan Park
PEARCES ROAD
7
DOGSTHORPE
WELLAND
NEWARK
Cemetery
School
BEECHWOOD CLO
OAKLEAF RD
CHERRY TREE GROVE
HAWTHORN RD
SYCAMORE AVENUE
ROWAN AV
LARCH AVENUE
DERBY GS
BAKERS GDS
GRACECHURCH
MANSFIELD CT.
DELAMERE
CLOSE
NOTTINGHAM WAY
WEYMOUTH WAY
ALDSWORTH CL
FARINGDON CL
SHERBORNE
EYE
SWAN
BURFORD WY
FRANKLYN CRESCENT
OXNEY
ROAD
MARRIOTT CT
LYVELL GDS
AUGUSTA CL
THE MAPLES
Peterborough Regional College
GILDENBURGH AV
HILL CL.
PO
REEVES WAY
BISHOPS CLO
BROAD CLOSE
VINEY CL
THE
WOODLAND
PERKINS PARKWAY
Perkins Engines
Superstore
Playing Fields
THE BROADLANDS
PALMERS RD
WESTMINSTER PL
EMPSON RD
NEWARK ROAD
The Newark Centre
Playing Fields
EDGERLEY DRAIN ROAD
F l a g   F e n
8
ASHCROFT GDS
BAR WAY
SHIRE GRO
ROWER CLO
HERITAGE COURT
Boys School
Eastern Industry
Playing Fields
Playing Fields
BROADWAY GDS
COLLEGE PK
DUNSTAN CT
ROSRIC CL
TATTUN
DROVE
DANES ROAD
REEVES
Eastholm Girls School
FRANK PERKINS PARKWAY
Primary School
Westcombe Square
THE SQUARE
VICARAGE FARM ROAD
Flag Business Exchange
LEOFRIC SQ
ADAM CT
NEWARK ROAD
GRESHAM SQUARE
STOREY'S BAR ROAD
F l a g   F e n
9
WESTFIELD GROVE
NORMAN
GREEN GATE
FLAG FEN ROAD
KINGSLEY RD
CHESTER RD
COBBET Sch.
RASEN CRT.
HEXHAM CRT.
FONTWELL CT.
BANK
WETHERBY WAY
PADHOLME ROAD
ROUNDHOUSE CLOSE
STORE PK
BELGIC SQ
EAST
FOURTH DRIVE
FlagFen Museum
MELLOWS
DE BEC CL
MELLOWS CL
ROYCE ROAD
CARR ROAD
BOONGATE
TYRELL PARK
Car Auction Complex
Fenlake Business Centre
FENGATE
THIRD DRIVE
Star CL.
BUCKLER CL
BURTON ST
BURNT CT.
Ch.
GLENTON ST
STAR MEWS
MALLORY RD
Showcase Multiscreen Cinema
FORTY ACRE RD
BOONGATE
NEWARK ROAD
NEWTON WAY
Milton Business Park
MORRIS ST.
NENE ST
ATKINSON
WESTGATE
PH
FENGATE
POTTERS WY
HARVESTER WAY
FIRST DRIVE
ST. DAVID'S SQ
SECOND DRIVE
Caravan Park
Swimming Pool
Athletics Track
PARKWAY
FENGATE
NURSERY LA.
Greyhound Stadium
N o r t h   B a n k
R I V E R   N E N E
10
J
K
L
M
© G I Barnett & Son Ltd.

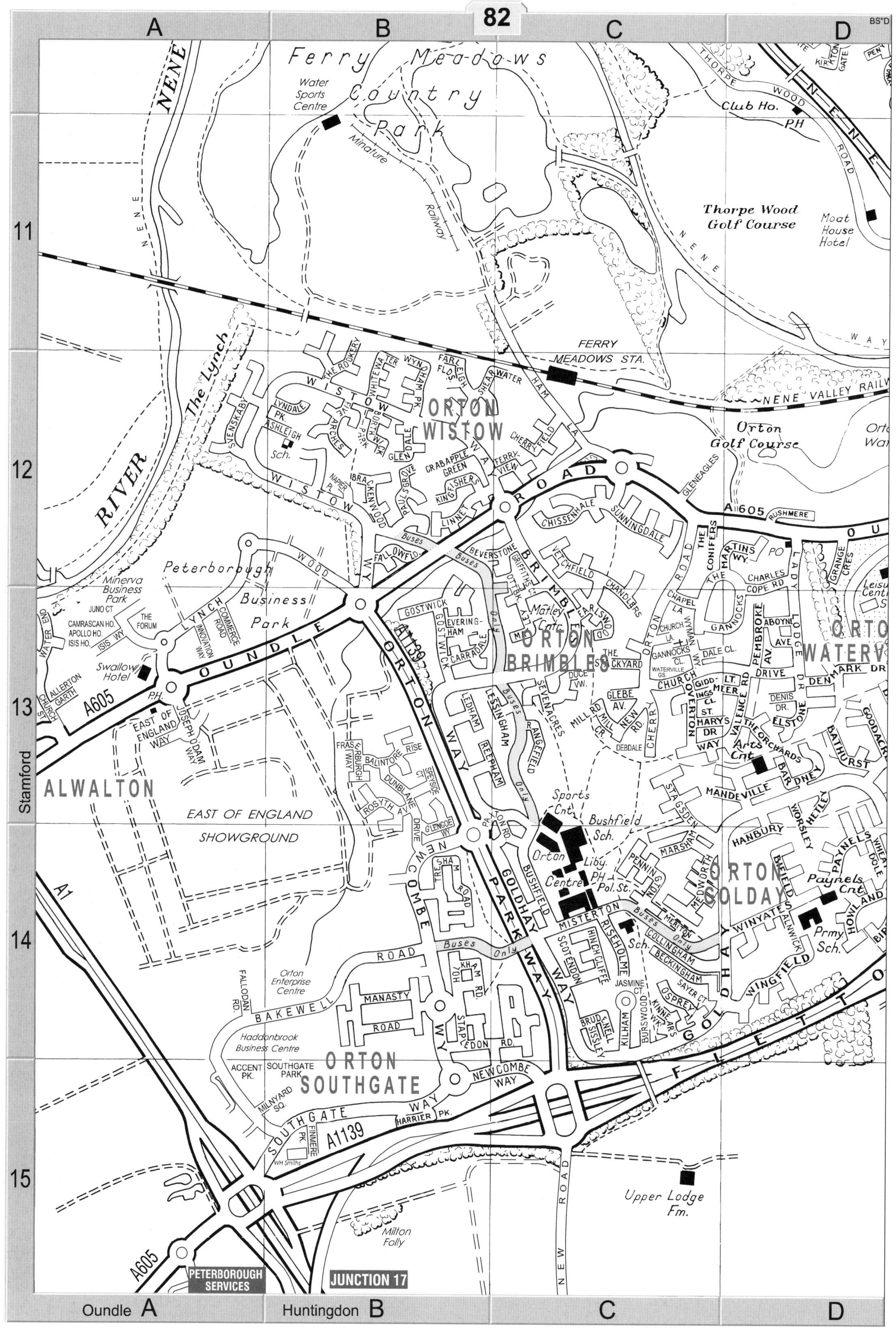

82
A B C D
BS"D
NENE
Ferry Meadows Country Park
Water Sports Centre
Minature
Railway
Club Ho.
PH
NENE ROAD
KIRK GATE
PEN
Thorpe Wood Golf Course
Moat House Hotel
NENE
11
The Lynch
RIVER NENE
WISTOW
THE ROOKERY
WHITLEWA TER
WYNDHAM PK.
FARLEIGH FLDS.
SHEARWATER
ORTON WISTOW
FERRY MEADOWS STA.
NENE VALLEY RAILW
Orton Golf Course
Orto War
LYNDALE PK.
ASHLEIGH
Sch.
SVENSKABY
BRACKENWOOD
NAPIER
IBRA
GLENDALE
BURNWICK PK.
PAUL'S GROVE
CRABAPPLE GREEN
KING'S
LINNET
FISHER
FERRY VIEW
CHERRY FIELD
BRIMBLE ROAD
CHISSENHALE
SUNNINGDALE
GLENEAGLES
A 605 RUSHMERE
12
WISTOW
FALLOWFIE
Buses
Buses
BEVERSTONE
GRIFFTHS
OTTBK
VETCHFIELD
CHANDLERS
THE CONIFERS
THE MARTINS WY.
PO
CHARLES COPE RD.
OU
Peterborough Business Park
WOOD
COMMERCE ROAD
INNOVATION WAY
GOSTWICK
EVERING- HAM
Matley Cntr.
EARLSWO
CHAPEL LA
CHURCH LA
WYMAN
GANNOCKS
GRANGE CRES
ORT WATERV
Minerva Business Park
JUNO CT.
THE FORUM
LYNCH
GOSTWICK
CARRADALE
ORTON BRIMBLES
THE BACKYARD
GANNOCKS GS
WATERVILLE GS
DALE CL.
ORTON OVERTON
LT. MEER
ABOYNE AV.
PEMBROKE DRIVE
LEIS Centr S
CAMRASCAN HO.
APOLLO HO.
ISIS HO.
ISIS WY.
OUNDLE
DUCE VW.
GLEBE AV.
NEW RD.
CHURCH DR
GIDD GS
CL
DENIS DR.
ELSTONE
DENMARK DR
13
WATER END
ALLERTON GARTH
Swallow Hotel
PH.
A605
Stamford
CHURCH
A 605
EAST OF ENGLAND WAY
JOSEPH DAM WAY
ORTON WAY
EDHAM
LESSINGHAM
REEPHAM
SEVENACRES
RANGEFIELD
MILL RD.
MILL CR.
DEBDALE
CHERRY
ST. MARYS DR WAY
VALENCE RD.
THE ORCHARDS
BAR
DNEY
BATHURST
GOODAC
ALWALTON
EAST OF ENGLAND SHOWGROUND
FRASER
FRENBURGH WAY
BALINTORE RISE
DUNBLANE
ROSYTH AV.
SPEYSIDE
GLENGOE
Buses
Sports Cntr.
Buses Only
PAXTON RD.
Bushfield Sch.
STA GSDEN
MANDEVILLE
MARSHAM
HANBURY
ARTS Cntr
WORSLEY
PAYNELS
HEILEY
DOLE
14
A1
NEWCOMBE
TRESHAM ROAD
GOLDHAY PARK WAY
Orton Centre
Liby.
PH
Pol. St.
PENNING
MEDWORTH
MEARTON
Buses Only
ICOLLINGHAM
RISEHOLME Sch.
MISTERTON
HINCHCLIFFE
SCOTENDON
BECKINGHAM
ORTON GOLDAY
BFIELD
WINYATES
ALNWICK
WINGFIELD
GOLDHAY
Paynels Cntr.
Prmy. Sch.
HOWLAND
WHEAT
BIR
15
Orton Enterprise Centre
FALLODAN RD.
BAKEWELL
MANASTY ROAD
STAPLEDON
ROAD
KH. M
KH. M RD.
JASMINE CT.
BRUD SISSLEY
KILHAM
SNELL
SAYER CT.
BURSWOOD
KINNEAR
OSPREY
NEWCOMBE WAY
FLET TO
Haddonbrook Business Centre
ACCENT PK.
SOUTHGATE PARK
MILNYARD SQ.
ORTON SOUTHGATE
STAPLEDON WY.
WAY
HARRIER PK.
SOUTHGATE WAY
FINMERE
WH Smiths
A1139
NEW ROAD
Upper Lodge Fm.
A605
PETERBOROUGH SERVICES
JUNCTION 17
Milton Folly
Oundle A
Huntingdon B
C
D

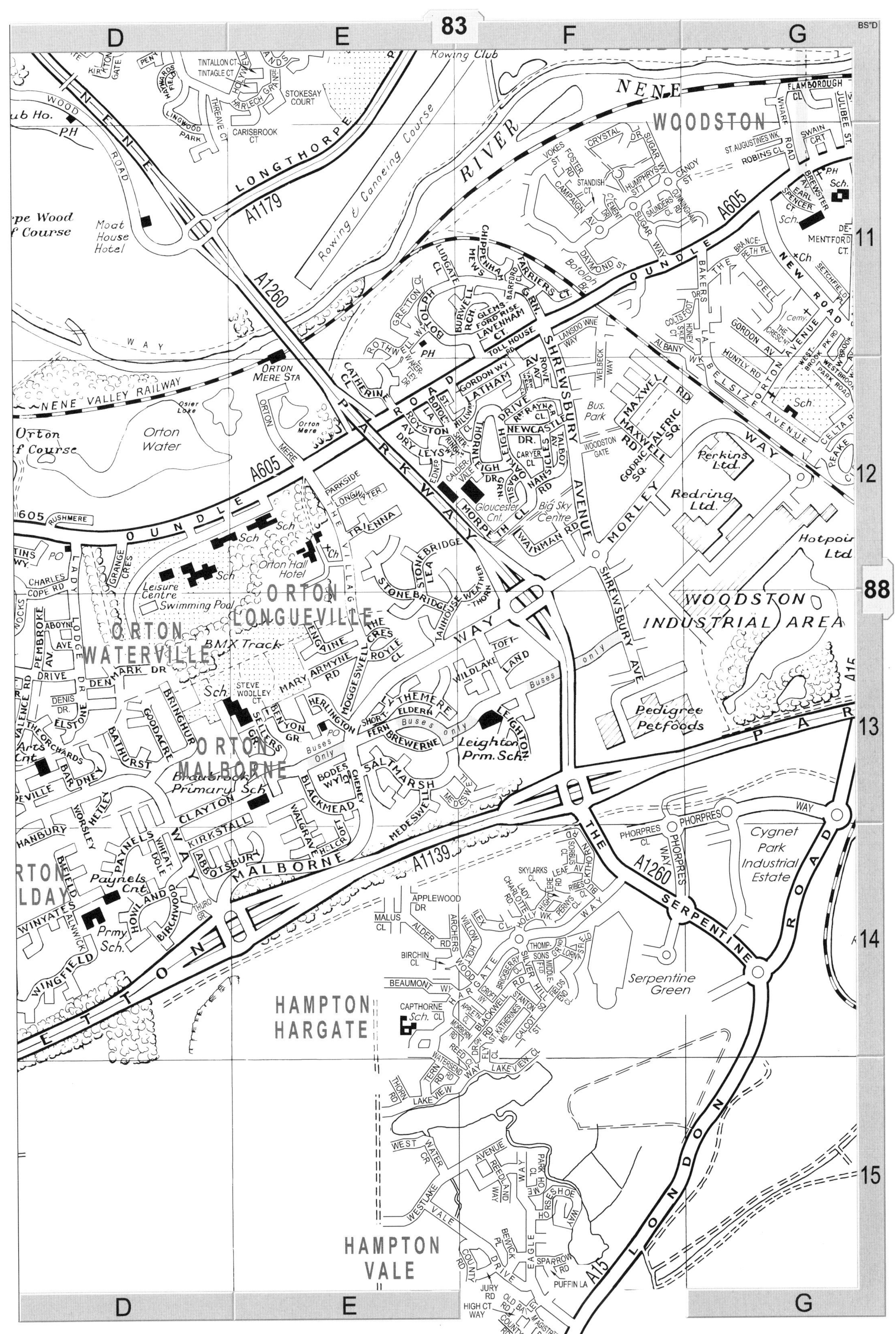
83
D E F G
NENE
WOODSTON
RIVER
Rowing Club
Rowing & Canoeing Course
Moat House Hotel
A1179
A1260
Orton Mere Sta
NENE VALLEY RAILWAY
Osier Lake
Orton Mere
Orton Water
A605
ORTON LONGUEVILLE
ORTON WATERVILLE
Leisure Centre
Swimming Pool
BMX Track
ORTON MALBORNE
Braybrook Primary Sch
A1139
HAMPTON HARGATE
HAMPTON VALE
WOODSTON INDUSTRIAL AREA
Pedigree Petfoods
Redring Ltd.
Perkins Ltd.
Hotpoint Ltd.
Cygnet Park Industrial Estate
Serpentine Green
LONDON ROAD
A15
A1260
SERPENTINE
THE PARKWAY
OUNDLE ROAD
SHREWSBURY AVENUE
BELSIZE AVENUE
NEW ROAD
A605
Leighton Prm. Sch.
Big Sky Centre
Gloucester Cnt.
11
12
88
13
14
15

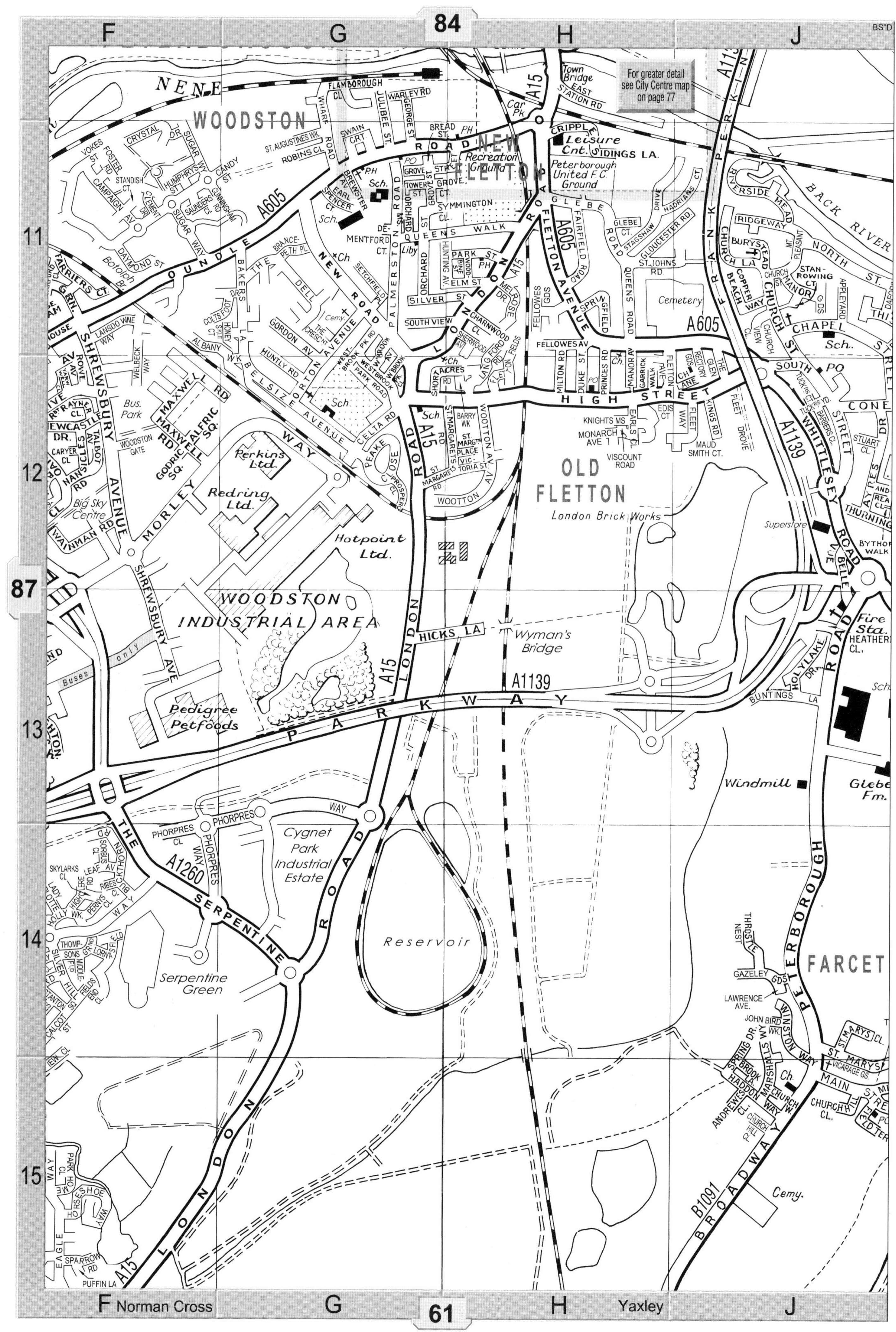
84
F G H J
BS"D
NENE
WOODSTON
For greater detail
see City Centre map
on page 77
Town Bridge EAST STATION RD.
Car Pk
CRIPPL
Leisure Cnt. SIDINGS LA.
FLAMBOROUGH
WHARF RD.
JULIBEE ST.
WARLEY RD.
SWAIN CRT.
BREAD ST.
PH
Recreation Ground
Peterborough United F.C. Ground
BACK RIVER
NORTH ST.
RIVERSIDE MEAD
RIDGEWAY
BURYSTEAD
COPPER WAY
MANOR
STAN ROWING
APPLEYARD
CHURCH ST.
VOKES
CRYSTAL
DR.
SUGAR WAY
FOSTER RD.
STANDISH
HUMPHRYS ST.
CANDY ST.
ST. AUGUSTINES WK.
ROBINS CL.
BREWSTER
EARL SPENCER
Sch.
DE- MENTFORD CT.
PO GROVE
TOWER ST.
ORCHARD GROVE
SYMMINGTON
GLEBE CT.
ST.JOHNS RD.
GLOUCESTER RD.
STAGSHAW DRIVE
HADRIANS CT.
FAIRFIELD RD.
SPRINGFIELD
RECTORY VIEW
CHURCH VIEW
CHAPEL
Sch.
SOUTH
PO
CONE
11
CAMPAIGN AV.
DAYMOND ST.
SUGAR WAY
CUNNINGHAM
SAUNDERS
CLEMENT ST.
Boroph
OUNDLE
A605
NEW ROAD
Ch
Sch.
PALMERSTON RD.
NEW ROAD
SETCHFIELD
QUEENS WALK
Liby
PARK
PINEWOOD
ELM ST.
SILVER ST.
SOUTH VIEW
CHARNWOOD
MELROSE
FELLOWES
GLEBE ROAD
QUEENS ROAD
FLETTON AVENUE
A605
A15
Cemetery
A605
CHURCH
MT. PLEASANT
THI
HARRIERS CT.
SHREWSBURY AVE.
HOUSE AV.
ROWE AV.
LANSDOWNE WAY
WELDECK WAY
THE DELL
BAKERS LA.
DRS.
COLTSFOOT
HONEY
ALBANY WK.
GORDON AV.
HUNTLY RD.
BELSIZE AVENUE
Cemy.
WEST BROOK
WESTBROOK
PARK ROAD
SHORT ACRES
LANGFORD
FELLON FIELDS
FELLOWES AV.
MILTON RD.
DUKE ST.
PRINCES RD.
GARRICK WALK
FLETTON AVE.
GLEN GDNS.
KINGS RD.
FLEET WAY
South
TUCKS YD.
BARBERS CT.
STUART CL.
AYRES
REA CL.
THURNING
NEWCASTLE DR.
TALBOT CL.
CARYER CL.
NANSEN RD.
GODRIC SQ.
MORLEY RD.
MAXWELL RD.
MAXWELL SQ.
ALFRIC SQ.
THE CRESCENT
HUNTLY RD.
MORTON AVENUE
WEST BROOK
CELTA RD.
ST. MARGARETS
BARRY WK.
ST. MARGARETS PLACE
WOOTTON AV.
HIGH
STREET
KNIGHTS MS.
MONARCH AVE.
EARLS CL.
EDIS CT.
MAUD SMITH CT.
FLEET DRIVE
A1139
BYTHORM WALK
12
Big Sky Centre
WAINMAN RD.
Bus. Park
WOODSTON GATE
Perkins Ltd.
Redring Ltd.
WAY
PEAKE
CLOSE
PROSPER
A15
WOOTTON
VIC- TORIA ST.
VISCOUNT ROAD
OLD FLETTON
London Brick Works
Superstore
87
Hotpoint Ltd.
SHREWSBURY AVE.
WOODSTON INDUSTRIAL AREA
A15
LONDON ROAD
HICKS LA.
Wyman's Bridge
A1139
Fire Sta.
HEATHER CL.
HOLYLAKE DR.
ROAD
BELLE V'E
Buses only
BUNTINGS LA.
Sch.
13
Pedigree Petfoods
PARKWAY
Windmill
Glebe Fm.
THE BLACKTHORN RD.
PHORPRES CL.
PHORPRES WAY
WAY
Cygnet Park Industrial Estate
SERPENTINE ROAD
PETERBOROUGH ROAD
SKYLARKS CL.
LEAF AV.
RIBESCL.
PENNYS WAY
A1260
THRISTLE NEST
GAZELEY GDNS.
14
THOMP. SONS CL.
SILVER FLD.
LADY LOTTIE HOLLY WK.
MIDDLE HILLS
THE FIELDS
Serpentine Green
Reservoir
FARCET
LAWRENCE AVE.
JOHN BIRD WK.
SPRING DR. WY.
WINSTON WAY
ST. MARYS CL.
VICARAGE GS.
MAIN STREET
15
PARR WAY
HORSESHOE WAY
EAGLE
SPARROW RD.
PUFFIN LA.
A15
LONDON ROAD
ANDREWS CL.
HADDON CL.
MARSHALLS WAY
BROOK
Ch.
CHURCH W.
CHURCH TILL PL.
CHURCHILL CL.
B1091 BROADWAY
Cemy.
F Norman Cross G 61 H Yaxley J

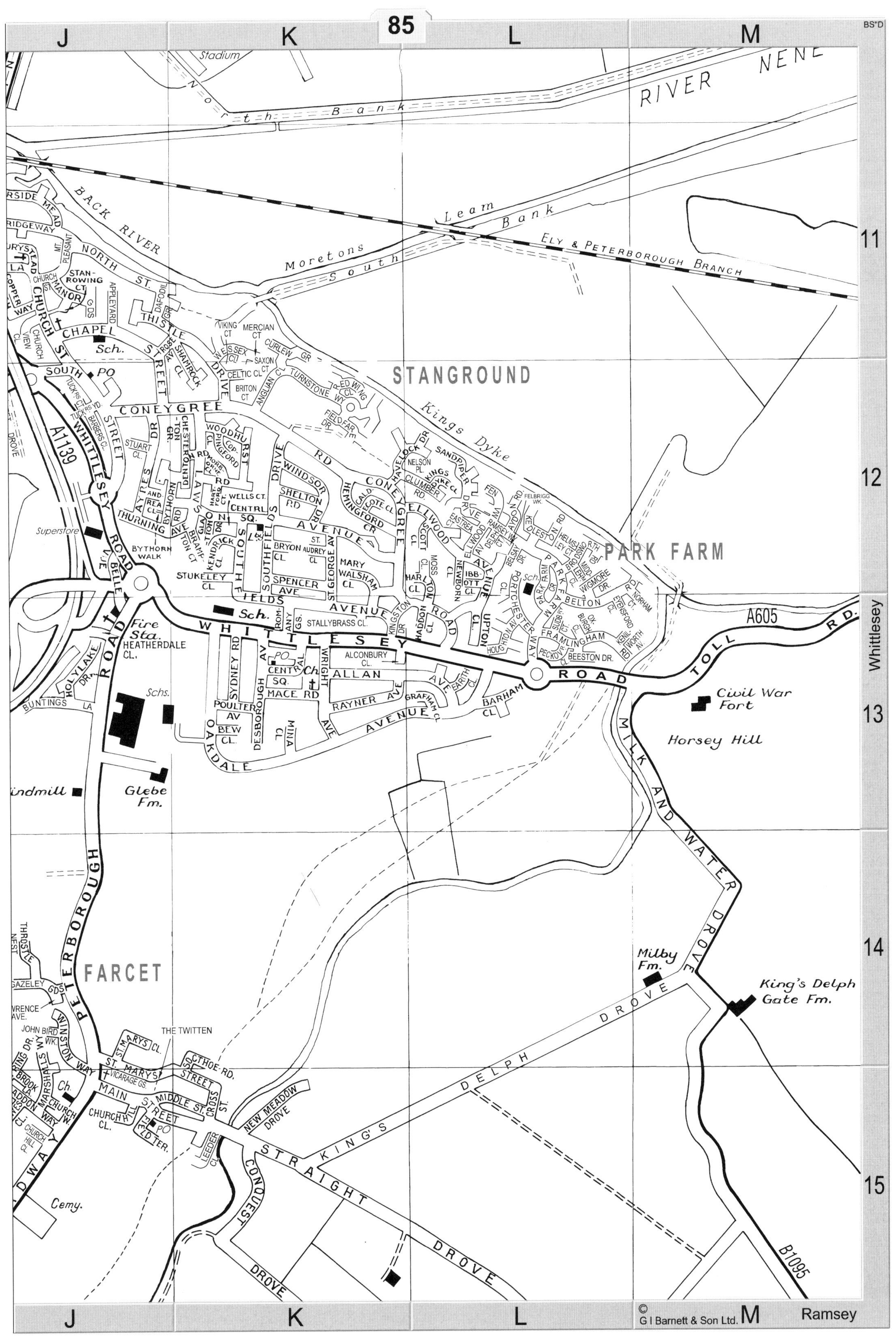
85
J   K   L   M
BS"D
RIVER NENE
Stadium
North Bank
Leam Bank
BACK RIVER
Moretons South Bank
Ely & Peterborough Branch
RSIDE MEAD
RIDGEWAY
URYSTEAD
LA
MT PLEASANT
NORTH ST.
COPPER WAY
CHURCH ST.
STAN-ROWING CT.
MANOR
G DS
APPLEYARD
CHURCH VIEW
CL.
CHAPEL
Sch.
THISTLE STREET
DAFODIL
ROSE
SHAMROCK CL.
DRIVE
VIKING CT
MERCIAN CT
WESSEX CL
CURLEW GR.
SAXON
CELTIC CL.
ANGLIAN CT.
TURNSTONE WY.
RED WING
STANGROUND
Kings Dyke
SOUTH
PO
CONEYGREE STREET
CHESTERHOLM
TON GR.
ROSE DR.
STUART CL.
AYRES DR.
AND REA CL.
NORHAM
BYTHORN CT.
AVE
HART RD.
GLAOON
WOODHURST
COP.
PINGFORD
MORE RD.
KENDRICK CL.
HIGGS
SOUTHFIELDS
DRIVE
WELLS CT.
CENTRL. SQ.
SHELTON RD.
WINDSOR
RD
HEMINGFORD CR.
RD
CONEYGREE
BRANT
STUKELEY CL.
FIELDS
BRYON AV.
AUDREY AV.
ST.
SPENCER AVE
MARY WALSHAM CL.
AVENUE
ST. GEORGE AV.
HAVELOCK DR.
SANDPIPER CL.
NELSON PL.
KINGS DYKE CL.
CLUMBER
FEN
ELLWOOD
SCOTT
CASTREA
RD
NOQUAY
RAMSEY
DELPH
KEOSES
NO LEY
HELMSDON RD
FELBRIGG WK.
PARK FARM
WIGMORE DR.
NORHAM
EVENSFORD
KINIL RD.
PARK FARM
BELTON
PORTCHESTER WAY
FRAMLINGHAM
BEESTON DR.
HARLTON CL.
MOSS CL.
IBB OTT CL.
NEWBORN
UPTON CL.
HOUGH
PECKO
A1139
WHITTLESEY ROAD
BYTHORN WALK
Superstore
THURNING
BELLE
Fire Sta.
HEATHERDALE CL.
ROAD
HOLYLAKE DR.
BUNTINGS LA
Schs.
Windmill
Glebe Fm.
WHITTLESEY
Sch.
ROM
ANY GS.
STALLYBRASS CL.
AVENUE
SYDNEY RD
AV
PO
CENTRAL SQ.
Ch
WRIGHT RD.
ALCONBURY CL.
ALLAN
MACE RD.
KINGSTON
DR
HADDON ROAD
ERITH
AVE
BARHAM CL.
ROAD
A605
Whittlesey
TOLL RD.
POULTER AV
DESBOROUGH
MINA
RAYNER AVE
AVE
GRAFHAM CL.
AVENUE
OAKDALE
BEW CL.
Civil War Fort
MILK AND WATER DROVE
Horsey Hill
PETERBOROUGH ROAD
FARCET
THROSTLE NEST
GAZELEY GDS.
LAWRENCE AVE.
JOHN BIRD WK.
WINSTON WAY
THE TWITTEN
RING DR.
MARSHALL
BROOK LA
HADDON WAY
CHURCH VW.
CHURCH CL.
CHURCH HILL
Ch.
ST MARYS CL.
ST MARYS
VICARAGE GS.
CTHOE RD.
STREET
MAIN STREET
MIDDLE ST.
CROSS ST.
LEEDER CL.
FLD TER.
PO
NEW MEADOW DROVE
Milby Fm.
King's Delph Gate Fm.
DELPH DROVE
STRAIGHT DROVE
KING'S DROVE
CONQUEST DROVE
Cemy.
B1095
© G I Barnett & Son Ltd.
Ramsey
11
12
13
14
15
J   K   L   M

PETERBOROUGH INDEX TO STREETS

Abbey Road F.5
Abbotsbury D.14
Abbotts Grove............................E.2
Aboyne Avenue D.13
Acacia Avenue J.6
Accent Park B.15
Acer Road J.7
Acland Street G.9
Adam Close L.9
Adderley....................................E.6
Addington Way E.4
Ainsdale Drive E.4
Airedale Close H.7
Albany Walk................................F.11
Albert Place H.10
Alconbury Close K.13
Alder Road E.14
Aldermans Drive.......................G.9
Aldsworth Close K.7
Alexandra Road G.7
Alfric Square F.12
All Saints Road H.8
Allan Avenue K.13
Allen Road G.7
Allerton Garth A.13
Allexton Gardens K.6
Alma Road H.8
Almond Road H.6
Almoners Lane G.9
Alnwick D.14
Amanda Close G.10
Amberley Slope E.4
Ambleside Gardens G.4
Andrea Close J.12
Andrewes Close J.15
Andrews Crescent G.5
Anglian Close K.11
Angus Court F.9
Anthony Close H.6
Apollo House A.13
Appleton Close F.14
Applewood Drive E.14
Appleyard J.11
Apsley Way................................D.10
Arbury Close...............................D.9
Archers Wood E.14
Artingdale D.9
Artis Court D.9
Arundel Road E.5
Ascot Drive J.7
Ash Close J.6
Ash Park....................................E.2
Ash Road J.7
Ashburn Close C.1
Ashcroft Gardens J.8
Ashfields F.10
Ashleigh....................................B.12
Ashton Road..............................E.8
Aster Drive F.4
Astore Park K.9
Atherstone Avenue E.8
Atkinson Street J.9
Auborn Gardens E.9
Aubretia Avenue F.4
Audley Gate E.9
Augusta Close............................L.7
Avon Court G.5
Axiom Avenue F.8
Aydon Road L.12
Ayres Drive J.12
Azalea Close D.10

Back Lane L.5
Bader Close E.7
Bagley End J.5
Baker Gardens J.7
Baker Street H.10
Bakers Close F.11
Bakers Lane F.11
Bakewell Road A.14
Bala Court F.4
Balintore Rise B.13
Balmoral Road E.5
Bamber Street G.8
Barbers Close J.12
Barbers Hill...............................E.1
Bardney D.13
Barford Close F.11
Barham Close L.13
Barkston Drive...........................J.7
Barn Close E.4
Barnard Court D.9
Barnard Way..............................D.9
Barnes Way E.4
Barnstock D.7
Baron Court F.3
Barrowfield K.7
Barry Walk H.11
Bartram Gate G.5
Basil Green F.12
Bathurst D.13
Beaulieu Court L.5
Beaumont Way E.14
Beauvale Gardens G.4

Beckets Close G.6
Beckingham C.14
Bede Place H.7
Bedford Street............................J.8
Beech Avenue G.9
Beech Lane L.5
Beechwood Close J.7
Beeston Drive L.13
Belgic Square K.9
Belham Road G.6
Belle Vue J.12
Belsay Drive L.12
Belsize Avenue G.12
Belton Road L.12
Belvoir Way J.6
Benedict Square E.4
Benland D.7
Berkeley Road E.9
Berry Court G.8
Bettles Court.............................H.7
Beverstone B.12
Bevishall...................................G.5
Bew Close K.13
Bewick Place F.15
Bickleigh Walk D.9
Bifield D.14
Birchin Close E.14
Birchtree Avenue H.6
Birchwood.................................D.14
Birkdale Avenue E.4
Bishop's Close K.8
Bishop's Road H.10
Bishopsfield F.5
Blackdown Garth.......................F.4
Blackmead E.14
Blackwell Road F.14
Blandford Gardens K.6
Blind Lane D.9
Bluebell Avenue H.6
Bodesway E.14
Boongate J.9
Boongate K.9
Boroughbury.............................H.9
Borrowdale Close G.4
Borthwick Park B.12
Boswell Close............................G.6
Botolph Green E.11
Bourges Boulevard....................G.7
Bower Close J.8
Bowling Alley F.6
Bowness Way H.4
Boxgrove Close M.5
Bozeat Way E.7
Brackenwood B.12
Brackley Close F.9
Braddon Street E.7
Bradegate Drive K.6
Bradwell Road D.9
Bramall Court E.9
Brampton Court K.12
Branston Rise K.6
Brassey Close G.7
Braybrook D.14
Bread Street G.11
Breamore Gardens E.9
Brendon Garth G.5
Bretton Centre D.7
Bretton Gate D.8
Bretton Gate E.8
Bretton Green D.7
Bretton Way C.9
Brewerne E.13
Brewster Avenue G.11
Briar Way...................................J.8
Brickberry Close F.14
Bridge Street H.10
Bridgehill Road F.2
Bright Street G.9
Brigstock Court E.7
Brimbles Way C.12
Bristol Avenue E.4
Briton Court K.12
Broad Close K.7
Broadway H.9
Broadway J.15
Broadway Gardens J.8
Brocklesby E.9
Brocklesby Gardens E.9
Brodsworth Road L.12
Brook Lane J.15
Brook Street H.9
Brookfield Home Park D.4
Brookfurlong E.7
Broom Close...............................H.6
Brotherhood Close F.6
Brownlow Road H.7
Brudenell C.14
Brynmore D.5
Buckland Close..........................E.9
Buckle Street J.9
Buckminster Place K.6
Buckthorn Road F.14
Bull Hotel Road H.9
Buntings Lane J.13

Bure Close G.6
Burford Way K.7
Burghley Road H.8
Burghley Square H.9
Burmer Road G.7
Burswood C.14
Burton Court J.9
Burton Street J.9
Burystead J.11
Bus Station Road H.10
Bus Way E.13
Bushfield...................................C.14
Buttermere Gardens G.4
Buttermere Place G.4
Byron Close K.12
Bythorn Road J.12
Bythorn Walk J.12

Calcot Street F.14
Caldbeck Close G.4
Caldecote Close L.12
Cambri Avenue G.8
Cambrian Way F.5
Camelia Close F.4
Campaign Avenue F.11
Campbell Drive...........................G.3
Campion Road H.6
Camrascan House A.13
Candidus Court E.2
Candy Street F.11
Canonsfield D.3
Canterbury Road E.4
Canwell E.3
Canwell F.3
Capthorne Close........................E.14
Caravan Parks L.7
Carisbrook Court D.11
Carleton Crescent F.5
Carlton Close E.10
Carr Road K.9
Carradale B.13
Carron Drive D.4
Carters Close C.9
Cartmel Way L.5
Caryer Close F.12
Castor Road A.8
Cathwaite H.5
Catley H.5
Cattle Market Road H.9
Cavendish Street........................J.9
Caverstede Road F.5
Cecil Road H.7
Cedar Gardens H.6
Celta Road G.12
Celtic Close K.12
Central Avenue J.7
Central Sqaure K.12
Central Square K.13
Cerris Road H.6
Chadburn H.5
Chain Close H.7
Chancery Lane L.5
Chandlers C.12
Chantry Close............................H.8
Chapel Lane C.13
Chapel Lane E.4
Chapel Street (Peterborough) ...H.9
Chapel Street (Stanground) J.11
Charles Cope D.13
Charles Cope Road D.13
Charles Street............................J.9
Charlton Court E.10
Charnwood Close H.11
Chatsfield D.2
Chatsworth Place E.9
Chaucer Road F.6
Chelmer Garth G.5
Cheltenham Close J.7
Chelveston Way F.8
Cherry Orton Road C.13
Cherryfield C.12
Cherrytree Grove J.7
Chester Road J.9
Chesterton Grove K.12
Chestnut Avenue H.6
Cheviot Avenue F.5
Cheyney Court E.13
Chiltern Ridge F.5
Chissenhale C.12
Church Drive C.13
Church Hill Close J.11
Church Lane J.11
Church Lane (Orton Brimbles) ...C.13
Church Lane (Werrington) E.4
Church Street (Alwarton) A.13
Church Street (Peterborough) H.10
Church Street (Stanground) J.11
Church Street (Werrington) J.11
Church View Close J.11
Church Walk (Marholme) B.5
Church Walk H.9
Church Walk (Farcet) J.15
Churchfield Court F.6

Churchfield Road F.5
Cissbury Ring E.4
City Road H.9
Clare Road G.7
Clarence Road G.7
Clarendon Way..........................D.1
Clavering Walk E.2
Clay Lane K.5
Clayton D.14
Cleatham D.8
Clement Drive F.11
Cleve Place M.4
Cleveland Court G.4
Clifton Avenue G.9
Clipston Walk F.8
Clumber Road............................L.12
Cobbet Place..............................J.9
Cobden Avenue G.8
Cobden Street G.8
Coleridge Place G.6
College Park J.8
Collingham C.14
Coltsfoot Drive F.11
Coneygree Road J.12
Coningsby Road.........................D.5
Coniston Road F.4
Conquest Drove K.15
Conway Avenue F.5
Copeland D.9
Copper Beech Way J.11
Coppingford Close K.12
Copsewood.................................E.3
Corfe Avenue F.5
Cosgrove Close E.7
Cotswold Close G.5
Cottesmore Close F.8
Cotton End D.8
Council Street............................F.6
County Road F.15
Coventry Close E.4
Coverdale Walk E.3
Cowgate H.10
Cowper Road G.6
Crab-Apple Green B.12
Crabtree H.5
Craig Street H.9
Cranemore D.3
Cranford Drive E.8
Crawthorne Road H.9
Crawthorne Street H.9
Crescent Bridge G.10
Cripple Sidings Lane H.11
Crocus Grove H.6
Croft Way F.14
Cromwell Road G.8
Cropston Road K.6
Cross Street H.10
Cross Street K.15
Crowhurst E.3
Crowland Road M.3
Crowland Road ....Eye Inset
Crown Street G.6
Croyland Road F.5
Crystal Drive F.11
Cumbergate H.10
Cunningham Road F.11
Curlew Grove K.12
Cypress Close D.10

Dafodil Grove J.11
Dalby Court J.6
Dale Close C.13
Danes Close J.8
David's Lane D.3
Davids Close D.3
Daymond Street F.11
De Bec Close J.9
Deacon Street G.9
Deacons Croft............................E.7
Debdale C.13
Deene Court E.8
Deerhurst Way L.5
Deerleap D.8
Delamere Close K.6
Delapre Court L.5
Demontfort Court G.11
Denham Walk............................F.8
Denis Drive................................D.13
Denton Road K.12
Derby Drive J.7
Derwent Drive G.5
Derwood Grove D.3
Desborough Avenue K.13
Dickens Street...........................J.9
Dingley Court E.8
Doddington Drive D.9
DOGSTHORPE...........................J.6
Dogsthorpe Grove H.8
Dogsthorpe Road H.7
Donaldson Drive G.4
Donegal Close............................F.4
Dorchester Crescent K.7
Dovecote Close H.6
Dover Road F.5

Down Gate D.10
Dragon Fly Close F.15
Drain Road G.2
Drayton D.8
Dry Leys E.12
Dryden Road G.6
Duce View C.13
Dudley Avenue E.5
Duke Street H.12
Dukes Mead E.4
Dunblane Drive B.13
Dunsberry D.6
Durham Road J.9
Dyson Close G.9

Eagle Way F.15
Eaglesthorpe G.7
Eames Gardens K.7
Earith Close L.13
Earl Spencer Court G.11
Earls Court H.12
Earlswood C.13
East of England Way A.13
East Station H.11
East Station Road H.10
Eastern Avenue J.6
Eastern Close K.6
Eastfield J.8
Eastfield Grove J.8
Eastfield Road J.8
Eastgate J.9
Eastleigh Road J.9
Eastrea Court L.12
Edenfield E.12
Edgcote Close E.8
Edgerley Drain Road L.8
Edgerley Drove L.5
Edinburgh Avenue E.4
Edis Court H.12
Edwalton Avenue G.9
Egar Way D.9
Eldern E.13
Elizabeth Close H.8
Ellindon E.6
Elliot Avenue D.9
Ellwood Avenue L.12
Elm Street H.11
Elmfield Road H.7
Elmore Road E.9
Elstone D.13
Elter Walk G.4
Ely Close E.4
Empson Road L.8
Enfield Gardens E.8
English Street G.8
Ennerdale Rise F.4
Eskdale Close G.4
Essendyke D.6
Everdon Way E.8
Everingham B.13
Exchange Street H.10
Exeter Road H.7
EYE M.4
Eye By-Pass J.5,K.5,L.5
Eye Green Industries M.4
Eye Road K.7
Eye Road L.6-M.4
Eyebrook Gardens G.4
Eyebury Road M.6
Eyebury Road ....Eye Inset
Eyensford Close L.13
Eyrescroft D.6

Fairchild Way H.6
Fairfield Road H.11
Fairmead Way F.10
Fallodan Road A.14
Fallowfield (Orton Wistow) B.12
Fane Road F.6
Far Pasture E.2
FARCET J.14
Faringdon Close K.7
Farleigh Fields B.12
Farley Garth F.7
Fawsley Garth F.7
Felbrigg Walk L.12
Fellowes Avenue H.11
Fellowes Gardens H.11
Fen View L.12
Fenbridge Road E.3
FENGATE J.10
Fengate Close J.9
Ferndale Way J.5
Ferry Hill A.10
Ferryview C.12
Ferryview D.12
Festival Court E.8
Field Terrace J.15
Field Walk J.9
Field Walk J.9
Fieldfare Drive K.12
Fields End Close F.14
Figtree Walk H.6
Finchfield L.6
Finchley Green G.8
Finmere Park B.15
First Drove K.10
Fitzwilliam Street H.9

Five Arches B.12
Flag Fen Road J.8
Flamborough Close G.10
Flaxland D.7
Fleet Drove J.12
Fleet Way J.12
Fletton Avenue H.11
Fletton Branch G.12
Fletton Fields H.12
Fletton Parkway C.15
Flore Close F.8
Fontwell Court K.9
Forty Acre Road K.10
Foster Road F.11
Fountains Place ....Eye Inset
Fourth Drove L.9
Foxcovert Road E.3
Foxcovert Road
   (North Werrington) D.1
Foxcovert Walk E.2
Foxdale G.6
Foxley Close E.4
Framlingham Road L.13
Francis Gardens G.6
Frank Perkins Parkway J.11
Frank Perkins Way K.8
Franklyn Crescent K.7
Fraserburgh Way B.13
Freston H.5
Fulbridge Road F.4
Fulbridge Road G.6
Fulham Road G.9
Furze Ride H.6

Gallions Close F.5
Gannocks Close C.13
Garrick Walk H.12
GARTON END H.7
Garton End Road H.7
Garton Street H.7
Gascoigne D.3
Gatenby E.3
Gaydon Court E.8
Gazeley Gardens J.14
Geneva Street H.9
George Street G.10
Georgian Court G.10
Giddings Close C.13
Gildale F.3
Gilldenburgh Avenue K.7
Gilmorton Drive K.6
Gilpin Street G.7
Gladstone Street G.7
Glamis Gardens E.9
Glastonbury Close L.5
Glatton Drive K.12
Glebe Avenue C.13
Glebe Court H.11
Glebe Road H.11
Glencoe Way B.14
Glendale B.12
Gleneagles C.12
Glenton Street J.9
GLINTON D.1
Glinton By-Pass C.1
Glinton Road A.1
Globe Street H.10
Gloucester Road H.11
Godric Square F.12
Goffs Mill D.9
Goldcrest Court J.6
Goldhay Way C.14
Goldlhay Way D.14
Goodacre D.13
Goodwin Walk E.2
Goodwood Road C.9
Gordon Avenue G.11
Gordon Way F.12
Gorse Green H.6
Gostwick B.13
Gottsmill D.9
Gracechurch Court J.7
Grafham Close L.13
Grafton Avenue E.9
Granby Street H.10
Grange L.7
Grange Avenue L.7
Grange Crescent D.12
Grange Road F.9
Gransley Road F.7
Granville Street H.8
Grasmere Gardens F.4
Gravel Walk H.10
Gray Court F.6
Great Northern Cottages G.7
Green Lane H.8
Green Man Lane B.5
Green Road L.4
Greenacres D.3
Greengate Close J.8
Greengate Court J.8
Greenham D.8
Gresham Square L.9
Gresley Way F.7
Gretton Close E.11
Griffiths Court C.12
Grimshaw Road H.7

Groom Close H.5
Grove Court G.11
Grove Lane D.10
Grove Street G.11
Grovelands G.10
Guilsborough Road ....Eye Inset
GUNTHORPE F.4
GUNTHORPE G.4
Gunthorpe Ridings G.4
Gunthorpe Road G.4
Gurnard Leys D.5
Guthlac Avenue F.5

Hacke Road F.9
Haddon Close L.13
Haddon Road G.9
Hadley Road F.5
Hadrians Court J.11
Hall Lane E.3
Hallaton Road K.6
Hallfields Lane G.4
Halton Close L.12
Ham Lane C.12
Ham Lane D.12
Hampton Court F.7
HAMPTON HARGATE F.14
HAMPTON VALE E.15
Hanbury D.14
Hankey Street G.8
Hardwick Court E.9
Harebell Close J.5
Hargate Way E.15
Harlech Grange D.10
Harrier Park B.15
Harris Street G.7
Harrison Close D.9
Hartford Court K.12
Hartwell Way E.7
Harvester Way J.10
Harwood Gardens E.9
Hastings Road E.5
Haweswater Close G.4
Hawkeshead Way G.4
Hawthorn Road J.7
Haywards Field D.10
Hazelcroft D.3
Heath Row J.5
Heather Lane H.6
Heatherdale Close J.13
Heaton Close E.9
Hedgelands E.2
Hedgelands E.3
Helmsdale Gardens E.4
Helmsley Close L.12
Helpston Road A.1
Heltwate E.6
Heltwate Close E.6
Hemingford Crescent K.12
Henry Court H.8
Henry Street H.8
Henshaw L.7
Henson Street J.9
Hereward Close J.10
Hereward Road J.9
Heritage Court J.8
Herlington E.13
Herrick Close G.6
Hetley D.14
Hexham Court J.9
Hickling Walk G.4
Hicks Lane G.13
High Court Way F.15
High Street, Eye M.5
High Street, Fletton H.12
Highbury Street H.8
Highclere Road F.14
Hill Close K.7
Hillward Close F.12
Hinchcliffe C.14
Hodgeson Avenue D.2
Hodney Road L.4
Holcroft E.14
Holdfield E.7
Holditch Street G.9
Holgate Lane E.2
Holkham Road B.14
Holland Avenue F.5
Holland Close F.5
Holly Walk F.14
Holmes Road D.1
Holmes Way G.5
Holywell Close D.10
Holywell Way D.10
Home Pasture E.2
Honeyhill H.5
Honeysuckle Court F.11
Horton Walk E.8
Houghton Avenue L.13
Howland D.14
Hoylake Drive J.13
Humphrys Street F.11
Hunting Avenue G.11
Huntly Grove H.8
Huntly Road G.12
Huntsmans Gate C.9
Hurn Road C.4
Hurn Road D.3

Hyholmes D.6
Hythegate F.3

Ibbot Close L.12
Ihlee Close G.5
Ilex Close F.14
Illston Place K.6
Irchester Place F.8
Isham Road F.8
Isis House A.13
Isis Way A.13
Itter Crescent G.6
Ivatt Way F.7
Ivy Grove F.4
Ixworth Close L.5
Ixworth Close M.5

Jasmine Close C.14
Jellings Place H.8
John Bird Walk J.14
Johnson Walk G.6
Jordon Mews H.9
Jorose Way D.9
Joseph Odam Way A.13
Jubilee Close E.6
Jubilee Street G.10
Juniper Crescent D.9
Juno Court A.13
Jury Road F.15

Keats Way F.6
Kedleston Road L.12
Keeton Road G.6
Kelso Court E.5
Kendale Close H.4
Kendrick Close K.12
Kenilworth Avenue L.13
Kennett Gardens G.5
Kent Road G.9
Kesteven Walk J.9
Kestrel Court D.9
Keswick Close G.4
Key Theatre H.10
Keys Park L.6
Kildare Drive F.8
Kilham C.14
Kilverstone E.1
Kimbolton Close H.9
King Street H.10
King's Delph Drove K.15
Kings Gardens H.7
Kingsbridge Court D.2
Kingsfishers B.12
Kingsley Road J.8
Kingston Drive L.13
Kinnear's Walk C.14
Kipling Court F.6
Kirby Walk E.8
Kirkmeadow D.6
Kirkstall E.14
Kirkton Gate D.10
Kirkwood Close G.10
Knights Mews H.12
Knole Walk E.9

Laburnum Grove J.6
Lady Charlotte Road F.14
Lady Lodge Drive D.12
Ladybower Way G.4
Lakeside F.3
Lakeview Close F.15
Lambes Court D.3
Lammas Road H.6
Lancashire Gate J.10
Lancing Close E.4
Landsdowne Way F.11
Langford Road H.12
Langley E.6
Langton Road K.6
Larch Grove J.7
Larklands E.10
Larks Green D.3
Larkspur Walk F.4
Latham Avenue F.12
Lavender Crescent H.6
Lavington Grange L.7
Lawn Avenue H.6
Lawrence Avenue J.14
Lawson Avenue K.12
Laxton Square H.9
Lea Gardens G.10
Leaf Avenue F.14
Ledbury Road E.9
Ledham B.13
Leeder Close F.15
Leighton F.13
Leinsters Close F.9
Leiston Court M.5
Leofric Square K.9
Lessingham C.13
Lethbridge Road G.5
Levens Walk D.9
Lewes Gardens F.4
Lichfield Avenue E.4
Lilac Road J.6
Lime Tree Avenue G.8

PETERBOROUGH INDEX TO STREETS (Continued)

Lincoln Gate ...H.9
Lincoln Road ...C.1
Lincoln Road ...D.4
Lincoln Road ...E.5
Lindisfarne Road ...L.5
Lindridge Walk ...D.9
Lindsey Close ...F.5
Ling Garth ...H.5
Lingwood Park ...D.10
Link Road ...G.9
Linkside ...E.5
Linnet ...B.12
Lister Road ...G.6
Little Close ...L.5
Little Johns Close ...C.9
Littlemeer ...D.13
Livermore Green ...D.2
Loder Avenue ...C.9
Loder Way ...D.9
London Road ...G.12
London Road (Hampton) ...F.15
Long Causeway ...H.10
Long Pasture ...E.3
LONGTHORPE ...D.10
Longthorpe Close ...D.10
Longthorpe Green ...E.10
Longthorpe Parkway ...E.11
Longwater ...E.12
Lonthorpe House ...C.9
Lornasfield ...F.14
Lower Bridge Streeet ...H.10
Lowick Gardens ...F.8
Lowther Gardens ...F.4
Loxley ...D.3
Luddington Road ...F.5
Lutton Grove ...F.7
Lyme Walk ...E.8
Lynch Wood ...A.13
Lyndale Park ...B.12
Lynton Road ...G.7
Lythemere ...E.13
Lyvelly Gardens ...L.7

Mace Road ...K.13
Magee Road ...G.5
Magistrates Road ...F.15
Magnolia Avenue ...D.9
Main Street ...J.15
Malborne Way ...E.14
Mallory Road ...L.9
Malus Close ...E.14
Malvern Road ...F.4
Manasty Road ...B.14
Mancetter Square ...E.5
Mandeville ...D.14
Manor Avenue ...H.12
Manor Drive ...H.4
Manor Gardens ...J.11
Manor House St. ...H.9
Mansfield Close ...J7
Manton ...D.9
Maple Grove ...J.7
Mardale Gardens ...G.4
Marholm Road ...A.10
Marholm Road ...E.5
Marine Avenue ...F.5
Market Place ...H.10
Market Way ...H.9
Marlowe Grove ...G.6
Marriott Court ...K.7
Marshalls Way ...J.15
Marsham ...C.14
Marsham ...D.14
Martin Court ...E.3
Martins Way ...D.12
Martinsbridge ...L.7
Mary Armyne Road ...E.12
Mary Walsham Close ...K.12
Maskew Avenue ...G.7
Maud Swift Close ...J.12
Maxwell Road ...G.12
Mayfield Road ...H.7
Mayor's Walk ...F.9
Mead Close ...E.5
Meadow Grove ...H.5
Meadow Road ...F.1
Meals Gate ...G.4
Medbourne Gardens ...J.6
Medeswell ...F.14
Medworth ...C.14
Medworth ...D.14
Meggan Gate ...D.10
Megnell Walk ...E.9
Melford Close ...E.10
Mellows Close ...J.9
Mellows Close ...J.9
Melrose Drive ...H.11
Mendip Grove ...G.5
Mercian Court ...K.12
Merelade Grove ...D.2
Meriton ...C.14
Mewburn ...D.5
Meynall Walk ...E.9
Mickle Gate ...D.10

Middle Pasture ...E.2
Middle Street ...J.15
Middlefield ...F.14
Middleham Close ...L.12
Middleton ...D.8
Midgate ...H.9
Midland Road ...G.9
Mildmay Road ...F.6
Milk and Water Drove ...M.13
Mill Crescent ...C.13
Mill Road ...C.13
MILLFIELD ...G.8
Milnyard Square ...B.15
Milton Road ...H.12
Milton Way ...C.9
Mina Close ...K.13
Minster Precincts ...H.10
Misterton ...C.14
Moggswell Lane ...E.12
Moggswell Lane ...E.13
Monarsh Avenue ...H.12
Monks Drive ...M.5
Monks Grove ...D.3
Montague Road ...F.6
Monument Street ...H.9
Moores Lane ...L.4
Moorfield Road ...F.9
Morbon Road ...E.14
Morborne Close ...K.12
Morland Court ...E.3
Morley Way ...F.12
Morpeth Close ...F.12
Morpeth Road ...E.9
Morris Street ...J.9
Moss Close ...L.12
Moulton Grove ...E.7
Mount Pleasant ...J.11
Mountbatten Way ...E.7
Mountsteven Avenue ...F.5
Mowbray Road ...C.5
Muskham ...D.8
Muswell Road ...F.8
Myrtle Avenue ...J.6
Myrtle Close ...J.6
Myrtle Grove ...J.6

Nab Lane ...G.5
Nansicles Road ...F.12
Napier Place ...B.12
Naseby Close ...E.8
Nathan Close ...E.9
Neaverson Road ...D.1
Nelson Place ...L.12
Nene Parkway ...D.10
Nene Street ...J.9
Nene Way (Pathway) ...A.11
NETHERTON ...F.9
NEW ENGLAND ...G.7
New England Barracks ...F.7
NEW FLETTON ...H.11
New Meadow Drive ...K.15
New Road (Orton Brimbles) ...C.13
New Road (Orton Southgate) ...C.15
New Road (Peterborough) ...H.9
New Road, Orton ...G.11
NEWARK ...K.7
Newark Avenue ...J.7
Newark Hill ...K.7
Newark Road ...K.9
Newark Road ...L.7
Newborn Close ...L.12
Newborough Road ...J.4
Newby Close ...E.9
Newcastle Drive ...F.12
Newcombe Way ...B.14
Newcombe Way ...B.15
Newmarket Close ...J.7
Newstead Close ...M.3
Newton Court ...G.5
Newton Way ...K.10
Nichol's Avenue ...F.9
Nicholas Taylor Gardens ...D.9
Nightingale Court ...H.4
Norburn ...E.6
Norfolk Street ...G.8
Norham Court ...L.13
Norman Road ...J.8
Normanton Road ...K.6
North Bank ...K.10
NORTH BRETTON ...D.6
North Station ...G.9
North Street (Peterborough) ...H.9
North Street (Stanground) ...J.11
North Terrace ...L.7
Northam Close ...M.3
Northampton and Northbank
  Road ...K.9
Northfield Road ...G.6
Northminster Road ...H.9
Norton Road ...G.7
Norwood Lane ...J.4
Nottingham Way ...J.7
Nursery Close ...H.8
Nursery Lane ...K.10

Oak View ...D.9
Oakdale Avenue ...K.12
Oaklands ...H.8
Oakleaf Road ...J.7
Oakleigh Drive ...F.12
Occupaption Road ...G.7
Odecroft ...E.7
Old Bailey Road ...F.15
Old Close Mews ...H.8
OLD FLETTON ...H.12
Oldbrook ...D.5
Olive Road ...J.6
Orchard Close ...F.9
Orchard Mews ...G.11
Orchard Street ...G.11
Orme Road ...F.8
Orton Avenue ...G.12
ORTON BRIMBLES ...C.13
ORTON GOLDHAY ...D.14
ORTON LONGUEVILLE ...E.13
ORTON MALBOURNE ...D.13
Orton Meadows ...D.12
Orton Mere ...E.12
Orton Parkway ...B.13
ORTON SOUTHGATE ...B.15
Orton Water ...D.12
ORTON WATERVILLE ...D.13
ORTON WISTOW ...B.12
Orwell Grove ...G.5
Osier Lake ...D.12
Osprey ...C.14
Osric Court ...J.8
Otterbroek ...C.13
Oundle Road ...A.13
Oundle Road ...F.11
Outfield ...D.5
Overstone Court ...F.7
Overton Road ...D.13
Overton Way ...C.13
Oxburgh Close ...L.13
Oxclose ...D.6
Oxford Road ...G.7
Oxney ...K.7
Oxney Road ...K.7
Padholme Road ...J.9
Padholme Road East ...K.9
Palm Court ...H.6
Palmers Road ...L.8
Palmerston Road ...G.11
Papyrus Road ...E.4
Park Crescent ...H.8
PARK FARM ...L.12
Park Farm Crescent ...L.13
Park Farm Way ...L.12
Park Home Road ...F.15
Park Lane ...J.9
Park Road ...H.8
Park Street ...H.11
Parkside ...E.12
PARNWELL ...L.6
Parnwell Way ...L.7
Partridge Grove ...D.3
PASTON ...G.5
Paston Lane ...F.6
Paston Parkway ...G.4
Paston Riding ...G.5
Patterdale Road ...H.4
Paulsgrove ...B.12
Pavilion ...L.5
Paxton Road ...B.13
Paynels ...D.14
Paynesholm ...H.5
Paynesholm ...H.5
Peacock Close ...D.3
Peacock Way ...C.10
Peake Close ...G.12
Pearces Road ...M.7
Peckover Close ...L.13
Peddars Way ...D.10
Pelham Close ...C.9
Pembroke Avenue ...D.13
Pembroke Grove ...D.1
Pendleton ...E.7
Pennine Way ...F.5
Pennington ...C.14
Penrith Grove ...H.4
Percival Street ...G.9
Perkins ...K.9
Pernys Close ...F.14
Pershore Way ...Eye Inset
Peterborough Branch ...F.11
Peterborough Road ...J.14
Peterborough Road ...L.5
Peterborough Road (Eye) ...L.6
Peveril Road ...H.6
Phorpres Close ...F.14
Phorpres Way ...F.14
Pine Tree Close ...J.6
Pinnys Way ...M.7
Pipe Lane ...J.9
Pipistrelle Court ...E.4
Pittneys ...G.5

Pitton Close ...G.5
Playing Field ...L.5
Ploverly ...E.3
Pope Way ...G.6
Poplar Avenue ...J.6
Popley Court ...H.8
Portland Avenue ...G.6
Portman Close ...F.8
Potters Way ...J.10
Poulter Avenue ...K.13
Pratt Avenue ...G.5
Priestgate ...H.10
Primrose Close ...H.6
Prince's Gardens ...H.8
Princes Gate ...H.8
Princes Road ...H.12
Princes Street ...H.8
Priors Gate ...D.3
Priory Road ...F.9
Prospero Close ...G.12
Provident Place ...L.8
Puffin Lane ...F.15
Pyecroft ...H.7
Pyhill ...E.6

Queen Street ...H.10
Queens Drive West ...H.8
Queens Gardens ...H.8
Queens Road ...H.11
Queens Walk ...G.11
Quinton Garth ...F.8

Ragdale Close ...K.6
Raleigh Way ...E.7
Rangefield ...C.13
Rasen Court ...K.9
Ratcliffe Court ...K.6
RAVENSTHORPE ...E.7
Rayner Avenue ...K.13
Rector's Way ...G.5
Rectory Gardens (Glinton) ...C.1
Rectory Gardens (Old Felton) ...J.12
Rectory Lane ...C.1
Redbridge ...D.2
Redgate Close ...L.6
Redmile Walk ...J.6
Redwin Close ...K.12
Reed Close ...F.15
Reedland Way ...F.15
Reepham ...B.13
Reeves Way ...J.8
Regdale Close ...K.6
Regency Way ...G.10
Ribes Close ...F.14
Richmond Avenue ...E.5
Ridgeway ...J.11
Ridings ...H.4
Rightwell ...D.8
Rightwell East ...D.7
Rightwell West ...D.7
Ringstead Road ...G.5
Ringwood ...D.9
Ripon Close ...E.4
Risby ...E.6
Riseholme ...C.14
Rivendale ...E.4
River Lane ...G.10
Rivergate ...H.10
Robert Avenue ...G.6
Robert Rayner Close ...F.12
Robin Hoods Close ...C.9
Robins Close ...G.11
Rock Road ...G.7
Rockingham Grove ...E.5
Roller Skating Rink ...K.9
Rolleston Garth ...J.6
Romany Gardens ...K.13
Rose Avenue ...J.11
Rosemary Gardens ...G.6
Rosyth Avenue ...B.13
Rotheby Grove ...K.6
Roundhouse Close ...K.9
Row Avenue ...F.12
Rowan Avenue ...J.7
Rowing Club ...F.10
Rowland Court ...E.2
Royce Road ...K.9
Royle Close ...E.13
Royston Avenue ...E.12
Rudyard Grove ...G.4
Rushmere ...D.12
Rushton Avenue ...D.3
Russell Street ...G.9
Rydale Court ...G.4

Saddle Court ...G.6
Saddlers Close ...C.1
Sages Lane ...E.5
Salisbury Road ...E.4
Sallows Road ...H.7
Saltersgate ...L.7
Saltmarsh ...E.13
Sandford ...E.7
Sandringham Road ...F.6

Sapperton E.2
Saunders Close.......................F.11
Saville Road F.8
Saxby Gardens J.6
Saxon Court K.11
Saxon Road J.9
Sayer Court C.14
Scalford Drive J.6
School Close D.8
Scotendon C.14
Scotney Street.......................F.6
Scott Close L.12
Scotts Road C.1
Seabright Way C.9
Searjeant Street G.8
Second Drove........................K.10
Serlby Gardens E.9
Serpentine Green F.14
Setchfield Place G.11
Severacres C.13
Severn Close G.5
Sewage Farm Road L.10
Seymour Place.......................H.5
Shakespeare Avenue G.6
Shamrock Close K.12
Sharma Leas D.4
Shearwater B.12
Sheepwalk H.5
Sheldrick Walk D.3
Shepherds Close E.4
Sherborne Road K.7
Sheridan Road G.6
Sheringham Way F.12
Sherwood Avenue H.11
Shire Grove J.8
Shortacres Road G.12
Shortfen E.13
Shrewsbury Avenue F.12
Silver Hill F.14
Silver Lake D.12
Silver Street G.11
Silverwood Road G.8
Sissley C.14
Skaters Way E.3
Skylarks Close F.14
Smallwood E.7
Socthoe Road........................K.14
Soke Parkway D.9
Somerby Garth K.6
Somerville D.2
Sorbus Close.........................F.14
South Bank K.11
South Parade F.9
South Street J.10
South Street J.12
South View G.11
South View Road F.6
Southfields Avenue K.12
Southfields Drive K.12
Southgate Park......................B.15
Southgate Way B.15
Southlands Avenue H.7
Sparrow Road F.15
Spencer Avenue K.12
Speyside Court B.13
Spinney Walk D.9
Spinney Walk E.9
Spring Drive J.15
Springfield H.11
Springfield Road......................G.8
Springnall D.8
Squires Gate G.4
St. Alban's Drive L.5
St. Audrey Close K.12
St. Bees Drive........................L.5
St. Benedicts Close C.1
St. Benet's Gardens ....Eye Inset
St. Botolph Lane......................E.12
St. Davids Square K.10
St. Georges Avenue K.12
St. James Avenue G.7
St. John Fisher School J.8
St. John's Road H.11
St. John's Street H.9
St. Judes Close E.8
St. Katherines Mews F.14
St. Margaret's Place H.12
St. Margaret's Road H.12
St. Mark's Close H.9
St. Marks Street H.9
St. Martins Street H.8
St. Mary's Close J.8
St. Marys Close......................J.14
St. Marys Drive C.13
St. Marys Street J.14
St. Michael's Walk M.5
St. Olave's Drive M.5
St. Pauls Road G.7
St. Peters Road H.10
Stagsden C.13
Stagsden D.14
Stagshaw Drive H.11
Stallybrass Close K.13
Stamford Road A.4
Stamper Street.......................D.9
Stan Rowing Court J.11
Standish Court.......................F.11

Stanford Walk E.8
STANGROUND.......................L.12
Staniland Way E.3
Stanley Road H.9
Stanrowing Court....................J.11
Stanton Square F.14
Stanwick Close.......................G.10
Stapledon Road B.14
Star Close J.9
Star Road J.9
Stathern Road K.6
Station Road G.9
Staverton Road D.3
Staxton Close B.5
Steve Wooley Court E.13
Stimpson Walk E.3
Stirling Way D.5
Stokesay Court E.10
Stone Lane...........................G.7
Stonebridge E.13
Stonebridge Lea E.12
Storrington Way E.4
Story's Bar Road L.9
Straight Drove........................K.15
Stuart Close J.12
Stuart Court...........................J.8
Stukeley Close K.12
Stumpacre D.6
Sturrock Way E.6
Sudbury Court........................L.13
Suffolk Close E.9
Sugar Way............................F.11
Summerfield Road G.8
Sunningdale C.12
Sunnymead D.2
Superstore K.8
Sutton Court E.3
Svenskaby A.12
Swain Court G.11
Swale Avenue G.5
Swallowfield E.3
Swan Gardens K.7
Swanspool E.7
Sweetbriar Lane E.2
Sycamore Avenue J.7
Sydney Road K.13
Symmington Close G.11

Tait Close J.8
Talbot Avenue F.12
Tanhouse.............................F.13
Tansor Garth.........................E.8
Tantallon Court G.8
Tarrant D.2
Taverners Road G.8
Teanby Court C.9
Temple Grange E.2
Tennis Centre D.5
Tennyson Road G.6
Tern Road E.15
The Aracade H.9
The Barracks F.7
The Broadlands......................L.8
The Conifers C.12
The Covert E.10
The Crescent (Orton) E.12
The Crescent (Woodston) G.11
The Cresset D.7
The Dell G.11
The Drive F.10
The Forum A.13
The Gannocks D.13
The Glen J.12
The Green (Werrington) E.4
The Green Wheel (Pathway) B.6
The Leys.............................D.10
The Lindens H.9
The Maples L.8
The Mead E.5
The Orchard F.4
The Orchards D.13
The Paddocks D.23
The Pentlands G.4
The Rookery..........................B.12
The Serpentine F.14
The Square K.8
The Stackyard C.13
The Steynings E.4
The Steynings F.4
The Twitten J.15
The Willows C.1
The Woodland K.8
Third Drove L.10
Thirlemere Gardens G.4
Thistle Drive J.11
Thistlemoor G.7
Thomas Close C.9
Thompsons Ground F.14
Thornemead F.3
Thorney Road......................Eye Inset
Thornleigh Drive F.12
Thornton Close.......................G.4
THORPE.............................E.9
Thorpe Avenue F.9
Thorpe Gate F.10
Thorpe Lea...........................G.10
Thorpe Meadows F.10

Thorpe Park Road E.10
Thorpe Road F.10
Thorpe Wood Road C.10
Thorseby Close E.9
Threave Court D.10
Throstlenest J.14
Thurlaston Close E.10
Thurning Avenue J.12
Thuro Grove D.14
Thursfield E.3
Thurston Gate D.10
Tilton Court J.6
Tintagle Court E.10
Tintern Rise L.4
Tirrington D.9
Tiverton Road E.9
Toftland F.13
Toll Gate D.8
Toll House Road F.11
Topmoor Way G.5
Touthill Close H.9
Tower Street G.11
Towler Street H.9
Tresham Road B.14
Trinity Street H.10
Troutbeck Close G.4
Tucker's Court J.12
Tuckers Yard J.12
Tudor Close G.5
Turnstone Way K.12
Turves Road M.4
Turves Road M.3
Twelvetree Avenue D.2
Twyford Gardens K.6
Tyesdale D.8
Tyler's Mews..........................E.4
Tyrrell Park L.9

Uldale Way G.4
Ullswater Avenue F.4
Uplands E.2
Uplands E.3
Upton Close D.10
Upton Close L.13

Vale Drive E.15
Valence Road D.13
Vere Road G.7
Vergette Road D.1
Vergette Street H.8
Vermont Grove G.10
Vetchfield C.12
Vicarage Farm Road K.9
Vicarage Gardens J.15
Victoria Place E.8
Victoria Street (Old Fletton) H.12
Victoria Street (Peterborough) H.8
Viking Court K.12
Vine Walk E.8
Viney Close K.8
Vineyard Road H.10
Vintners Close F.9
Virginia Close D.10
Viscount Road H.12
Vokes Street F.11

Wainman Road F.12
Wainwright D.3
Waitacre L.7
Wake Road J.9
Wakerley Drive E.12
Walcot Walk D.9
Walgrave E.14
Walkers Way C.9
Walsingham Way L.5
Waltham Close K.6
Waltham Walk M5
WALTON..............................E.5
Walton Park E.5
Warbon Avenue G.7
Ward Close J.9
Warley Road..........................G.10
Warwick Road........................E.5
Water End (Alwalton) A.13
Water End (Marholme) B.5
Water End (Peterborough) F.10
Watergall D.6
Waterloo Road H.8
Watersend Road.....................E.15
Waterworks Lane B.2
Watt Close G.4
Waveney Grove G.5
Wayford Road D.10
Weatherthorn F.13
Websters Close C.1
Wedgwood Way E.5
Weedon Close G.5
Welbeck Way F.12
Welbourne...........................F.3
Welbourne Lea F.3
Welland Close H.6
Wellkington Street J.9
Wells Close E.4
Wells Court K.12
Welmore Road C.1
Wentworth Street H.10
WERRINGTON........................E.3

Werrington Bridge Road F.2
Werrington Grove E.4
Werrington Mews E.4
Werrington Park Avenue.............E.4
Werrington Parkway D.4
Wesleyan Road H.6
Wessex Close K.11
West Parade F.9
West Water Crescent E.15
Westawe D.7
Westbrook Avenue G.12
Westbrook Park Avenue.............G.11
Westbrook Park Close F.12
Westbrook Park Road F.11
Westcombe Square K8
Westerley Close E.8
Western Avenue H.6
Westfield Road F.8
Westgate G.9
Westlake Avenue E.15
Westminster Gardens M.5
Westminster Place L.8
Westmoreland Gardens H.9
WESTWOOD.........................E.7
Westwood Park Close...............F.9
Westwood Park Road F.9
Wetherby Way K.9
Weymouth Way K.6
Whalley Street........................J.9
Wharf Road G.10
Wheatdole D.14
Wheel Yard H.9
Whisted Street J.9
White Cross E.7
Whitepost Road L.4
Whitewater B.12
Whittington L.7
Whittlesey Road J.12
Whitwell H.5
Wicken Way E.7
Wigmore Drive L.12
Wilberforce Road G.6
Wildlake F.13
Willesden Avenue F.6
Williamson Avenue G.9
Willonholt E.7
Willoughby Court K.6
Willow Avenue J.6
Willow Holt F.14
Wilton Close F.8
Wilton Drive F.8
Wimborne Drive K.7
Windermere Way G.4
Windmill Street.......................G.8
Windrush Drive G.5
Windsor Avenue E.6
Windsor Drive K.12
Wingfield.............................D.14
Winslow Road E.9
Winwick Gardens F.8
Winyates.............................D.14
Wisteria Way F.3
Wistow Way B.12
Wistow Way D.12
Witham Way G.5
Woad Close M.5
Woburn Close.......................D.10
Woodbine Mews J.9
Woodbine Street H.11
Woodbyth Road H.7
Woodcote Close H.6
Woodcroft Road A.3
Woodfield Road F.9
Woodhall Rise E.2
Woodhurst Road....................K.12
Woodpecker Close H.5
WOODSTON.........................F.11
Woodston Gate F.12
Woolaston Road E.7
Woolfellhill Road L.4
Woolgard D.9
Wootton Avenue G.12
Wordsworth Close G.6
Worsley..............................D.14
Wright Avenue K.12
Wulfric Square E.6
Wycliffe Grove D.2
Wyman Way C.13
Wyndham Park B.12

Yarwell Close F.12
Yew Tree Walk D.9
York Road............................G.7

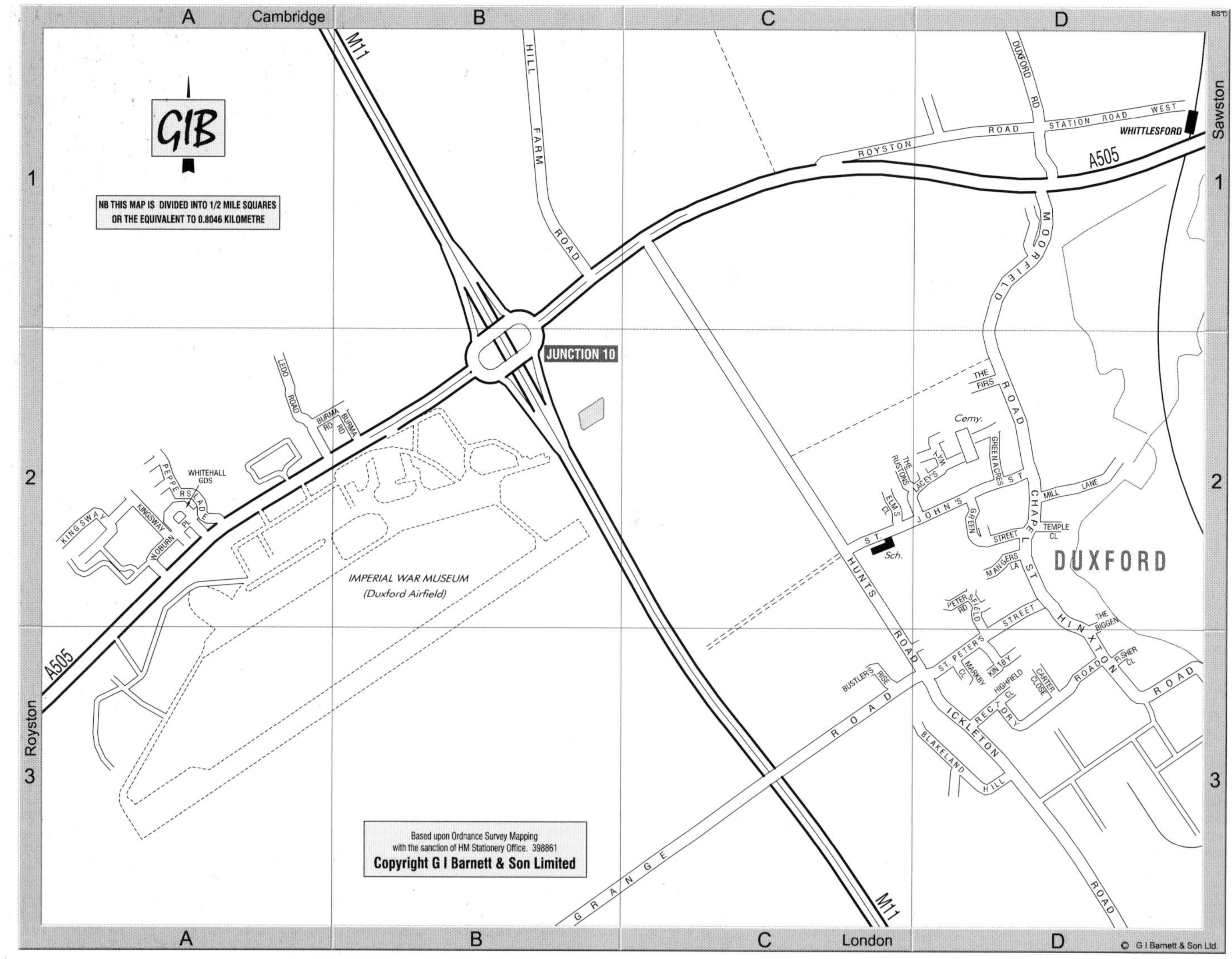

DUXFORD INDEX TO STREETS

Blakeland Hill D.3
Burma Road A.2
Bustler's Rise C.3

Carter Close D.3
Chapel Street D.2

Duxford Road D.1

Elms Close C.2

Fisher Close D.3

Grange Road B.3
Green Street D.2

Greenacres D.2

Highfield Close D.3
Hill Farm Road B.1
Hinxton Road D.2
Hunts Road..........................C.2

Ickleton Road D.3

Kingsway............................A.2
Kintby D.3

Lacey's Way D.2
Ledo Road A.2

Managers Lane....................D.2
Markby Close D.3
Mill Lane D.2
Moorfield Road D.1

Pepperslade A.2
Petersfield Road D.2

Rectory Road D.3
Royston Road......................C.1

St John's Street C.2
St Peter's Street D.3
Station Road West D.1

Temple Close D.2
The Biggen D.2
The Firs..............................D.2
The Rustons C.2

Whitehall Gardens A.2
Woburn Place A.2